HISTORICAL PERSPECTIVES
ON CONTEMPORARY EAST ASIA

Edited by
Merle Goldman
Andrew Gordon

Historical Perspectives on Contemporary East Asia

HARVARD UNIVERSITY PRESS

Cambridge, Massachusetts, and London, England   2000

Library of Congress Cataloging-in-Publication Data

Historical perspectives on contemporary East Asia / edited by Merle Goldman, Andrew Gordon.
    p.   cm.
   Includes bibliographical references and index.
    ISBN 0-674-00097-8 (alk. paper) — ISBN 0-674-00098-6 (pbk. : alk. paper)
    1. East Asia—History—19th century.   2. East Asia—History—20th century.
  I. Goldman, Merle.   II. Gordon, Andrew, 1952–
  DS515 .H57 2000
  950.4—dc21   00-024008

Contents

Preface

This collection of essays has been inspired by James Crowley's edited volume *Modern East Asia: Essays in Interpretation,* published in 1970. The essays in that work were scholarly and thought-provoking, based on the most recent research, and widely used in introductory courses in modern Chinese and Japanese history. Thirty years have passed since those essays were written; new research materials, many new monographs, different themes, and a variety of approaches, encompassing social and cultural as well as political and economic interpretations, have appeared in the study of East Asian history. Therefore, we thought it was time to produce a new set of essays, in the hope that they might be comparably useful for new generations of students. With the exception of Ernest Young, this volume has a new roster of writers, and Young's essay, with its greater emphasis on cultural issues, is very different from his essay in the 1970 volume. Moreover, an essay about the development of social organizations and their impact on politics in the first half of China's twentieth century by Keith Schoppa, which was not a separate topic in the previous volume, has been added to this volume. Furthermore, since Korea has become an important actor in East Asia, we have added an essay on Korea by Carter Eckert.

We have asked each author to distill from his or her ongoing research an interpretive essay on some aspect of the history of modern East Asia. The coverage ranges over the nineteenth and twentieth centuries and touches on political, social, economic, cultural, and international issues. Our goal falls between that of a textbook and a specialized monograph. We make no claim to cover all the important topics in the history of East Asia over the past two hundred years. This collection is designed to address provocative questions concerning the experience of particular nations and of East Asia as a whole. It is also designed to be used in college courses in tandem with a textbook.

The essays can be read or grouped in several ways. They can be read as separate packages of the modern history of each country. They also can be read as the history of events occurring across countries. Most of the authors have addressed some common questions and come up with a number of variations on common themes. One overarching theme that occurs within and across the national groupings is the Western effort over the past two centuries to open or integrate Asian nations into a global economic and diplomatic system. The opening essay by Warren I. Cohen stresses that the push from outside to "open" East Asia economically and politically has been a persistent feature of modern history. He also points out the strengths within the indigenous societies that prevented China, Japan, and Korea from being totally overwhelmed by Western imperialism. Other authors emphasize the internal pressures for change within these countries. In looking at the late nineteenth century, Carter Eckert and David Howell stress that important changes were under way in Korea and Japan before the Western advance. They describe well-grounded nationalist discourses with long histories, which shaped nationalist or reformist movements in modern times. Mary Rankin focuses on the profound political and social changes also going on in China that were accelerated by the Western impact.

Ernest Young emphasizes that for China to accept the protocols of Western-style state-to-state international relations was to accept a lowering of its "Middle Kingdom" status in the world. By contrast, the new order for both Japan and Korea could be understood as a kind of elevation, if (and only if) the new national unit could participate not as a colony but as an independent nation-state. In the twentieth century, however, both before and after World War II, a theme common to the chapters by Merle Goldman and Andrew Nathan, Andrew Gordon, Cohen, and Eckert is the great unease among both the rulers and masses of people in East Asia over their integration into the world economic system. They saw integration as a process that might compromise national integrity.

Regionalism is another important theme, particularly in the chapters on China, but it has noteworthy comparative implications as well. Rankin, Young, and Schoppa stress the development of increasing autonomy—social, political, economic, and even cultural—of local Chinese elites. Some of this regionalism also existed in Japan's Meiji revolution, which was led by a small group of domains in the southwest. These domains opposed the shogunal order located in north-central Japan. But, as Howell shows, this tension was ultimately and fairly easily contained by the revolutionary samurai who remade both institutions and culture in relatively inclusive, though not democratic, ways. And regionalism is scarcely mentioned by Sheldon Garon or Gordon, reflecting the fact that it has not been a dominant theme in twentieth-century Japanese history. The case of Korea falls somewhere in between those of China and Japan. There is, of course, the divide between South and North Korea in the post–World War II era, and in South Korea itself there has been a persistent, politically significant regional divide. Unlike in China, however, wholesale dispersal of power to localities has not occurred. In this regard, Korea's experience is closer to Japan's. This contrast may be related to size: one Chinese province, Sichuan, is larger in population than either Japan or Korea.

Virtually all the essays stress nationalism as a powerful motivating force in modern East Asian history. Nevertheless, nationalism has diverse roots and takes a variety of forms in different contexts. It has been neither the exclusive nor even the primary possession of any particular social group or political ideology. The authors discuss regional nationalism and centrist nationalism, anticolonial nationalism, emperor-centered or imperialist nationalism, militarist or fascist nationalism of the Guomindang or wartime Japan, Communist and revolutionary nationalism of the People's Republic of China, and developmental nationalism of postwar South Korea, Japan, and post-Mao China.

In addition, most of the essays point out the tension between nationalist liberation, whether from Western or Japanese domination, and reverence for, or defense of, what people construed to be the "traditions" of their nations. Young in particular describes the ongoing tension in the early twentieth century between calls for a cultural revolution, on the one hand, and unease at the implied loss of Chineseness in the modernizing attack on the past, on the other. Eckert identifies similar tensions in Korea, but they are between the local and cosmopolitan orientation of elites. They revered Chinese culture as universal, but they prided themselves on being better or more fully imbued with Chinese culture than the modern Chinese themselves. When modernizing projects, based on a Western model, enter such an intellectually polarized context, they are seen to hold danger as well as promise. Both Howell and Eckert highlight a crucial point concerning the ideological co-dependence of empire and colony: Howell shows that the Meiji state won control over a society whose people were often suffering under the impact of modernizing programs by offering empire as the nationalistic goal that made it all worthwhile; Eckert stresses that Korea's colonial subjugation to Japan in the first half of the twentieth century was a formative experience for modern Korean nationalism.

Several contributions stress what might be called "transwar" continuities. They reveal that pre–World War II forms of modernity persisted well across the wartime divide of 1945 throughout Asia and even the revolutionary divide of 1949 in China. These continuities are the focus of William Kirby's analysis of the common aspirations for industrialization and the structures of the two "party-states" of China's Guomindang and the Communist Party of prewar and postwar vintage. They are likewise the thrust of Garon's and Gordon's arguments about state-society relations and the socioeconomic structure of transwar Japan. The Goldman–Nathan essay, however, points out that Mao Zedong's utopian impulses made his rule, especially from the late 1950s till his death in 1976, a sui generis episode in China's modern history, or at least a derivative of the millennium movements in China's premodern history.

In the postwar era, versions of the developmental state, a regime committed above all to mobilizing capital and human resources on behalf of a national project of economic development, were found throughout most of East Asia. Although in Mao's China the emphasis was on development as ideology, his successors resumed China's more pragmatic pre-1949 economic developmentalism, which held sway in Japan and Korea since the 1950s. In all three nations, the state was a powerful force in relation to society, the economy, and culture. The state was most intrusive in China, while in Japan and Korea, as well as in that other part of China, Taiwan, a middle class emerged and democratic procedures were gradually introduced that increasingly made it possible for their populations to hold their governments accountable.

The essays which examine East Asia since World War II highlight the problematic status of liberalism, as distinct from mass participation and mobilization. A middle class and critical voices did not appear in China, as Goldman and Nathan point out, until the post–Mao Zedong era, when the Deng Xiaoping–Jiang Zemin regime relaxed the state's controls over virtually everything except politics and religious groups perceived as potentially political. Another crucial difference has been the place of political parties. Whereas they acted as intermediaries between state and society in Japan for much of the twentieth century, and in South Korea in the latter twentieth century, one party has functioned as the monopolistic superintendent of the state, and through it of society, in China and North Korea. In both Japan and

South Korea, critical voices gained force as some of the social, environmental, and political costs of rapid economic developmentalism became clear. In both cases a politics of accommodation co-opted these critiques, though the Korean experience appears far more contentious. A more energetic democratic movement of middle classes has emerged in postwar Korea, perhaps because they were more repressed than in postwar Japan.

These essays in the modern history of East Asia raise the question of whether the twenty-first century may witness "the end of history," if that phrase, as coined by Francis Fukuyama, is understood to mean the unchallenged triumph of the norms and practices of a Western-style liberal capitalism. The modern history of East Asia has presented the dramatic, sometimes devastating and sometimes uplifting spectacle of extremely varied experiences of modernity, both within Asia and between Asia and the West. But East Asia at the start of the twenty-first century is more closely integrated than ever before into a global economy and political order dominated by the West. Nevertheless, even if China as well as Japan and Korea generally continue to move in a liberal, capitalist direction, it is likely that the experiences of the past centuries, as described in these essays, will shape distinctive futures for the citizens of each of these countries.

Merle Goldman
Andrew Gordon

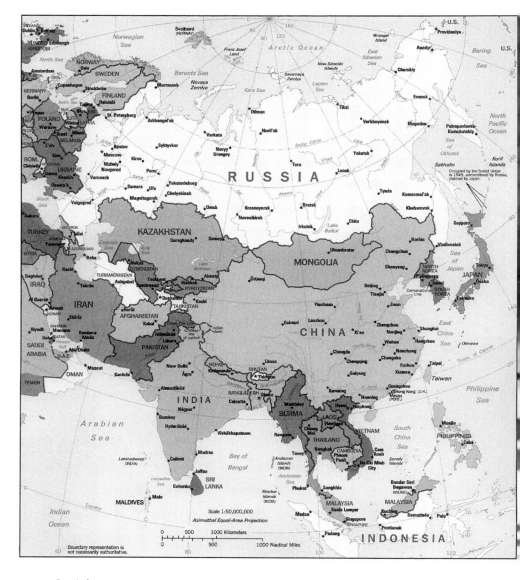

1. Asia

2. East Asia and surrounding territories

CHAPTER 1

The Foreign Impact on East Asia

WARREN I. COHEN

Prior to the nineteenth century, Westerners engaged the countries of East Asia only when their presence was welcomed or tolerated by Asian governments. They came primarily in search of opportunities to trade and, in far smaller numbers, to preach Christianity. Few reached Korea, and those who established themselves in China and Japan on occasion offended their hosts. At various times Western merchants and priests could be and were expelled or executed in all three countries. Neither the Vatican nor the great powers of Europe could protect their subjects from the laws of Asian states or the caprice of Asian rulers. Simply stated, the conditions under which Westerners operated in China, Japan, and Korea were determined exclusively by the rulers of those countries. East Asians participated in the global economic and diplomatic systems on their own terms.

The mid-nineteenth century was a watershed in the history of international relations. The East Asian order over which China had been at least nominally dominant for thousands of years shattered. Western power proved itself superior to that of Asia, largely owing to advanced military technology, improvements in military discipline and supply, and the co-opting of native forces on the Indian subcontinent. By force and intimidation, the West, led by Great Britain, dictated the new terms of contact in a series of treaties that included fixed tariffs and extraterritoriality—the exemption of foreigners from local law. The erosion of central power in China and Japan facilitated the Western intrusion. By 1870, most of East Asia had been opened to Western goods and ideas.

Resistance to the Western-organized international system, to what Asians called the "unequal treaties," remained strong. Korea, into which Western influence dribbled indirectly from China, had repelled all efforts to force open its doors to trade with the Europeans and Americans. Powerful provincial forces in Japan remained determined to "expel the barbarians." China had preserved its territorial integrity, and students of statecraft were already preparing to strengthen the country and enable it to stand up to its tormentors. The victory of the West was neither total nor final.

To the student of international relations, these events followed a pattern that has pervaded most of human history: the constant struggle of states for wealth and power. It is less a story of wicked imperialists and innocent victims—although there was no shortage of either—than it is a reminder that all states seek to expand their power and influence; that they perceive threats when other states do the same; and that conflict is as "natural" as peace.

Rising Powers: Japan and the United States

The most striking development of the last third of the nineteenth century was not the continued exaction of privileges by the West from its Asian victims, but rather the rapid recovery of Japan from the doldrums of the late Tokugawa years. It was Japan that forced Korea to open its doors and ultimately dominated that country. It was Japan that became China's great tormentor. And it was Japan that stopped the Western advance into East Asia, checking the Russian march into Korea and Manchuria in the early years of the twentieth century and intimidating Great Britain and the United States as well.

The power of Japan's central government, the Tokugawa shogunate, had been in decline before an American fleet arrived and "persuaded" the Japanese to sign their first treaty with the West. The influx of foreign diplomats and merchants that followed served as a catalyst for the overthrow of the Tokugawa. The government's response to the challenge of the West was deemed by most Japanese to have been inadequate, and many feared that Westerners would run rampant over Japan as in China. The perception of an external threat to the Japanese polity drove rival provincial forces into alliance against the shogunate. Together they defeated it in 1868 and carried out the nominal "restoration" of imperial power, uniting the country behind the symbol of the Meiji Emperor.

Japan's new leaders learned much about international relations from the West and were determined to join the ranks of the great powers. Toward this end they recognized the need for a strong central government and a strong military. Once they were able to defend themselves against the Americans and the Europeans, they would rid themselves of the unequal treaties imposed on them by the West and establish themselves as the dominant power in East Asia.

Qing leaders and the Chinese who worked with them also understood that to compete with the West, China had to modernize its military technology and accelerate industrialization. The absence of central direction proved fatal to the Qing self-strengthening program. Li Hongzhang, the most successful modernizing official, built an arsenal, an army and a navy, a steamship company and a railroad, a textile plant and a coal mine, but he, rather than the nation, was the principal beneficiary of his efforts. These assets increased his personal wealth and power greatly; they were not always available when needed elsewhere in China. In 1884, for example, when Qing forces attempted to block French advances in Vietnam, Li failed to come to their aid, preferring not to risk his own men and ships. China was forced by France to surrender its status as overlord of Vietnam. And just as Li was unmoved by the plight of those who fought the French, they remained on the sidelines as he struggled against the Japanese in the decade that followed.

Korea provided the principal arena in which the contest for primacy in East Asia was fought between China and Japan. Much of Korea's misfortune was geographically determined: its territory was easily accessible to larger and more powerful Asian neighbors and, following Russia's expansion to the Pacific, of interest to the tsar's officials as well. But Korea's internal affairs had much to do with its inability to organize effective resistance against those who would deny its independence.

Although a faction had emerged in Seoul that favored modernization and looked to Japan as an example, the predominant influence in Korea in the 1880s remained Chinese. It was Li Hongzhang who negotiated Korea's first treaty with the United States and persuaded the Koreans to accept it in 1880. The Qing still perceived Korea as their vassal, and Li hoped that a Western stake in Korea would forestall the expansion of Japanese influence. The Korean queen looked to China for support and was unsympathetic to Japanese-inspired change. A failed coup attempt in 1882 also appears to have been aimed at the reformers and their Japanese supporters.

In brief, the two principal factions in Korean politics had each compromised their country's independence by seeking foreign support. At this point, the Russians urged the court to look to them for protection as a means of breaking loose from Chinese control. Some Korean political figures even looked to the United States, hoping the Americans might help them preserve their independence. Instead of mobilizing the support of their own people, Korean leaders turned frantically to one or another of the foreign contenders in their efforts to gain or retain power.

A rebellion in 1894 prompted the king to petition for Chinese help, but the Japanese quickly moved troops into Seoul. A few days later China and Japan declared war on each other. At last Li Hongzhang's navy steamed into action, only to be destroyed by a Japanese fleet that was better trained, equipped, and commanded. In control of the seas, Japan reinforced its troops easily and drove the Chinese out of Korea. And the Japanese army did not stop at the Yalu but marched into Manchuria and on into the Shandong Peninsula. There was little to stop it from continuing to Beijing. The Qing were forced to sue for peace, and Li negotiated with the great Japanese statesman Ito Hirobumi.

Ito demanded Chinese recognition of the independence of Korea; the cession of Taiwan, the Pescadores, and the strategically important Liaodong Peninsula in southern Manchuria, China's gateway to Korea; and in addition a huge indemnity and new commercial concessions. The Qing had no choice but to accept the terms offered. Most threatening to the Qing court was the loss of the Liaodong Peninsula, which would put the shadow of Japanese troops over Beijing. Fortunately for China, Russia had its own aspirations in the region and won French and German support for its demand that the peninsula be left in Chinese hands. Japan was not ready to challenge the Europeans and backed off, but the Japanese would not forget.

The debacle in Korea, the failure of China's modern military forces, and the harshness of Japanese peace terms devastated the Qing court. It was apparent that self-strengthening had failed. Japan had exposed China's weakness, and now the Europeans, especially the Russians, were eager for new territorial and commercial concessions. The Russians expected to be rewarded for helping China retain the Liaodong Peninsula. Others would demand comparable concessions. The Chinese empire was on the verge of dismemberment, the "slicing of the Chinese melon." By the end of 1898, China was divided into spheres of influence, controlled by foreigners, filled with foreign officials, merchants, investors, and troops. Annexation of these spheres and the end of China's existence as an independent state were only a step away.

Although their role had not been as important as that of Great Britain, Americans had been involved in East Asia from the moment of their nation's conception. They had made their presence known in every port city of the region, dominating the carrying trade to China in the 1840s. They led the way in the opening and modernizing of Japan and were the first Westerners to obtain a treaty with Korea. Americans were everywhere, and their Asiatic Fleet indicated their government's intention to protect its citizens and their interests; but the United States had claimed no territory as its colony and had no sphere of interest in East Asia at the time of Sino-Japanese War.

In the course of the American crusade to liberate Cuba in 1898, the United States, aided by Filipinos rebelling against Spanish imperialism, defeated Spain in the Philippines as well as in Cuba. Spain surrendered, and the U.S. government had two choices: it could leave the islands in the hands of the Filipinos, or it could replace Spain as the imperial power in the Philippines. It chose empire. America would rule the Philippines as Britain ruled India, France ruled Indochina, and Holland ruled Indonesia. Overcoming ferocious Filipino resistance, the United States became an imperialist power in Asia.

Among the reasons for the American decision to take the Philippines was fear in the business community that European and Japanese imperialists, as they carved their spheres of influence in China, would deny opportunities to Americans. Now the United States would have a foothold in the region, a position from which Americans could compete with others for the resources and markets of East Asia. As the historian Richard Leopold contended, "The desire for the Philippines and a concern for China became mutually supporting."[1]

Businessmen concerned with China remained uneasy, demanding more vigorous action by their government. Leading commentators on foreign affairs, including the navalist Alfred Thayer Mahan, wrote about the importance of East Asia in the world balance of power. To appease its critics, Washington issued its "Open Door notes" in 1899 and 1900. The United States asked those powers with spheres of influence in China not to discriminate against American trade within those spheres or interfere with the work of the Chinese Imperial Maritime Customs Service, an important source of Qing income. The American notes also asked that China's territorial integrity be preserved. It was a modest initiative designed to satisfy both businessmen who sought to expand their interests in China and romantic nationalists eager to see their country play a larger role in the world.

The United States was asking the other nations with interests in China to pursue a policy of self-denial in the areas under their control. In return for equal treatment for their exports, the Americans offered nothing. The

United States, however, was not challenging the existing spheres of influence, nor seeking to compete in railroad or mining development, crucial to the Russians and Japanese. There was nothing to be gained by rejecting the American request, and little to be lost by endorsing it with qualifications that protected the interests dearest to each nation. The various addressees replied evasively, but the American government pronounced itself satisfied.

Although John Hay, the American secretary of state, persuaded himself that his country had contributed to the preservation of the Chinese empire, no expressions of gratitude came from Beijing. At the time the Open Door notes were formulated, relations between China and the United States were tense as a result of discriminatory practices against Chinese emigrants to the new American territories of Hawaii and the Philippines. Benevolent feelings toward China did not motivate Hay, nor did the Chinese have any illusions.

Japan's victory over China in 1895 and the American victory over Spain in 1898—and especially the imperial acquisitions of both victors—indicated the determination of Tokyo and Washington to join the competition for wealth and influence in the region. European dominance over East Asia was to prove short-lived, as the rising powers, Japan and the United States, began to assert themselves.

Boxer Interlude

The terms imposed on China by the Japanese after their victory in 1895 and the aggressive actions of the Western powers in the years that followed had a strikingly disruptive impact on coastal China. Foreigners overran the country, digging mines, building railroads and factories, treating the Chinese with contempt in their own land. Educated Chinese and others in the port cities understood that China was not faring well in the world competition for wealth, power, and status.

The years between 1895 and 1900 were years of intellectual and political ferment in China as scholars and officials struggled to find the means to preserve their country's independence and restore its historic grandeur. The dreams and schemes of reformers and revolutionaries came to naught. Unrest intensified, especially in north China, as the Chinese government found no way to check foreign intrusions. Into this void moved a crypto-nationalist movement, the "Boxers," to harass foreigners, especially missionaries, and native converts to Christianity.[2] Eager to divert the Boxers from anti-dynastic activities, the Qing court supported them in their actions against foreigners with the modern arms of the imperial army. The result was war with Japan and the West in the summer of 1900, a war that China could not win and that ended in August with the occupation of Beijing by a foreign expeditionary force.

China's borders remained intact, but the Chinese were forced to pay an enormous indemnity to the victors. This indemnity, added to that exacted by the Japanese in 1895, put an extraordinary burden on Qing finances, greatly inhibiting the dynasty's ability to rule and retarding the country's effort to industrialize.[3] In addition, China had to grant its conquerors the right to station troops between Beijing and the sea—new protection for foreigners in north China and new monuments to China's weakness.

In the Light of the Rising Sun

Russia posed the principal threat to China and the shaky balance of power that had emerged in East Asia in the last years of the nineteenth century. The Russians had exploited the unrest in China to move their forces into Manchuria. They were deeply involved in the internal affairs of Korea. In general, they left no doubt that they intended Russia to be the dominant power in East Asia.

Neither the Chinese nor the Koreans had the means to deny the Russians their objectives. The Americans and British were troubled by Russian actions, and opposed them diplomatically, but neither country imagined a vital interest in Korea or Manchuria. The Japanese, however, did perceive a threat to their security, as well as to their economic interests in the region. Japan's aspiration to join the great powers, to be treated as an equal, was also being challenged by Russian intransigence.

In 1901 the Japanese proposed joint action against Russia to the Americans, but the United States was unwilling to use force to achieve its goals in East Asia. The British, however, had concluded that their interests would be served best by an alliance with Japan, and in January 1902 the Japanese accepted Britain's offer. As an ally of Great Britain, Japan found that its leverage with the Russians and its world standing increased significantly.

Nonetheless, the Russians rejected a Japanese proposal for the division of spheres of influence, an offer of Manchuria for Korea. The Japanese broke off diplomatic relations in 1904 and attacked the Russian fleet at Port Arthur. The Russians suffered a disastrous defeat. Their forces in East Asia were outnumbered and outgunned, and the logistical problems of moving reinforcements from Europe to the Pacific proved overwhelming. The beginnings of the revolution of 1905 further weakened the Russian war effort.

Fortunately for the Russians, the Japanese were having problems of their own, particularly a shortage of funds. Confronting a shortage of manpower as well, they asked the American president, Theodore Roosevelt, to broker a peace accord. Roosevelt's initial delight over Japan's military success, his contention that Japan was serving the ends of the United States, had given way to recognition that Japan might prove to be an even more formidable opponent of American interests in East Asia than Russia. The Western powers operating in the region would have important interests in Europe, the Middle East, South Asia, and Africa—"divided interests, divided cares." Japan would focus on East Asia and have "but one care, one interest, one burden."[4] It would be good to end the war while Russian power remained sufficient to maintain a semblance of a balance of power in the region. The ensuing Treaty of Portsmouth gave Japan a de facto protectorate over Korea and a valuable sphere of influence in Manchuria. Its navy dominated the shores of northeast Asia. Conqueror of Russia, ally of Great Britain, it had increased its stature in the world enormously: Japan had become a great power.

It was evident to Asian and Western observers alike that Western domination of East Asia would not endure forever. The Japanese, struggling to rid themselves of the capitulations forced on them by the Americans and Europeans, had succeeded. In 1894 they had won revision of the unequal treaties, ended the extraterritorial privileges Westerners had enjoyed in Japan, and also gained important concessions on the road to tariff autonomy, achieved fully in 1911. They had the strongest army in East Asia and the most powerful navy in the Pacific. In the age of imperialism, in which Darwinian thought influenced the foreign policies of the world's leaders, the Japanese had proven themselves to be competitive. They were the only Asian imperialists.

The Koreans had attempted to stay clear of the Russo-Japanese War, but the Japanese sent troops to seize Seoul and all points of strategic value on the peninsula. Korea became a Japanese protectorate. No country would come to Korea's rescue. In 1905 Tokyo forced the Koreans to give Japan control over their foreign affairs and to accept a Japanese resident-general who would be de facto ruler of the country. The Japanese intended to remake Korea in their own image.

Enraged by the Koreans' lack of gratitude and by the resistance movement that grew rapidly, the Japanese decided to annex the country in 1910. The pace of economic exploitation accelerated, and the whole country was organized to serve Japan's interests, economic as well as strategic. The Japanese could proceed quickly and ruthlessly in large part because of their confidence that the rest of the world would not interfere. In a secret convention in 1907, the Russians had formally accepted Japanese control of Korea in exchange for Japan's recognition of Russia's special interests in Outer Mongolia. Both the British and the Americans were more concerned about Japanese activity in Manchuria, where their economic interests were far greater than in Korea.

The Japanese government was responsive to Western complaints about events in Manchuria. Japanese diplomats and businessmen considered good relations with the Americans and British to be important: bankers in London and New York provided the loans with which Japan paid the bills for war with Russia—and Western capital and markets would be important to the development of the Japanese empire for years to come. The approach of the Foreign Ministry and financial sector focused on the wealth Japan might accumulate in China through cooperation with the West and a benign paternalism toward China. The Japanese army, however, was less interested in commercial and financial affairs or in accommodating the Chinese or any of the Western powers. Charged with defense of the empire, it was determined to maximize Japan's position, tolerating no opposition—and it was the army that controlled the situation in the field.

Ultimately it was the Americans who troubled the Japanese. American naval power was also growing, as was the demand of American businessmen, journalists, and missionaries in China that their government restrain Japan. And another issue, that of the mistreatment of Japanese who migrated to the United States, was creating tension in the relationship. Public anger directed against the United States for its racism narrowed the options of the Tokyo government, to the advantage of the army's inclination to ignore American complaints. By 1907, Japanese naval war plans portrayed the United States as a potential enemy.

Fortunately for Japan, Roosevelt did not accord American business interests in East Asia a high priority. He recognized the growth of Japanese power and was eager to direct it toward continental expansion, away from the Philippines, Hawaii, and the west coast of the United States. He worried about anti-Japanese activities in California. It was one thing to mistreat Chinese immigrants, whose government could do little to protect them; it was quite another to mistreat Japanese. Central to Roosevelt's policy toward East Asia was his determination to avoid conflict with Japan. In 1908 the Japanese ambassador in Washington and the American secretary of state negotiated an agreement in which both sides affirmed their desire for friendly relations. The Japanese agreed to redirect emigration to the Asian mainland and explained that they no longer considered southern Manchuria part of China: it was the defensive bulwark of their continental empire. The Americans raised no objections; they accepted Japan's dominant role on the continent.

Nationalist Challenges to Imperialism

In 1905, encouraged by Japanese success against Russia and angered by American mistreatment of Chinese immigrants, Chinese students organized an anti-American boycott, arguably the first sustained nationalist movement in Chinese history. Certainly the Chinese had ample reason to be outraged by American racism, but the organizers were concerned with larger issues than U.S. immigration policy: they sought to strike a blow for Chinese prestige. Lacking the military power necessary to strike at the imperialists, they harnessed the resources available, using an organized public opinion against that power least likely to respond with force.

Another major sign of burgeoning Chinese nationalism was the "rights recovery" movement, an effort to wrest control over the construction and operation of railroads from foreigners. The movement spread across the country between 1904 and 1907 and generated mass support. In terms of capturing control of railroad development, the movement failed, but as a school for nationalist organizers, it played an important role.

In 1911, to the surprise of the major powers with interests in China, the Qing dynasty was overthrown and a republic proclaimed. Although Japanese leaders were divided over the appropriate response, none of them favored the emergence of a strong China. The Japanese army in Manchuria immediately devised schemes for separating Manchuria and Mongolia from the rest of China. The Foreign Ministry and important business interests perceived opportunities for economic advantage in all of China by pursuing less overtly aggressive policies. Other Japanese imagined a revivified China assisting Japan in ridding Asia of Western imperialism.

The Americans, British, French, and Germans were concerned primarily with maintaining their privileges in China. They would work with anyone who would honor the treaty system they had imposed in the nineteenth century. The Russians saw an opportunity to weaken Chinese authority over Outer Mongolia—and did so. Otherwise, the Republic of China fared reasonably well. Japanese army plans for Manchuria and Inner Mongolia were aborted, and the Western powers withheld recognition only briefly.

The war that began in Europe in August 1914 had dramatic consequences for China. Suddenly the European powers were too busy to interfere in Chinese affairs. Unfortunately for China, Japan was not. Yet neither were the Americans, who perceived themselves as China's champions. The confrontation between the rising Pacific powers, Japan, and the United States was approaching.

As allies of the British, the Japanese promptly overran German possessions in East Asia, including the German concession in Shandong. In January 1915 they went further, presenting China with their notorious Twenty-one Demands. China was to become a Japanese protectorate, to be exploited much as Japan had exploited Korea just before annexation. Clearly, Tokyo assumed that the war in Europe had left it with a free hand, and the Japanese were moving rapidly to capitalize on the opportunity.

Objections to the Japanese moves came from London and Washington. But the Japanese were well aware that the British could not oppose them in any significant way and that the Americans, given their limited interests in the region, were hardly likely to do more than express displeasure. For the moment, the fifth and most obnoxious group of demands was dropped, but the Chinese were forced to accept the others immediately.

In 1917 both the United States and China intervened in the world war on the side of the British and their allies. Approximately 100,000 Chinese laborers assisted British, French, and American forces in France, suffering several thousand casualties. When the war ended in 1918, Chinese diplomats went to the peace conference at Versailles with great hopes based on their country's role in the war and the anti-imperialism explicit in the Fourteen Points enumerated as a basis for a lasting peace by the American president, Woodrow Wilson. Wilson's call for self-determination, presumably for all the world's people, was the catalyst for much of the nationalist fervor in East Asia in 1919.

The Koreans exploded first. With the Japanese serving as unwitting tutors, traditional xenophobia had evolved into modern nationalism. Many Korean nationalists went into voluntary exile, in both China and the West. But the activities of the exiles had little impact on Japanese imperialism. Only slightly more effective were the freedom fighters operating out of

Manchuria and the Russian Maritime Provinces. But on March 3, 1919, Korean nationalists organized their first great act of resistance as approximately 2 million people across the country demonstrated for independence. Japanese troops opened fire on the participants and torched the schools and churches to which they fled for refuge. They killed nearly eight thousand people. Scores of thousands were injured or arrested. No Western government came to the rescue.

The Chinese dreamt of ridding themselves of all the symbols of their semicolonial status, but regaining control of the former German concession in Shandong was their minimal demand. At Versailles, however, the Chinese representatives learned that Japan had signed secret treaties with its European allies that bound them to support Tokyo's claims. Wilson was China's only hope—but, troubled by a Japanese threat to quit the peace conference rather than yield on Shandong, he abandoned his support for the Chinese position.

In China the decision at the peace conference to transfer control of Shandong to Japan prompted outrage. Beginning with a demonstration in Beijing on May 4, 1919, hundreds of thousands of students took to the streets throughout China, committing acts of violence against allegedly pro-Japanese members of the government and organizing a boycott of Japanese goods. They had become the ingredient necessary for the cementing of what the revolutionary leader and first president of the Republic, Sun Yat-sen, called China's "loose sands" into a powerful nationalist force.

Conferences in Washington and Moscow

Tensions between Japan and the United States troubled leaders of both countries. They had succeeded in finessing the immigration issue and other problems caused by racism in America. The Japanese had outmaneuvered the Americans easily when Roosevelt's successor attempted to reduce their influence in Manchuria by having Americans buy the Russian- and Japanese-controlled railways. Wilson's apparent unfriendliness at the time of the Twenty-one Demands created anxiety in Tokyo, but the two governments papered over their differences in the Lansing-Ishii agreement of 1917. New issues, however, arose between them at Versailles, and before the end of 1919, these issues and new immigration problems generated a brief war scare. A banking consortium agreement in 1920, in which the United States implicitly accepted Japan's sphere of interest in Manchuria, ended the crisis.

Both Japanese and American war planners recognized that their countries had many issues that divided them and might lead to military confrontation. In particular, the navies of the two countries watched each other very carefully. The Japanese were deeply concerned by the enormous growth of the U.S. Navy during the world war. The United States had emerged suddenly as the greatest naval power in the world, and its capacity to outstrip Japan in an arms race was all too obvious. Japanese leaders were also aware that their British allies could not be counted on against the Americans. The security of the empire was at stake.

Japanese naval building worried analysts in the United States. Agitation for disarmament was intensifying in postwar America. Its leaders concluded that the only way to provide for their nation's security *and* satisfy the public clamor for disarmament was to reach agreement with Japan to end the incipient arms race. They understood that the arms race could not be separated from other issues, including the Anglo-Japanese alliance, Japanese imperialism in China, and the balance of power in East Asia. At the invitation of the United States, in 1921 the British, Chinese, Japanese, and five lesser European states joined the Americans at a major conference in Washington.

From the American vantage point the conference was a tremendous success. Rejecting a suggestion that they join the Anglo-Japanese alliance, the Americans succeeded in replacing it with a harmless four-power nonaggression pact in which they and the French joined the British and Japanese. More satisfying to the American public was a five-power treaty in which Italy joined the other four in an agreement to limit the size of their respective navies, thus checking the arms race. The naval agreement left Japan secure in its home isles while limiting the ability of the Japanese navy to conduct offensive operations in the eastern Pacific.

The conference then turned to the matter of China—of great power competition in the western Pacific and Chinese aspirations. Sentiment in the United States favored Chinese challenges to Japanese and European infringements on China's sovereignty, and the Chinese and American delegations worked closely together; but the principal concern of American officials, like their Japanese and European counterparts, was protection of their interests in China. Ultimately, the participants in the conference agreed not to interfere in the internal affairs of China, to allow the Chinese to unify and modernize their country in their own way and at their own pace. To Americans, this was the solution to coexisting with Japanese power in East

Asia. All the states with significant interests in the region—except Soviet Russia—were committed to peaceful competition without prejudice to the future of China.

The Chinese were less satisfied. At best the participants were promising no *further* encroachments on Chinese sovereignty. Most of the attributes of sovereignty that China had been forced to surrender over the previous eighty years had not been retrieved. To politically involved Chinese, the conference had served the ends of the imperialists but had done little for China. The point was underscored in Moscow, where representatives of Sun Yat-sen's Guomindang (Nationalist Party) and the Chinese Communist Party attended a Comintern-sponsored "Congress of the Toilers of the Far East."

The failure of communist revolutions in Europe had led Lenin and some of his colleagues to look to Asia as an arena in which their vision might succeed. Lenin sent Soviet agents to China to find worthy collaborators. Under pressure from Chinese, Japanese, and Korean radicals—and in the context of the Washington Conference, the Comintern convened its "Toilers of the Far East" meeting in January 1922. It was a way of asserting Soviet interest in any Pacific settlement—of reminding the powers that Russia also had interests in East Asia.

The Guomindang "Revolution" and the Great Powers

The Soviet government had much to fear from a powerful anticommunist Japan on its border and much to gain from the emergence of a China strong enough to confront Japan. But after the death of Yuan Shikai in 1916, the Chinese state had disintegrated. Respect for the authority of the government in Beijing declined with distance from the city. Various military men became regional warlords, obstacles to a united China. Realizing that the nascent Communist Party had no power and little influence, the Russians ultimately chose to support Sun's efforts to unite the country. In 1923 Sun and a Soviet representative announced that Russia would provide the Guomindang with aid. Arrangements were made to have the Guomindang form a coalition with the Chinese Communists. And in 1924 the Soviets further ingratiated themselves with Chinese nationalists by surrendering some of the privileges of the unequal treaties.

Lenin died early in 1924, and Sun's death followed a year later, but the Guomindang-Soviet alliance held. Russian arms and advisers enabled Jiang

Jieshi (Chiang Kai-shek), Sun's principal military aide, to beat back attacks by nearby warlord armies. Well equipped, well led, and highly motivated, Jiang's forces began to extend their control over south China. And then in May 1925 their cause received an unintended boost from the foreign community in Shanghai when demonstrators against Japanese imperialism were fired upon by British troops, killing an estimated dozen and wounding a score more. The incident led to a spontaneous outburst of anti-imperialist, antiforeign sentiment that spread from Shanghai through China's cities and ultimately to the countryside—the "May Thirtieth Movement." A few weeks later, as Guomindang and Communist organizers mobilized thousands of workers, peasants, students, and soldiers in antiforeign demonstrations and strikes in Guangzhou, British troops killed more than fifty marchers. These incidents greatly strengthened the Guomindang-Communist alliance, winning enormous support for its cause throughout the country.

As Jiang's forces fought their way toward the Yangzi, they met with little foreign interference. The British, whose interests were greatest in the region and who had been targets of much of the antiforeign agitation, chose to come to terms with the Guomindang. In December 1926 they indicated a willingness to revise the unequal treaties. The Americans followed suit. The Japanese, concerned primarily with Manchuria, also acted with restraint. But a crisis arose when Chinese forces in Nanjing attacked foreigners and foreign property, including the American, British, and Japanese consulates. With over a hundred Western and Japanese warships in the region and thousands of foreign troops on hand, the threat of a major intervention to stop the Guomindang advance loomed.

On the same day that he received demands for reparations and punishment of the offenders from the foreign powers, Jiang ordered the arrest and massacre of hundreds of Communists and labor leaders in Shanghai. At a critical moment in his relations with Japan and the West, he perceived an urgent need to initiate maneuvers that ultimately enabled him to best Stalin and decimate the Communists before they could eliminate him. Because of the timing, the foreign policy issue and the internal political issue became intertwined: too recalcitrant a response to the foreign powers might provoke intervention, and too conciliatory a response surely would result in charges that he had sold out to the imperialists.

The Japanese, who had the clearest understanding of the turmoil within the Guomindang, counseled patience. They believed that they could work with Jiang, that he would respond reasonably to their determination to preserve their interests in China. Less enamored of Jiang, but lacking a feasible alternative, the Americans and British followed the Japanese lead. In March 1928 Jiang accepted American terms for settling the Nanjing incident.

Suddenly, in May, Japanese troops clashed with Guomindang troops in Shandong, undermining the efforts of Japanese statesmen. When the government in Tokyo attempted to retrieve the situation by forcing the principal northern warlord to return to Manchuria, the Japanese army assassinated him in a vain effort to take complete control of the region. Neither military nor civilian authorities in Japan supported the efforts of the army in the field, but no Japanese leader was willing to accept Chinese sovereignty over Manchuria, precluding an understanding with Jiang.

Guomindang forces soon gained control of most of China, and diplomatic recognition followed. In July 1928 the United States signed a treaty granting tariff autonomy to China and constituting recognition of Jiang's Nanjing regime. By the end of the year, all of the major powers had recognized the new government and negotiated treaties granting it tariff autonomy. On October 10, 1928, the Guomindang government was formally proclaimed. A few months later the Guomindang flag was raised over Manchuria. China was at least nominally reunited under the leadership of Jiang Jieshi. The revolutionary vision of Sun Yat-sen had been realized, treaty revision had begun, and the era of imperialist domination of China might have ended.

Crisis in Manchuria

It was in Manchuria that Chinese hopes for an end to imperialism were dashed, and it was, of course, the Japanese who were responsible. Jiang was determined to drive the Soviets and Japanese out of China's northeastern provinces. An effort to seize the Soviet-controlled Chinese Eastern Railroad in 1929 provoked a strong military response, and the Chinese were forced to back off. They then focused their efforts against the Japanese.

No Japanese leader—and few knowledgeable Japanese—were willing to countenance the loss of Japan's privileges in Manchuria. Japan's Kwantung army in Manchuria, disgusted by what it perceived as Tokyo's appeasement of Jiang, offered its own response to Chinese nationalism. On September 18, 1931, after setting off an explosion on the Japanese-owned and operated South Manchuria Railroad in order to allege Chinese provocation, Japanese troops began the conquest of the region. The age of Japanese militarism had dawned and with it a new threat to Western interests in East Asia. While it crushed nationalism in Korea and fought it in China, Japan asserted its claim to lead nationalist movements throughout the rest of Asia, promising to preserve the continent for Asians, to free it from Western influence.

Japan was the dominant power in East Asia in the 1930s, as it had been since the world war. Japanese military power, resorted to increasingly by Tokyo and its men in the field, dictated the international affairs of the region. Japanese leaders were determined to control the resources and territory they deemed essential to their nation's security. After they consolidated their hold on Manchuria, the Japanese gradually edged toward full-scale war with China. Jiang's government was unable to respond effectively, and it received minimal support from the outside world.

The major Western states—France, Great Britain, and the United States— were drowning in the depths of the Great Depression, desperately eager for the crisis in East Asia to pass without need for their involvement. The League of Nations, to which the United States did not belong, could not act without strong British leadership, which was not forthcoming. From the United States came admonishments, first gentle, then increasingly harsh, to no avail. Words would not stop the Japanese army, but the international community had nothing more to offer. The vision of a collective security regime, embodied in the League, evaporated as each of the great powers determined that its interests in Manchuria were not sufficient to justify the risk of war with Japan. In 1933 Japan withdrew from the League, underscoring the impotence of the organization.

For a brief time Jiang could find solace in the relationship he was developing with Germany. He had been pleased with German economic and military advisers with whom he had worked in the late 1920s, and in 1933 new ties were established with the Germany of Adolf Hitler. Several senior German military officers provided Jiang with valuable advice, and before long all of the major German corporations were operating in China, helping to modernize its infrastructure and industry. The Chinese navy and air force were remodeled along German lines, but the promised U-boats and the Messerschmitt and Stuka aircraft never arrived. The new self-strengthening movement was interrupted when Hitler decided to ally with Japan instead.[5]

For its part, the Soviet Union was eager to strengthen China against Japan to enhance its own security, and Stalin concluded that no man had a better chance of unifying the country than the man who had outmaneuvered him in 1927. He helped free Jiang when he was seized by his own forces in the "Xi'an incident" of 1936, and Jiang grudgingly moved toward an accommodation with the Communists in a united front against Japan. The willingness of Jiang, the Communist leader Mao Zedong, and disparate warlords to submerge the past and abandon their ambitions was minimal, but they could not stem the tide of patriotic fervor that was sweeping urban Chinese.

Few Japanese believed that a united China was in their interest, and the Communists were viewed by most Japanese with more loathing than the Guomindang. Several Japanese leaders, military as well as civilian, had long favored reaching a settlement with Jiang to preclude a Communist victory in China and to keep Soviet influence out of Asia. The possibility of a Guomindang-Communist united front generated new anxieties. The Japanese army was a powder keg awaiting a spark. That came in July 1937.

War Comes to Asia

The Japanese government was not seeking war with China in 1937. Even the Army General Staff hoped to avoid any major confrontation with the Chinese. Nonetheless, minor skirmishes in the vicinity of Beijing in July escalated into full-scale warfare. Japanese officers in China were eager to strike, and the mood in China precluded further appeasement by Jiang. Seeking a rapid victory, the Japanese poured troops into China. World War II had begun in Asia.

The ensuing battle for control of the Yangzi Valley, from Shanghai to Nanjing, lasted nearly five months and cost the Chinese approximately 250,000 casualties, 60 percent of the men they had put into the field. In December the Japanese took Nanjing, where officers unleashed their troops for a two-month orgy of looting, rape, and murder—atrocities unsurpassed in the history of modern warfare—subsequently referred to as the Rape of Nanjing. China's best-trained and equipped forces had been decimated and its capital lost to the enemy. By its actions at Nanjing, the Japanese army wrecked mediation efforts by Hitler aimed at preventing the spread of communism in China.

Jiang had hoped for intervention by the League or the Americans, but as in 1931, little but words of comfort came from those quarters. The Europeans were focused on the activities of Hitler and Mussolini, much closer to home, and the Americans were wallowing in the profound neutralist and pacifist mood that had captured the country after the failure to stop Japan in Manchuria. Initially, only the Soviets, fearful of a Japanese attack on their Asian lands, provided significant aid.

In the late summer of 1939, however, Soviet support for China dropped sharply. After signing a nonaggression pact with Hitler's Germany in August, the Soviets were less concerned about having to fight a two-front war. During the week the pact was signed, Soviet and Mongolian troops repelled a Japanese attack on the border between Mongolia and Manchuria. In a counteroffensive they destroyed the Japanese force. Stalin concluded that he had little further need to keep the Chinese in the field.

The coming of war in Europe in September 1939 left the Chinese in desperate straits. The Soviets had turned their backs on China's plight, and the Americans now focused their attention on events across the Atlantic. Britain was fighting for its survival. China stood virtually alone, and the question was how long it would be before Jiang was forced to succumb to Japanese pressure. Against overwhelming odds, Jiang and his forces in Chongqing and Mao and his forces in and around Yan'an held out.

The Japanese increasingly looked southward, eager to exploit opportunities created by Hitler's pressures on Britain, France, and the Netherlands. In September 1940 they forced the French to allow Japanese forces to move into Indochina. A few days later they concluded the Tripartite Pact, the Axis Alliance, with Germany and Italy, intended to intimidate the United States by threatening a two-ocean war if the Americans intervened in either the European or Asian conflict. The signing of the pact was an event of enormous importance for Japan's relations with the United States—and, indirectly, of tremendous benefit to China. No words, no act, could have been more effective in convincing Americans of their stake in the outcome of the Sino-Japanese War than Japan's decision to ally with Nazi Germany.

In the months following the signing of the Tripartite Pact, the United States began supplying large-scale aid to China. In 1941 China also became eligible for lend-lease, the aid program originally designed to provide Great Britain with the means to defend itself—and many millions of dollars' worth of military equipment was allocated for China. At the same time, the United States began to apply economic sanctions against Japan, first cutting off the sale of scrap iron, then freezing Japan's assets in the United States in July 1941, and imposing a partial oil embargo in August.

American military leaders, unready for war and anxious to avoid a showdown with Japan, succeeded in getting President Franklin Roosevelt to authorize the licensing of some Japanese oil purchases. Although Roosevelt had rejected an appeal for a meeting with the Japanese prime minister in June, the United States agreed to negotiations aimed at reaching a modus vivendi. Most American leaders were interested in reaching an understanding that would prevent war with Japan and allow them to concentrate on the war they considered more dangerous to the United States—the war in Europe.

Throughout the autumn of 1941, Japanese and American diplomats met in Washington. But as Japan's oil reserves were consumed, time was running out. If the Americans would not provide the oil essential to Japan's war machine, it would have to be found elsewhere—and soon. The American Pacific fleet at Pearl Harbor would have to be destroyed to preempt interference in Japan's conquest of Southeast Asia and its control of Indonesian oil. The failure of diplomacy would necessitate war—and diplomacy failed.

Fear that Jiang would surrender if the United States appeased Japan stiffened the American negotiating position. The British, too, were apprehensive, and their prime minister, Winston Churchill, warned Roosevelt that a Chinese collapse would increase the danger to British and American interests in East Asia. In Washington and London there was also concern that a Japan freed from Chinese resistance would attack the Soviets, facilitating a Nazi victory as Hitler's armies pounded Leningrad and Moscow.[6]

And so war came to America in the form of a brilliantly executed Japanese attack on Pearl Harbor on the morning of December 7, 1941, "a date," Roosevelt told his countrymen, "which will live in infamy." Japanese leaders had little expectation of defeating the United States, but they saw no alternative to war if Japan was to maintain the momentum of its imperial expansion. They anticipated dealing a blow to American naval power sufficient to buy the time to build an impregnable position in East Asia. As they planned construction of a Greater East Asia Co-prosperity Sphere, they hoped the Americans would not be willing to pay the price of trying to take it away from them. It was a gamble the Japanese military was willing to take.

The Pacific War

Japan conquered Southeast Asia with remarkable speed in the six months following the attack on Pearl Harbor. But defeat of its fleet by the U.S. Navy in the Battle of Midway in June 1942 ended its offensive in the eastern Pacific. In the months that followed, Japan fought tenaciously to hold on to every inch of territory it had seized; but slowly the Americans brought their superior wealth and power to bear and pushed the Japanese back, island by island. American submarines conducted a ruthless war against Japanese shipping, Tokyo was firebombed in March 1945, and it was only a matter of time before the Japanese military would be forced to admit defeat.

In May 1945, Germany surrendered. Japan was alone, and U.S. planes began a massive bombing offensive that finished off Japan's navy and industrial base. But the Japanese gave no indication of their willingness to surrender. American leaders knew that victory over Japan was in reach. The questions that remained were when and at what cost. As Washington looked for a strategy with which to end the war, it concluded that Jiang, husbanding his resources to fight the Chinese Communists, would not be much help. Roosevelt turned to the Soviet Union and, at Yalta in February 1945, won a pledge from Stalin to abrogate the Soviet-Japanese nonaggression pact and attack Japanese forces within three months of the end of the war in Europe. In return Roosevelt promised to gain Jiang's agreement to restore tsarist privileges in Manchuria—a small price for the United States to pay.

In July 1945, after Roosevelt's death and the surrender of Germany, Churchill, Stalin, and President Harry Truman met at Potsdam and issued a declaration calling on Japan to surrender and spelling out their terms. Akira Iriye, the leading historian of Japanese-American relations, has argued that "the Potsdam declaration should have been accepted immediately and unequivocally by the Japanese government, for it gave them what they were seeking, 'a peace on the basis of something other than unconditional surrender.'"[7] Committing possibly the greatest mistake in recorded history, the Japanese government delayed its decision, and, unintentionally, the prime minister indicated that Tokyo did not take the declaration seriously.

Assuming continued fierce Japanese resistance comparable to that encountered at Iwo Jima and Okinawa, and determined to end the war quickly and at minimal cost in American lives, Truman ordered the air force to drop the first atomic bomb. On August 6, 1945, the people of Hiroshima were struck by the most horrible weapon mankind had ever devised.

Still the Japanese military refused to surrender. Two days later Soviet troops invaded Manchuria and overran the depleted Japanese army there. On August 9 a second atomic bomb obliterated Nagasaki—and still the Japanese military opposed surrender. It took five more days and the intervention of the emperor to move the Japanese government to accept the Allied peace terms. The war in Asia was over—and the stage was set for the next great confrontation in East Asia.

The Cold War in East Asia

In Washington, especially among American military leaders, apprehension emerged about Soviet intentions in Manchuria and Korea. Stalin clearly was determined to assert Soviet power in East Asia, and Roosevelt had conceded Soviet influence in Manchuria and claims to territories the Japanese had wrested from the tsar in 1905. But Roosevelt was dead, and some of his advisers thought he had conceded too much. The men who had crafted the victory over the Axis powers would not countenance a Soviet challenge to their perception of the security of the United States and its interests across the Pacific.

The disposition of forces at the end of the war allowed the United States to deny the Soviets—or any other nation—a meaningful role in the occupation of Japan. On the mainland, however, the situation was quite different. Soviet troops were dominant in the Northeast, and Stalin's diplomats drove hard bargains in negotiations with the Chinese. Although the Soviets had been China's principal supporters early in the war, Jiang had not hesitated to seize the opportunity to eliminate Soviet influence in Xinjiang when Germany attacked the Soviet Union. When the balance shifted in Stalin's favor, he forced Jiang to accept the "independence" of Outer Mongolia—which had been in the Soviet orbit since the 1920s—and Soviet control over Manchurian railways and ports.

In Korea, Soviet troops did not take advantage of the late arrival of American forces but withdrew north of the thirty-eighth parallel, the point at which Soviet and American planners had agreed to divide their zones of occupation. Stalin was not ready for a confrontation with the United States. The Japanese were disarmed and expelled from north and south, but the Koreans, anticipating independence, found their country divided and occupied, the freedom promised in the victors' Cairo Declaration of 1943 postponed. Throughout the country Koreans of all political persuasions staged demonstrations, almost unanimously outraged by the denial of their independence.

Increasingly, in the months following Japan's surrender, the Soviet Union and the United States viewed each other as potential adversaries, with enormous ramifications for the peoples of East Asia. Koreans and Chinese began to look to one or the other of these great powers to achieve their own political ends, linking their own civil strife to the growing enmity between the Americans and the Soviets.[8]

At the end of the war in Asia, the principal concern of the Americans, widely shared by their allies and Asians generally, was to eliminate Japan as a military threat. The men responsible for atrocities or deemed responsible for starting the war were tried as war criminals. Japan was stripped of its empire, and its military and civilian population overseas was repatriated. Its armed forces were demobilized. The Japanese were denied a centralized police force, which might take on a paramilitary character, and Japan's arms industry was dismantled.

A second important American objective was the democratization of Japan. In practice that meant remaking Japan in America's image—a New Deal for Japan. In 1946 the Japanese were forced to accept a constitution drafted primarily by the staff of the Supreme Commander of Allied Powers, General Douglas MacArthur. Most striking among its provisions, and in accord with the highest American priority, Article 9 required the Japanese to renounce war as an instrument of national policy and consequently the right to maintain military forces. The pacifism of this article was embraced by the Japanese people, perhaps more eagerly than any other reform imposed by their conquerors.

From 1948 to 1950 the Americans looked for a way to end the occupation, to return control of Japan to the Japanese before they became hostile to the American presence. American leaders were confident that the Japanese could be relied on to oppose communism and to work with the United States and its allies against the spread of Soviet influence. Washington was also eager to have the Japanese economy recover so that it would cease to be a drain on American resources. American policy planners saw Japan as central to an integrated regional economy, the "workshop" of Asia, the engine of Asian economic growth. A few went further and wanted to see Japan rearm so that it could defend itself and support the containment policy of the United States.[9]

The Soviet Union was not eager to see a free and independent Japan resume its place in the world order. Japan alone had been a terrible threat to East Asia for half a century. The prospect of a powerful Japan allied with the United States could only produce nightmares in the capitals of the Soviets and their friends. Indeed, there were few Asians who wished to see Japan unfettered. Consequently, the Soviets refused to sign a peace treaty with Japan to end the occupation, and the Americans, lacking support from their friends, chose not to proceed unilaterally. Although the occupation continued, there was little doubt that the Japanese had regained de facto control of their domestic affairs by 1950.

In China at the end of the war, Jiang Jieshi confronted a serious problem:

the challenge of the Chinese Communists. He was determined to rid the country of Mao's followers, but he realized that external forces, Soviet and American, might pose obstacles. He had outmaneuvered Stalin once, in the 1920s, and might succeed a second time. The Americans, his wartime allies, were almost as troublesome. Relations had soured during the war, and Jiang could not be certain of the course of the post-Roosevelt leadership in Washington.

Neither the Soviets nor the Americans had a clear plan for coping with the civil strife they anticipated in China. Mao had not been Stalin's choice to lead the Chinese Communists, and he had purged the party of those most likely to be subservient to Moscow. He had demonstrated during the war that he would not sacrifice the interests of his forces to serve those of the Soviet Union.[10] Jiang, by contrast, had conceded Stalin's demands regarding Manchuria and Mongolia. Stalin preferred to work with the Communists, to envision a communist revolution sweeping Asia, but he was not prepared to sacrifice the gains he had won from Jiang on behalf of a prickly, uncontrollable Mao. Stalin's ambivalence was reflected in Soviet actions immediately following Japan's surrender. Very early, Mao confessed to party cadres that "Soviet policy cannot be understood."[11]

American policy was similarly muddled, largely because policy makers were contemptuous of Jiang and suspicious of Mao. Leaning toward support of Jiang despite wartime criticism of his repressive government, the Americans tried to mediate between the competing parties to prevent a civil war. They hoped that "moderates" in both parties would create a centrist regime, unsullied by the fascist tendencies they saw in Jiang's Guomindang or the threat of pro-Soviet communist totalitarianism they perceived in a Maoist government.

From mid-1946 through mid-1949, a civil war raged in China. The Americans and Soviets watched each other carefully, but neither side sent in its own forces. The Americans disengaged gradually, but continued to provide Jiang's government with a modicum of support. The Soviets gave the Chinese Communists access to surrendered Japanese weapons, but held back until it was apparent that the Communists would win with or without their support. In effect, the two great powers deterred each other, and neither considered the outcome of the battle of vital importance to its own security—so long as the other stayed out. In the context of the emerging cold war, the Americans were relieved to see the Soviets withdraw from China and gambled on Chinese nationalism to keep a Maoist China from becoming an "adjunct of Soviet power."[12] The Soviets were equally relieved when the United States chose not to intervene to rescue Jiang from defeat. When the end was in sight, both Washington and Moscow sought ways to reach accommodation with the incoming regime, which was beholden to neither of them.

As a committed Marxist-Leninist, Mao had no reservations about aligning his country with the Soviet Union in its confrontation with the Americans. In June 1949 he publicly denounced the United States and declared that China would lean to the side of the Soviets. But Mao and Zhou Enlai, his principal aide and diplomatist, were very much aware that the United States was better able than the Soviet Union to provide the assistance they needed for the reconstruction and modernization of China. As Chinese patriots, they were unwilling to become dependent on Stalin. If the Americans would refrain from further interference in China's internal affairs and treat China with respect, as an equal, Mao and Zhou might be receptive to overtures from Washington.

American leaders were divided over the possibility of a useful working relationship with the People's Republic of China, but Dean Acheson, the secretary of state who dominated the policy process in 1949, was clearly receptive to the idea. He despised communism and led his country's preparations for conflict with the Soviet Union, but he also despised Jiang. He was intrigued by the argument that China's Communists might be kept from becoming an instrument of Soviet policy. Domestic political considerations handicapped his efforts, but he kept the door open until catastrophe in Korea slammed it shut late in 1950.[13]

Stalin was conscious of the attraction of American wealth and power to some Chinese leaders. He had no intention of supporting a regime that might play him off against the Americans. Unable to install a more malleable leader, he kept Mao at arm's length until assured he could count on Chinese support in any conflict with the United States. Mao and his comrades had a simple choice: commit themselves to the Soviet Union and gain Soviet support against any external threat, or gamble on the goodwill of the avowedly anticommunist government in Washington. They chose Moscow.

When Stalin finally agreed to receive Mao in December 1949, the ensuing negotiations were difficult and demeaning for Mao. After two months, Mao gained the alliance that would protect him from the Americans and their new Japanese friends without surrendering China's independence. In return he was forced to concede the loss of Mongolia and to leave Manchurian ports in Soviet hands until 1952. The ideological bonds between Stalin and Mao scarcely intruded on each man's relentless pursuit of his nation's interests.

The Sino-Soviet alliance of 1950 upset Acheson's plans for reaching an accommodation with the People's Republic, but the Americans still intended to extricate themselves from the Chinese civil war by abandoning the rump regime Jiang had established on Taiwan. They anticipated the Communist takeover of Taiwan in the summer of 1950 and assumed that recognition of Mao's government would follow soon afterward. No one in Washington expected friendly relations with Beijing, but Acheson was persuaded that a working relationship was possible. Eventually, he predicted, Soviet imperialism would drive the two Communist states apart. The United States wanted to be in position to drive home the wedge.

One signal the Americans sent Mao came in their announcement of a "defensive perimeter" in the Pacific which excluded Taiwan. American leaders indicated publicly that Taiwan was not essential to the security of the United States. But the defensive perimeter proclaimed by the Americans also excluded the entire Asian mainland, raising questions about how the United States might respond to an attack on the intensely anticommunist Republic of Korea (ROK), which had been established south of the thirty-eighth parallel. Acheson declared that the South Koreans would have to defend themselves or turn to the UN.

In Korea, the mutually hostile regimes that had emerged on the peninsula in 1948 were at each other's throats, each eager to attack the other and unify the country under its own control. From the end of 1948 to June 1950, there were constant cross-border skirmishes initiated by both sides. Several times in 1949, Kim Il Sung, leader of the Communist North, begged Stalin to give him the means to attack the South. Stalin demurred, apprehensive about provoking a confrontation with the United States. The Americans denied the southern regime the offensive capability it desired. But in the spring of 1950, noting the withdrawal of American troops from Korea and the fact that Korea was outside the announced defensive perimeter of the United States, Stalin decided to give the northern Communist regime the supplies and military advisers it needed to overrun the South.

With the approval and support of Mao Zedong, Kim prepared a massive invasion of the South. Kim was confident that he could gain control of all of Korea quickly, before the Americans could muster a response. Stalin, with so many signals of a lack of American interest in Korea, bet there would be no response: he gave Kim the green light to attack. They were wrong, and the world, most especially the Korean people, paid a terrible price for their miscalculations.

On June 25, 1950, Korean Communist forces swept across the thirty-eighth parallel and quickly threw back the outnumbered and less well equipped southern army. But to the dismay of Kim, Stalin, and Mao, and despite its decision to place Korea outside its defensive perimeter, the United States chose to come to the aid of the ROK. American leaders perceived a direct threat to Japan and to the credibility of the United States as a defender of its friends. Remembering the failure of the League to stop Japan in Manchuria in 1931, they were determined to see the UN succeed. The League's inaction had been followed by further aggression and World War II. Never again. If Stalin was testing the will of the United States to resist Soviet expansion, the Americans accepted the challenge.

Most of those who fought against Kim's armies were Koreans or Americans, but fifteen other members of the UN also sent troops, most notably the British and the Turks. Together they beat back North Korean attacks and launched a successful counteroffensive in mid-September, driving the northerners back across the thirty-eight parallel in less than a month. Kim's government now faced the possibility of complete destruction.

The Chinese were apprehensive. If the Americans rolled back the North Koreans and eliminated the Communist state on China's border, they might continue their offensive into Manchuria. They might then attempt to overthrow the Communist government of China and return Jiang to the mainland. The Americans had already ordered ships to the Taiwan Strait to prevent Mao's men from attacking Taiwan. Profoundly concerned, Chinese leaders warned the Americans that if UN forces crossed the thirty-eighth parallel into North Korea, China would intervene against them.

Contemptuous of Chinese power and eager for an opportunity to demonstrate that they could reverse the spread of communism that once seemed to threaten all of Asia, American leaders ordered their troops across the thirty-eighth parallel. The plan was to annihilate North Korean forces and unite all of Korea under a noncommunist government. But they had underestimated Mao.

Mao was convinced that China would have to fight the United States eventually, and he preferred to fight the Americans in Korea rather than on his own soil. A grateful Stalin offered air support, then withdrew the offer, fearful of provoking the United States. Nonetheless, Mao sent Chinese "volunteers" across the Yalu into Korea. Eventually Soviet air support did arrive surreptitiously. Chinese troops quickly drove UN forces back down the peninsula, across the thirty-eighth parallel, reeling back to Pusan in defeat. China had taught the United States an important lesson.

Eventually, the Americans and their allies drove the overextended Chinese back across the thirty-eighth parallel. In July 1951 both sides reluctantly accepted a truce that brought the border between northern and southern regimes close to where it had been before the war started. It took two years of acrimonious negotiations and occasional fighting before an armistice agreement was reached in 1953. Even then a peace treaty proved elusive.

The Chinese had demonstrated to the world that they could not be ignored. Their intervention prevented the unification of Korea under a government likely to be hostile to them. But the price of Chinese intervention was high. Chinese casualties are estimated at over 800,000. For decades the Chinese and the Soviets argued bitterly over the $2 billion bill the Soviets presented Beijing for the aid they gave to China's military. And the Americans reentered the Chinese civil war, reenlisting on the side of Jiang's rump regime, and preventing Beijing from sending its forces to conquer Taiwan.

The confrontation between China and the United States ended American efforts to reach an accommodation with Beijing. As Chinese killed Americans in Korea, a hostile American public perceived China as a rogue state, a dangerous aggressor for whom there was no place in the UN and with whom the United States should not have diplomatic relations. The Americans continued to recognize Jiang's government on Taiwan as the legitimate government of all China. Jiang was clearly the principal beneficiary of the American and Chinese interventions in the war between the rival Korean states.

The Japanese also gained significantly from the war. Most of the goods and services required by UN forces in Korea were procured in Japan, providing an enormous stimulus to the Japanese economy. Japanese minesweepers, part of a growing "defense" establishment of dubious constitutionality, cleared Korean harbors of mines that baffled the U.S. Navy, facilitating the landing of UN troops. And in 1951, ignoring the objections of China and the Soviet Union, the United States and forty-seven other states signed a treaty of peace with Japan, leading to the end of the occupation. On the same day, the Japanese were required to sign a security treaty that allowed the Americans to maintain bases, troops, and ships on Japanese soil and in Japanese waters. In return they would be shielded by the American "nuclear umbrella."

After the Korean War, the central tension in the cold war in East Asia was between the United States and China. The principal flash point was the Taiwan Strait. The Americans stationed warships in the strait for nearly two decades after the Korean War. American aid to the Guomindang on Taiwan resumed, much of it military. Twice, in 1954 and again in 1958, Mao provoked confrontations by ordering attacks on Guomindang-held islands off the coast of China. On both occasions the United States intervened and forced him to back down. In 1954 the Americans signed a mutual defense pact with Jiang. Mao's efforts, however, were not unrewarded. In the United States and in the capitals of its allies there was widespread unease with the prospect of a major war over a handful of tiny islands of no strategic value. American leaders were compelled to mute their belligerent rhetoric and negotiate with the People's Republic. In 1958 they forced Jiang to announce that his mission of ending Communist rule of the mainland would not require the use of force. Mao had succeeded in creating tension between Taibei and Washington and in increasing doubts about American policy toward China among its Western allies.

A major additional side effect of the strait crisis of 1958 was an intensification of the discontent that had been growing in the Sino-Soviet relationship. The Chinese were still angry over Soviet looting of Manchuria after World War II and the terms of Soviet economic and technical assistance. A Soviet offer of military advisers and requests for submarine basing rights and a radio station on Chinese soil to broadcast to Soviet submarines aroused Mao's suspicions. In the late 1950s Soviet foreign policy struck Chinese leaders as excessively cautious; nor were they pleased by Soviet domestic policies such as de-Stalinization. Worst of all, Soviet advice to avoid provoking the United States irritated Mao. The Soviet failure to support their operations against Taiwan led the Chinese to suspect Soviet indifference to China's interests. The ultimate indignity was the suggestion by Nikita Khrushchev, the Soviet leader, that Mao accept the two-Chinas policy toward which the United States had moved—in other words, surrender Taiwan in return for American recognition of the People's Republic. Angry exchanges, focused primarily on ideological differences, led to the recall of Soviet technicians from China in 1960 and an unsuccessful Soviet effort to sabotage China's nuclear weapons program.[14] In the years that followed, relations became increasingly hostile.

As Mao and Khrushchev drove each other and their countries apart with harsh rhetoric, China was rent internally by divisions within the Communist Party, especially over issues such as the pace of agricultural and industrial change and the value of intellectuals to the state. The "Hundred Flowers" and "Great Leap Forward" campaigns of the late 1950s were followed by the "Great Proletarian Cultural Revolution" that exploded in the mid-1960s. The Cultural Revolution brought China's economic development to a halt and damaged the reputation it had won in world affairs since 1949. And despite the tenuous position of China in an international system in which it had succeeded in antagonizing both superpowers, the country's foreign policy apparatus was destroyed and all but one of China's ambassadors was recalled from abroad.

In 1968 a warning bell sounded for any Chinese leader concerned about national security. Soviet military intervention crushed a heretical reform movement in the Communist Party of Czechoslovakia. Shortly afterward, the Soviet leader, Leonid Brezhnev, pronounced the "Brezhnev Doctrine," claiming the right to use force in defense of Moscow's conception of socialism. As the Soviets proceeded to mass troops along their borders with China in Xinjiang and Manchuria, tensions increased.

In March 1969 clashes between Soviet and Chinese patrols in the vicinity of Chenbao Island in the Ussuri River between Manchuria and Siberia resulted in heavy casualties on both sides. After the Chinese rejected Moscow's demand for negotiations, Soviet forces marched into Xinjiang in August. Fearful of a preemptive strike against their nuclear installations in the region, the Chinese agreed to meet with the Soviets, defusing the crisis but doing little to improve Sino-Soviet relations.

Mao was persuaded that the Soviet threat was serious and became receptive to the idea that accommodation with the United States might be useful to counter Soviet pressure. The Americans, shaken by their battering in Vietnam in the late 1960s, began to perceive the Chinese as potential allies against the Soviets and as a source of support for their efforts to extricate themselves from the war in Vietnam. Each side moved cautiously, aware of opposition to rapprochement in both countries. As had been the case in the 1950s, Taiwan was the irresolvable issue. In 1971, however, the Americans and Chinese found compelling reasons to compromise. The winning formula was "one China, but not now." The Americans acknowledged the fact that Chinese on both sides of the strait insisted on one China and expressed their expectation that the future of Taiwan would be determined peacefully, by the Chinese themselves, at some later time. In 1971 the United States supported the seating of representatives of the People's Republic in the UN. Gradually the Americans moved to disengage themselves from Taiwan, to which they were bound by the mutual defense treaty of 1954.

By the mid-1970s, China and the United States had clearly ceased to be adversaries. The leaders of both countries had concluded that cooperation against the Soviet Union was of greater immediate importance than the many issues that still divided them. The cold war in East Asia was virtually over as the United States accepted defeat in Vietnam and began to pull back from the peak of its military involvement in the region. It remained, however, the dominant power there, retaining overwhelming naval superiority in the western Pacific and bases in Japan and Korea. Most East Asian leaders welcomed the American presence as a source of stability, a means both of containing communism and of preventing a revival of Japanese power.

The Resurgence of East Asian Economic Power

The cold war was not the only activity in East Asia in the years between the Communist victory in China's civil war and the moment when the Americans finally recognized the People's Republic. These were also years of extraordinary economic activity. Japan led the way with an astonishing burst of growth that took it from dependency on the largess of the United States to becoming one of the world's largest economies and Washington's most feared commercial rival. The Japanese were not alone. South Korea reluctantly came to terms with its former tormentor and used both Japanese capital and the Japanese development model to launch its own highly successful industrialization. Singapore, Hong Kong, and Taiwan, all primarily ethnic Chinese entities, outperformed many larger states, including the People's Republic of China. By 1977, America's trade across the Pacific had surpassed that with its traditional partners across the Atlantic. The economic importance of East Asia had increased enormously. It promised to be central to the international economic system, as it had been before the nineteenth century.

Coping with the United States remained Japan's most important and most difficult challenge. No other country could equal American military power or provide a comparable market for Japanese exports. But the Americans had come to regret their efforts to prevent the rearmament of Japan and pressed constantly for the Japanese to rebuild their military for integration into the forces defending the "Free World" against the "international Communist conspiracy." The Japanese parried these thrusts easily, pointing to the limitations of the constitution the Americans had imposed on them and domestic political opposition to revising the relevant provision. The Japanese had the weaker hand, but they played it very well.

Japan's leaders understood the importance of their American connection. In the context of the cold war, it was sensible to be aligned with the United States, to let Americans fight Japan's battles. Equally important was the market for Japanese goods provided by the United States and the easy access Americans gave Japan to the world's most advanced technology. It was an era in which the economy of the United States and support to America's friends provided an extremely high rate of world economic growth, a climate favorable to Japanese exports. As a result of shrewd industrial policy, Japan's growth rate soared.

By the 1960s, concern about Japan's becoming a financial burden to the American taxpayer gave way to fear of Japan as a commercial threat. By 1968 Japan had overtaken Germany to rejoice in having the second-largest economy in the world. Before long, some Japanese would dream of overtaking the United States, of Japan as number one. It was not an outcome Americans were prepared to countenance, nor was Japan's economic power a comfort to the neighbors it had once attempted to dominate.

Friction over trade issues began to trouble relations between Washington and Tokyo. To most American leaders, the political-military considerations of the cold war greatly outweighed trade matters, but in the 1960s complaints from domestic industries hurt by Japanese competition could no longer be ignored. Added to these irritations was Japan's unhappiness with America's war in Vietnam. Particularly irksome was the use of Okinawa as a staging ground for the American assault on North Vietnam in the late 1960s. The Japanese demanded the return of Okinawa, but the American military would not surrender its bases there. The territorial question soon became enmeshed in disagreements over trade.

In 1969 the Americans offered to return Okinawa in exchange for a Japanese agreement to limit textile exports to the United States. The Japanese prime minister, Sato Eisaku, accepted President Richard Nixon's offer and agreed to allow the United States to maintain bases on Okinawa and to reintroduce nuclear weapons in an emergency. Nixon thought Sato had promised also to limit textile exports. Both sides were delighted with the handling of Okinawa's reversion, but the textile settlement quickly collapsed. For over a year tense negotiations between the two countries embittered their relations. In the summer of 1971 came what the Japanese called the "Nixon shocks."

In July 1971 Nixon dramatically informed the world that his national security adviser had visited Beijing secretly and that the United States was proceeding toward rapprochement with China. The Japanese were given less than one hour's notice of this remarkable shift in American policy, although every advocate of rapprochement in the American government had underscored the importance of keeping Tokyo informed.[15] Nixon had taken his revenge on Sato, who, faithful to his American ally, had long resisted popular demands for accommodation with China. This was shock number one.

In August Nixon struck again, imposing a surcharge on all U.S. tariffs in an effort to improve the trade balance. He began a process that ultimately forced the revaluation of the yen upward against the dollar, a de facto devaluation of the U.S. dollar to make American goods more competitive. Washington had sent Tokyo a clear message: it would no longer subordinate its economic interests to its foreign policy objectives.

The Nixon shocks changed the nature of the Japanese-American relationship. The Japanese could no longer count on benign neglect in Washington's response to Japan's commercial expansion. And if anger over trade issues frayed the alliance, could Americans newly enamored of China be relied on to provide for Japan's security? To some Japanese leaders it was evident that the United States was turning to China for insurance against the growing power of Japan. Japan would have to fend for itself in the international arena.

In fact, Japanese-American relations, though frequently roiled by economic issues, remained reasonably constant. The Japanese could not easily find a substitute for the American market or a cheaper source of protection. Few Americans were prepared to contemplate a hostile Japan, however useful rapprochement with China might be for America's confrontation with the Soviet Union.

The Japanese model was followed with relative ease by South Korea. In the colonial era, Japan had viewed Korea as an integral part of its economic system and had laid the foundations for a modern industrial infrastructure on the peninsula—although most of the industry was in the north. The Japanese had also created institutions, similar to their own, approximating what Chalmers Johnson and others have called the developmental state,[16] a bureaucratically run regime focused on economic growth. Virtually all Korean officials and businessmen spoke Japanese and had contacts in Japan that proved enormously valuable after 1965, when Park Chung Hee's military dictatorship forced the people of South Korea to swallow a treaty of normalization with Japan.

Park was determined to build a wealthy and powerful nation. Economic development was his mission, and foreign-educated Korean technocrats and American advisers helped him refine and implement his ideas. Korea's development would have to be export-driven, given the relatively small size of the domestic market. Its comparative advantage lay with its well-disciplined, low-wage work force, kept in line by Park's troops and the dreaded Korean CIA. By 1981, Korea's exports had soared from $42 million in 1962 to an incredible $20 *billion.* Its construction industry, having demonstrated its excellence in Vietnam, won most of the contracts for projects in the oil-rich Middle Eastern states. Park had driven South Korea into the front ranks of the world's economic powers.

Park's assassination in 1979 was followed by another military coup, headed by a general who lacked Park's intelligence and reputation for rectitude. He and the general who succeeded him succumbed to corruption, and neither could carry out the adjustments required by the changing international economic climate. A bailout by the Japanese in 1983 facilitated recovery from the doldrums that struck immediately after Park's death, but Korea was forced to open its markets as a price for Japanese and other foreign assistance. Brutal repression of an uprising in the less prosperous southern city of Kwangju radicalized students and workers, many of whom believed that the American military in Korea, linked closely to the Korean troops sent to Kwangju, was complicit in the death of thousands of demonstrators.

Korea was rescued from the vicissitudes of the 1980s by a combination of middle-class anger, American pressure, and the example of "People's Power" overthrowing dictatorship in the Philippines in 1986. The military chose to accept political reform and elections in the late 1980s, but the nascent South Korean democracy, though an important force in the world economic system, was not free of its core problems, not least among them the security threat from the North.

Taiwan, arguably, had been the greatest beneficiary of the Korean War—and especially of Chinese intervention in that war. Japan's economy had benefited greatly from American procurement policies, but the very survival of the regime on Taiwan derived from the change in American policy, the rapid reversal of Washington's decision to abandon the island to the Communists. American economic and military assistance to Taiwan resumed, and American industrial goods, factories, and equipment flowed there in the 1950s and early 1960s. Once it became clear that Taiwan had become an American protectorate, Japanese and American companies seeking low-priced goods arrived to buy whatever Taiwan could produce. Jiang's technocrats concluded that export promotion was the answer to Taiwan's needs. Like the Japanese, they concentrated on achieving rapid economic growth, adjusting the island's productive structure in relation to the opportunities they saw in the international economy. Slowly they shifted the focus of planning from Jiang's dream of recovering the mainland to creating a solid base for a de facto independent Taiwan. Between 1959 and 1965, when American economic assistance began to be phased out, Taiwan's foreign trade increased at a phenomenal rate.

In the mid-1960s, partly in response to American pressures, Taiwan moved away from state-owned enterprises to private enterprise and allowed direct foreign investment. Multinational corporations seeking cheap labor flocked to the island, producing goods there for export. Taiwan created the world's first export-processing zone in 1966. An enormous flow of private foreign investment followed, with funds coming from the United States, overseas Chinese everywhere, Japan, and western Europe.

The 1970s required some painful adjustments. First came the shock of Chinese-American rapprochement and the fear of abandonment and isolation that accompanied it. Then came a huge increase in world oil prices and a worldwide recession in 1973. Several major U.S. corporations, forced by Beijing to choose between doing business on the mainland or on Taiwan, chose the larger potential of continental China. And finally came trade tensions with the United States, beginning in 1977.

Shrewdly, Taiwan's leaders invited some of the world's leading multinationals to operate on the island under concessionary conditions, giving other countries and influential companies a stake in its future. Its lobbyists in Washington, second only to the Israelis in sophistication and accomplishment, protected Taiwan's interests. And to cut production costs, its industries began to move to Southeast Asia to take advantage of cheaper labor there. By 1979 tiny Taiwan was the twenty-first–largest trading country in the world, and it soon was second only to Japan in the amassing of foreign currency.

In the years that followed, despite losing its seat in the UN and its mutual defense pact and official relations with the United States, Taiwan continued to thrive. It benefited from a combination of excellent leadership, skillful lobbying and diplomacy, and a buoyant world economy to which it was an important contributor. And with prosperity, political conditions improved as the Guomindang confounded its critics by moving toward democracy.

Potentially the greatest impact on the world economy was the decision of China's leaders, in the late 1970s, to abandon self-reliance and to seek the rapid modernization of their industry through increased contact with the outside world. China had not been an important member of the world trading community since the Great Depression, and many of its leaders opposed contact with the West, fearing dependence on outside, ideologically hostile forces. The leading advocate of opening China to the world was Deng Xiaoping, one of the party leaders who had been purged early in the Cultural Revolution. By the close of 1978, Deng emerged as China's paramount leader. He won the support of party leaders less receptive to integration in the world economy, less comfortable abandoning the Soviet-style planned economy, but well aware that Mao's utopian visions had brought the country to ruin.

The leadership's decisions to accept foreign loans, foreign aid, and foreign direct investment attracted billions of dollars into the country. American, European, and Japanese businessmen were eager to explore China's vast market and to invest in industries that would benefit from the country's enormous supply of low-wage, nonunionized labor. Technology that China might have required another generation to develop on its own was immediately available.

Deng also moved quickly to cement rapprochement with the United States, a process that had slowed in the mid-1970s. He and the Americans put aside continuing differences over Taiwan and established formal diplomatic relations early in 1979, opening the floodgates for investment in China. In the years that followed, the contribution of the United States to China's modernization was enormously important. American universities trained thousands of Chinese scientists, competing with American businessmen in the transfer of technology to a country so recently their nation's enemy. As China's export industry grew, the United States became its principal market, absorbing as much as a third of the manufactured goods China shipped abroad.

China's economic growth and the speed with which it became a major trading state and an important participant in world capital markets was extraordinary. Its growth rate for the years 1978 to 1993 was the fastest of any country in the world. Despite continued low per capita income, the gross national product of China's billion-plus people overtook that of Germany, placing China third behind the United States and Japan. Many analysts predicted it would have the world's largest economy in the twenty-first century. Its trade surplus with the United States also grew rapidly, creating a new source of friction between the two countries.

Clearly, as the world entered the last decade of the twentieth century, the economies of East Asia had regained an importance lost centuries before, when the West industrialized and they did not. Militarily, China alone seemed likely to emerge as a great power in the foreseeable future—although Japan certainly had the necessary wealth and industrial base. Korea and Taiwan were already major players. Before the twenty-first century was over, East Asia seemed likely to regain its place as the locus of the world's economic power.

On the Eve of the Next Millennium

The men and women who lived through the last years of the twentieth century witnessed one of the major events in world history—the collapse and disintegration of the Soviet empire. They were also witnesses to one of the great triumphs of the human will—the election of Nelson Mandela as president of South Africa, marking an end to the apartheid regime that had shamed that nation. Only one event in East Asia was of comparable iconic import—the Tiananmen massacre, the brutal suppression of the democracy movement in China in 1989.

For the peoples of East Asia there were other events of unusual, even extraordinary significance. South Korea and Taiwan both emerged as stable democracies. In 1994 a war between an impoverished but possibly nuclear North Korea and the United States was narrowly averted. Attempting to intimidate Taiwan, China provoked a confrontation with the United States in 1996. The people of Hong Kong, many profoundly troubled by the events at Tiananmen, watched as the People's Liberation Army (PLA) marched into their city and China resumed sovereignty over it in 1997. And before the century ended, the economic miracles of East Asia began to unravel as currencies tumbled, banks failed, stock and real estate values fell, and unemployment rose. The stability of some of the region's regimes seemed less certain as the legitimacy that came with prosperity was threatened. Of gravest concern was the possibility of East Asia's economic troubles resulting in a worldwide depression. The price of globalization could prove to be very high for all concerned.

The expectation that the future would belong to East Asia, that the locus of power was returning to where it had been before the brief era of Western dominance, had to be reconsidered. It was, of course, entirely possible that at the next turn of the business cycle, the Asian dragons, big and little, would surge forward and dominate international trade. It was conceivable that the shaky Chinese banking system would be repaired in time to allow the continued rise of China's economic and military strength, as well as its political influence. One might even assume that eventually a strong, competent Japanese government would emerge and revitalize that nation, whose economy was in the doldrums for most of the 1990s—and whose well-being is so critical to the region. But the mood in the region was less confident in 1999 than it had been in 1990.

A striking feature of the 1990s, of enormous significance for East Asia, was the resurgence of the American economy. It had been clear throughout the decade that all of the states that feared China—or Japan, or North Korea—perceived the presence of American military power as a source of security. Before century's end, the United States was again being pressed into the role of economic hegemon, at the very least as the market of last resort.

China, however, was increasingly dissatisfied with American preeminence in the region. American support for Taiwan posed a major obstacle to Beijing's hopes for reunification. The United States retained sanctions against China for its transgressions at Tiananmen long after all the other major industrial states had resumed business as usual, and constantly criticized China's human rights abuses. Some Chinese leaders argued that the United States was seeking to "contain" China, to prevent it from taking its rightful place among the world's great powers, its rightful place as the dominant power in East Asia. And China was too big, too powerful, for the United States to dictate the terms of contact.

Before the decade ended, the United States and China backed away from their confrontation in the Taiwan Strait and groped clumsily toward what they called a "strategic partnership." However vague the term, it was vastly superior to the moment in 1996 when the Chinese found it necessary to remind Americans that the PLA had missiles that could destroy Los Angeles. But tensions eased by an exchange of presidential visits in 1997 and 1998 flared again in May 1999 when American planes, bombing Belgrade as part of NATO's effort to stop ethnic cleansing in Kosovo, mistakenly destroyed the Chinese embassy in the Yugoslav capital. In retaliation, the Chinese government encouraged violent demonstrations against the American embassy in Beijing. The episode, combined with American concerns about Chinese spying in the United States, threatened to derail efforts in both Washington and Beijing to cooperate on issues of vital concern to both countries.

At this point, in July 1999, Lee Teng-hui, Taiwan's democratically elected president, roiled the waters further by announcing that henceforth relations between Taibei and Beijing would have to be conducted on a "special state-to-state" basis. "Clarifications" issued by his aides suggested that Taiwan would no longer accept the one-China formulation to which Taiwan, China, and the United States had adhered since the early 1970s. Neither Lee's remarks nor those of his aides constituted a declaration of independence, but they outraged Chinese leaders determined to bring Taiwan under China's control. In the weeks and months that followed, Washington worked frenetically to prevent violence in the strait, assuring Beijing of continued American commitment to the one-China principle and simultaneously attempting to persuade Lee to soften his remarks. Throughout the episode, Bill Clinton, the American president, had to be wary of a Congress eager to support democratic Taiwan and mistrustful of the People's Republic.

At least as volatile as the Taiwan Strait standoff between Beijing and Taibei is the situation on the Korean Peninsula. The rapid economic decline of the Communist regime since the death of Kim Il Sung in 1994 and the persistence of famine in the country suggest that the condition of Pyongyang is terminal. Yet its military forces remain powerful, and its missile and nuclear technology pose an increasing risk to all the states of the region—and conceivably to the United States as well. No one can predict the peaceful reunification of Korea with any confidence or be sure that the Communists will go quietly into the night. Nor can anyone be certain that the great powers—China, Japan, and the United States—will manage Korean affairs wisely.

Though hardly a passive or inconsequential participant in the affairs of the region, Japan is the nation least likely to disrupt the existing fragile international structure. Japanese leaders continue to rely on the United States for their country's security, having drawn a step closer with the new U.S.-Japan security guidelines agreed upon in 1997. At the same time, they are loath to give offense to their Chinese neighbors. Economically, Japan remains dominant in East Asia, and it has the human and industrial potential with which to compete with the United States worldwide. At least one analyst, the historian Walter LaFeber, sees renewed confrontation between Japan and the United States as likely.[17] Most observers, however, are more sanguine.

The struggle for wealth and power in East Asia continues, with Chinese-American relations likely to remain central. The importance of avoiding a cold war between China and the United States is obvious. Should the world be spared that calamity, the answer to the related question of whether China will be a responsible member of the international community or attempt to use its growing power to maximize its own position, ultimately destabilizing the region, is likely to define the twenty-first century in East Asia.

Selected Readings

The Chinese system of managing Western traders, its destruction in the Opium War, and the Western imposition of the treaty system are all most easily approached in John Fairbank, ed., *Cambridge History of China: Late Ch'ing, 1800–1911,* pt. 1 (Cambridge: Cambridge University Press, 1978). See also James Hevia, *Cherishing Men from Afar: Qing Guest Ritual and the Macartney Embassy of 1793* (Durham, N.C.: Duke University Press, 1995), for a challenging explanation of the conduct of Qing diplomacy.

The era of Japanese dominance is most accessible in W. G. Beasley, *Japanese Imperialism, 1894–1945* (Oxford: Clarendon Press, 1987). For Japan's role in the post–World War II international economy, see Takashi Inoguchi and Daniel I. Okimoto, *The Political Economy of Japan,* vol. 2, *The Changing International Context* (Stanford: Stanford University Press, 1988); and Stephen D. Cohen, *An Ocean Apart: Explaining Three Decades of U.S.-Japanese Trade Frictions* (Westport, Conn.: Praeger, 1998).

For Korean affairs, see Bruce Cumings, *Korea's Place in the Sun* (New York: W. W. Norton, 1997); and Don Oberdorfer, *The Two Koreas* (New York: Addison Wesley Longman, 1997). Both books are also useful for the American role in Korea.

Comprehensive surveys of the U.S. role in East Asia are Warren I. Cohen, *America's Response to China,* 4th ed. (New York: Columbia University Press, 1999); and Walter LaFeber, *The Clash: A History of U.S.-Japanese Relations* (New York: W. W. Norton, 1997).

For an understanding of twentieth-century Chinese foreign relations, start with Paul A. Cohen, *History in Three Keys: The Boxers as Event, Experience, and Myth* (New York: Columbia University Press, 1997). Michael H. Hunt,

Frontier Defense and the Open Door (New Haven: Yale University Press, 1973), focuses on 1895–1911. The diplomacy of republican China has not been studied adequately. In addition to William Kirby, *Germany and Republican China* (Princeton: Princeton University Press, 1984), John W. Garver, *Chinese-Soviet Relations, 1937–1945* (New York: Oxford University Press, 1988), provides insight into the policies of Jiang and Mao. For the years since 1949, a useful volume is Thomas W. Robinson and David Shambaugh, eds., *Chinese Foreign Policy: Theory and Practice* (Oxford: Clarendon Press, 1994).

CHAPTER 2

Social and Political Change in Nineteenth-Century China

MARY BACKUS RANKIN

Historians confer images on centuries. Thus China in the eighteenth century is known for prosperity, peace, and the elegant courts of three great autocratic Manchu emperors; it was the "High Qing." The nineteenth century, in contrast, is often characterized in terms of dynastic decline. Rulers were weak, government corrupt, and armies ineffectual. Scholars decried moral decay. Rural misery gave rise to massive rebellions—long considered portents of dynastic collapse. The weakened Qing dynasty could not resist Western invaders.

One set of explanations of why China was seemingly so slow to appreciate the Western threat suggests a cultural conservatism encompassing traditional scholarly contempt for barbarians and the military, Confucian resistance to change, and a Sinocentric worldview formalized in a tributary system through which rulers of peripheral domains acknowledged the superiority of the "Middle Kingdom." From the Opium War (1839–1842) to the end of the century, Chinese only reluctantly and haltingly accepted Western military and industrial technology to strengthen the country. They were still slower to accept the Western-style international system of legally equal states, which followed diplomatic practices incompatible with Qing emperors' ideas of their own centrality. Officials and scholars were even more reluctant to undertake fundamental restructuring of government, education, and the economy.[1]

Numerous Chinese Marxist historians, by contrast, emphasize the semi-feudal nature of Qing China. The meaning of feudalism in this interpretation is not derived from European history, but instead signifies a political system controlled by the oppressive imperial government and an agrarian socioeconomic system based on small-scale household production in which peasants' surplus was extracted by landlords. These historians also stress that imperialism retarded Chinese development, and additionally blame Confucianism for the rigid traditionalism, superstition, and backwardness that they see in the old society.

Such narratives include some obvious historical realities. The Qing dynasty (1644–1911) did become weaker, domestically and internationally. During the nineteenth century there were six major rebellions and countless lesser uprisings. China was defeated in four wars with Western countries or Japan. Foreigners accumulated territorial concessions and trading rights in "treaty ports," as well as legal immunities, economic rights, and religious privileges. Several decades of military and diplomatic humiliations occurred before the dynasty seriously mobilized for change. Nonetheless, Confucianism was not as conservative and backward-looking as is often supposed, and tradition was not static. Processes of change were under way in Chinese society and politics.

The nineteenth-century changes fell into two categories: the slow, cumulative changes in society begun long before Western imperialists forcibly entered China and the more pronounced deviations incorporating foreign practices. Indigenous changes with pre–nineteenth-century roots continued, but the old trajectories were interrupted in the middle of the century by both massive rebellions and imperialist military and economic intrusion. These almost simultaneous crises produced a historical disjuncture, after which some of the main phenomena of twentieth-century Chinese history began to appear: imperialism, state-building, modernization, mobilizations within society, nationalism, and revolution. These processes unfolded unevenly as people reacted to a series of late nineteenth-century crises that led toward still more profound historical reorientations beginning in the late 1890s.

Much of the social change during the nineteenth century did not involve the rise of new classes such as the bourgeoisie or proletariat familiar to students of European history. Instead it took place in practices, processes, and relationships: more scholar-gentry deriving income from trade or doing specialized work such as managing water control; merchants enjoying higher status more comparable to gentry; more peasants producing for the market but also more slipping down into an itinerant subclass of transport workers and vagrants; modest alterations in gender relationships; and adaptation of lineage organization to business purposes. Toward the end of the century, however, men with specialized Western educations and professional skills appeared; these were the forerunners of new social groups emergent at the beginning of the twentieth century.

Political change was more difficult because it impinged on imperial authority. The basic structure of the Qing centralized bureaucratic monarchy persisted throughout the century despite many small modifications in government practice and organization. The autocratic ruler and his chief councilors presided over a complex central bureaucracy of six boards and numerous agencies. Bureaucratic authority descended through provincial administrations headed by governors-general and governors to counties headed by magistrates. Even though more and more posts were purchased, government examinations remained the approved method of recruiting officials, who were then appointed, evaluated, and rotated from the center.

The conquering Manchu dynasty adopted not only this effective Chinese-style bureaucracy but also Confucian ruling practices. The emperor fulfilled a solemn ritual role as the link between heaven and earth. Government examinations based on the Confucian classics recruited men into the bureaucracy and ensured that education reinforced orthodox morality. Government also influenced the social hierarchy by conferring gentry status through the examination degrees. To benefit the populace as a whole, the rulers sought to maintain order, promote prosperity, ensure minimum levels of subsistence through welfare and famine relief, and keep taxes low so as not to burden the people unduly.[2]

The throne could, in theory, intervene anywhere in government and society. During the eighteenth century, vigorous emperors, assisted by some remarkable activist officials, sought to extend the reach of the central state into society. By the nineteenth century, the increasingly populous, commercialized, urbanized, and diverse society had become harder to keep under control. Within government itself, emperors were constrained by bureaucratic procedures even more than before. At the same time, two heritages of the seventeenth-century Manchu invasion continued to affect politics even though the Qing no longer behaved like a conquest dynasty. Latent tensions still existed between Chinese officials and their Manchu and Mongol counterparts, and the court banned any public debate within society and any associations of scholars that could remotely be considered political. Those who even appeared to violate these prohibitions or oppose Manchu rule risked execution. But as government corruption, natural disasters, poverty, and social unrest increased at the end of the eighteenth century, prominent literati as well as officials began to express alarm and discuss solutions.

There were two overlapping reformist phases in the nineteenth century. The first, ascendant in the early decades, was internally focused. Officials and concerned literati sought to make government more honest and effective so it could resolve mounting domestic problems and benefit the people. Existing Confucian reform agendas seriously addressed, but could not solve, the intractable social and economic problems that foreshadowed massive rebellion. Because the old domestic problems never disappeared, Confucian reformism continued through the rest of the century. It shaped the policies of the 1860s Restoration after the Taiping Rebellion, but thereafter was overshadowed by externally driven reform.

In the second phase, which gathered momentum in the 1870s, reform was propelled by the growing threat of Western imperialism. Foreign methods were appropriated for Chinese purposes, and traditional conceptions were combined with Western ideas. The term "modern" was not yet part of the Chinese vocabulary, but some officials pursued "self-strengthening" of the Chinese state by technically modernizing military organization and armaments and introducing mechanized industry, transportation, and communication. This official reformism soon included modifying classical education to better prepare men to govern, introducing subjects such as science and Western languages in a few new schools, and adding government offices to represent China abroad or promote self-strengthening at home.

The new reformism did not, however, follow a single trajectory. The more volatile aspects arose not from government programs but from the treaty port press, gentry involved in public affairs, and patriots distressed over defeats by France in the 1880s and Japan in the 1890s. Reform was politicized; demands for change reflected long-accumulating frustrations of scholars and lower officials lacking political influence as well as emerging national consciousness and incipient societal mobilization. The 1898 Reform Movement signaled the advent of open oppositional politics; radical reformers who briefly dominated the government during the One Hundred Days during the summer of 1898 aspired to change the nature of Qing political power as well as alter bureaucratic structure and government policies.

Historians analyzing nineteenth-century Chinese history have argued over whether to emphasize internal events or stress the Western impact, alternatively viewed as subjugation to capitalist imperialism or as a positive stimulus to necessary modern reform.[3] Despite the different interpretations, international and domestic events were actually so interwoven that neither operated independently. The effect of Western imperialism, however, was more transformative. Chinese had to react to situations that they had not encountered before. Westerners introduced new technology, new types of social and political organization, new ideas, and new conceptions of relationships. Old questions could then be reformulated: How much education should women receive? How active a role should government play in the economy and society? Are localities best governed by centrally appointed bureaucrats or local men? Should more officials and literati be allowed to express opinions to the throne? Latent tensions became manifest as Chinese conceived of hitherto unimagined solutions. International trade provided opportunities for enterprising merchants but introduced new economic instabilities into peasants' lives. Assertive Westerners intruded into more and more localities. Political loyalties were also strained as military defeats aroused patriotism. By the end of the century, disagreements over how to defend China from foreigners had not only eroded faith in government leaders but also produced pressure to transform the government structure. Society slipped further from official control as information and ideas were conveyed through the press and telegraph, people traveled more rapidly on steamboats, the first short railways appeared before 1900, and foreign trade stimulated new Chinese businesses.

The mid–nineteenth-century disjuncture did not require rejecting all of the past. Existing processes, ideas, and practices were often redirected and redefined, thereby leading to new results. Even though Confucianism justified authoritarian, paternalistic family structures and autocratic imperial rule, it was more flexible in practice than in theory. By the nineteenth century, there were numerous schools of scholarship with differing intellectual, literary, and historical agendas. Confucianism penetrated all levels of society, interacting with Buddhism and Daoism (themselves fractured into different sects) and countless popular cults. Interwoven popular and elite cultures produced a Chinese culture characterized by regional, ethnic, and class variation while incorporating basic norms of authority, hierarchy, and gender. Officials often tolerated divergent practices if they did not seem subversive, and traditional social institutions such as lineages proved adaptable to new uses. Because considerable adjustments could occur within existing systems, social and cultural flexibility as well as rigidity may have discouraged rapid structural change. Conversely, small incremental alterations in existing practices and institutions could lead toward modernity as people adjusted to changing times.

A Changing Traditional Society

The dramatic crises of the nineteenth century occurred amidst slow but cumulative economic and social changes with roots in the Ming dynasty

(1368–1644). The interacting demographic and commercial growth was most fundamental. Population surged from about 250 million around 1750 to well over 400 million in 1850. Trade increased along with population. By the late eighteenth century, there were long-distance markets in grain. Indigenous banking, credit, and trade organizations expanded throughout the nineteenth century. Cities along the coast and the Yangzi River, such as Canton and Suzhou, became economic as well as administrative centers. New towns and local markets appeared in commercialized areas. Land could be more easily bought and sold, but the economic arrangements of ownership and tenancy became increasingly complex. Instead of concentrating in a great capital city as in Tokyo, the urban populace was spread throughout regional urban hierarchies commercially tied together. Peasant families produced rice, cotton, silk, and woven cloth for the market. While often living at the margins of subsistence, they were not isolated in self-sufficient communities. A free and mobile labor force also developed as almost all legal restrictions on geographic movement disappeared during the eighteenth century.

By the nineteenth century, trade was too large for close government supervision, although the Qing still maintained a few monopolies such as salt. Hugely rich salt merchants moving in high circles were vulnerable to imperial whims. All well-off traders expected official requests for contributions, for which they often received patronage in return. Nonetheless, the Qing state generally favored commerce, and officials usually saw advantages in regulating trade through price mechanisms rather than direct control. Commerce, however, failed to evolve into capitalism along European paths for many reasons. Most important, China did not exploit the mineral sources of energy that powered European industrial capitalism.[4] Capital accumulation was also discouraged by population pressure on resources, the small scale of peasant farming, and merchant preference for spreading investments over several enterprises to diminish risk and avoid official exactions. Because class lines had become so permeable, successful merchants could relatively easily join the more prestigious gentry instead of pursuing exclusively mercantile class interests. Even so, Western traders encountered a commercialized, urbanized agrarian economy.

As commerce developed and trade became more interchangeable with gentry occupations, the status of merchants rose. Wealth lacked the prestige of examination degrees, but it could be made respectable through philanthropy and cultivated lifestyles. Trade became a major means of upward social mobility as successful merchants used profits to finance education, donate to the community, and purchase degrees that reduced government harassment and might lead to official posts. By the later nineteenth century, the term *gentry-merchant* was applied to both individuals and cooperating groups of degree holders and traders.

The increasing number of people aspiring to gentry status weakened the longtime connection of scholars to government service, thereby modifying the nature of the gentry. As education spread and the number of men qualified to compete in the examinations increased, the chances of passing and holding office declined because the number of high degrees and regular official posts remained much the same. Educated men had to find alternative careers, ranging from teaching, scholarship, and art to management, trade, publishing, and more marginal literate occupations such as legal pettifoggery. Competition for office became even more acute when the government expanded sales of ranks and degrees to raise money during the Taiping Rebellion. From 1865 to 1900, about half of all middle-rank local officials had purchased their posts compared to 29 percent in 1840.[5] Men who passed the still prestigious examinations were frustrated by long delays in obtaining office. Receding opportunities for government service contributed to malaise and alienation among the literati toward the end of the century. The uncertainties of official appointment probably also encouraged some men to decide that Western education opened greater opportunities than the classical curriculum.

The surplus of educated men also contributed to the increase in societal organization. Local historical gazetteers record growing numbers of elite-financed and managed schools, charitable institutions, temples, shrines, and other organizations for community needs such as water control and fire fighting. Villages had their own religious and community associations. Lineage organizations, trade guilds, and native-place associations of merchants, workers, scholars, and officials employed in cities away from home similarly increased. Secret societies and cults spread, and militia proliferated in times of disorder. When Chinese came in contact with Western institutions in the treaty ports, their societal organizations were complex and dense, and the accelerated expansion of organizations after the Taiping Rebellion reflected both domestic tendencies and impetus from abroad.

Geographic mobility increased as well; people of all classes traveled for numerous reasons. There was permanent migration to underpopulated frontiers or hill country in the interior. As these lands filled up, more surplus population moved to the cities or went abroad from the southeast coast to

Southeast Asia and, after the mid-nineteenth century, the Americas. In the second half of the century, new waves of internal migration occurred into areas depopulated by the Taiping and other rebellions. In addition, there was constant temporary migration: men (mostly) of all classes traveled between their home areas and the cities and towns, where they found short- or long-term employment; poor boatmen, coolies, and peddlers eked out a living along trade routes; and refugees fled warfare and natural disasters. With transportation improved, tourism became a pastime of cultured elites.

For the poor, geographic mobility was often associated with social marginality. The poorest men had little hope of acquiring land or even marrying and being part of respectable village society. When they left villages to seek employment, their needs for protection and community contributed to the increase in popular sects and secret societies. Volatile combinations of a rootless social stratum, religious or religiously infused popular organizations, and general economic insecurity produced uprisings. Sects and secret societies were usually peaceful, but the pressure from Beijing on officials to root out subversion and heterodoxy caused tension with this growing social segment.

Geographic mobility also interacted with urbanization. Men left villages to become urban handicraft workers. Portions of the populace sojourned in cities while maintaining their native-place registrations. Within elite society, officials could not serve in their home provinces, merchants did business away from home, and scholars and artists sought wealthy patrons. Many merchants, in particular, became bi-residential. They were urbanites, with commitments both to the city where they did business and to their often more rural home areas, where lineages fostered ritual kinship solidarity. They could identify with and act as links between communities in both places without being fully a part of either.

In much of China, the gentry had already moved permanently to larger market towns and county seats for greater safety and more social and cultural opportunities than rural life offered. As the number and size of cities grew, burgeoning urban culture continued to foster diverse lifestyles challenging literati high culture and classical scholarship. Cities became centers for business, entertainment, and pleasure; wealth in itself acquired greater value; fiction was written for a broadening urban audience. Elites and commoners interacted somewhat differently than in rural settings. Differences in wealth were normally greater, but cultural mixing was encouraged as rich and poor lived more closely side by side and enjoyed the same festivals and operas. At the same time, the influx of rootless poor into cities could foster social antagonisms.

Urban and commercial expansion also opened new cultural space for women. Most important, the rise of print culture encouraged elite families to educate girls and gave women opportunities for self-expression through poetry from the seventeenth century onward. Education and writing opened opportunities for gentry women to develop companionable relationships with fathers and husbands and to enlarge their circle of friendships. As travel became commonplace, it was easier to leave the house to visit friends and relatives, attend religious festivals, and make pilgrimages to monasteries. Women at home took charge of households as husbands sojourned in distant parts. During the eighteenth century, Qing policy strongly supported the revival of the cult of chastity by conferring honors on widows who never remarried. Scholars revived emphasis on womanly virtue, and argued whether women might display literary talents publicly or only use their abilities within the household to nurture the virtue that would sustain men in their worldly pursuits. Elite women were educated, but male anxiety over their public appearances and the conflicts between their literary aspirations and domestic work caused frustration and insecurity.[6] On balance, however, it seems probable that, despite the efforts to reinvigorate the Neo-Confucian moral precepts relegating elite women to the inner chambers, the seventeenth-century momentum toward more education and somewhat freer public appearances was not seriously interrupted in practice.

The effects of nineteenth-century disorder on women remain to be studied, but there is fragmentary evidence that their horizons were not substantially narrowed. Gazetteers record occasional donations by women for local public projects, most often a bridge or religious institution. Women were also able to turn male emphasis on chastity to their advantage by, for instance, advocating lineage charitable estates to support poor widows.[7] Principles holding that women were subordinate to men and their proper place was in the home remained firm, but the practice varied. The small but receptive gentry audience for missionaries who advocated girls' schools and decried footbinding in the late nineteenth century suggests a growing uneasiness among fathers and husbands over the restrictions endured by daughters and wives. Chinese reformers had much to change when they began in the 1890s to demand that women be educated and contribute to strengthening China, but they were not addressing a situation as bleak as their dark rhetoric suggested.

In rural areas, however, economic and social change often produced stress that undermined both local stability and official efforts at nurture and control. Nineteenth-century China was beset by contentiousness and lawlessness. Immigrants settling the hills had their own swashbuckling, violent way of life, which produced tensions with the more prosperous and stable original inhabitants in the fertile valleys. Lineage, village, and ethnic feuding became endemic in some regions. Sects and secret societies provided a degree of solidarity and security for the rural poor, but also smuggled, racketeered, and protected workers along transport routes. The rural populace increasingly brought civil suits before the magistrates' courts, particularly over the complex issues of land-ownership and inheritance. This practice fostered the ad hoc expansion of formal civil law through substatutes appended to theoretically immutable statutes of the Qing Code. The old profession of low-status litigation masters (pettifoggers) spread further to help commoners to prepare and present plaints. Less positively, the flood of litigation, particularly in commercializing areas, burdened magistrates with unmanageable piles of cases and contributed to the small-scale social friction in the countryside.[8]

These local disorders indicated larger problems, dating back to the eighteenth century, lying behind the midcentury rebellions. Population increases were not matched by increases in per capita production. The rural populace living at the margins of subsistence was vulnerable to natural disasters and economic dislocations. Overpopulation also led to deforestation and farming on marginal land. Because the government lacked money to deal with the worsening ecological problems, irrigation and flood prevention systems declined, and silting raised some riverbeds above the level of adjacent land. As a result the Yellow River repeatedly overflowed levees onto the flat North China Plain, causing great misery to the inhabitants and impeding grain shipments to the capital by damaging the Grand Canal.

Finally, commercialization, urbanization, population increase, and rural instability combined to alter relationships between the state and local societies. Unlike in Tokugawa Japan, localities in Qing China did not have a degree of formal autonomy, and officials were not local men. In practice, however, social size and complexity undercut government authority. Instead of expanding to keep pace with societal growth, the regular bureaucracy was supplemented by auxiliaries: clerks of central boards, private legal secretaries to officials, merchant tax farmers, clerks and runners of the county sub-bureaucracy, and low-level local functionaries carrying out directives in small jurisdictions. The small bureaucracy thereby retained its basic structure and did not need higher taxes to handle more work.

The unquantifiable, but probably large, increase in local clerks and runners was essential to the operation of local government. They were often not as corrupt as their reputations suggested. Even so, this reliance on low-paid functionaries who were not accountable to regular bureaucratic disciplinary procedures made considerable room for extortion and for preferential treatment of those who had close connections with this level of the *yamen* (bureaucratic) staff. This was an old and continuing problem that weighed heavily on the legitimacy accorded local governments.[9] Beginning in the late eighteenth century, societal elites in county seats or market towns increasingly assumed financial and organizational responsibility for local welfare and other social services that the underfunded bureaucracy could not supply. They mainly cooperated with magistrates, but the latent tension between societal initiatives and official authority, and the sharp competition between reputable local elites and the sub-bureaucracy, became more manifest at the end of the nineteenth century.

Cohesion between state and society was still fostered by cultural identities and the long-standing connections between gentry and government. Commerce was also slowly fostering economic integration. Even so, societal organization was increasing more rapidly than the size of the government, and state ability to mobilize resources declined. Poverty in some areas was beyond the capacity of welfare systems to solve. It is important to remember that social and economic relationships and activities occurred in multitudinous local contexts. Diverse local practices and structures did not necessarily fit generalized characterizations of China as a whole or conform to the unitary aims of state policies. The decentralized, local, fractionated nature of much of the change perhaps hindered national strengthening more than did tradition.

Disruptive social changes gathered momentum as the already fragile prosperity of the high Qing ended. One hundred and fifty years of moderate inflation gave way to deflation around 1820.[10] The rural impact was worsened by a simultaneous drain of silver from the country to pay for opium imports. When scarce silver became more valuable in terms of the plentiful copper coins, peasants who used copper to pay taxes calculated in silver needed more coins to pay the same assessment. Landlords, caught between peasants paying rent in copper and tax collectors calculating liability in silver, were also squeezed. In the 1830s and especially the 1840s, numerous small uprisings in the normally relatively stable lower Yangzi River Valley formed a prelude to the intersecting midcentury crises of foreign wars and massive rebellions.

The Two-Pronged Midcentury Crisis

From the 1840s through the 1860s, government and society faced enormous strains from domestic rebellion and foreign attack. These internal and external threats exacerbated each other. Both revealed the decay of existing armies and weak leadership at court. Nevertheless, given the magnitude of problems, the dynasty's ability to survive is even more striking than the disarray.

Imperialist Invasion

The Qing had experience with Europeans since its founding, but these contacts were peripheral to governance. Circumstances changed in the later eighteenth century, when the British East India Company aggressively expanded purchase of Chinese tea for the English market and subsequently increased opium imports to China to pay for the purchases. East India Company officers chafed at the regulation of the Canton trade through a group of Chinese monopoly merchants known as the Cohong, but two British missions to Beijing failed to liberalize trade policy or establish diplomatic relations. As addiction spread and smuggling increased, the rapidly expanding opium imports wreaked social havoc. Tensions came to a head when Imperial Commissioner Lin Zexu came to Canton determined to end opium imports and eradicate addiction. These events led to the Opium War (1839–1842), followed by the Second Opium (Arrow) War (1856–1860), which established the semicolonial treaty port system.

This familiar narrative of the Opium Wars does not explain why the Qing was so resistant to Western-style diplomatic relations. A conventional explanation stresses the cultural hegemony exercised by China within its tributary system of international relations. Peripheral rulers were included in this sphere by affirming Chinese cultural centrality and their own inferiority. Sinocentric assumptions, traceable to China's experiences with barbarian tribes in antiquity, were not challenged by these weaker neighbors. The elaborate symbolism of tributary ritual reinforced the hierarchical relationships and inhibited pragmatic responses to new situations. The Chinese, therefore, had difficulty accepting the concept of diplomatic equality between sovereign states. Moreover, because this system tied foreign trade to tribute missions, the Qing government failed to appreciate the importance Westerners attached to trade itself.[11]

This interpretation has been challenged from a number of viewpoints. Historians using Manchu-language archives have discovered that the Qing court's conception of international relations was not so Sinocentric. Qing emperors ruled a vast Chinese and Inner Asian empire; they were Confucian monarchs in China, but had important ethnic, marital, or religious ties with Manchuria, Mongolia, and Tibet and drew upon teachings of the Yellow Sect of Tibetan Buddhism to reinforce claims to divine universal rulership. To maintain hegemony in Inner Asia as well as over Japan and Southeast Asian kingdoms, the Qing engaged in complicated negotiations and relied on military force as well as ritual and cultural ideology. Diplomatically, only relations with Korea and Vietnam fitted the tributary model, and foreign trade with Southeast and Inner Asia flourished outside this system. Practices of the European states were thus not totally alien to Qing experience.[12]

The diplomatic clash between Britain and China has alternatively been described as originating between two expansive "imperial formations" with "universalistic pretensions."[13] Each side was buttressed by ideology, and each used its own diplomatic rituals to maneuver for ascendancy. The Qianlong Emperor, who personified the civilized autocracy of the eighteenth-century Qing court more than any other Manchu ruler, and Lord Macartney, who had served the British Empire in the West Indies, South Africa, and India, knew they were arguing over incompatible ways of representing power as they discussed whether Macartney should *koutou,* or kneel on one knee, in the audience of 1893. Neither side won this encounter, and both misinterpreted the outcomes because they misread unfamiliar cultural cues.

As the British increasingly intruded along the south coast, the early nineteenth-century emperors became less inclined to negotiate, and both sides sought to resolve their differences by force. The timing of the two Opium Wars is important in understanding China's initial slowness to appreciate Western military superiority. The Qing rulers of the nineteenth century were not aware that the once formidable Qing armies had degenerated, and this degeneration accelerated as troops became addicted to opium. During the same period, European military organization and technology improved through repeated conflicts, capped by the Napoleonic Wars. Since European technological superiority had only recently been achieved, it was not surprising that China underestimated the force of a small number of ships and troops far from their own country. Most important, the government's main attention, virtually all its military strength, and much of its funds were devoted to suppressing rebellions from 1850 to the mid-1870s. Although it was the chief target of British imperialism in East Asia, China could not devote its main resources to resisting this onslaught. Both Opium Wars ended after the Qing felt its capital was threatened. In 1860 British and French troops actually invaded Beijing and looted and burned the magnificent Summer Palace on the outskirts.

The treaties concluding these two wars established a system of foreign privileges maintained by gunboat diplomacy and extended through more wars during the rest of the century. "Semicolonial" quite accurately summarizes the system. The 1842 Treaty of Nanjing opened five treaty ports to trade, ceded Hong Kong to Britain, guaranteed Western officials equality with their Chinese counterparts, allowed foreigners to be tried by their own consuls, and passed these privileges on to other Western countries through the most favored nation principle. Later agreements gave foreigners more concessions and allowed them to travel to more parts of China. Britain gained economic access without the draining administrative responsibilities of absorbing another large colony in addition to India. China entered the emerging world economy and the increasingly global system of Western-style international relations, but in a subordinate position. The unequal treaties opened the way for modernizing influences and new economic impetus from foreign trade, but they constrained China's actions, disrupted the economy, and eroded sovereignty.

Most immediately, the first Opium War contributed to social conditions that fostered rebellion. Workers along old transport routes saw jobs disappear as trade moved from Canton to Shanghai. Secret societies expanded, pirates moved inland, and militias that had been mobilized against the British did not disband. The fears awakened by foreign invasion fed a more general social malaise. Anti-Manchu sentiments were also aroused in the Canton area when Manchu banner troops harassed the local populace and the British victory undermined Qing prestige.

The Great Rebellions

From 1850 through 1873, there were five enormous uprisings: the Taiping (1850–1864), the Nian (1853–1868), Muslim rebellions in the northwest

(1862–1873), and two rebellions of Chinese Muslims and ethnic minorities in southwest provinces (1854–1873). These rebellions devastated large areas, caused perhaps 60 million deaths, and brought the dynasty close to collapse. Only 10 to 20 percent of the populace remained in some counties of Zhejiang and Jiangsu provinces, where opposing armies fought repeatedly. Towns and villages were flattened, fields wasted, and waterworks destroyed.

Each rebellion was a magnification of traditional types of unrest. The Taiping was the largest and most complex. Its leader, Hong Xiuquan, never succeeded in acquiring the lowest civil service degree, but did encounter a British missionary and his Chinese assistant while in Canton for the examinations. Hong idiosyncratically appropriated the Christian message as a personal revelation and claimed to be Jesus' younger brother. Nonetheless, Taiping ideology also incorporated millenarian visions of popular Buddhist sects promising that the Eternal Mother would save true believers at the apocalyptic inauguration of a new era.[14]

A particularly receptive audience was found within the miserably poor, violence-plagued Hakka society in the infertile hills of Guangxi Province. The incorporation of anti-Manchuism into their message and an abortive effort to establish a theocratic, regulated, egalitarian society after their capture of Nanjing in 1853 suggest that the Taipings can be called revolutionary. Some twentieth-century revolutionaries, notably Mao Zedong, claimed to be the heirs of what they saw as the beginnings of populist peasant radicalism and anti-Manchu nationalism, culminating in the twentieth century.[15] Mao may indeed have been inspired by stories of the Taipings, but there seems to be little evidence for drawing direct lines between their uprising and twentieth-century revolutions.

The Taiping movement itself suffered from poor governance and reluctance to adjust radical ideology to win over local societies. Directives prohibiting common customs, outlawing festivals, separating families, and removing restrictions on women intensified opposition. Taiping armies, moreover, moved through the Yangzi provinces as destructive invaders. They found collaborators, but taxes and requisitions, destruction of crops, disruption of trade, starvation, and disease outweighed the appeal of only partly implemented land redistribution and other egalitarian policies. Undercut by its own shortcomings, the Taiping movement nevertheless raised a serious ideological challenge to the imperial state—one which incorporated some foreign alternatives derived from Christianity and some contact with Westerners.

The Nian uprising was a more traditional disorder in part of the North China Plain. It arose in another harsh environment beset by banditry, smuggling, feuds, and natural disasters. To survive, villagers formed bandit bands to attack other settlements and militias for defense. Such groups, based in walled villages, formed an alliance that controlled as much as ten thousand square miles for over a decade.[16]

The northwest rebellion of the militant Muslim New Teaching Sect arose against official oppression. Both sides slaughtered inhabitants of captured cities. Governor-General Zuo Zongtang, a particularly stern example of the able midcentury officials to whom the Qing owed its survival, engaged in a long campaign to regain control, a campaign that was noteworthy for systematic extermination of the rebels. The southwestern risings stemmed from a more multifaceted combination of poverty and natural disasters, complaints of minority groups against government cultural discrimination and coercion, and anger over corruption and taxation shared by Chinese within the poor populace. These risings, too, resulted in many deaths. The southwest rebellions underlined the limits of the optimistic assimilationist policies of the eighteenth century. The northwest risings and their suppression came closer to total religious and cultural war, pushing the state toward only partly successful assimilation efforts in that area.

None of the uprisings solved underlying social and economic problems, particularly in impoverished places such as the Guangxi highlands and the Nian areas. The northwest and Lower Yangzi region did recover in contrasting ways. In the northwest, which the Qing considered a vital link in the Inner Asian part of its empire, the government focused on establishing firmer control. It created the province of Xinjiang, sent out more disciplined officials, promoted trade, and encouraged increased Chinese immigration. Xinjiang became more integrated with China, but the sentiments of the local populace were often ignored, and ethnic tensions remained. In the lower Yangzi, much of the change arose from within society as legacies of the Taiping Rebellion interacted with effects of international commerce. Wealthy families fleeing the Taipings arrived in Shanghai as the city was becoming the center of foreign trade. These refugees invested and formed new networks there. Merchants shifted their operations to the rising regional metropolis of Shanghai, while the once dominant lower Yangzi cultural and trade centers of Suzhou and Yangchou recovered slowly from the rebellion. By contrast, the badly damaged silk-producing areas of northern Zhejiang Province soon prospered because of foreign trade. As commercial hierarchies and scholarly networks radiated from Shanghai, differences grew between areas that fell within its economic orbit and those that did not.

Recovery in the countryside varied from place to place. In the most prosperous parts of the lower Yangzi region, well over half the land was rented. Absentee landlords often owned scattered plots, and further complications arose when rights to the surface and subsoil were divided among multiple owners. These many-layered landholding systems were thrown into confusion when so many people died or fled and land registers needed to identify holdings were destroyed during the rebellion. After the war, new people took over abandoned land and disputed older claims. With labor scarce and land plentiful, rent reductions and tax remissions were offered to bring fields back into cultivation, and tenants sometimes flouted landlord authority. Elsewhere, as around Suzhou, big landlords retained their land and cooperated to found rent-collection bureaus. Local officials intervened more in landlord-tenant relations, at first by reducing rents but later by helping to collect them so landlords could pay their taxes. Tenants eventually lost leverage throughout the region as population pressure built up again. As rents rose, collective protests also increased by the end of the century.[17]

Rural organization did not simply revert to its midcentury character, however. Sericulture and considerable other rural production was now bound up with foreign trade. Landlords had other business and commercial interests that might be more profitable than landholding. Such changing economic involvements oriented wealthy landholders still more strongly to cities and exposed them to Western practices. The trend was in the direction of the more pronounced rural-urban divisions and declining profitability of land-ownership that characterized the republican period.

Despite all the new and continuing agrarian problems, victory over the rebellions allowed the Qing to preserve both the dynasty and the spacial unity of the empire for another forty years. This delay forestalled dismemberment of China by imperialism. When nationalism emerged at the end of the century, it attached Chinese identity to the space defined by the Qing empire rather than to more homogeneous regions within it. More immediately, though, the Taiping Rebellion marked the end of the good old days for many scholar-gentry. It painfully revealed the insecurity of life. Surviving refugees returning from Shanghai found their homes destroyed, mulberry trees cut down, and fields overrun by weeds. Literati feared further disorder and attributed unrest to government corruption and misrule. Distressed over moral decay in government, members of this politically aware social group resolved to revive their home counties.

The government itself emerged intact but shaken. The Taiping Rebellion had shown the ineffectiveness of the state's armies and so drained the treasury that even the emperor economized on clothing. Yet despite all the indications of weakness, the state showed a remarkable resiliency. The Qing was saved by provincial officials and gentry who organized new militia-based armies, by the adoption of some Western military technology, and by revenues from new internal customs. After the Taipings were defeated, many of the dynasty's officials who defeated the Taipings, led efforts to reform and strengthen government so as to better order society. Power, however, had significantly shifted away from the center. With officials bent on reform, literati in the provinces eager to take part in public affairs, and Westerners with a firm foothold in the treaty ports, the stage was set for the often unpredictable political turns of the rest of the century.

Dealing with Crisis: Bureaucratic Politics to 1860

The nature of Beijing politics was also affected by the crises. From the beginning of the dynasty, Qing rulers were determined to prevent recurrence of the contentious literati factionalism of the late Ming. The strong autocratic rulers of the mid-Qing encouraged detached scholarship but did not welcome blunt criticism. Moreover, they hunted out and severely punished suspected anti-Manchu subversives. Nonetheless, as rural rebellions arose and government corruption intensified at the end of the eighteenth century, officials and scholars called for revitalized moral leadership. They discussed problems privately and proposed reforms to improve the government's financial condition, make administration more efficient, and promote the people's livelihood.

While the undeniable existence of problems opened a slightly larger window for opinion expression, non-officials were still strictly forbidden to form societies to discuss state affairs. Early nineteenth-century reform was, therefore, pursued within tolerated bureaucratic networks based on patronage, home province, year of passing the examinations, and friendships cemented by shared connoisseurship and aesthetics. Responses to the perceived social and administrative crises revolved about two long-established reformist approaches: statecraft *(jingshi)* and moral censure *(qingyi)*. Statecraft was characterized by practical proposals to "order the world" by improving administration. Officials and establishment-literati thus sought to follow their seventeenth- and eighteenth-century predecessors in realizing long-standing moral commitments to strong, effective, and equitable Confucian government.[18] Moral censure, submerged after the fall of the Ming, did not resurface until the nineteenth century. It was outspoken, crusading, self-righteous policy criticism from lower-ranking or somewhat marginalized officials seeking to expunge corruption and ineptitude, so dangerous in a time of crisis. Both strands were prominent in socially and politically troubled times, and both aimed to strengthen the existing political system. The reform agendas overlapped, but the political styles and implications were clearly different. Statecraft helped the makers of policy govern well. Moral censure involved criticism of the policy makers, and had a destabilizing, oppositionist potential.

During the first of two early nineteenth-century reform phases, some high officials and their statecraft advisers attempted to reinvigorate eighteenth-century efforts to rationalize administration. During the 1820s, priority was placed on abolishing the Grain Transport Administration, responsible for the inefficient and expensive shipping of grain to Beijing via the increasingly dilapidated Grand Canal. The political maneuvers preventing this reform suggest that the barrier to moderate administrative change was not so much ideological conservatism as vested interests and factional rivalries. Disillusionment over the 1820s failure influenced the second phase, begun in the 1830s. Frustrated official reformers with blocked careers saw themselves more as fringe critics than empowered participants in government. Their maze of networks and personal ties converged on a loosely organized friendship society known as the Spring Purification Circle, whose annual rituals gathered together disenchanted bureaucratic activists. These militants, concerned over wrongful exercise of autocratic power, believed that repression of criticism in times of trouble was more dangerous to the dynasty than issue-oriented factionalism. Some found inspiration in seventeenth-century literati political movements. Although their goal was to regenerate the dynasty, they implicitly threatened a basic principle of Qing autocratic governance: the prohibition against literati gathering to discuss state affairs.[19]

When militant reformism became mixed up with foreign relations over the question of opium, the results were explosive. After militants gained the support of the Daoguang Emperor, Imperial Commissioner Lin Zexu, who was strongly connected to moral censure networks, led a crusade in Canton against both opium imports and Chinese addicts in the belief that resolute action would cause the British to abandon the trade. This miscalculation pushed the Qing into the Opium War, and the resulting defeat would leave its mark on domestic politics for the rest of the century. Each subsequent foreign attack focused political discourse on defense, and the split between pro-war militants, symbolized by Lin Zexu, and policy makers favoring peace negotiations as the most realistic course was replayed in changing contexts. The militants' increasingly vicious attacks on peace negotiators weakened the bureaucratic hierarchical order, encouraged factionalism, and eroded restrictions on expressing opinion.

Foreign affairs also interacted with other recurrent issues of bureaucratic politics. Latent rivalry between Han Chinese and Manchus within the bureaucracy was reinforced because high Manchu officials, who were particularly concerned over the threat to Beijing, favored making peace with the British. After the war, the Daoguang Emperor, disillusioned with moralistic militancy, shifted his support to the Manchu grand councilor Muchanga, who had supported the peace treaty. Muchanga attempted to tighten central control within the bureaucracy by putting his own protégés into provincial posts. He thereby accentuated tensions between the administrative center and provincial officials in the course of his struggle with the moral censure militants. When the new emperor dismissed him in 1850, the militants recovered their influence in the bureaucracy. By then, however, social unrest in Guangxi Province was overshadowing foreign affairs, and the main effect of these bureaucratic maneuvers was to make way for the more marked swing toward decentralization that accompanied the Taiping Rebellion.

The first Opium War had already reinforced the drift of initiative and responsibility from the government center to societal elites. Lin Zexu and other militant officials cooperated with prestigious literati in the Canton academies who organized a militia bureau to resist the British troops. Some village elites also assembled their own defense forces. The political impact was threefold. Official policy in Canton, influenced by local literati anxious to defend their homeland and academies, diverged from that of leaders in Beijing more interested in protecting the capital and court. Militias, organized first against foreigners and then against bandits, secret societies, and rebels, would become a vehicle for local initiatives during the Taiping Rebellion. Finally, ambush of a British patrol by village militiamen in 1841 was inflated into a great popular victory by militants who asserted that the resolute Chinese people could defend the country were it not for cowardly officials in Beijing. When revived in the later nineteenth century, this powerful emotional argument against central policy makers would deepen alienation from government.[20]

Although the tensions arising from imperialist incursions were obscured by the need to suppress the great rebellions, they resurfaced after internal peace was restored. At midcentury, dissent remained within the bounds of bureaucratic patronage politics; protagonists identified their agendas with the best interests of the dynasty and ultimately depended on imperial support. Nonetheless, literati reformers, practical or militant, engaged in more open political debates with a collective impact on policy. They were only intermittently successful, but they began a process that culminated after 1900, when broader political dissatisfaction would be redefined in terms of constitutionalism and self-government in open political contests leading toward revolution against the Qing.

The Emergence of New Contexts and Political Agendas

Together the rebellions and the two Opium Wars reconfigured the social and economic landscape of much of China. The beginnings of major twentieth-century processes of state-building, industrialization, societal mobilization, nationalism, and revolution emerged in the new contexts. Old patterns obviously continued, but changing traditional attitudes and practices were modified by becoming part of new processes in shifting circumstances. The argument, so dramatically made in 1867 by the Mongol scholar-official and imperial tutor Grand Secretary Woren that Western learning would subjugate the Chinese by undermining their culture, waned. Modernity, however, did not become the positive value and fashionable condition desired by many intellectuals until the early twentieth century. Much of the change arose unplanned from circumstantial, cumulative, not completely self-conscious processes within many arenas: the central or provincial administrations, treaty ports and foreign capitals, local scholarly and managerial networks, popular sects and secret societies. Different groups with their own agendas often diverged and interfered with one another.

Incorporation into International Systems

In contrast to the midcentury period of rebellions, during the last three decades of the nineteenth century the impetus for domestic change often came from abroad. In 1864, when the new British-managed Imperial Maritime Customs began to publish fairly reliable statistics, net imports were valued at 46,210 customs taels and exports at 48,655. In 1899 the figures were 264,748 and 195,785. This increase meant that more agricultural production and trade was aimed at international markets and more Chinese were coming in contact with foreigners. The corresponding increase in Maritime Customs revenues from 7.872 million to 22.870 million customs taels played a significant part in the shift of state revenues from land taxes to trade taxes.[21] During the same years, the Qing government was drawn reluctantly into the diplomacy of the Western-dominated world state system. A decisive break with the old tribute system came in the 1880s. To counter Japanese encroachments, the court transferred responsibility for Korean relations from the traditionalist Board of Rites to Governor-General Li Hongzhang. Li had organized the Anhui Province army against the Taipings and promoted several major self-strengthening economic projects. Subsequently he became the official most associated with, and most blamed for, the Qing's often controversial foreign relations. In this instance he sent troops and actively intervened in Korean politics, in effect abandoning the noninterventionist practices of the traditional tributary system for ones closer to the intrusiveness of Western imperialism.

In both trade and diplomacy, the Qing was hampered by concessions in the unequal treaties and increasing foreign encroachment as more European countries as well as Japan pressed demands. Closely spaced diplomatic crises, wars, and invasions kept the government on the defensive and aggravated social unease. In a long-standing, shifting debate, some historians have emphasized negative economic effects, blaming foreign trade and imperialism for distorting the economy, stifling native industry, transferring profits abroad, and further immiserating the rural populace by replacing handicrafts with foreign imports. Others, while acknowledging the humiliations and inequities, have stressed foreign contributions to development. Foreign investors introduced modern technology, provided capital, and fostered an entrepreneurial environment. Treaty ports provided legal protections for Chinese firms and exposed Chinese to new practices and ideas. These forces launched China on the path to modernity.[22]

Foreign intrusion actually had both positive and negative effects on China's often interrupted efforts at economic development. Technology essential to industrializing and raising per capita productivity came from abroad. Some modern private enterprises contributed; the foreign-owned, Chinese-edited newspaper *Shenbao*, for instance, pioneered metal-type printing and lithography. Yet much of the relatively limited technology transfer of the second half of the nineteenth century came through the officially sponsored, merchant-managed arsenals, naval yards, steamship companies, telegraphs, and textile mills. These first steps led toward more substantial industrialization after 1900, but revealed problems with both state and private economic organization.

Corruption invaded the system of "official supervision and merchant management" through which government-sponsored enterprises were administered. More fundamentally, projects initiated by individual provincial governors-general did not have full backing from Beijing. Because of the court's ambivalence toward modernization, other officials sought to divert profits of successful enterprises. Merchants became increasingly wary of participating in official ventures. At the same time, their new expertise further increased their status, and foreign contacts gave them safer alternatives for investment. Men began to pour into Shanghai after the Opium War to seek profits in foreign trade, and some of these poor adventurers became rich. The entrepreneurial self-made merchants of Shanghai, with their powerful native-place associations, were further removed from official control than the wealthy members of the Canton Cohong during the early nineteenth century. Foundations were indirectly laid for merchant participation in Shanghai city affairs, the constitutional movement, and the 1911 revolution.

In rural areas, foreign trade brought prosperity to some places and decline to others, but more generally increased economic instability. Peasant households might be able to adjust or substitute production in response to market changes. Thus if imports undercut one crop or handicraft, they shifted to another. While evidence is lacking as to whether household incomes rose or fell in the long run, the required adjustments undoubtedly further strained families living at the margins of subsistence. Many households could use the labor of their women and children to get by, but could seldom accumulate reserves. The impact of international markets on tea production in Fujian Province provides one example of destabilization.

Tea had long been produced in the hills of northwest Fujian.[23] Therefore, commercial routes, market centers, and middlemen linking small-scale tenant farmers to urban markets already existed when export began in the late eighteenth century. After the 1850s, production boomed in response to British demand. New market centers were established, middlemen multiplied, and credit facilities became more complex. While living standards probably improved, social turmoil increased as settlers migrated to tea-producing areas. With tea replacing rice farming, food shortages occurred, overcultivation worsened erosion, and gender roles were upset when women found jobs outside the home in tea processing. This highly volatile tea boom collapsed suddenly at the end of the 1880s because of new competition from highly capitalized tea plantations in northern India. Chinese tea continued to be produced for sale abroad, but could no longer compete successfully with either Indian tea or the Japanese tea that had also entered foreign markets. The boom and bust contributed to social insecurity as indicated by exacerbated feuding and further growth of secret societies and sects in this turbulent province.

This history of Fujian tea also provides insights into factors limiting economic development. There was no overall coordination of China's decentralized production units and no structural transformation to a more capital-intensive and organized mode. Well-developed indigenous market mechanisms expanded to facilitate international trade, but the Chinese type of commercial organization was not well suited to competition in capitalist world markets. Small tea-farming households could not generate the capital needed to compete with colonial tea plantations in India. The boom was too brief to produce a capital surplus essential for structural change. Private efforts by Fujian gentry and officials were too isolated and transitory to standardize production and advance technology.

The other part of the problem was the underfinanced, understaffed Qing government, which was ambivalent toward foreign trade, was accustomed to largely laissez-faire policies with respect to much domestic commerce, and had little leverage over foreign merchants. Unlike the Japanese developmental state operating in a far smaller country, it did not provide national coordination, technical advice, quality control, and standards to rationalize tea-growing practices. This inability to promote private economic activity limited the economic foundations from which the bureaucracy sought to strengthen the state in the late nineteenth century.

Strengthening the State

State-strengthening meant promoting recovery from the midcentury rebellions as well as circumscribing foreign intrusion. Policies after the Taiping Rebellion initially were defined within an old reformist narrative of dynastic restoration based on the long-established agenda of the agrarian-based imperial bureaucratic state sensitive to popular welfare. Restoration required both reasserting internal military and political control and securing the foundations of the polity through morally infused, honest, benevolent government.[24] Plans to sponsor relief, revive agriculture, rebuild dikes, lighten some land tax burdens, and promote Confucian education partly succeeded. The extent of the domestic tasks was, however, beyond the capacity of the bureaucracy despite such excellent provincial and local officials as the statesman, general, and scholar Zeng Guofan, who played so large a part in suppressing the Taiping Rebellion and reviving society afterward. Moreover, Confucian conceptions of limited benevolent government did not address the economic and social roots of rural distress in demography, productivity, and class.

Confucian benevolence was even less appropriate for resisting imperialist intrusions. By the 1870s, new initiatives aimed at foreign problems overlay Restoration reforms. The Qing government had originally bought and manufactured foreign armaments to use against internal rebels. Subsequently, "self-strengthening" and "foreign affairs" embraced military and industrial projects, Western-style diplomatic relations, and knowledge to strengthen China against foreigners. The resulting hybrid reformism could fit into expandable conceptions of practical statecraft, and eventually acquired a sensible rationale in the slogan "Chinese learning for fundamentals, Western learning for practical use." By the 1890s, self-strengthening was being further redefined as a broader pursuit of "wealth and power," which had become the concern of people outside as well as within the government. As "practical use" focused on "wealth and power," preserving the state emerged as a goal that officials such as Li Hongzhang and the famous reformist governor-general Zhang Zhidong combined with loyalty to the dynasty. This late nineteenth-century self-strengthening thereafter changed and expanded into the more self-consciously modernizing state-rebuilding of the Qing New Policies of 1902–1911. Governments after the republican revolution, most notably the Nanjing regime (1927–1937), would continue efforts to strengthen the state and extend control into society.

Did the Qing in the late nineteenth century haphazardly initiate processes similar to the state-building that historians have defined in early modern Europe? In Europe this process was stimulated by warfare between emerging states and was entwined with the rise of capitalism and nationalism. It involved improved military technology and organization, creation of technically skilled government bureaucracies, more efficient taxation, and formation of police forces capable of maintaining order.[25] The nineteenth-century

Chinese context was unlike early modern Europe. China already had a formidable bureaucracy. Commercial activity abounded, but capitalism per se was weak. Moreover, this modernizing formula fit poorly with still influential Confucian concepts of good government. Nonetheless, the Western intrusion, as well as domestic disorder, pushed the Qing toward more extractive and coercive models of state power and more fundamental army reforms. Chinese could also look back to their own statist Legalist heritage, much of which had been incorporated into practices of the centralized bureaucratic monarchy. China did not duplicate the European path, but there was enough movement toward state-strengthening in the quarter century following the great rebellions to suggest a foundation for the governmental activism of the New Policies period. Was this really as slow a reaction to imperialism as is generally assumed, or was it actually fairly rapid?

Despite continuing military weakness against foreign adversaries, the Qing army was better able to control internal disorder than it had been for a hundred years. The court also partly restored central authority within the bureaucracy by rotating strong provincial governors-general to new posts and disbanding the large regional armies they had commanded during the rebellions. Powerful Li Hongzhang was brought close to the capital as governor-general of Zhili Province. New central and local government bureaus were established. The province of Xinjiang was organized with a traditional Chinese bureaucratic structure in the northwest.

State revenues increased as the Qing broke loose from its self-limiting system of fixed land taxation. By the 1890s, over half of tax collections came from trade, mainly from the Imperial Maritime Customs and new taxes, known as *likin*, on goods entering domestic markets. Since the beginning of the century, revenues had nearly doubled to 90 million taels, although provincial governments retained much of the *likin* revenue. Beijing's revenue needs were never met. Nonetheless, more by happenstance than design, the Qing cleared the way for subsequent experiments with modern fiscal administration by abandoning its old tax policies during the second half of the nineteenth century.

These achievements were, however, limited. Although some Confucian scholars still refused on principle to compromise with Western ways, cultural loyalties were increasingly compatible with pragmatic appropriation of useful Western practices. Ironically, as the number of officials supporting self-strengthening increased, the task was complicated by bureaucratic politics as well as foreign intrusions. The total range of problems facing the government was great; competing pressures on limited funds were enormous. Money spent to promote industry in Shanghai left less to extend state authority in the northwest. The building of a modern navy was delayed by Empress Dowager Cixi's desire to rebuild the Summer Palace. Disagreements over allocating scarce funds aggravated factional competition for political power.

Such rivalries not only undercut self-strengthening but also reflected unclear political leadership arising from structural divisions of authority in Beijing. Cixi's influence during the last four decades of the century began with her manipulations of the succession to the throne in 1861 and 1875 that enabled her to become regent for two young emperors. Initially only marginally legitimate, Cixi maneuvered to check rivals among the Manchu princes. She relied on shifting groups of favored advisers, and improved her reputation with Chinese literati-officials by allowing a wider range of officials to express opinions in memorials to the throne. Ambiguities over where power lay worked against the instituting of consistent policies and new initiatives.[26]

Cixi was above all a skilled court politician intent on maintaining her position. Her modest encouragement of self-strengthening was initially enough to gain support from literati proponents and progressive governors-general—and one of these governors-general, Li Hongzhang, was associated with her from the mid-1880s to the mid-1890s. At the same time, she sought to prevent the political authority of the Manchu court from shifting to reformist Chinese officials in the provinces. Therefore, she tried to satisfy different groups in the capital by approving reform plans without transferring much money from old bureaucratic agencies to new ones staffed by Li's foreign affairs protégés. Li and other modernizing Chinese provincial officials went along with these methods because they retained limited latitude to follow their own agendas rather than having to cooperate with progressive princes at court "to restructure power from the center out."[27] Instead of creating a consistent progression toward self-strengthening, policy wavered as political cross-currents moved in different directions.

The literati demoralization arising from blocked careers, fear of rebellion, concern over foreign attacks, and unease over Cixi's role was even more corrosive. Considerable numbers of literati wondered whether officials cared about the people's well-being and, especially after the mid-1880s, believed that the court was isolated from the opinions of those who were not in the empress dowager's inner circle. Moreover, officials holding the highest examination degree were increasingly upset by competition from men who had purchased rank for office. After being expanded to raise money to suppress the midcentury rebellions, this irregular route to officialdom was subsequently also used by men educated in Western skills instead of the traditional examination curriculum. The Qing did not effectively counteract the bureaucratic malaise, which eroded the commitment of scholar-gentry to the state and was connected to new reformist initiatives arising within society.

Societal Organization: Impetus from Below

Societal organization on the local level expanded more and more rapidly during the second half of the nineteenth century, and eventually connected local activists to issues affecting the whole country. The impetus came from factors also affecting the central government: rebellion, foreign penetration, and literati malaise. Societal activities in the commercialized and urbanized areas of central and south China eroded Beijing's authority, interacted with alienation growing inside the bureaucracy, and fostered the view that local men could provide better direction of local affairs.

The proliferation of social organizations began with institutions long sanctioned by the government: gentry-directed local welfare organizations, bureaus for water control, schools, commercial guilds, and the native-place associations of sojourning merchants and gentry. These organizations were neither strictly autonomous nor private; local leaders constantly interacted with officials in usually cooperative relationships. Nonetheless, their power was not simply conferred by the state. It also derived from their status in local society and community services. Governmental authority was contingent on allowing local leaders scope to plan and manage their community's affairs as long as their organizations were officially sanctioned and did not directly challenge state power.[28] As multifarious duties increasingly devolved to county magistrates during the nineteenth century, the initiative in this ambiguous relationship shifted toward social elites and their growing local organizations.

These changes, however, occurred locally in only some places; they most often assumed new trajectories in areas most affected by the Taiping Rebellion or foreign intrusion. In the lower Yangzi, post-rebellion reconstruction was mainly carried out through traditional institutions, but the magnitude of the Taiping destruction inspired a more intense, determined activism.

Local initiatives assumed their own momentum, sometimes amalgamating elite-directed public services into complexes of charitable and educational institutions. Networks of gentry involved in these complexes might gain substantial local power. The institutions also provided public spaces where members of local elite establishments might meet to discuss "affairs"—including governmental matters of interest to gentry, such as the administration of examinations in the provincial capital of Zhejiang.

Additional impetus for local elite management came from literati returning home, some committed to helping their families and localities after the rebellions, others dismissed or withdrawing voluntarily from the uncertainties of Beijing politics, still others frustrated with the drift of government. Such men looked upon their participation in local affairs as the pursuit of statecraft goals of social well-being from outside the bureaucracy. They reinforced the critical, vaguely alienated mood of some literati networks and broadened the range of local elite public activity. Yan Chen, a frustrated dismissed official from northern Zhejiang, for example, dominated public welfare and educational organizations in his county for well over a decade after the Taiping Rebellion. He gathered information about social conditions by talking to people as he traveled about the county administering a program to support infants in poor families and also acted as defender of the populace and spokesman for the gentry in an effort to reform local grain tribute tax collection. As he presents himself in his autobiography and the gazetteer he edited, he appears much like a benevolent official outside the government.

After the main damage of the Taiping Rebellion was repaired, local activity expanded geographically when gentry extended their fund-raising and organizational expertise to causes outside their home areas. This outward reach through networks and connections became evident in the lower Yangzi provinces in the late 1870s when a prolonged drought caused severe famine in north China. Li Hongzhang organized a famine bureau in Tianjin to coordinate relief and solicit donations, particularly from wealthy Shanghai merchants. Gentry in Hangzhou, Suzhou, and several other cities took further initiatives in organizing special committees, collecting contributions, and sending their own representatives to dispense these funds in the famine area. Shanghai newspaper reports indicate the pride that these men took in their efforts and encouraged contributions by listing the donors in Zhejiang and Jiangsu provinces. Thus, societal activities began to spread beyond the administrative boundaries in which they had normally been confined. Literati activists, habitually oriented to both China and locality, facilitated this outward thrust.[29]

The roles of the treaty ports, especially Shanghai, and the treaty port press were still more important. After the Opium Wars, Shanghai became a magnet for scholar-gentry as well as for merchants and workers who constituted the main part of communities of sojourners totaling hundreds of thousands by the end of the century. Those who visited were exposed to an increasingly vigorous Chinese-foreign hybrid culture and urban cosmopolitanism that would become the Shanghai trademark. Even some landlords and peasants who never went to the city were pulled into its commercial orbits as silk and other items were produced for export. Networks radiating from Shanghai began to draw together a new macro-regional elite.

One of the most important contributions by treaty ports to societal mobilization was to provide legal protection in foreign concessions for the nascent press. Chinese-language daily papers appeared in Hong Kong and Shanghai in the early 1870s. Although they were too few in number before the 1890s to be vehicles for the open political debate identified with emerging civil societies in France and England, their political role in China was important. These newspapers encouraged public involvement and publicized projects undertaken by multiplying gentry-merchant reformist networks. By publishing editorials criticizing officials, offering views on current affairs, drawing connections between specific events and general issues, and simply making information more readily available, they encouraged readers to discuss affairs of state. *Shenbao* in Shanghai and *Xunhuan ribao* in Hong Kong moved public opinion out of the confines of private literati networks and bureaucratic channels and developed a readership interested in political issues.

In addition to promoting Western technology, industry, and education during the 1870s and 1880s, these papers presented the literati critique of a corrupt government, isolated from public opinion, in which evils spread downward from an autocratic apex through uncaring officials to clerks who directly exploited the people. *Shenbao* in particular spread information about local elite public activities and defended gentry against officials. Some editorials also advocated public discussion of official policies, and eventually in the late 1880s called for a parliament. Some editorials suggested that initiatives by local men were more likely to succeed than official ones and even urged public discussion to correct governmental faults.[30]

Burgeoning locally based activism encouraged the desire of gentry and merchants for greater participation in local government. About the same time, a handful of literati authors revived seventeenth-century Chinese critiques of centralized autocracy that advocated *fengjian* (an old Chinese concept of "feudal" governance distinct from both European feudalism and the Marxist designation of precapitalist China). They proposed modestly reorganizing state power by institutionalizing gentry participation in local administration. These indigenous formulations resonated with the interest among a few scholars of Western affairs in participatory local government as one source of the power of countries such as England. During the 1900s the old theories would merge into adaptations of Western and Japanese conceptions of self-government. In addition, the practices and experiences of elite participation in running local affairs would carry over into both private associations and the chambers of commerce, educational associations, and other institutions officially mandated by the Qing in its New Policy reforms of the 1900s. Before then, the incremental geographic expansion of local activities would become mixed up with nationalism arising from defeats in wars with France and Japan during the 1880s and 1890s.

Nationalism and Oppositional Public Opinion

Nationalism increasingly penetrated political discussion during the last quarter of the nineteenth century. It arose in a number of ways: debates over defense against imperialist invaders, experiences with foreigners in the treaty ports, and angry local reactions to missionaries, traders, and gunboats penetrating the interior after the Taiping Rebellion. It precipitated open political opposition to the government at the end of the century but did not inspire a unified movement. Like self-strengthening, nationalism combined with other agendas that could either foster identification with the state or encourage suspicions of it. The defeats in the Sino-French (1884–1885) and Sino-Japanese (1894–1895) wars were crucial in shaping attitudes of critical literati officials and scholar-gentry. Public outrage over the peace treaties focused especially on the territorial provisions. China recognized French suzerainty over Annam in 1885. Still more shockingly in the 1895 treaty, China ceded Taiwan to Japan and recognized Korea's independence, thereby opening the way for Korea's annexation by Japan in 1910. These very tangible losses, followed by the international scramble for more territorial spheres of influence in China during the late 1890s, raised public fears that China would be dismembered and its people left helpless.

Modern Chinese nationalism is often contrasted to traditional locally based, culturally inspired resistance to invasion, characterized as antiforeign, xenophobic, or conservative culturism. After China was defeated by

Japan in 1895, the loyalties of radically reformist scholars such as Liang Qichao shifted from dynasty to state. They adopted goals of national wealth and power and appropriated social Darwinist ideas of national struggle for survival. In arguing for fundamental reform, they denounced many aspects of traditional culture and sought to change the populace into educated citizens to build a strong China. National strength would thereafter be a dominant political goal in the twentieth century.[31] This approach brings out the importance of nationalism in modern China and links it to state-building and modernity. It explains important aspects of twentieth-century nationalism in China, but tends to overstate differences between traditional views and modern nationalism. It also fails to address why nationalism was so closely linked to political protests and revolution at the end of the Qing and often also during the Republic.

Some scholars studying nationalism worldwide have further linked nationalism to the modern state by suggesting processes by which people transfer loyalties from small traditional communities to the nation, which thereby becomes the overriding "imagined community"—often constructed against a threatening foreign Other. Its political expression, the nation-state, extends its reach into society and uses modern technology and organization to mobilize the populace for survival in international competition. Other theorists dispute this close identification of nationalism with modernization and the state by arguing that people can simultaneously identify with the nation and other communities based on locality, kinship, gender, ethnicity, religion, or class. National loyalties are, therefore, pluralistic, dynamic, and changing. They may adhere to existing identities without replacing them, and a national community may emerge from building upon and reinterpreting changing traditions.[32]

As applied to Chinese history, the more pluralistic view undermines the distinction between traditional-conservative-xenophobic Chinese culturism and modern-progressive-Western nationalism. Nationalism-as-process unfolds instead through various additions to or rejections of old loyalties and diverse encounters with foreigners. If emerging Chinese nationalism is not overly identified with the rise of a modern state and is not considered inevitably antithetical to a mythic static cultural tradition, it can also be connected to older antiforeignism and a patriotic heritage combining loyalties to culture, dynasty, and territory. The international context adds still another dimension. Nationalism arose in China against imperialism. Because China was not a colony, anti-imperialism could not lead to a nationalist revolution against colonial power as occurred in other parts of the world during the twentieth century. Instead, political anger against imperialists turned against the foreign Manchu Qing (and subsequently against republican governments) for failing to protect the country. Nationalism thus could foster opposition to, rather than support of, the state.

Popular nationalism did not develop so clearly in the late nineteenth century. Attacks on foreigners were common, but few could be called protonationalistic. They frequently reflected specific interests of such groups as gentry community leaders, sects and secret societies, transport workers, or peasant producers instead of manifesting the generalized nativist anxiety and hostility that were magnified beyond control in the Boxer Uprising. Yet even if horror stories about missionaries dismembering children were not nationalistic, they contributed to the perception of foreigners as menacing Others and reinforced the feeling that China was increasingly under siege. Once political mobilization began in the early twentieth century, foreigners were demonized in different ways during urban clashes that more clearly contributed to emerging popular nationalism.

Commitments of officials such as Li Hongzhang to strengthening China can be called nationalistic, but they did not require reordering the structure of state power. By the end of the century, elite activism spreading from localities to the center provoked a more transformative process. The treaty port press and gentry activists intermingled old militant visions of militia defending the country with spreading commitments to adapting Western techniques. Politically marginalized men in and out of office and critics seeking a role in state policy making combined the goals of self-strengthening with those of patriotically inspired political participation.

The Sino-French War, which followed several minor foreign incursions in the 1870s, was crucial to the emergence of oppositional nationalism among morally censorious literati within the bureaucracy and a broader spectrum of scholars outside. Although militant opposition to Western learning was receding, a variety of critics during the war enlarged on other themes of the early nineteenth-century moral censure narrative: foreign threats to Chinese territory, traitors in high office, the people as the true defenders of the country, and upright militant reformers returning government to its proper path. Perception of mounting foreign dangers, in effect, added defense of race and territory to conceptions of governing to benefit the people.

Journalism fundamentally altered the political dimensions of the 1880s mobilization by both molding and expressing opposition within society.

From the protection of the Shanghai International Settlement, *Shenbao* attacked the Qing officials responsible for the peace treaty and advocated popular mobilization for defense more strongly than could militants in Beijing. It addressed a wider audience and continued its attacks after the court cut off criticism within the capital in 1885. Two edicts ordered officials to discipline the newspaper, but to no avail. Thus the moral censure critique of defense policy was no longer as centered within the bureaucracy as during the Opium Wars.

The abundant critical rhetoric of both the Sino-French War and the Sino-Japanese War of 1894–95 drew upon twelfth-century Chinese history for familiar examples of heroic resistance to foreign invasion and traitorous officials who compromised with the enemy. At the same time, writers in the 1890s increasingly invoked such concepts of the Western state system as political sovereignty, economic rights, and territorial integrity. They used phrases, such as China's being "cut up like a melon," that were soon incorporated into social Darwinist rhetoric. Little differentiated this mixture from nationalism.

The oppositional thrust to this nationalism-in-process was dramatized in the vitriolic attacks on Li Hongzhang, who was accused of selling out the country through the peace treaties he negotiated to end both wars. Advocates of war constantly urged mobilizing the populace and warned that without resolute and immediate action China would be dismembered and destroyed. They depicted the Chinese people as more determined defenders of the country than high officials and even perhaps the throne itself, as an 1895 *Shenbao* editorial hinted. Particularly during the Sino-Japanese War, the rhetorical romanticization of the people's resolve in popular tracts and the treaty port press amounted to an attack on the government. By implication, saving China required finding a way to reject the policies of those who wielded central authority.[33] Thus, by the end of the war the press had spread the idea that the populace must join in saving China, foreshadowing the emphasis on citizen participation in reformist and revolutionary public opinion after 1900. Growing numbers of scholars in and out of government began to doubt that the Qing state in its current form could embody the China that had to be saved.

Despite the furor, patriotic public opinion failed to affect policy. Consequently, critics became interested in a second reformist conception of participation in government: the expression of views in Western-style parliaments. Since at least the early 1880s newspapers had referred to European (and after 1890 the new Japanese) parliaments. While scholars with knowledge of the West were interested in assemblies as a source of national power, younger members of the reconstituted moral censure network in Beijing were attracted to deliberative institutions as vehicles for literati public opinion. Authors of 1890s reform tracts, some of whom had connections to this network, also suggested modest political restructuring. Even though Chinese literati advocated parliaments to foster solidarity between the ruler and the ruled, deliberative bodies convened for this purpose would be a check on autocracy in the Chinese context. Since the throne and high officials responsible for the peace treaties were not willing to take account of criticisms raised both within and outside the bureaucracy, the politically aggressive, nationalistic reformism precipitated by the 1895 defeat and cession of Taiwan to Japan was infused with opposition to those dominating government.

Thus state-strengthening split just as it was gathering momentum in the government. One set of advocates, including Li Hongzhang, accommodated to the political situation at court and the changes in the bureaucracy. The other, composed of participants in patriotic moral censure politics, was reinvigorated by the wars with France and Japan. The men of this persuasion were attracted to reforms that would increase their participation in policy making, and they interacted with aroused scholars in the provinces and treaty ports. The radical potential became evident in the open political contestation of the late 1890s when state leaders lost control over policies to strengthen China.

Political Conflict

China's defeat by Japan sparked a remarkably rapid politicization of public affairs. Radicalism intensified from the end of the war through mid-1898, initially abetted by more moderate official reformers such as Governor-General Zhang Zhidong, who employed radicals to carry out educational and other reforms in Hunan until they became too disruptive. The new, specifically reformist press spread iconoclastic philosophy, nationalistic messages, and calls for political and social restructuring. These ideas appeared more fully in the treatises of individuals such as the reformer, utopian philosopher, and constitutional monarchist Kang Youwei; Liang Qichao, who was the most widely read reformist and constitutionalist publicist of the late 1890s and 1900s; and Yan Fu, who found in English and French liberalism possibilities for releasing popular energies to strengthen China. Liang's section on women in his famous 1897 tract on reform illustrates the sudden iconoclasm. Liang bitterly condemned footbinding, the subservience expected of women, and what to him was their frivolous poetry. He urged that they must break out of their traditional confinement to become vigorous and educated and contribute to national strength. Although he still envisioned women acting within the family, he redefined female morality in nationalistic rather than Confucian terms and drastically changed the debate over their proper roles.

The division of authority in the court after the Guangxu Emperor came of age in 1889 had opened the way for cooperation between the young emperor and critics of the peace treaty. These contacts led to the One Hundred Days of reform in the summer of 1898, during which a group of radical reformers within and outside the bureaucracy led by Kang Youwei gained influence over the emperor and sought to use his authority to enact fundamental structural changes and replace officials who opposed them.

Although the One Hundred Days failed, politics had already changed permanently during the longer reform period from 1896 to mid-1898. The throne could not effectively reimpose the long-standing Qing ban on scholar associations after the appearance of numerous societies. The press had widely discussed Beijing's domestic policies, and patriotic scholars had ignored the already battered restrictions on representing opinion to the throne. Elite activists in the provinces had participated in national politics. The view implicit in the ferociously critical rhetoric during the Sino-Japanese War—that national survival justified defiance of state authority—was expressed through political activity. This shredding of basic principles of Qing rule went far beyond the nineteenth-century shifts in initiative from state toward society, setting the stage for decades of conflict between governments and social forces.

Historians have concentrated on reformist activities in Beijing, Shanghai, and Hunan, but associations, schools, and newspapers also appeared in other parts of the country. The impetus arose from a mixture of patriotic anxiety, expanding experiences of societal elites in local affairs, and growing contacts with Westerners and their practices. Society had changed since the Taiping Rebellion. With the shock of defeat by Japan, politics suddenly caught up with society.

Many officials and societal elites favored reform, but the failure of the One Hundred Days revealed deep divisions over apportionment of political power and brought out the differences between radically reformist scholars and more moderate official and gentry reformers. What in effect was an abortive radical coup at court during the summer of 1898 precipitated the

September countercoup backed by those who felt threatened: Cixi, ideological conservatives, officials whose posts were abolished, opponents of the moral censure faction, Manchus alarmed by assertive Chinese reformers controlling the government, and reformers who thought the pace of change too fast. With the emperor under house arrest, another wave of disillusioned reformers fled the capital. Executions provided reformist martyrs. Not only leading figures but also the considerable number of societal elites who were somehow associated with reform in the provinces had reason to fear a conservative reaction. Political anxiety tinged with anti-Manchuism persisted as the court replaced Chinese provincial officials with Manchus and rumors of plans to depose and kill the emperor circulated. Concern over China's future also remained intense as foreign powers competed for more territorial and economic concessions and Westerners traveled still more widely about China after the Sino-Japanese War.

In this uneasy atmosphere, three events during 1900 set the stage for further political reorientations during the last decade of the Qing. The greatest was the Boxer Uprising, a popular sectarian movement, mixing martial arts and spirit possession. It spread among rootless young men congregating in the market towns of impoverished northwestern Shandong Province. This initially localized anti-Christian movement acquired new volatility and unexpected political significance when antiforeign Manchu princes and ultraconservative officials became convinced that the magic powers claimed by the Boxers might enable them to expel Westerners from China. With this encouragement, already uncontrollable Boxer forces broke loose from their rural base and headed for the capital to support the dynasty and eradicate foreigners.[34]

The Western allied army sent to rescue besieged foreigners quickly defeated the numerous but unorganized and poorly armed Boxers in August 1900. The foreign occupation of Beijing ended the anti-technological fantasies spun from Boxer assertions of invulnerability to bullets. Once the ultraconservative backers of the Boxers were discredited, the moderate reformers still in the bureaucracy obtained Cixi's support for comprehensive administrative change. The moderate reformers joined with reformers in south and central China who shared their opposition to the court's pro-Boxer policy. Although events of late 1898–1900 had reinforced distrust of the Manchu court among Chinese elites, chances for cooperation between high officials and societal leaders in pursuit of modernizing reform improved until tensions reappeared in the mid-1900s.

In addition, two small radical uprisings in the summer of 1900 pointed toward future intractable conflict between Qing state modernizers and revolutionary or reformist movements in society. The revolutionary Sun Yat-sen launched his second short-lived republican anti-Manchu uprising with secret society leaders in Huizhou, Guangdong. Radical reformers in Hunan with ties to Liang Qichao were arrested and executed just before a planned uprising to restore the Guangxu Emperor to power with the aid of secret society allies. Though weak, these risings brought radical violence into the elite reformist repertoire and, in Sun's case, solidified commitment to anti-Manchu republican revolution against the Qing.

The interaction of radicalism and more establishment elite reformism was exemplified by the National Society, formed in Shanghai a month before the Hunan rising. Some members knew of the planned uprising, but this remained a loosely organized discussion group. Prominent reformist literati and incipient revolutionaries came together in opposition to the Qing court. Their open public gatherings coexisted with a frustrated radical subtext. Thus the National Society foreshadowed the uncertain division between reformers and revolutionaries sharing nationalistic commitments and anti-government rhetoric in the emerging urban elite. During the next decade politics would change further as students at modern schools and professionals with specialized educations joined members of the old scholar-gentry elite. Nonetheless, the conflicts after 1905 between the Qing political center and decentralized elite societal movements reflected the disagreements over the locus of power and the relationships between state and society that had surfaced in the 1890s.

Although few Chinese would have anticipated the rapid changes during the final decade of the Qing dynasty, retrospectively we can see that nineteenth-century developments prepared the way. The nationalistic movements for reform and revolution at the end of the Qing did not burst forth newborn to challenge static tradition after the particularly humiliating defeat by Japan. Part of what is called dynastic decline during the nineteenth century can be attributed more accurately to long-term population increase and the attendant expansion of commerce and societal organization. The Qing government structure was gradually being rendered inadequate to deal with social problems and complexities arising from quantitative growth. Reluctance to expand the bureaucracy reflected not only Confucian advocacy of light government but also the interests of gentry-literati who, despite their ties to the political center, sought a degree of informal autonomy within their home areas.

In addition, the Qing declined in the narrower sense of diminished imperial authority. Even the two competent emperors of the first half of the nineteenth century ruled more by balancing bureaucratic factions than had their eighteenth-century predecessors. Autocracy waned and literati politics revived as problems facing government became more intractable. None of the three emperors between 1850 and the end of the century controlled policy. The throne became a more unstable, politicized, and fragmented institution. Policies became more inconsistent as latent hostility between Manchu and Chinese officials became more open and aspirations for a political voice grew at the fringes of official power. Mobilization against Western penetration was delayed.

Both the long-term expansions and cyclical decline were among the causes of the midcentury rebellions that severely disrupted society and increased bureaucratic decentralization, opportunities for gentry to organize independent community defense, and diversion from the foreign menace. Organizing late nineteenth-century history in terms of twentieth-century themes such as nationalism, state-building, societal mobilization, modernization, and revolution underplays more indigenous phenomena such as continuing localism. Nevertheless, it was the impact of Western imperialism that turned internal trajectories in new directions.

The transformative effect of Western intrusion did not arise simply from the Chinese forsaking conservative tradition for modern foreign ideas and practices or from imperialism undermining the Chinese society and economy. Rather, the political, military, social, and cultural interactions between Chinese and Westerners initiated processes that modified or redirected Chinese practices, relationships, beliefs, and loyalties. Multidirectional international and domestic forces altered contexts, reconfigured power relationships, produced new interests, and modified cultural assumptions. As Chinese perceived new threats and opportunities, they combined useful existing practices with new methods to pursue new goals. Chinese merchants could use their sophisticated trading methods and organizational experience as the foundation for adapting profitable Western business practices. Statecraft expanded to include self-strengthening, and local societal organization encouraged ambitions for self-government in parts of China. The long-accumulating literati malaise fostered oppositionist patriotic reformism. The mixing of Chinese and Western, traditional and modern meant that rapid changes in the early twentieth century retained connections with the flexible Chinese heritage while moving in directions opened up by the encounter with imperialism.

Despite the continuing foreign encroachment, the record during the last decades of the nineteenth century suggests that the Qing government had considerable strengths as well as weaknesses, as would be shown by the New Policies of the 1900s (see Chapter 6 by Ernest Young). Why then did its administratively directed modernization not lead to successful state-building after 1900? One answer is that the reformist impetus was coming from many directions within the large, diverse Chinese society as well as from government. Old oppositionist tendencies and local orientations continued to encourage mobilization for new goals. New social groups emerged alongside existing gentry and merchant elites. Segments of these changing elite strata had become politicized, and the press both expressed and led assertive public opinion.

Officials and the court had little time to centralize power and assume leadership of modernization. When they did so after 1900, it was too late. Scholar-gentry had helped the Qing survive the Taiping Rebellion, but many of their elite descendants were now questioning the Qing political system. As also happened to the Russian imperial government at about the same time, a strategy of reform undermined rather than strengthened the state. Beijing's efforts would intensify opposition and foment conflict. Qing state-strengthening would be overtaken by revolution.

Why did an enduring "civil society" not emerge from the nineteenth-century background of gentry-merchant mobilization? One cannot speak of such a development during almost the entire Qing, when the government prevented any formal political association or discussion and made all outside criticism dangerous. There was, however, a range of permitted local extra-bureaucratic organizational activity for trade, welfare, and other local community affairs. The growth of such organizations, patriotic concerns, and the minuscule but vocal press of the later nineteenth century did create a basis for rapid expansion of public activity after 1902, when state policy decisively changed. Along with both new state-authorized and entirely private organizations would come a new open politics in which urban elites began to demand not only recovery of national rights but also new rights of political participation and the rule of law. A still indeterminate Chinese variety of civil society appeared incipient at the end of the Qing.

Circumstances then seem to have been more favorable to the emergence of such a social-political "society" than at any other time in the twentieth century. Since the government ignored public opinion, the nationalism associated with gentry political mobilization certainly did not promote state authority. Moreover, Chinese political culture did not appear inevitably authoritarian in the processes of selection and interaction with foreign ideas, institutions, and practices at the beginning of the twentieth century. The Qing was still strong enough to maintain a fair degree of the order necessary for civic institutions to develop. Gentry were still socially powerful, and the affinities, areas of agreement, and relationships between officials and societal activists from the same social backgrounds contributed to the government's relative tolerance of critics or opponents.

Such cooperative possibilities would be submerged by the clashes described in Chapter 6 between societal elites in the provinces and the centralizers in the Qing court and the new Beijing ministries. Combinations of revolutionaries, frustrated reformers, and constitutionalists could overthrow the Qing, but the fragile alliances would not be cohesive enough to persist and dominate republican events. Participatory aspirations did not disappear but were contingent on larger circumstances. As subsequent chapters show, the political weight of what came to be described as liberal groups diminished as the republican environment soon became unfavorable and political goals changed.

Selected Readings

Bernhardt, Kathryn. *Rents, Taxes, and Peasant Resistance: The Lower Yangzi Region, 1840–1950.* Stanford: Stanford University Press, 1992. A comprehensive treatment of the changing structure of land-ownership, rents, and taxation in the lower Yangzi core. It provides an important new perspective by showing the decline of landlord power vis-à-vis peasants and the state during the Republic and gives new information on the interaction of the Taiping government with the local populace.

Cohen, Paul A. *Discovering History in China: American Historical Writing on the Recent Chinese Past.* New York: Columbia University Press, 1984. A sensible, thorough critical analysis of such issues as tradition and modernity, imperialism, and the Western intellectual and cultural impact on China as framed by historical scholarship and debates of the 1970s and 1980s.

———. *History in Three Keys: The Boxers as Event, Experience, and Myth.* New York: Columbia University Press, 1997. Provides three accounts of the Boxer Rebellion of 1900: those of historians, the participants, and the popular myths about the movement. A superb meditation on the nature of history, historical writing, memory, and myth.

Crossley, Pamela Kyle. *Orphan Warriors: Three Manchu Generations and the End of the Qing World.* Princeton: Princeton University Press, 1990. This work traces three generations of a Manchu bannerman family in Zhejiang from the mid-eighteenth century to the 1930s. The author argues that Manchus, living apart in garrison communities, were never thoroughly sinicized and developed a stronger sense of ethnic identity as their world fell apart at the end of the Qing.

Duara, Prasenjit. *Rescuing History from the Nation: Questioning Narratives of Modern China*. Chicago: University of Chicago Press, 1995. An exploration of how twentieth-century historical narratives have often privileged the modern nation-state and submerged conflicting narratives from the past or from localities. The sophisticated and persuasive theoretical perspectives on nationalism, modernity, and history in the first two chapters are followed by detailed studies of specific Chinese topics with additional discussion of India.

Esherick, Joseph W. *The Origins of the Boxer Uprising*. Berkeley: University of California Press, 1987. This outstanding social history sets the origins of the Boxer movement in the local geographical and social environments and traces processes through which small groups formed and coalesced. It emphasizes popular culture and conflicts with Chinese Christians backed by missionaries rather than connections to old Chinese sects and finds no antidynastic motives.

Fairbank, John K. *Trade and Diplomacy on the China Coast: The Opening of the Treaty Ports, 1842–1854*. Cambridge, Mass.: Harvard University Press, 1953. A classic, detailed work on the beginnings of the treaty port system, from which many of the author's influential ideas about Chinese culture, diplomatic relations, and Western impact ultimately derive.

Goodman, Bryna. *Native Place, City, and Nation: Regional Networks and Identities in Shanghai, 1853–1937*. Berkeley: University of California Press, 1995. An outstanding, detailed urban social history focusing on the native-place associations of sojourners. Arguing for the interaction of local and national identities and interpenetration of the traditional and the modern, the book presents many original ideas about the development of nationalism and changes in the urban power structure.

Hevia, James L. *Cherishing Men from Afar: Qing Guest Ritual and the Macartney Embassy of 1793*. Durham, N.C.: Duke University Press, 1995. A postmodernist cultural reassessment of this famous diplomatic encounter arguing against the prevailing view that an inwardly focused, culturally conservative Qing court failed to appreciate the significance of Western technology or the Western military threat. This thesis and some translations in the long analysis of guest ritual are controversial. The book contains many useful insights, however, and provides an excellent summary of persuasive new interpretations of Qing tributary foreign relations.

Huang, Philip C. C. *Civil Justice in China: Representation and Practice in the Qing*. Stanford, Calif.: Stanford University Press, 1996. A reinterpretation of traditional Chinese law, judicial practices, and their rationality based on archival research. Huang argues that magistrates' courts heard civil as well as criminal cases and based decisions on the Qing Code rather than simply mediating. He suggests a tripartite division between a formal realm of the district courts and Qing Code, an informal realm of community mediation, and a third realm that combined the two.

Kuhn, Philip A. *Rebellion and Its Enemies in Late Imperial China: Militarization and Social Structure, 1796–1864*. Cambridge, Mass.: Harvard University Press, 1970. This is a detailed examination of gentry-led militia organization against the Taiping rebels in southwest and central China. Its analyses of the militarization of local societies, the expansion of gentry power, devolution of central power, and the possible implications for future self-government have been influential.

Mann, Susan. *Precious Records: Women in China's Long Eighteenth Century.* Stanford: Stanford University Press, 1997. A broad study of many aspects of women's activities and lives during the eighteenth century. It shows the complexities of gender relations rather than simply stressing female subjugation, and considers some of the ways women related to society as a whole and to the state.

Polachek, James M. *The Inner Opium War.* Cambridge, Mass.: Council on East Asian Studies, Harvard University, 1992. This is a unique history of bureaucratic factions and politics during the first half of the nineteenth century. It describes the rise of moral censure *(qingyi)*, its relationship to the Opium War, and the interplay between the politics in Beijing and local social groups in Canton.

Rankin, Mary Backus. *Elite Activism and Political Transformation in China: Zhejiang Province, 1865–1911.* Stanford: Stanford University Press, 1986. This reinterpretation of late Qing history is based on detailed study of elite social activism and politicization in Zhejiang Province. It traces connections between expanded public activities to repair the damage of the Taiping Rebellion, more outwardly oriented initiatives arising from patriotic and other concerns of the 1880s and 1890s, and finally the uses of new institutional structures by local men after 1900 and the state-societal political conflicts of the last Qing decade.

Rowe, William T. *Hankow: Conflict and Community in a Chinese City, 1796–1895.* Stanford: Stanford University Press, 1989. This work and its companion volume are major urban studies of the city of Hanzhou in the nineteenth century. Rowe provides voluminous detail on urban life with special emphasis on the effects of commercial expansion and makes comparisons with European history.

Schwartz, Benjamin. *In Search of Wealth and Power: Yen Fu and the West.* Cambridge, Mass.: Belknap Press, 1964. This is an enduring study, based on deep knowledge of Chinese and Western political thought, of a pervasive rationale for reform in the late nineteenth century. It contributes to understanding intellectual and cultural exchanges by showing how Yan Fu selected and reinterpreted writings of—especially English—liberal thinkers to suggest how Chinese could form groupings that would contribute to national strengthening.

Skinner, G. William, ed. *The City in Late Imperial China.* Stanford: Stanford University Press, 1977. This volume combines several interpretive articles by Skinner analyzing Chinese urban structure and development with more specific articles by other authors on particular aspects or cities. It remains an important contribution not only to Chinese urban history but also to Chinese social history in general.

Spence, Jonathan. *God's Chinese Son: The Taiping Heavenly Kingdom of Hong Xiuquan.* New York: W. W. Norton, 1996. This highly readable kaleidoscopic narrative history captures the drama of the rebellion and the ambiguities of imperialist intrusion in the mid-nineteenth century while providing a wealth of detail. Historical insights emerge through the narration rather than through overt analysis.

CHAPTER 3

Visions of the Future
in Meiji Japan

DAVID L. HOWELL

The story of Japan's modern history conventionally begins in 1853, when Commodore Matthew C. Perry led a squadron of American naval vessels into Edo Bay and forced Japan's emergence from more than two centuries of relative isolation from the Western world. Although Perry does not really deserve his starring role in Japan's modernization drama, there is no question that the encounter with Western imperialism was the catalyst for one of the most remarkable political, economic, and social transformations in modern history. The diplomatic troubles of the 1850s and 1860s set off a chain reaction of domestic crises the likes of which had not been seen since the founding of the Tokugawa *bakufu* in 1603. For more than 250 years the *bakufu*, or military government of the Tokugawa shoguns, governed Japan according to a complex distribution of authority. The shogun derived his legitimacy from the powerless emperor, on whose behalf he nominally ruled, but shared actual control with the lords of about 270 semiautonomous domains. Its unwieldy institutional structure notwithstanding, Japan under the Tokugawa was politically stable and relatively prosperous. The crises, however, some of them long in the making, brought down the entire structure of the regime in 1868. The result was the Meiji Restoration and Japan's entry into the ranks of self-consciously "modern" nations.

No country has been so successful at implementing modernity as a matter of public policy as Meiji Japan. Soon after its establishment, the regime embarked on a program of rapid institutional and economic development designed in the first instance to preserve Japanese independence in the face of Western imperialism and in the long run to win Great Power status for Japan itself. By the end of World War I, it had achieved both goals. But the very fact of this accomplishment lends an air of inevitability to the enterprise and consequently obscures just how contentious both the goals and the means of their attainment were.

To help us better understand how the Meiji leaders accomplished these goals, this essay begins by surveying the paths not taken by Meiji Japan. Disaffected samurai, crusaders for parliamentary democracy, and peasant rebels challenged the state's effort to build an authoritarian, westward-looking industrial and military power. The state's vision prevailed in the end, partly because the regime quashed the alternatives, sometimes brutally. But repression alone does not explain its triumph. Enough people became convinced of the urgency of the state's goals to support them, at least implicitly.

To preserve Japan's national independence, the Meiji regime had to rally the support of the people. It did this in part by delivering economic growth and a measure of political stability, and in part by fostering nationalism and a yearning for Western-style "modernity." The goal was to maintain national unity in the face of challenges in the international arena. Creating a unified nation meant creating a uniform one, in which differences among the people were subordinated to their common character as subjects of a modern nation-state. But to the extent that the people answered the state's call and embraced a notion of "modernity," they did so in the expectation that they would be full participants in the nation-building project. This paradox gave rise to a fundamental tension in late nineteenth-century Japanese politics between the people's desire to join in the crafting of a new order as self-aware subjects and the state's need to homogenize the population under its direction. This tension was finally resolved only with the discovery of nationalism's natural element, empire, an arena in which diverse actors eagerly embraced their common identity as Japanese.

Past and Future in the Meiji Restoration

The turmoil of the fifteen years between Perry's arrival and the Restoration of 1868 prompted many Japanese people to wonder how they might turn the crisis to Japan's advantage. The West was necessarily a part of the future they imagined—for some a model to emulate, for others a malevolent agent that would rob Japan of its national essence—but for all a force to reckon with. The world the Western powers were then creating—the world of industry and imperialism, trade and technology—*was* the future, whether the Japanese liked it or not. Even the most xenophobic elements in late Tokugawa politics came to realize this stark truth sooner or later.

Looking to the future for a vision of society was new to mid–nineteenth-century Japan. Previously idealists and policy makers alike had called for a return to the putative golden age of the early seventeenth century, immediately after Tokugawa Ieyasu's founding of the regime. To be sure, the object of their longing was often as much a fantasy as the forward-looking visions of later thinkers, but it is significant nonetheless that they pointed to a supposedly known past rather than a necessarily unknowable future as the template for tinkering with the body politic. Once the modern West burst onto the scene, a return to Ieyasu's age quickly lost its attraction even as a rhetorical device, much less a concrete model on which to base policy. And so people began to think about the future. They imagined the previously unimaginable possibility of a world not run by the Tokugawa *bakufu*—a world that was not a variation on the theme of Ieyasu's reign. For some this "future" appeared as a wholehearted embrace of the West, while for many others it took the guise of the distant past, a millennium earlier, when the emperor ruled directly.

This reconsideration was not sparked entirely by the encounter with the West. From the mid-eighteenth century onward, Japanese thinkers had developed a vocabulary for situating Japanese culture vis-à-vis that of China, the source of classical learning. Such inquiry into the nature of Japanese culture was known as nativism *(kokugaku)*.[1] Nativist thought was not originally intended as a critique of the Tokugawa system, much less a call to bring it down. Far from being insurrectionary, it was often not even obviously political: Motoori Norinaga (1730–1801), the greatest nativist scholar, devoted himself to the study of philology and poetics. In his studies of the classics of Japanese literature and history, such as the eleventh-century *Tale of Genji* and the eighth-century history of Japan, the *Kojiki* (Record of ancient matters), he suggested the possibility of a distinctively Japanese spirit, which manifested itself through the language. Through the efforts of Hirata Atsutane (1776–1843) and others, nativism evolved in the early nineteenth century into a popular intellectual movement with increasingly political overtones. Atsutane's many supporters in the countryside were attracted to his equation of agricultural work with religious practice, which reaffirmed the importance of the rural community while at the same time suggesting a link to the nation as a whole. In contrast to those who sought answers to contemporary problems in Ieyasu's time, the nativists looked beyond the Tokugawa order in search of the "essence" of Japaneseness. They found it in the remote past, the Age of the Gods *(kamiyo)*. Blurring history, politics, and religion, the nativist past was infinitely remote and hence infinitely pliable. In the face of crisis, the habits of thought fostered by nativist scholarship were directed toward politics and that most "essentially" Japanese of institutions, the imperial court.

The Meiji Restoration was carried out not by intellectuals, nativist or otherwise, but rather by an alliance of coldly pragmatic politicians and passionately loyal activists formed in response to diplomatic pressure and domestic unrest. The activists, known as *shishi,* or "men of high purpose," were mostly very young, low-ranking samurai. As a group they were more inclined to violent action than quiet introspection. They were not nativists for the most part, at least not in the sense of being affiliated with a formal school, such as the Ibukinoya, through which Hirata Atsutane and his successors disseminated nativist writings and recruited new disciples. But their concerns, as reflected in slogans such as *sonnō jōi* (revere the emperor, expel the barbarian), resonated with those of many participants in the nativist movement. In fact, however, the *shishi*'s concept of loyalty to the throne had a different provenance from the nativists'. It entered the political vocabulary via the heterodox Neo-Confucianism of the Mito School, which originated in the domain of the same name. Its lord headed a collateral branch of the Tokugawa house, and the last Tokugawa shogun, Yoshinobu, was born into the Mito house. Accordingly, while Mito activists were prominent in a number of anti-*bakufu* incidents—most notably the assassination in 1859 of the shogunal regent, Ii Naosuke—their concept of imperial loyalty grew out of an attempt to shore up the *bakufu*'s rule, not to topple it. To them national consciousness was symbolized by the emperor, and it transcended but did not negate loyalties to individual feudal lords. Only in the 1860s—by which time it had become clear that the *bakufu* could not respond to the challenges of the time—did *shishi* from other domains reinterpret the concept of "revere the emperor" *(sonnō)* to signify an explicit anti-Tokugawa stance.

In contrast, the core supporters of Hirata nativism came from a very different social stratum than the *shishi*. Although a number of samurai were attracted to nativism, most supporters were relatively well-to-do peasants and Shinto priests. They were drawn to nativism initially not because of fear for Japan's national independence but because of a concern that rural society was on the brink of collapsing from the strains of an increasingly commercialized rural economy. Their conception of imperial loyalty was more religious than political; for them the imperial court was the national institutional manifestation of an intensely local identification of agricultural work with religious devotion. The opening of treaty ports, however, and Japan's concomitant entry into world markets (especially for silk and other textiles) in 1859 further destabilized village society and thereby drew many Hirata nativists into the world of politics. Given that they shared the rhetoric of imperial loyalty with the *shishi*, it is no surprise that many nativist activists saw themselves as being part of the loyalist political project.

Many *shishi* died before the Tokugawa *bakufu* fell in 1868, victims of their own ethic of violent action. But a number of the survivors went on to become prominent in the Meiji government, and others who did not survive, such as Yoshida Shōin and Sakamoto Ryōma, nevertheless left a lasting influence on the leadership of the new regime. In contrast, few of Atsutane's disciples enjoyed anything more than short-lived prominence in the new order, despite their support for the *shishi*'s cause. After the Restoration, nativist leaders were installed as specialists in religious policy; as such they spearheaded a vicious persecution of Buddhism and attempted to establish Shinto as the state religion. Within a decade, however, they were shunted aside as antimodern reactionaries, victims of their own doctrinaire insistence on the unity of politics and religion.

The significance of nativism thus lies less in its direct role in bringing about the Meiji Restoration than in its role in opening the world of national political discourse to village elites and other commoners. In the short run this helped to ensure the success of the restorationist forces, but in the long term fostered one thread of tension that would divide Japan in the 1870s and 1880s, as conflict arose over the question of who would participate in the nation-building project and to what extent.

The final decade and a half of Tokugawa rule was a time when people from all walks of life became involved in politics simply by taking some sort of action. "Action" could mean anything from assassination to quiet discussion of current events. Naturally, the assassins have gotten more press, but it would be wrong to underestimate the significance of the quieter activists in fostering a mood amenable to radical political change. Beginning at about the time of the Perry mission, for example, village leaders, doctors, petty samurai, and others throughout Japan began keeping records of current affairs—generally based on rumors or secondhand reports—which they circulated among themselves in the form of letters. These letters were the main source of information on current events to reach the countryside before modern newspapers became widely available in the 1870s. Although the men who compiled them did not generally engage in editorializing, they had come to see national politics and international diplomacy as processes that had an immediate impact on their lives. This sense of a direct, personal connection with national and international affairs was new to late Tokugawa Japan.[2]

Nativist networks formed an important part of the informational infrastructure that supported the *shishi*'s political agenda. Yashiro Hirosuke, a nativist in Hirayama village in western Musashi Province (Saitama Prefecture), for example, used visits to the Hirata Academy in Edo (Tokyo) as an opportunity to collect information about goings-on in the *bakufu*, which he passed on to his sponsor, Saitō Jippei, the headman of Hirayama village. Another of Saitō's clients, Gonda Naosuke, went to Kyoto, where *shishi* leaders recruited him to gather intelligence in Edo and the surrounding countryside.[3] Moreover, Yashiro and others in Saitō's circle were connected to a group of nativists who beheaded three statues of fourteenth-century shoguns in Kyoto in 1863.[4] Cutting off a statue's head is not the same as cutting off a real one, but as an expression of discontent with the status quo it contributed indirectly to the success of the Restoration movement.

Below the politically aware village leadership, the attitude of the vast majority of Japanese toward the turmoil of the late Tokugawa years is harder to gauge. By the eve of the Restoration, however, a number of popular movements suggested that many common folk longed for a new future, too, one in which the emperor would spread his benevolence across the land. Mass pilgrimages to the imperial family shrine at Ise, the carnivalesque revelry of the *eejanaika* (what the hell!) movement, and violent "world renewal" *(yonaoshi)* protests all suggest such a longing. But it was longing without a clear sense of participation. The *eejanaika* movement was the cavalier response—"what the hell!"—of city dwellers and peasants to political upheaval, prompted in part by the distribution by *shishi* of amulets promising a better future. Similarly, the people calling for world renewal did not suggest that they themselves would do the renewing: the future was for the emperor to bestow upon them.

At the end of 1867, after much political maneuvering, the shogun Tokugawa Yoshinobu formally surrendered his authority to the fifteen-year-old Meiji Emperor on the understanding that he would remain part of a ruling council. A coup d'état by activists from the Satsuma and Chōshū domains put an end to that idea, and thus the Meiji regime was born in January 1868. Satsuma, in southern Kyushu, and Chōshū, in westernmost Honshu, had both emerged from a period of national economic turmoil in the 1830s and 1840s relatively well-off, which left them in a strong position to act once imperial loyalists came to dominate their politics in the last decade of the Tokugawa period. Although there was some dancing in the street, the coup was met mostly with cautious hope and quiet despair, as samurai authorities and common people alike waited to see if it would be a decisive turning point or merely another twist in the decade-old tale of domestic political ferment.

The odds were against the new regime. Forces loyal to the Tokugawa—or at least opposed to the Satsuma-Chōshū alliance—put up a struggle that raised the specter of Western intervention. As it turned out, the civil war was brief, in part because Yoshinobu and his key advisers chose to surrender rather than risk the sort of prolonged turmoil that would have prompted intervention. But even after quelling the civil war, the new government still directly controlled only about a quarter of the country's productive capacity. The economy as a whole was in disarray from the lingering trauma of entry into the world market and widespread crop failures in 1867 and 1868. Adding to the burden, peasant protests and samurai uprisings were a constant irritant for a decade.

While the fledgling regime sought to avert economic collapse and Western intervention, its immediate task was to attain a measure of control over the country—through military action when necessary, and otherwise through the appropriation of local administrative structures. It was a tall order, and surviving the vicissitudes required decisive leadership. Once the initial crisis was past, the state turned to the task of creating institutions based on the model of Western-style modernity, a process that took the remainder of the nineteenth century and culminated in the Meiji Constitution of 1889 and the Meiji Civil Code of 1898.

The Meiji state offered encouragement to those nativists who took the notion of a return to the past literally by creating an institutional structure that replicated, at least in name, the ancient age of direct imperial rule and the fusing of politics and religion. This concession, however, soon proved to be a hollow one, for it quickly became evident that taking a return to the past too seriously would jeopardize Japan's national independence; thousand-year-old institutions were simply not adequate to build a modern state. And if there was anything that the new regime—otherwise so uncertain of its future direction—was sure of, it was the need to preserve independence. Accordingly, by the early 1880s it had abandoned most trappings of the putative return to the ancient past. At the same time, however, the most critical symbol of that past—the imperial institution—was thoroughly larded with "traditions," some modeled after those of Western-style monarchy, others claiming to reflect authentic Japanese antiquity, but all very much inventions of the time. But however artificial, the imperial institution served as a powerful anchor of political loyalty throughout the tumultuous changes of the late nineteenth century, during which time Japan was remade as a modern nation-state.

Immediately upon its foundation, the regime embarked on a vigorous program of institution-building designed to fend off Western imperialism. Needless to say, this was an extremely complex and hazardous process, not least because the new regime was founded on a very shaky economic and military base. Since well before the Restoration, leaders of the *bakufu* and major domains had come to recognize the necessity of Western technology for defense. The prescient among them realized that importing arms would accomplish little in the long run without also building infrastructure and nurturing a cadre of experts familiar with all aspects of Western societies. The Meiji regime continued this program of defense-oriented Westernization under the slogan *fukoku kyōhei* (rich country, strong army).

The reforms introduced to build a state able to defend itself from imperialism utterly transformed the structure of the Japanese government and economy. First, the imperial capital was moved from Kyoto to Tokyo (as Edo was renamed in 1868) in a symbolic break with the long history of the ancient capital. In 1869 the lords of the most powerful domains, including Satsuma, Chōshū, and Tosa (whose men dominated the new government), surrendered their domain registers to the court, thereby giving the central government direct authority over their territories. Most other domains quickly followed suit, while the remaining domains were abolished two years later with the establishment of prefectures throughout the country. The abolition of the domains was of tremendous significance because it eliminated the decentralized administrative structure that had existed for centuries and replaced it with a highly centralized state. Achieving centralization gave the government control over all of Japan's tax revenues as well as the ability to implement reforms directly and uniformly throughout the country.

Major economic reforms included the elimination of restrictions on the buying and selling of land in 1870, followed in 1873 by the land tax reform, which stabilized government revenues by basing taxes—now payable in cash rather than in kind—on the value of land rather than on fluctuating agricultural yields. Together these policies gave cultivators clear title to their holdings, which encouraged efficient farming and hence economic growth. But they also opened the door to a dramatic increase in farm tenancy and the concomitant growth of a class of absentee landlords because the need to pay fixed tax bills in cash made it difficult for cultivators to ride out a poor harvest or two without mortgaging or selling their land. At the same time, the state began to commute samurai stipends to bonds, a process completed in 1876. This controversial policy stripped the hereditary warrior class of its most significant economic privilege. Although it was a necessary step toward making the state solvent, it was the source of much discontent, including a large number of violent protests.

In tandem with these political and economic reforms, the state dismantled the Tokugawa social status system, which had grouped people according to their obligations to feudal authority: samurai as warriors and administrators; peasants, artisans, and merchants as producers and distributors of commodities; and Buddhist clergy, outcastes, and miscellaneous smaller groups as providers of religious, penal, and other services. The dismantling of the status system was marked institutionally in the household registration law of 1871, which created a uniform roster of subjects regardless of previous status or domain affiliation. At the same time, a series of policies designed to efface status differences was implemented. Thus, in 1870 commoners were allowed the public use of surnames, a privilege previously restricted to the samurai and a small number of non-samurai elites; the outcastes were nominally liberated in 1871; and the visible emblems of samurai status, particularly the right to carry two swords, were eliminated by 1876. Moreover, in 1872 the government implemented universal conscription, which eliminated the samurai's monopoly over military service and with it their principal raison d'être.

In some ways the most significant reform for our purposes was the creation of a national school system in 1872, which mandated sixteen months (raised to six years by 1907) of compulsory primary education for both boys and girls. This policy reflected a general feeling that industrial and military development required a literate and numerate populace. It also was the first critical building block in the creation of a meritocracy in which boys (but only boys) could rise from humble beginnings to serve the nation as officials or industrialists. The policy was striking both in its ambition and in the often bitter opposition that it provoked among peasants. Many people in the countryside failed to see the utility of spending huge sums to build schools and hire teachers—the expenses for which were borne by the localities—and then forgoing children's important contribution to the household economy to impart skills that few of them (particularly girls) would ever have occasion to use. Less visibly but perhaps more significantly, the education policy undermined the communities of knowledge that had long existed in rural areas. For in fact literacy levels on the eve of the Restoration—estimated very roughly at perhaps 30 percent for men, 10 percent for women—were quite high for a preindustrial society. They were the product of informal schools—called *terakoya* (temple cottages) because many were run by Buddhist clerics—that dotted the countryside. These schools imparted basic literacy to most pupils and introduced those who could afford to study longer to the classics of Chinese and Japanese philosophy, history, and literature. Their teachers and advanced students participated in the sorts of networks that had supported the rise of nativism and the spread of circulating news reports. Lacking central control, they were the foundation of an extremely diverse public sphere of scholarly inquiry and debate in the early modern period. The centrally mandated schools eventually displaced this independent intellectual realm through the creation of a regular hierarchy of primary and secondary schools, all teaching a standardized curriculum, albeit to a much broader segment of the population than before.

As challenging as all of these reforms were, creating a modern nation-state entailed much more than building modern institutions, symbolized by a modern monarchy. Rather than simply imposing new institutions on the Japanese people, the state had to persuade them of their urgency and necessity. In other words, getting people to follow the state's program was not enough; they had to be taught to think in terms of it as well. A central element of this project was the reform of customs. Customs *(fūzoku)*, particularly outward markers of social status such as clothing, hairstyle, and a samurai's two swords, served to situate individuals within the early modern order and, more generally, to distinguish "civilized" Japanese from neighboring "barbarian" peoples, such as the Ainu of Hokkaido. Customs as markers of civilization and barbarism further situated Japan within a broader East Asian world, for a similar attitude (albeit with different normative customs) prevailed elsewhere throughout the region, as revealed, for example, in the Qing dynasty's insistence that Chinese men adopt the Manchu queue.

Insofar as the Meiji effort to preserve national independence entailed persuading the Western powers that Japan was "civilized," the logic of Japanese understandings of the relationship between customs and civilization demanded that customs be reoriented to fit new, Western standards. Government leaders, including the emperor himself, quickly adopted Western clothing and hairstyles as symbols of their acquiescence to the new standards. The embrace of Western civilization spread quickly throughout the upper echelons of Japanese society—or at least male society, which had always been considered the principal locus of civilization. By the late 1870s, only rustics and the elderly in major cities failed to sport Western-style haircuts.[5] Members of the cultural avant-garde could be seen at trendy Tokyo restaurants such as Seiyōken in the Ueno district, tucking into novel food items like beefsteaks washed down with beer and wine. In the meantime, members of the Meiji Six Society (Meirokusha) earnestly debated the merits of such proposals as adopting the Western alphabet and making Christianity the official religion, while a future education minister, Mori Arinori, argued that making English the language of public discourse was "a requisite of our independence in the community of nations."[6]

Much of this impulse can be dismissed as mere faddism; and indeed within about a decade Japan saw a reaction against unbridled Westernization. Yet beneath the surface of passing fashion lay a more profound effort to encourage the Japanese people to internalize new notions of civilization while at the same time preventing them from moving in uncontrollable directions. This effort is revealed neatly in a series of laws enacted by the Justice Ministry in 1872, the *ishiki kaii jōrei*, or customs regulations. The customs regulations penalized a series of "uncivilized" but common practices, such as public urination and mixed bathing, while trying to stem the spread of unauthorized experiments with novel fashions, such as women's cutting their hair and thereby liberating themselves from unwieldy traditional coiffures. The regulations were not necessarily successful in eradicating "uncivilized" habits—certainly public urination remains common even today, at least among taxi drivers and drunken businessmen—but in any case they are significant less for their degree of efficacy than for the way they represent the state's effort to encourage the Japanese people to internalize new standards of behavior, standards that, however trivial they may appear, were part of a larger package of political, economic, and social reforms designed to secure Japan's position vis-à-vis the West. By the end of the nineteenth century, this effort had succeeded in compartmentalizing "uncivilized" customs into clearly delineated spaces, most notably urban slums, which were seen as existing apart from mainstream society.

The Nostalgic Vision of the Satsuma Rebels

Although there was by no means unanimity among the Japanese people about the nature of the new regime and the sort of future its institutional reforms presaged, in a sense the first decade of the Meiji era passed so quickly that the nation was carried along with the current of change almost willy-nilly. The state—whose leadership itself was hardly united—was so busy tinkering with old institutions and creating new ones, then tinkering with those too, that the only thing beyond debate was the need to preserve national independence, which by the mid-1870s meant revising the unequal treaties imposed on the *bakufu* by the Western powers. No one with any influence, whether within the government or outside it, questioned the validity or urgency of that goal. Furthermore, by the end of the first decade of Meiji, all but the most recalcitrant elements in society recognized that the key to winning treaty revision was the creation of a "modern" state, as defined in relation to the West. Accordingly, in the years immediately after the Restoration, the priority was to adopt a generic "modernity," with the question of precisely what sort of "modernity" that would be—German or British or a new uniquely Japanese version—to be answered later.

Once the basic reforms were in place, disaffected samurai forced their way to the top of the national political agenda, in effect demanding an immediate answer to the modernity question. The new regime had been troubled since its founding by peasant uprisings—hundreds of them, often quite violent—sparked by resistance to policies ranging from the creation of the school system and the imposition of conscription to the liberation of the outcastes and attempts to contain cholera outbreaks. But these uprisings, however irritating, posed no fundamental threat to the regime or the premises of its rule. Such was not the case with samurai-led rebellions. Part of the samurai threat lay in the fact that the coup d'état that brought about the Meiji Restoration was itself a kind of large-scale samurai rebellion, led by the forces of Satsuma, Chōshū, and their allies. Government leaders thus understood firsthand the power of a few thousand determined and heavily armed samurai. Of the hundreds of samurai protests that occurred between 1868 and 1877, the half dozen serious enough to threaten the stability of the regime were led mostly by men who had been prominent in the Restoration movement but had later broken with the Meiji government. The leaders of these rebellions were sympathetic to the Meiji project of preserving national independence but feared that the state was taking Japan too far from the ideals of the old order. Their followers were more akin to peasant protesters, rising in an attempt to reverse specific policies they found injurious. The objectionable policies, of course, were those that stripped them of their hereditary privileges and economic supports: the commutation of stipends, prohibitions on bearing swords in public, and exhortations to wear Western-style clothing and hairstyles. In particular, the economic hardships they faced when trying to make a go of farming or commerce led many to feel they had little to lose by taking up arms against the state.

The Satsuma Rebellion of 1877 was the last and by far the most serious of the samurai uprisings. Putting it down took seven months and nearly bankrupted the state. Satsuma was the heartland of the Restoration; the domain's financial, military, and human resources helped to bring down the Tokugawa order. The rebellion was led by the charismatic Restoration hero Saigō Takamori, whose life was emblematic of the selfless loyalty and sincerity of the *shishi*. Saigō had been a central figure in the Meiji government until the end of 1873, when he and a number of others within the ruling circle left over the failure of a scheme to provoke war with Korea.[7]

Saigō returned home to the Satsuma capital of Kagoshima apparently intending to retire to a quiet life of fishing, hunting, and soaking in hot springs. It was not to be. The local samurai population was full of malcontents. Saigō's return, with a large contingent of Satsuma men from the Imperial Guard and national police force following close behind, gave them the leader they were looking for. Shortly after arriving in Kagoshima, Saigō founded the first of what would become a network of "private academies" *(shigakkō)*, which started out as vocational schools but very quickly turned into military training centers for samurai youths. Scholars are divided on Saigō's intentions—some think he planned all along to raise an army, others insist that the academies were more like martial arts Boys' Clubs—but in either case radical prefectural officials soon assumed responsibility for the academies. Before long Saigō's supporters in the prefectural government refused to implement national policies such as the universal education law and land tax reform, while in the meantime the academies evolved into a full-fledged military force hostile to the central government.

Satsuma's hotbed of antigovernment feeling derived from the domain's central role in bringing about the Restoration. Moreover, its samurai population was much larger than in other parts of Japan, comprising nearly a quarter of the entire population (in contrast to a national average of about 6 percent). The proportion of warriors was so high because the Satsuma domain had included in its retainer band a large number of *gōshi* (rustic samurai), rural reservists who combined farming with an existence at the very edge of samurai society. The *gōshi*'s marginal position made them particularly vulnerable to the economic impact of policies such as the land tax reform and the commutation of samurai stipends, and sensitive to the loss of their privileged social status.

The rebellion itself was sparked by a rumor that the government planned to have Saigō assassinated. Although Saigō appeared a reluctant rebel, once the uprising began, he quickly assumed leadership. After some early victories, his army made a series of strategic blunders—a pointless siege of the neighboring Kumamoto Prefecture's castle the worst among them—and was pushed back to Kagoshima. Once it became obvious that the war was lost, Saigō committed suicide rather than suffer the indignity of being captured.

The Satsuma Rebellion was the closest Japan came to a civil war since the brief, reluctantly fought struggle following the coup d'état of 1868. In putting it down, the government demonstrated its will and capacity to act decisively against any insurrectionary challenge, even one led by the Great Saigō. To be sure, it took all the king's horses and all the king's men to put Japan back together again. The entire conscript army plus police auxiliaries, 65,000 men in all, fought against a core Satsuma force of 12,000 men, supplemented by 10,000 sympathizers from other domains. The war to suppress these rebels cost the government 42 million yen, or 80 percent of its annual budget, 6,000 killed and 10,000 wounded.

Saigō's death also marked the end of a distinctive vision of the future, in which Japan would remain faithful in its modernity to the ideals of the status-based feudal order of the Tokugawa era. This vision is revealed in a series of memorials Saigō submitted to the throne in 1871: he advocated such policies as the formal adoption of Shinto as the official state religion, with a concomitant proscription of both Christianity and Buddhism; a land tax based on agricultural yields (he suggested a rate of 50 percent); government investment to preserve the agricultural base of the economy; and a tax on manufacturing, the revenues from which would go to paying samurai stipends.[8]

The government did not adopt any of his proposals. Indeed, in retrospect they appear reactionary or at least unrealistic. But Saigō was not trying to arrest Japan's encounter with Western-style "modernity." Rather, his goal was to guide it in the direction least disruptive to Japan's social and political traditions. The cornerstone of Saigō's vision was the preservation of the essential elements of the early modern status system, bolstered by reverence for the imperial institution. To achieve his goal of maintaining an agricultural economy would necessarily delay industrial development, and the development that did occur was to be geared more explicitly and exclusively toward defense. Saigō's vision of foreign relations rejected the market-seeking imperialism of the Great Powers, but did not rule out colonial expansion, so long as it was "defensive"—that is, designed to create a protective buffer around Japan at the expense of countries such as Korea and Ryūkyū (present-day Okinawa).

Such a vision was not completely unrealistic. In fact, during its final years in power the Tokugawa *bakufu* had tried to impose just such a model on the country, combining a minimal package of innovations to satisfy Western demands for trade with enough industrial development to guarantee national security. Given that the powers were not particularly interested in colonizing Japan directly, such an attitude—cordial but not particularly accommodating to the West—might have succeeded in creating a Japan less isolated than during the Tokugawa years, yet free of aspirations to prominence in the international arena. Considering that Japan in 1877 was still materially and militarily far from becoming an industrial power, Saigō's vision appears more pragmatic than reactionary.

But once the Meiji leadership had settled on the path of Western-style modernity, Saigō's high-tech feudalism could not be accommodated. The formative experience of Saigō's opponents was the Iwakura Mission of 1871–1873, in which important figures in the leadership, including Ōkubo Toshimichi, Iwakura Tomomi, Kido Takayoshi, and Itō Hirobumi—but not, significantly, Saigō or other later opponents of the regime—traveled around the world, seeing firsthand both the awesome power of the West and the abject conditions of regions that had fallen under its direct control. The mission's charge was to revise the treaties with the Western powers if possible but also to study Europe and America in an attempt to discern the bases of their technological and military strength. Although the embassy failed to renegotiate any treaties, the journey left a deep impression on its members, not least the sense that the sort of minimalist engagement with the West advocated by Saigō and others would not be enough to preserve Japanese independence. The envoys were particularly taken with Germany, partly because of the warm reception given to them by Bismarck. (In contrast, Queen Victoria could hardly be bothered to receive the embassy.) More important, they were struck by the similarities between Germany and Japan. Both had only recently been unified politically, and like Japan, Germany was a late-comer to industrialization. The German victory over France in the Franco-Prussian War of 1870 duly impressed the embassy as well. Perhaps the most remarkable feature of the mission's experience, however, was that it never seemed to occur to the Japanese that any of the minor powers they visited—the Netherlands, Denmark, or Switzerland—might be an appropriate model for Japanese modernization. Their sights remained set on Britain, France, the United States, and Germany.

Because the gap in wealth and productivity between Japan and the West was if anything greater than they had expected, the mission returned home convinced that the path to military and industrial strength would be long. In contrast, those leaders who had not accompanied the mission saw fewer barriers to the achievement of parity with the powers. The divergence between the Iwakura group and those who had stayed home came to a head over a plan to provoke Korea into war. The idea was to use gunboat diplomacy to force Korea—the last isolated East Asian nation—to make diplomatic and trade concessions very similar to those made by Japan to the Western powers. Trade was less a goal than the creation of a buffer between Japan and an expansive Russia, to be achieved by mobilizing disaffected and underemployed samurai. Opponents of the plan generally had no objection to its goals but merely to its timing, for they felt that Japan was too weak and vulnerable to waste resources on such a risky venture. And indeed, Japan forced the unequal Treaty of Kanghwa on Korea only three years later (see Chapter 4). In the meantime, however, the government had broken decisively, leaving Saigō and other future opponents of the regime outside the ruling circle.

The Democratic Vision of the Freedom and Popular Rights Activists

The defeat of the Satsuma rebels eliminated one alternative to centrally directed development. A second challenge, sparked in part by the same Korean crisis that had precipitated Saigō's break with the oligarchs, emerged in the mid-1870s. The Freedom and Popular Rights Movement (*jiyū minken undō*) was a loose alliance of former samurai and relatively well-to-do commoners who agitated for some form of parliamentary democracy. The movement eventually succeeded in forcing the authorities to accede to constitutional government, though the result fell well short of mass democracy.

Although the popular rights movement is usually discussed in the singular, in fact it was an extremely diverse phenomenon. National leaders included politicians such as Itagaki Taisuke and Gotō Shōjirō, onetime members of the ruling circle whose personal commitment to democracy was questionable. The rank and file included big-city journalists, former samurai, and a heterogeneous mix of landlords, village officials, and rural notables. In general, however, supporters of the movement tended to be young, prosperous, and relatively well educated men, perhaps four fifths of whom came from rural areas.

In much the way that the rhetoric of imperial loyalty had led rural nativists in the 1850s and 1860s to lend at least implicit support to the *shishi*'s anti-Tokugawa activism, the disparate elements of the Freedom and Popular Rights Movement were united by a mutually expedient but essentially superficial commonality of language. Itagaki Taisuke's conception of "democracy," though deliberately cloaked in Western terminology, in fact derived from the Confucian idea of the loyal subject's duty to remonstrate with his lord in order to protect him from the machinations of "venal ministers" (the "venal ministers" in this case being Ōkubo Toshimichi, Iwakura Tomomi, and others who had opposed the plan to provoke Korea into war). Nevertheless, Western ideas about democracy and natural rights, once translated into Japanese and popularized by passionate democrats such as Nakae Chōmin, Ueki Emori, and a host of liberal journalists and orators, took on a life of their own. In particular, rural activists believed that they themselves were the "people" on whom a democratic future would be built. They were not republicans calling for an end to monarchy but rather local elites asserting their own relevance in the face of rapid social and economic change. Significantly, aside from a few radical ideologues, no one in the movement was particularly concerned with winning a voice in government for the mass of the Japanese people, including women.

The movement took shape shortly after Itagaki and Gotō left the government at the end of 1873, angry that the plan to invade Korea had been rejected. From a base among disaffected Tosa samurai, it quickly broadened to incorporate people from a variety of class and geographic backgrounds. Responding in part to the movement's evident appeal, in 1875 the state mandated popularly elected prefectural assemblies, which had no lawmaking powers but did serve as a forum for political activity. By 1880, some sixty petition drives had yielded a quarter million signatures calling for the creation of a national assembly. The vitality of this grassroots movement owed less to the halfhearted leadership of Itagaki and Gotō than to the efforts of liberal journalists, who persisted in their calls for a constitution in the face of strict press and libel laws implemented in 1875 and 1877.

In late 1881, after much internal wrangling, the government announced that the emperor would bestow a constitution upon the nation by the end of the decade. This decision arose in part from a sense that constitutional government, including at least the trappings of parliamentary democracy, was a necessary part of the package of institutions that made the Western powers "modern." It was also a pragmatic strategy, rooted in the realization that the best way to deflate the popular rights movement was to give it what it asked for, but on terms dictated by the state. The key was framing the constitution as a "gift" given freely by the emperor to the people. As a gift, the document was not a matter of public debate; only the emperor himself—in reality, oligarchs acting in his name—could decide its content. As a result, the constitution was drafted in strict secrecy, mostly by the oligarch Itō Hirobumi, working from the Prussian model. Promulgated in 1889, it went into effect the following year.

The government's promise of a constitution marked the beginning of a new stage in the popular rights movement. Itagaki founded the Liberal Party (Jiyūtō), which became the main focus of local political activism during the early 1880s. Itagaki's ambivalence toward his own movement made the Liberal Party's national organization weak and ineffective; its real strength lay in the 149 local party branches that dotted the countryside. These branches served as the institutional nexus between purely local issues and national politics. A good example of this link is the Fukushima Incident of 1882, in which the centrally appointed governor of Fukushima Prefecture, Mishima Michitsune, battled with the local branch of the Liberal Party over a road-building project. At heart the incident was little more than a conflict over pork barrel politics, but the standoff between the authoritarian governor and the raucous prefectural assembly quickly came to symbolize a contest between tyranny and democracy. The governor had a group of party leaders arrested, prompting a crowd of ten thousand people to attack a police station; Mishima responded by calling in the army, with the result that more than two thousand people were arrested. Later, a small group of radicals even hatched a scheme to assassinate Mishima and thereby supposedly incite a popular rebellion that would topple the central government. (Just how killing Mishima would spark a revolution was something the conspirators never thought through very carefully.) The plot, known as the Kabasan

Incident, was quickly uncovered and suppressed, but it is remarkable that a ruckus over a road could escalate into a revolutionary plot in less than a year.[9]

Also remarkable was the dedication of many rank-and-file activists in the Freedom and Popular Rights Movement. The Learning and Debating Society, founded in 1880 in Itsukaichi, a village in the hills west of Tokyo, counted among its members the mayor, a former mayor, the principal of the local school, and other prominent figures in the community. They pledged to "develop liberty and improve society," in part by reading and discussing translations of Western philosophical works. In 1881 one member even wrote a complete draft of a national constitution, which included protections of citizens' rights within a framework that recognized the emperor's sovereignty.[10] The extraordinary enthusiasm of the Itsukaichi learners and debaters was mirrored by numerous similar groups throughout Japan, many of whom undertook constitution-writing projects of their own.

It is difficult to explain this ardor. On the surface it appears obviously to reflect a gnawing hunger for democracy. Why else would busy people give up their evenings to read difficult foreign books and draft fundamental laws they knew no government would ever adopt? The problem with democracy—and democracy movements—however, is the tension between altruism and self-interest. People who make their own decisions sometimes make petty and self-serving ones. Many of those in the Meiji countryside who rallied around the banner of liberty and democracy did so not to protect the rights of the weak but to further their own interests, often at the expense of others.

The link between democracy and self-interest helps to explain the troubling presence of outlaws in the world of local politics during the popular rights period. In the Nagoya area, for example, gangsters were prominent in both the local Liberal Party branch and a rival organization, the Patriotic Fraternal Society (Aikoku Kōshinsha).[11] The bosses and their gangs were around long before the Freedom and Popular Rights Movement ever emerged, so it would not be fair to call them a product of the movement. Still, local and prefectural politics gave the bosses a natural arena, for they were masters of the personal connections and regional economic concerns that drove local politics. Accordingly, aspiring politicians realized they could gain much from alliances with gambling ring bosses. Through the bosses, they could tap into ready-made networks of men at the village level, who could rally supporters and, if necessary, use strong-arm tactics to help reluctant or misguided voters make prudent decisions at the ballot box. The presence of outlaws in the Freedom and Popular Rights Movement does not deny the Fukushima and Itsukaichi activists' commitment to democracy. But it does remind us that the point of the movement was less to promote democracy as an abstract ideal than to create a forum for rural elites to participate in the building of a modern nation, which to them—as to rural nativists in the waning years of the Tokugawa regime—was a process grounded in the world of local communities and economies.

Unlike in the case of the nostalgic vision of Saigō Takamori or the moral vision of the Chichibu rebels (examined later in this chapter), a decisive moment of defeat is difficult to posit for the Freedom and Popular Rights Movement. The incidents at Fukushima, Kabasan, and Chichibu (which had an important popular rights element to it) are all worthy candidates, but only if one assumes that broad-based democracy was the genuine goal of the movement. Seeing the struggle as one over participation complicates any interpretation of the results. On the one hand, the activists got much of what they had asked for: a constitution, a popularly elected House of Representatives in the Diet, and a measure of local self-determination in the form of village and prefectural assemblies. On the other hand, the terms of local elites' participation in the nation-building project changed subtly but decisively. Economic change made the village a less insular entity, and the gradual intrusion of state power into the fabric of village and even household life altered the nature of the popular rights activists' role as community leaders.

Former activists became mayors, prefectural assemblymen, and Diet representatives; many no doubt were satisfied that they had all the democracy they or Japan needed. But as a class, the local notables who had participated in the nativist salons of the 1860s and democracy discussion groups of the 1880s found themselves assigned a new role as the local arm of central authority. They helped to implement movements on behalf of rural improvement and moral suasion campaigns cooked up by social bureaucrats and expert busybodies in Tokyo. Without question, many felt themselves to be full participants in the nation-building project through their role as the local face of centrally directed campaigns; no doubt many found ways to transform policies they were meant merely to administer. Nevertheless, the version of democracy they came to practice was quite different from the one they had envisioned in the heady days of the 1870s and 1880s. Japanese democracy developed in complicity with the state, beholden to power in a way that made political activism and intellectual engagement in dialogue with, yet independent of, the state difficult. That sort of democracy was doomed the moment the emperor announced his gift of a constitution.

The Moral Vision of the Chichibu Rebels

A final challenge to the state's program of centrally directed development was mounted by peasants who embraced what we might call a moral vision of politics, in which ordinary Japanese offered their loyalty and taxes to the state in exchange for benevolent rule. The character of the moral vision, which owed much to Tokugawa peasants' ideas of the nature of political authority, is revealed most vividly in the Chichibu Rebellion of 1884.[12] The protesters' defeat was akin to the collapse of samurai resistance after the Satsuma Rebellion: whatever resentments or unfulfilled hopes individuals may have continued to harbor, distinctively samurai and peasant visions of modernity lost all political cogency.

The origins of the Chichibu Rebellion lay in the transformative effects of Japan's entry into the world market in 1859 and the land tax reform of 1873. Times were generally good for Japan's farmers in the late 1870s. Steady inflation brought increased prices for their products, while land taxes went down (the tax rate was lowered by 17 percent in 1877), leaving them with both higher gross incomes and a smaller tax burden relative to income. Moreover, strong demand for Japanese silk in European markets encouraged many farmers to switch from grain to silk. The state, eager to maintain a positive balance of trade, also encouraged farmers to take up silk production. Japan alternated between positive and negative trade balances during the 1870s and 1880s; silk accounted for about 44 percent of exports during this period.[13] Farmers shifted to sericulture, particularly in relatively mountainous areas suited to growing mulberry trees (silkworms eat mulberry leaves—lots of mulberry leaves) but not to rice cultivation. The Chichibu district of western Saitama Prefecture, northwest of Tokyo, was one such area.

The main drawback to the expansion of silk production was that starting from scratch was quite expensive. Mulberry trees take several years to mature, and land given over to mulberry cannot readily be switched back to grain. Moreover, raising silkworms is extremely labor-intensive and hence draws women (tending silkworms was seen as women's work) away from other activities. But the prospect of higher incomes seemed enough in the 1870s to encourage many peasants to go into debt, mostly by mortgaging their land, to cover the start-up costs of converting from grain cultivation to silk production. In the inflationary economy of the late 1870s, the decision seemed a reasonable one, but government retrenchment in 1881 dried up the cash supply, leaving farmers with diminishing incomes but unchanging tax and debt burdens.

The Matsukata Deflation, as the retrenchment was called, hurt peasants throughout Japan, but perhaps most severely in areas like Chichibu, where many farmers had gone out on a financial limb to take up silk production. In Chichibu, the deflation began to hurt around 1883, when silk prices collapsed, falling by more than 50 percent from 1882 to 1885.[14] The rebellion in Chichibu, like smaller but similar protest movements in other silk-growing districts, was caused not by the financial hardship of plummeting prices per se so much as by the fact that the collapse came on the heels of a prolonged period of rising expectations. In the late summer and early autumn of 1884, desperate farmers in Chichibu held meetings to request government assistance in winning debt renegotiations or reductions from creditors. They were following a well-established precedent; Tokugawa era peasants had often looked to the state to intervene in private conflicts over debt. The Chichibu farmers may have been encouraged by the mixed signals they received from Tokyo: although troops had forcibly put down a number of movements for debt relief, the state had recently intervened on behalf of farmers in Hachiōji, a silk center south of Chichibu.

Although the impulse behind the peasants' meetings in Chichibu and elsewhere owed much to Tokugawa practices, there was a significant new feature: the presence of political parties, including both branches of the Liberal Party and ad hoc single issue groups. Their involvement threatened to turn specific grievances into national political issues, a fact recognized by the organizers of the Poor People's Party (Konmintō) in Chichibu and the Debtors' Party (Shakkintō) in nearby Gunma, who joined local Liberal Party branches even as they were setting up their own groups. The rush of malcontents to the Liberal Party ranks so alarmed the national leadership that it disbanded the party on the eve of the Chichibu Rebellion rather than be implicated in incendiary actions undertaken in its name.

Like the gamblers and gangsters of the Patriotic Fraternal Society in Nagoya, local notables who used personal connections and charisma to attract and keep followers were prominent in Chichibu and nearby districts. Generally called *kyōkaku,* or "chivalrous types," these men saw themselves as defenders of the poor and weak against the rich and powerful. But these

Robin Hoods were often closer to plain hoods—gamblers and thugs. Bosses *(oyabun)* could rely on the fealty of dozens or even hundreds of followers *(kobun)* distributed around a well-defined territory *(nawabari)*. Many were not professional gangsters so much as peasants or entrepreneurs who oversaw networks of underlings with whom they engaged in a range of activities, some perfectly legitimate, others downright criminal. The two principal leaders of the Chichibu Rebellion, Tashiro Eisuke and Katō Oribei, were both *kyōkaku*. Indeed, they were recruited to lead the movement precisely because of their personal networks both in the immediate vicinity and among Liberal Party members in the surrounding regions. Tashiro, who raised silkworms himself when not preoccupied with running his gambling den, characterized himself as a lawyer *(daigennin)*, an appropriate occupation for a man with his connections and charisma.

In any case, the mass meetings had little effect other than to create an angry mood in the villages of Chichibu. When autumn arrived with no sign of relief, a consensus emerged that violence was the only solution. On the first and second of November 1884, between seven and ten thousand rioters broke into and burned the offices and homes of moneylenders in an attempt to destroy records of their debts. The rebels were in control briefly, but once the army was called in they broke ranks and the uprising crumbled quickly. In fact, despite a great deal of damage to property, relatively few people were hurt during the rioting—another Tokugawa legacy, for peasant rebels in early modern Japan generally took great care to avoid physically harming people even as they freely destroyed and confiscated property. And owing to the movement's quick collapse, the army avoided shooting many people.

Chichibu stands out as a landmark incident. First, the state itself took the rebellion very seriously, mobilizing troops as soon as news of the incident reached Tokyo and promptly executing the ringleaders once it was put down. (One leader, Inoue Denzō, managed to escape to a village on the Okhotsk Sea coast of Hokkaido, where he lived a long and quiet life under an assumed name.) Second, at least some of the rebellion's leaders appear to have entertained ideas of overthrowing the Meiji state. A sign on an occupied government building read "Revolutionary Headquarters" *(kakumei honbu)*. Even if such sentiments were not widely shared among the participants, the very suggestion of revolution was alarmingly different from the usual pattern of peasant protests, which tended to focus on achieving specific and very limited goals. Third, many of the rank and file saw the movement not as an opportunity for revolution but rather as a time of "world renewal" *(yonaori)*. This sort of millenarian vision was common in the last years of the Tokugawa period, but singling out Itagaki Taisuke as the God of World Renewal who would bring prosperity and happiness to Japan was definitely a new twist. (Itagaki declined to be deified.) Revolutionary or millenarian, the challenge to the premises of the state's rule required a quick and harsh response despite the fact that the regime was never in any real danger.

The peasant rebels at Chichibu thought that the sort of implicit moral covenant that had guided relations between state and village society in the Tokugawa period still obtained under the Meiji regime. They thought that loyal service to the state through the payment of taxes and the performance of other duties entitled them to government intervention in times of dire need. They thought that benevolence was in fact the point of governance. They thought that showing their desperation by resorting to carefully choreographed violence would be met not with more violence but rather with conciliation. In short, they thought the Tokugawa rules of engagement in peasant uprisings were still valid.

Clearly, they did not appreciate the magnitude of the changes that had occurred. The point of governance was not to demonstrate the ruler's benevolence at all, but rather to establish the state's position within the community of nations. Internal dissent was seen not as an appeal to the morality of the monarch but rather as an insolent challenge to his rule. A new type of state brought with it a new style of response to disorder: no compromises, only brutal and swift suppression. Japan saw its share of riots and protests during the decades following Chichibu, but the people got the message. The idea of popular movement as a pas de deux between desperate subject and benevolent lord was gone. The peasants knew the next time they rose, the troops' guns would be loaded.

The Statist Vision and the Matsukata Deflation

The demands of national integration always prevailed over the interests or indeed the futures of the dispossessed, be they former samurai, small-fry local notables, the urban masses, or impoverished peasants. The state was more than the sum of its subjects, and the oligarchs as a group were confident that their authoritarian style of bureaucratic rule was suited to promoting the state's interests. In that respect they were not so very different from their Tokugawa predecessors. The main difference was their perception of the extent of the state's interests. Whereas the Tokugawa regime was concerned mostly with maintaining social order and seeing to it that people fulfilled their status-based tax and service obligations, the Meiji state routinely intruded into individuals' lives, telling them not just how to behave in the public realm but how to think like subjects of a modern nation-state.

The Meiji regime employed a variety of techniques in its attempt to instill in the people a sense of belonging in the national community. Since universal education and conscription gave it direct access to individuals at an impressionable age, it is hardly surprising that it was in school and in the military that Japanese learned reverence for the emperor, a standardized version of the Japanese language, and the discipline necessary for the functioning of modern institutions. A less direct means of creating modern subjects was the use of imperial pageantry, which succeeded in transforming the once shadowy sovereign into a figure at once intimately familiar and awe-inspiringly distant—a symbol of both the ties that bound the Japanese into a single "imagined community" and the state's power over the people. Creating a modern monarchy entailed first teaching the people who the emperor was, a goal achieved in part by parading the young sovereign around the country on a series of grand tours. Then the sovereign was raised back above the clouds as a sacred and inviolable figure, visible to most subjects only as an image in the official portrait distributed to schools.[15]

Schools, the army, and national pageantry were part of the nation-building project of every modern regime. An additional challenge facing the Meiji state in its effort to create a truly national sense of identity was its need to eradicate the vestiges of the institutions of the status system. That is why it eliminated Tokugawa era status categories, gave commoners surnames, liberated outcastes, allowed (indeed pressured) Buddhist priests to marry, divested samurai of their privileges and stipends, and so on. By stripping away intermediate levels of identity and the structure of precisely differentiated obligations toward the state, the state created a citizenry that was *essentially* equal in the sense that each individual had a direct relationship with the emperor as his subject, and each owed the emperor his or her undivided loyalty.

In addition to the symbolic task of creating a single, undifferentiated category of "imperial subject," the state had to deploy its bureaucratic power to ensure that the new relationship between emperor and subject had meaning at the level of actual political and economic affairs. That is why in 1884 the government undertook a rationalization of local administrative units, the first of many waves of amalgamation that have continued until the present. The rationalization was aimed in the first instance at reducing the cost of government, for having the country divided into tens of thousands of villages, towns, and cities was hopelessly inefficient. But the policy had the important side effect of bureaucratizing local government: village communities were subsumed within larger administrative units; although they continued to be important in the lives of their inhabitants, they lost meaning as political entities. Amalgamation thus eliminated the measure of political autonomy villages had enjoyed in the Tokugawa period and transformed local government from a critical mediating stratum to merely the lowest level of central control.

Among the side effects of the rationalization of local administration was heightened tension between commoners and recently "liberated" outcastes. In fact, discrimination against former outcastes may have become more virulent during the Meiji period, in part as a result of the reform of local administration. The inclusion of outcaste villages within larger administrative units raised issues concerning the education of outcaste children, rights to land, and access to common property resources. These problems exacerbated conflicts that arose when former outcastes tried to assert their formal equality with commoners by participating, for example, in local festivals on the same basis as other parishioners.

As diverse as the visions of the future we have examined were in other ways, none was opposed to a measure of economic development. Although wary of industrialization, Saigō Takamori and his samurai followers sponsored various schemes to improve agricultural productivity and thereby strengthen the economic foundation of the nation. The class of rural elites that supplied activists to the Freedom and Popular Rights Movement was composed of avid entrepreneurs who invested in cash-crop farming, commerce, and manufacturing. Likewise, the participants in the Chichibu Rebellion were enthusiastic advocates of economic development so long as they were among its immediate beneficiaries. Indeed, as a group they were rational profit-maximizers who had made some imprudent choices but were hardly ready to swear off production for the market. But a broad consensus about the desirability of development is not the same as a consensus about the methods or goals of growth. Granted that the transition from a feudal to a capitalist economy was bound to be painful even under the most compassionate regime, the Meiji state's policies often exacerbated the trauma, for industrialization and macroeconomic development were always more important to it than the fate of individual economic actors or indeed the welfare of entire regions.

The silk-spinning industry is a good example. Because silk was Japan's most important export, the government was eager to see the industry develop as rapidly as possible. To that end it underwrote the construction of several state-of-the-art factories, beginning with the Tomioka filature in 1873. Although the first Western-style factories were not profitable, by the end of the nineteenth century they were rapidly displacing the small, traditional workshops that had once been the mainstay of the industry. Moreover, since districts with long-established silk industries tended to retain traditional manufactories—switching to factory production was too expensive for local entrepreneurs—factories moved instead into areas with relatively new silk industries. Consequently, while modernization contributed to macroeconomic growth, it also drove traditional manufacturers into bankruptcy and undermined textile production in entire regions. From the standpoint of the oligarchs overseeing the national economic policy, this was an unfortunate but inevitable consequence of industrialization. The ups and downs of petty entrepreneurs or even of entire regional economies were ultimately not nearly as important as promoting the economic strength of the nation as a whole. After all, attaining a healthy industrial economy was a prerequisite to dealing effectively with the Western powers.

This basic pattern of modern industry developing under state sponsorship and displacing traditional manufacturing in the process was repeated any number of times, even in industries that produced neither export goods nor items of immediate national security importance, such as commercial fertilizer processing. In particularly critical areas, the state jump-started key industries, then turned them over to private entrepreneurs at fire sale prices. Although the process in effect taxed the Japanese people to put profits into the pockets of favored business interests, it did succeed in developing major industries and infrastructure. And since private investors were consistently reluctant to take substantial risks, it was probably the only route to quick success available at the time.

The Matsukata Deflation of 1881–1885 was the state's firmest statement of its vision of a future that favored industrial and military development over the immediate welfare of the Japanese people. It began when the finance minister, Matsukata Masayoshi, implemented a drastic retrenchment policy. In the long run the measure ensured Japan's financial health by putting the economy on a sound footing. In the short run, however, the

Matsukata Deflation caused a great deal of hardship for many segments of the population, particularly in the countryside. Immediately upon becoming finance minister in 1881, Matsukata began to reduce the volume of paper currency in circulation as a way to bring its value closer to that of gold and silver. Between 1881 and 1885 the note issue went from 159.4 million yen to 118.5 million, or slightly below the 1877 level. The measure brought about a recession that devastated farmers and handicraft producers but benefited the government, banks, and stronger businesses.

Matsukata's policy "established the strategy of giving priority to the modern sector . . . although inevitably at some cost to the average Japanese both at the time and for many decades later."[16] The cost alarmed even some major Meiji officials. For example, Inoue Kowashi, one of the architects of the Meiji legal system, was shocked by conditions in Osaka in 1885. Police officials there complained of being unable to handle the rapidly increasing beggar population, while prefectural bureaucrats concluded that for peasants the only alternative to outright starvation was to take to the road in a desperate search for work and food. Many were unsuccessful: in 1886 a total of 556 people in the area that now comprises Osaka and Nara prefectures were reported dead of starvation or diseases contracted while homeless.[17]

Matsukata's own attitude was to blame the victims. As he later recalled:

> At that time [1880] we fell into a condition which filled all classes of the country with anxiety. The real income of the government was reduced by nearly one-half. Among the people, those who lived on fixed incomes were suddenly reduced to dire straits. Bonds dropped sharply while commodity prices, especially the price of rice, rose to new heights. The land tax was in reality sharply reduced, while the value of land appreciated greatly. The farmers, who were the only class to profit from these circumstances, took on luxurious habits, causing a great increase in the consumption of luxury goods . . . Consequently imports from foreign countries were increased and the nation's specie supply further depleted. Merchants, dazzled by the extreme fluctuations in prices, all aimed at making huge speculative profits and gave no heed to productive undertakings. As a result, interest rates were so high that no one could plan an industrial undertaking that required any considerable capital.[18]

Matsukata's foisting the blame for the fiscal crisis upon the very people who suffered its remedy most acutely owed much to a long tradition in Confucian statecraft, in which economic dislocation was attributed to the masses' preference for wasteful luxury over the simple pleasures of dawn-to-dusk dirt farming. But whatever their provenance, his words are eloquent testimony to his utter contempt for the Japanese people's hardship—and indeed for anything that stood in the way of the industrial and military development that would raise Japan to Great Power status.

Japan in East Asia

In the end the statist vision of the future prevailed. By the early twentieth century, Japan had become a just barely democratic constitutional monarchy and an important military and industrial power. The state realized its vision in part by delivering a better quality of life to a significant portion of the population through improvements in living standards, health, education, and social and physical mobility. But these gains were realized only by systematically undermining other possible versions of Japan's future. This truth tempts us to read Japan's modern history as a story of unilateral repression, in which the masses (fatter and healthier though they may have been) were crushed under the jackboot of the police state. Such a story is attractive not only because it rings true but also because it absolves ordinary Japanese of their complicity in the dark episodes of their country's modern history. But saying that the Meiji state steamrollered competing visions of the future begs the question of how a uniformly repressive regime could stay in power with such apparent ease. Clearly, it had to offer something to exponents of the defeated visions to win at least their passive support.

That something was empire. Despite radical differences concerning the domestic political order, by the early twentieth century all but the most marginal groups in Japanese society took for granted the need for—and intrinsic desirability of—some kind of Japanese imperialist presence in East Asia. And why not? Imperialism is exciting and profitable—at least when you are good at it, and Japan was on a winning streak starting with the Taiwan Expedition of 1874 through to the early 1930s. If it brought hardship and injustice to Japan's imperial subjects, it was always easy to blame the victims for bringing their sorry state upon themselves. Since gunboat diplomacy and colonial aggrandizement had brought power and wealth to the Western powers, many Japanese politicians, intellectuals, and journalists assumed that, like telegraphs and waistcoats, this was another part of the do-it-yourself modernity kit.

Nonetheless, the government leadership was by no means unanimous in its attitude toward East Asia. The crisis over the plan to invade Korea in 1873 was merely the most spectacular of a nearly continuous series of disputes over foreign policy within the ruling circle. There was no master plan, no conspiracy to take over the world; the impetus behind many important decisions came when the government's hand was forced (or more often allowed to be forced) by events and the actions of individuals beyond its direct control. Yet beneath the surface of discord, most leaders assumed that an active Japanese presence in East Asia was desirable for defensive purposes as well as for the economic benefits that access to continental markets and resources would bring. And all felt that it would signal Japan's "civilized" aspirations to the Western powers.

The popular appeal of the empire-building project lay in its connection to an atmosphere of national crisis, carefully cultivated by government leaders, journalists, and other public figures. It was a sense that Japan's independence depended on its ability to establish a secure place for itself within the greater East Asian world. National crisis encourages people to put differences aside at least temporarily for the greater good; in late nineteenth-century Japan, national crisis was also nation-building crisis, and the differences put aside were those that had separated the status-based social order of the Tokugawa period from the modern imperial subjecthood of the Meiji era.

The unity fostered by the sense of national crisis helped to create Japanese nationalism, and nationalism is the special sauce that completes any recipe for a modern nation-state. When the Meiji state enacted policies in the name of the nation—to protect independence, to defend national honor—resistance all too easily appeared cautious, selfish, or even disloyal. As a key element in the nation-building project, the idea of Japanese prominence in East Asian affairs—whether accompanied by actual colonial expansion or not—had broad appeal. During the years immediately following the Restoration, dispossessed samurai were among the most enthusiastic advocates of an aggressive stance toward Korea. Saigō Takamori of course left the government over the proposal to invade Korea; although his personal ardor for war with Korea is open to question, he did see East Asia as an outlet for samurai energies. In 1874 another estranged Meiji leader, Etō Shinpei, led a group of northern Kyushu samurai in an abortive (and suicidal) scheme to invade Korea whether the government liked it or not. For Saigō, Etō, and their supporters, invading Korea had almost nothing to do with Korea itself; indeed, once Korea was forced to open itself to Japanese trade and diplomacy in 1876, the new relationship had little immediate impact on Japan's economy or its position vis-à-vis the West.

Most ordinary Japanese were too busy trying to make a living to worry about East Asian geopolitics. But a variety of push and pull factors combined to ensure that they would not remain aloof. For one thing, farmers, fishers, and entrepreneurs of various stripes were among the earliest Japanese to seek their fortunes away from home—first in Hokkaido and Sakhalin, later in Korea and Taiwan, and later still in Manchuria, Southeast Asia, and the Pacific islands. The need to defend the lives and economic interests of Japanese sojourners and migrants, particularly in Korea, sometimes led the government authorities to act against their own better judgment. The Sino-Japanese War of 1894–95 and the Russo-Japanese War of 1904–5 gave rural conscripts their first direct contact with fellow East Asians, though under circumstances that nurtured contempt and misunderstanding rather than amity and empathy.[19] Once Japan began accumulating possessions, particularly Taiwan (1895) and Korea (1910), colonial military and police service overseas gave peasant youths opportunities for career advancement and raw power—and with it a personal stake in Japan's imperialist project—that they would otherwise never have had. By the early twentieth century, even people who had no direct involvement in Japanese imperialism were beholden to the empire as a market, a source of cheap food, and an outlet for surplus population.

The impulse for Japanese involvement in East Asia was not solely the product of a desire for territorial or economic aggrandizement. In some cases imperialism was an idealistic endeavor, and for others—the early Meiji samurai, for example—it was an introspective enterprise that in the end had little to do with Asia at all. Activists in the Freedom and Popular Rights Movement were among the most enthusiastic and vocal advocates of Japanese engagement with East Asia. As a group, they embody the complex mixture of idealism and self-serving ambition that informed much of modern Japanese imperialism.

The liberals' embrace of empire reveals how a sense of national mission could subsume even those with radically divergent attitudes toward domestic politics. Democracy and empire were linked in the Freedom and Popular Rights Movement from the very outset. After all, Itagaki Taisuke's conversion to democratic thought occurred after the failure of the plan to invade Korea. But for many activists the initial attraction of East Asia lay in the presence of like-minded men in Korea and China, which raised for them the possibility of regional partnership to forestall Western imperialism. To be sure, the liberal educator and journalist Fukuzawa Yukichi made his famous exhortation to Japan to "leave Asia and enter Europe" *(datsu-A, nyū-Ō)* in

1885, a sign that he had become disillusioned by what he saw as the intractable backwardness of the Chinese and Korean regimes. But Fukuzawa's call is so famous and so in keeping with the image of a modern Japan permanently alienated from Asia that it is surprising to recall that Tokyo in the 1870s and 1880s was a mecca for liberal thinkers from throughout East Asia. Sun Yat-sen, the leader of the 1911 revolution in China, is the most famous of the East Asian sojourners. Like Sun, the Chinese diplomat and poet Huang Zunxian and the Korean Christian Yun Ch'i-ho saw in Japan a possible model for their own countries. Many Korean activists hopeful for a Meiji-style revolution in their own country cooked up insurrectionary plots from bases in Japan; some, including Yun and Kim Hong-jip, sought and received advice from Fukuzawa, who remained quite engaged with Asia despite his westward-looking posture. At the same time, the Chinese embassy in Tokyo was a meeting place for Japanese Sinophiles; even the oligarch Itō Hirobumi came by occasionally to get pointers on his poetic efforts in Chinese.

Yet a distinctly East Asian version of modernity, in which Japan played the benign role model, was not to be. For even among those liberal Japanese concerned about the plight of their fellows in China and Korea, a dangerous streak of arrogance can be discerned—a sense that Japan would "liberate" Asia whether the Asians liked it or not. In time it became increasingly difficult to distinguish between selfless idealists interested in the good of East Asia and cold pragmatists concerned only with Japan. The Black Ocean Society (Gen'yōsha) is a case in point. Founded in 1881 by former samurai of the Fukuoka domain, it began as a conventional popular rights organization but quickly became involved in affairs on the continent, particularly Korea. By the early twentieth century, the group's name was synonymous with the most virulent sort of right-wing ultranationalism. Deservedly so, for in addition to carrying out terrorist attacks within Japan, such as an attempt on the life of the politician Ōkuma Shigenobu, the group gathered intelligence for the Japanese army in Korea in the 1890s and later worked on behalf of annexation. Yet at the same time its leader, Tōyama Mitsuru, assisted Asian revolutionaries such as Sun Yat-sen, Kim Ok-kyun, and Emilio Aguinaldo.

By the end of the nineteenth century, many liberals had become disillusioned and abandoned the idealism that once guided their perception of Japan's role in East Asian affairs. They turned instead to a cynical view of international power politics, in part in response to what they saw as the hypocrisy of the Western powers. The classic example is the journalist

Tokutomi Sohō, who began as an enthusiastic supporter of the Freedom and Popular Rights Movement and Western-style liberal democracy, but later became an ardent nationalist and mouthpiece of the conservative government authorities. The turning point in Tokutomi's life came right at the end of the Sino-Japanese War in 1895, when he visited the Liaotung Peninsula, which was to be ceded to Japan as part of the peace settlement. "My trip to the Liaotung Peninsula was the first time I had set foot off Japanese soil," he later recalled, "and it was quite exciting . . . It was late April, and spring had just arrived. The great willows were budding; the flowers of North China were at the height of their fragrance. Fields stretched out before the eye; a spring breeze was blowing. As I travelled about and realized that this was our territory, I felt a truly great thrill and satisfaction."[20]

Soon afterward, however, the Triple Intervention by Russia, Germany, and France forced Japan to abandon its claims to Liaotung. Tokutomi was "vexed beyond tears" and returned home to Japan as quickly as possible. "As he was leaving, he picked up a handful of gravel from the beach at Port Arthur and carried this back to Japan in a handkerchief as a 'souvenir of what had been, for a time, Japanese territory.'" He regarded the shock of the Triple Intervention as the turning point in his life: "It is no exaggeration to say that the retrocession of Liaotung dominated the rest of my life. After hearing about it I became almost a different person psychologically. Say what you will, it happened because we were not strong enough. What it came down to was that sincerity and justice did not amount to a thing if you were not strong enough." The Triple Intervention convinced Tokutomi that "Japan's progress, the protection of the nation's security and interests, and whether or not Japan would have influence in the world, would ultimately depend upon military strength—and military strength alone."[21] It was a grim vision, but one that many Japanese had come to share.

Selected Readings

Beasley, W. G. *The Meiji Restoration.* Stanford: Stanford University Press, 1972.

Bowen, Roger W. *Rebellion and Democracy in Meiji Japan: A Study of Commoners in the Popular Rights Movement.* Berkeley: University of California Press, 1980.

Braisted, William R., trans. *Meiroku Zasshi: Journal of the Japanese Enlightenment.* Tokyo: University of Tokyo Press, 1976.

Crawcour, E. Sydney. "Economic Change in the Nineteenth Century." In *The Nineteenth Century.* Vol. 5 of *The Cambridge History of Japan,* ed. Marius B. Jansen. New York: Cambridge University Press, 1989.

Fujitani, Takeshi. *Splendid Monarchy: Power and Pageantry in Modern Japan.* Berkeley: University of California Press, 1996.

Harootunian, H. D. *Toward Restoration: The Growth of Political Consciousness in Tokugawa Japan.* Berkeley: University of California Press, 1970.

Huber, Thomas. *The Revolutionary Origins of Modern Japan.* Stanford: Stanford University Press, 1981.

Irokawa Daikichi. *The Culture of the Meiji Period,* trans. and ed. Marius B. Jansen. Princeton: Princeton University Press, 1985.

Jansen, Marius B., and Gilbert Rozman, eds. *Japan in Transition: From Tokugawa to Meiji.* Princeton: Princeton University Press, 1986.

Koschmann, J. Victor. *The Mito Ideology: Discourse, Reform, and Insurrection in Late Tokugawa Japan, 1790–1864.* Berkeley: University of California Press, 1987.

Lone, Stewart. *Japan's First Modern War: Army and Society in the Conflict with China, 1894–95.* New York: St. Martin's Press, 1994.

Najita, Tetsuo. *Japan: The Intellectual Foundations of Modern Japanese Politics.* Chicago: University of Chicago Press, 1974.

Robertson, Jennifer. "Sexy Rice: Plant Gender, Farm Manuals, and Grass-Roots Nativism." *Monumenta Nipponica* 39, no. 3 (Autumn 1984): 233–260.

Scheiner, Irwin. "The Mindful Peasant: Sketches for a Study of Rebellion." *Journal of Asian Studies* 32 (1973): 579–591.

Totman, Conrad. *The Collapse of the Tokugawa Bakufu, 1862–1868.* Honolulu: University of Hawaii Press, 1980.

Vlastos, Stephen. "Opposition Movements in Early Meiji, 1868–1885." In *The Nineteenth Century.* Vol. 5 of *The Cambridge History of Japan,* ed. Marius B. Jansen. New York: Cambridge University Press, 1989.

Walthall, Anne. *The Weak Body of a Useless Woman: Matsuo Taseko and the Meiji Restoration.* Chicago: University of Chicago Press, 1998.

Wilson, George C. *Patriots and Redeemers in Japan.* Chicago: University of Chicago Press, 1992.

Yates, Charles L. *Saigō Takamori: The Man behind the Myth.* London: Kegan Paul International, 1995.

CHAPTER 4

Korea's Transition to Modernity: A Will to Greatness

CARTER J. ECKERT

William James once suggested that a strong will, exemplified by "effort of attention," is the wellspring of energy that allows an individual to "stand this Universe" and attain "wished-for things."[1] Might one not say the same of countries or cultures? Certainly to encounter modern Korea in the speeches, policies, and writings of its political and intellectual elite during the last hundred years is to enter a realm dominated by what one might call, paraphrasing Nietzsche, a national "will to greatness." By this I mean a certain psychic presumption that Korea is inherently a great nation, both destined and entitled to play a leading role in the history of the world. One finds this premise most starkly in the public statements of Korean political figures and governments, but also, both explicitly and implicitly, in most Korean scholarly and nonscholarly writing about the "nation," whether in the late nineteenth century or today. Even in the darker periods of Korean history, as, for example, during the Japanese occupation (1905–1945) or after the Korean War (1950–1953), when the prospects for national development seemed dim, this sense of entitlement and destiny was never completely lost. Today in both North and South Korea it is so widespread as to have become a kind of Gramscian "common sense" in both societies that generally transcends specific political differences.

Despite the intrinsic difficulties of dealing with so abstract a subject, the Korean will to greatness would seem to merit some attention from scholars interested in Korea, as well as East Asia. Given its ubiquity and potential motivational power, it seems inconceivable, for example, that such a disposition has not played a role of some kind in Korea's remarkable transformation in the course of the past century. In keeping with the interpretive spirit of these essays, therefore, what follows are a few thoughts, admittedly subjective, about the historical origins and development of this sentiment, and its influence in the shaping of Korean modernity.

The Premodern Tradition

It is impossible to understand the Korean sense of national entitlement and destiny without first considering its precursors in the premodern period. Indeed, it is there that the origins of this feeling are to be found. Students and scholars familiar with Chinese and Japanese history would of course have no difficulty pointing to premodern signs of such a sentiment in those two countries. Chinese, after all, traditionally saw themselves politically and culturally as the center of the world, and by the twelfth century, the Japanese had begun to turn away from Chinese influence and develop a distinctive feudal society and culture that would eventually come to define what we think of today as traditional Japan.

Korea's distinctiveness from China is less immediately apparent than Japan's, and early works on Korea often tended to treat the country as little more than a miniature version of China, at best a model tributary state, at worst a poor man's attempt to emulate the great celestial empire to the west. Today Korea's distinctive character is generally recognized, at least by scholars, but the extent of that distinctiveness, including Korea's own special sense of place within the premodern East Asian world, is still often not fully understood and appreciated.

In fact, a key to understanding Korea's premodern tradition lies in grasping the interesting tension that lay between local and cosmopolitan interests and affinities, especially among the elite, throughout most of the peninsula's recorded history. From at least the seventh century, when the southeastern kingdom of Silla (57 B.C.–A.D. 935) unified the peninsula by subduing its rivals Paekche and Koguryŏ with Tang assistance and began importing Chinese institutions and culture on a large scale, the ruling elite of Silla, as well as their counterparts in the succeeding dynasties of Koryŏ (918–1392) and Chosŏn (1392–1910), continued to think of themselves and their country as participating in what in Western writing is often referred to as "Chinese" or "Sinitic" civilization, or the "Chinese world order."[2]

It is important to set these words off in quotation marks lest we fall into the modern fallacy of interpreting them in purely ethnic or national terms. For the elite of Silla, Koryŏ, and Chosŏn did not think in these ways. To be sure, they spoke of "revering China" *(chon hwa)* as a cardinal principle of state and society. But what did this mean? It certainly did not mean that they or their country were consigned to a permanent condition of inferiority and subservience to China in ethnopolitical terms, that is, to China the "nation-state," as modern parlance would have it. On the contrary, to the premodern Korean elite, "revering China" was the measure of their own greatness, the linchpin of their special sense of place in the world. It was a dynamic and creative ideological orientation.

To grasp how this orientation actually worked, one has to understand the Sinitic world from the Korean perspective. First and foremost, it was a universal world order. Although it originated in and radiated outward from China, it was by no means seen as something exclusive to China. Theoretically it embraced everything under heaven *(ch'ŏn ha)*, and non-Chinese individuals and societies could and did participate actively in it.

Second, it was seen primarily as a cultural phenomenon. In contrast to modern industrial capitalism, economics did not play a significant role in defining and maintaining the Sinitic world system. While economic exchange of various kinds took place among the participants in the system throughout its existence, even a total cessation of such exchange would not have brought the system to a halt.

Political relationships among member countries were certainly more important than economic connections, and there is no denying that Chinese military power helped support the imperial system as a whole. Yet here again one must note that at its core the system was not founded solely, or even primarily, on military might. Rather, the political relationships were embedded within a certain cultural orientation centered on the cosmological primacy of the Chinese emperor. Thus Koreans honored this shared cosmological vision in the form of regular tribute missions and solicitation of the emperor's formal recognition in the investiture of their kings. But apart from these infrequent ceremonial occasions, they paid little attention to their imperial suzerain in the conduct of their own internal affairs. For his part, the emperor, whoever he might be, was generally content once these formalities had been observed or, in the case of a new imperial dynasty, reestablished.

The Chinese, or whatever ethnic group happened to be ruling China, undoubtedly read more in the way of political subservience into these formalities than did the Koreans themselves. To the latter, however, the rituals were more complex. While they often helped buy or preserve the country's political integrity, especially when one of the non-Chinese peoples of the north such as the Mongols or Manchus sought to establish a new imperial dynasty, they were more often seen by the Koreans simply as morally correct behavior, in keeping with Korea's status as one of the civilized countries of the known world.

At the core of the Sinitic world system was a common belief in the superi-

ority of the traditional culture of China, especially that of the ancient Chou
dynasty, as the summit of human knowledge and experience. When Koreans talked about "revering China," what they really meant was revering this
cosmopolitan culture that ultimately transcended the spatial and temporal
boundaries of particular dynasties. In addition to paying homage by observ-
ing this formal political etiquette, the Korean elite expressed their respect for
the culture by importing many of the laws and institutions of China, and
above all by adopting the Chinese system of writing and making Chinese literature in the broadest sense the basis of their own educational system and
intellectual life. By the Chosŏn dynasty, the Korean elite were as thoroughly
saturated and well versed in this culture as anyone in China itself, and all
elite, formal writing was in classical Chinese. It was thus not unusual for
foreigners encountering Korea for the first time in the late nineteenth century to dismiss Korean literati culture as a mere imitation of its Chinese
counterpart.

They were, of course, wrong. From the Korean perspective, participating
in the Sinitic system and revering Chinese culture did not by any means imply a blind adherence to Chinese patterns and norms. Despite their cosmopolitanism, the Korean elite were always aware of their country's differences from China, some of which, such as their native language, as well as
food, clothing, and the customs of everyday life, were obvious. More important, the Koreans did not view the cosmopolitan culture as an inflexible or
static set of prescriptions, appropriate without interpretation or modification
for all times and places. The culture itself, moreover, as it came from China,
was varied and complex, filled with endless nuances, contradictions, and
possibilities of interpretation. The Korean elite thus felt free to pick, choose,
fashion, and even develop the culture according to their own local needs
and predilections. The result was a unique form of self-expression within
the context of a larger cosmopolitan tradition.

Such creative adaptation was clearly visible in Korea's history of legal and
institutional borrowing from China, which saw a major spurt after Silla's
unification of the peninsula in 661 and continued sporadically over the centuries, finally reaching a culmination in the Chosŏn dynasty. On the surface
the Chosŏn state looked much like its Ming counterpart, on which it had
been consciously modeled. Underneath, however, it was quite dissimilar
and reflected a very different society. The Ming-Qing system in China had
been established concomitant to and in support of a powerful emperor exer-
cising his will through a corps of bureaucrats, who were recruited through

an impartial state civil service examination system and dependent on and loyal to the imperial office. At heart it was an anti-aristocratic system, created to enhance imperial power.

The Chosŏn system functioned in an entirely different way. In fact its purpose was to preserve and protect aristocratic power. Since, and indeed before, the Silla unification, Korean society had been dominated by a strong aristocracy possessing its own resources in land and prestige, independent of the Korean king, and an extraordinarily strong status consciousness based on family bloodlines. Even while enthusiastically adopting Chinese laws and institutions, the Korean elite were careful not to disturb this bedrock social structure. Thus, although the Chosŏn bureaucrats, or *yangban*, as they had been known in Korea since the Koryŏ period, were selected by competitive state examination, as in China, the pool of eligible applicants for the examinations was strictly confined to certifiable members of a small number of patrilineal aristocratic lineages. These lineages, in turn, jealously guarded their monopoly over the bureaucracy, as well as the purity of their bloodlines, through strategic intermarriages, and by discriminating even against suspect members of their own class, such as the sons of remarried widows and the sons of concubines. In sum, the basic framework of Ming laws and institutions was adapted to the Korean elite's own local interests and sensibilities.

One finds a similar process of creative adaptation at work in Korean artistic and intellectual life. Korean ceramics, especially Koryŏ celadon, which is today justly acclaimed throughout the world for its unique beauty, was also praised as "first under heaven" by contemporary Chinese, and so admired by Japanese feudal lords that they forcibly transported whole villages of Korean potters to Japan during the Hideyoshi invasions of Korea in the late sixteenth century in order to secure these skills for themselves and their domains. Ceramics, however, are perhaps only the best-known example of Korean creativity within the Sinitic cultural world. Less known but equally impressive are Korea's achievements in other artistic and intellectual areas, including, not least of all, the varied and voluminous writings of Korean Neo-Confucian scholars during the Chosŏn period. There too Koreans carved out their own paths, whether in philosophy or statecraft, which were often in sharp contrast to contemporary trends in China.

One might be tempted to suppose that such modifications of Chinese institutions and thought would place Korea outside the orbit of Sinitic civilization. From the Chinese viewpoint, such adaptation was of course irrelevant so long as Korea fulfilled its formal tributary responsibilities to the emperor. To Koreans, adaptation was, first of all, a matter of practicality. Korea was not China, and the peninsula's own local peculiarities could not realistically be denied. Interpretation and debate were also an integral part of the civilized life, as noted earlier.

Furthermore, what was important to the Koreans in defining themselves as a civilized people was not the extent to which they measured up against any particular contemporary Chinese society, but rather the extent to which they lived up to the spirit of the Chinese classics by embodying the ideals of the Chou society of ancient times which Confucius and his disciples had extolled as a model. Culture for the Koreans was thus not the culture of contemporary China, though many were willing to acknowledge that one might learn something from it as well. Rather, culture meant the culture of the Chinese classics, which for the Koreans transcended any particular dynasty, and in a very real sense had little if anything to do with the physical or political China per se. The great culture in which all civilized countries participated had had its geographic origins in China, and its model society had also been located in China. But now, in what was generally referred to as a postclassical "later age" *(huse)* by Koreans and Chinese alike, both Korea and China were far removed from this almost mythic past, and no dynasty or country within the orbit of civilization, including China itself, could claim perfection. What one could do was respect the classical ideals and strive for perfection, and it was in fact this reverence and effort, as much as or more than the actual results, that determined a country's civilized standing.

This leads us to another notable aspect of the Sinitic world order as understood by the Korean elite. In addition to being universal and primarily cultural, the order was also hierarchical. Like the Chinese, the Koreans distinguished sharply between "civilized" *(hwa)* and "barbaric" *(i)* peoples on the basis of their respective mastery of and devotion to Chinese classical ideals, and Korean contempt for those deemed "barbarians" was consistent and profound. The other half of the common four-character compound that begins with "revere China" was in fact "expel the barbarians," who were regarded as only slightly higher on the scale of civilization than "beasts." Japan was of course not considered a barbaric society in the same sense as the continental tribes on the Sinitic frontier such as the Mongols and Jurchen/ Manchus. But the Koreans clearly saw themselves as superior to the Japanese, first, because they believed, with considerable justification, that the latter had historically imbibed much of their cosmopolitan culture through contact with Korea, and second, because Japanese society since at least the eleventh century had developed in ways that were quite alien to classical Chinese norms.

China had a certain obvious and natural precedence in the world hierarchy, given its political position in the civilized cosmology and its historical association with the origins of classical civilization. Nevertheless, one must distinguish here between the formal political hierarchy epitomized by the tributary system and what might be called a hierarchy of cultural status. The two were not always synchronous. In general, Koreans were willing to acknowledge China's political and cultural paramountcy for the reasons cited earlier, but China's position in the world hierarchy was not eternally fixed. A dynasty's political control of China invariably secured formal tributary obeisance from Korea, if only by force, but such political dominion did not automatically guarantee Korean acceptance of the dynasty's cultural superiority. Yu Insŏk, who was one of the last great defenders of the Sinitic world order at the end of the Chosŏn dynasty, explained China's position in that order as follows: "China is the great common ancestor of us all and the center of heaven and earth. If China stumbles and falls, the world will be in disarray and heaven and earth will disintegrate. Therefore, if China maintains its self-importance, taking care of itself so that it does not lose its status as the ancestor and center of us all, how in the world will all the branches of the family and component parts of the common body fail to respect and guard it?"[3]

The implication here is clear: the cultural hierarchy of the Sinitic world order was potentially subject to change; China could "stumble and fall" and "lose its status." By extension, therefore, the possibility also existed, at least from the Korean perspective, that Korea itself could rise to the top of the hierarchy. In the latter half of the Chosŏn dynasty, this is in fact exactly what happened. To the Korean elite, the Manchus who conquered Ming China in the early seventeenth century were northern barbarians, traditionally outside the circle of civilized countries. The Koreans supported the Ming to the bitter end, until they were finally compelled by force of arms in 1637 to acknowledge Manchu suzerainty and establish tributary relations with the new Qing dynasty which the Manchus had founded.

For nearly three hundred years thereafter, however, despite the Manchus' gradual assimilation into the Sinitic world, the ruling elite in Korea continued to look down on the Qing state as culturally inferior, and, as Chai-Sik Chung notes, took "particular pride in the fact that Korea was the only

country that remained to carry on the spirit of the fallen Ming dynasty."
King Sukchong, who ascended the Korean throne in 1674, actually had a
shrine erected within the royal palace as a sign of Korea's reverence for the
Ming spirit and the civilization it represented, and to thank Heaven for raising Korea "above the status of amoral beasts."[4] In 1704, in the latter part of
Sukchong's reign, another shrine, the Mandongmyo, was also built in the
countryside in accord with the final testament of Song Siyŏl, one of the period's most prominent *yangban*, to honor the memory of the last two Ming
emperors, and it continued to be a rallying symbol for pro-Ming literati in
Korea throughout the eighteenth and much of the nineteenth centuries.

When Western, and later Japanese, gunboats began to encroach upon the
peninsula in the mid-nineteenth century, Koreans had already experienced
more than a millennium of history as a unified, independent country with
only three dynastic changes. They had also carved out a place of honor for
themselves and their country within the only known civilized world. During
the previous two hundred years, moreover, the Chosŏn elite had seen China
"stumble and fall" from its exalted position in the Sinitic world hierarchy,
and had grown accustomed to thinking of their own country as the last refuge of civilization on earth, the "last remnant of the force of yang."[5] One
can hardly doubt that this sense of greatness would carry over into the period of Western and Japanese incursions and help shape the Korean response to modernity.

The Western Impact and Korean Response

The Korean elite's proud sense of themselves as the final bastion of civilization led them initially to take an uncompromising stance against the forces
that were impinging upon them from the West and Japan in the late nineteenth century. Contrary to what has become conventional wisdom today,
they did not underestimate the gravity of the threat before them. In a memorial to the throne in 1866, the same year that the American merchant
ship the *General Sherman* illegally sailed up the Taedong River toward Pyongyang, Yi Hangno wrote in a memorial to the throne that "today the calami-
ties of the Western barbarians have become so serious that those of the vast
waters of inundation and all ferocious animals do not exceed them." The
nature of the threat that Yi and others perceived, however, was essentially
moral, an affront to the fundamental principles of civilization. In whatever
guise they came, and despite whatever material goods and skills they of-

fered, the Westerners were at heart barbarians, and to deal with them, according to the prevailing Korean view, was the equivalent of "humanity" interacting with "beasts."[6]

To the Korean elite of this period, the Japanese were also little better than beasts themselves. As noted earlier, since at least the Silla unification, Koreans had never regarded their neighbors to the east as anything more than an inferior periphery of the Sinitic world, and the wholesale destruction and pillage wrought by Hideyoshi in the late sixteenth century had only cemented this view. With the Meiji Restoration in 1868, moreover, and the embrace of Western culture that followed, the Japanese had, from the Korean perspective, left the world of civilization entirely and become for all practical purposes one of the barbarians, no different in that sense from the despised Westerners. Like the latter, they had also invaded Korean waters with their gunboats in the 1870s and tried to force open the country to international trade. Even worse, they had violated long-standing tributary norms of the Sinitic world by, among other things, asking Korea to recognize the new Meiji sovereign as an "emperor."

During Japan's Tokugawa period (1600–1868), the question of how to address the Japanese ruler had never been an issue. The Chosŏn state had had no direct contact with Kyoto, and only very limited contact with the shogun in Edo, who was treated in diplomatic intercourse as a king within the Sinitic world order. Most of Korea's interaction with Japan, in fact, was with or through the island domain of Tsushima, which maintained a semi-tributary relationship with Korea. Now the Japanese were insisting that the old diplomatic framework be abandoned and the Koreans formally acknowledge the Meiji "emperor" as the head of the Japanese state. To the Chosŏn elite, imperial designation was a matter of moral principle, with profound cosmological implications in the Sinitic order. The title could be used only by the Chinese emperor. For the Japanese to appropriate it in such a way was to the Koreans absurd and contemptible, a clear sign that the former were losing their humanity. The Koreans thus at first refused to deal with the new Japanese government, and only the threat of military reprisal forced them finally to sign the Kanghwa Treaty of 1876, the first of many diplomatic and commercial treaties that would help push Korea inexorably into the non-Sinitic world.

One might easily imagine that the Korean sense of self-importance in the crumbling Sinitic world order would have left little or no room for a more flexible response to the Western impact in the late nineteenth century, but such was not the case. To be sure, the conservative *yangban* elite, epitomized by Yi Hangno and many others in the ruling Noron political faction, continued for the most part to denounce the Western and Japanese "barbarians" and to call for their expulsion, as well as for boycotts and prohibitions against foreign goods and customs. Indeed, the influence of this core elite, whose lineages had dominated the political system in Chosŏn Korea since the eighteenth century, should not be underestimated. Despite various changes in the structure of the state and eventually even the abolition of the state examination system in 1894, they retained a grip on many of the key levers of power and were often able to slow down or frustrate efforts at Westernization by reformist bureaucrats, or even by the king himself. The structural restraints on the Korean monarchy, as well as the timidity of Korea's last king, Kojong, did much in fact to help ensure the conservative elite's influence. Kojong had come to the throne as a minor, schooled by and hedged in by the *yangban* elite, his attitude toward Westernization basically ambivalent and vacillating; he was easy prey to the vociferous anti-Western *yangban* voices around him. This combination of monarchical weakness and *yangban* conservatism in the highest councils of government in the late nineteenth century did not serve the country well in its hour of greatest need and was an undeniable element in the complex of factors that eventually led to Korea's colonization by Japan.

But there were other voices in Korea that were more critical of the status quo and open to new ideas from the West and Japan. The dynasty, in fact, was suffering from numerous problems. Over the centuries, and particularly after the Hideyoshi invasions, the Chosŏn state had gradually lost control of its tax base to the *yangban* aristocracy, who used a variety of means to keep land in their possession (or under their control) and off the tax rolls. As the tax base shrank, the burden on the peasantry to supply state revenues increased accordingly, and the result was rural immiseration, a situation that was exacerbated by the ruling elite's physiocratic contempt for commerce and industry, and by active state efforts to prevent nonagricultural development and monetization of the economy. Eventually such financial mismanagement and economic bias led to rural protest. The nineteenth century was a period of almost continuous and widespread peasant uprisings, including three major rebellions: the Hong Kyŏngnae Rebellion of 1811, the Chinju Rebellion of 1862, and the great Tonghak Rebellion of 1894, the largest in Korean history, in which rebel forces actually succeeded for a time in occupying and governing a significant portion of the southwestern part of the peninsula.

Among the more educated classes of Chosŏn Korea, too, there was growing dissatisfaction with the current political, economic, and social situation. Hereditary groups traditionally held in low social esteem by the *yangban* elite—bureaucrats trained in specialized, technical skills, generally referred to as *chungin*, members of military lineages, and a burgeoning number of illegitimate *yangban* sons barred from political participation by reason of birth—were questioning the dynasty's unforgiving social system based on inherited status. Lineages with geographic roots in the recently settled northern provinces were also frustrated by what they perceived to be discrimination by southern lineages in the allocation of bureaucratic posts. Such discrimination in fact appears to have played a role in the Hong Kyŏngnae Rebellion of 1811, which arose in the northern province of P'yŏngan and was led by a disaffected literatus who felt he had been a victim of southern prejudice.

In the intellectual realm there was also contention and dissent. Indeed, there always had been. Despite a marked tendency among the ruling Chosŏn elite to regard any deviation in thought or policy from Neo-Confucian interpretations of the Chinese classics as "heterodoxy" *(sa)*, the fact is that these renderings had also been subject to continual reinterpretation by different generations of Korean literati. What constituted "orthodoxy" at any given time was therefore always open to a certain amount of variation and debate. Stepping outside that permitted range of orthodoxy could be fatal, especially in the quicksand of Chosŏn high politics, where careers and, indeed, lives often hung on the question of whether or not a particular view or policy was "orthodox." Outside the active political arena, however, there was more room for creative exploration of unconventional ideas, whether radical offshoots of the Neo-Confucian tradition such as the Wang Yangming school of Neo-Confucianism, popular at certain times in China but commonly regarded as a heresy in Chosŏn Korea, or even philosophical and religious thought deemed antithetical to the Neo-Confucian tradition, such as Buddhism and later Christianity. Although the scholars who were willing to consider such views were generally not part of the political or intellectual mainstream, and often produced their work in forced or voluntary exile or seclusion far from the capital, their very existence suggests that the larger Chosŏn intellectual world was by no means rigidly conformist. In the latter half of the dynasty there also developed a tradition of statecraft writing *(sirhak)*, again largely the work of non-mainstream scholars, who traced their intellectual lineage back to the seventeenth-century reformist writer Yu Hyŏngwŏn. Although they worked within the Neo-Confucian tradition, these scholars were less interested in disputing points of philosophy than in finding practical solutions to the serious political, economic, and social problems of their day.

By the nineteenth century, then, the Chosŏn system was experiencing a number of fissures, none of which, by itself or in combination, was of sufficient strength to bring down the dynasty, but which, once the country had been pried open by Western and Japanese threats, provided an indigenous space where the new civilization of the West could take root and grow. Most important here were the disaffected elements of the *yangban* class and secondary elite who were not only unhappy with their status in the existing system and therefore open to new ideas, but also sufficiently educated and well placed within the system to appreciate the changes that were taking place in the international sphere, and to take advantage of any opportunities that came their way.[7] Many such reformist-minded Koreans were inspired by the Western "new learning" *(sinhak)*, which for many in this early period was best exemplified by the laws, institutions, and values of Victorian England, the premier great power of the era, or by the United States, the first Western nation to establish formal diplomatic relations with Korea (in 1882), and the source of a subsequent influx of increasingly influential and successful Protestant missionaries.

When these young Korean reformers looked at the new civilization of the West, they saw a world that, despite radical differences, was not entirely dissimilar in certain key respects to the Sinitic world order in which they had been born and raised. Like the latter, the new world had universalistic pretensions, claiming to embrace all of humanity, and was therefore open to participation by all people and countries. From their background and perspective within the still existing Sinitic framework, the reformers in this period also tended to view the new world primarily as a cultural entity centered on the ideas of Western rationality and science (and, in some cases, Christianity), and they envisioned participation largely in cultural terms. They were not, of course, entirely oblivious to the political, economic, and even military aspects of the new order, but in good Neo-Confucian fashion, they tended to see these as natural manifestations of an essentialized cultural orientation that was diffused throughout the West.

The new world was also clearly hierarchical. Indeed, it was the common wisdom of the day, buttressed by a powerful current of social Darwinist thought, then reaching its apogee in the West, that some countries were more civilized or "fitter" than others. In 1875 the great Japanese educator Fukuzawa Yukichi (1834–1901), whose writings had helped work an intellectual transformation in Meiji Japan, published his *Bunmeiron no gairyaku* (An outline of a theory of civilization), in which he laid out a tripartite hierarchy of civilization and enlightenment *(bunmei kaika)* that encompassed all the nations of the world. Yu Kilchun (1856–1914), the most articulate and prolific of the early Korean reformers, who had come under Fukuzawa's patronage and influence in Japan and later studied and traveled in the United States and Europe, echoed his Japanese mentor in the late 1880s in a book about the challenge of modern Western civilization based on his personal experiences and observations. Borrowing heavily from Fukuzawa's work and vocabulary, Yu viewed the countries of the world in terms of their respective level of civilization or "enlightenment" *(kaehwa)*. The great powers of the West, England above all, represented the "enlightened" countries. The rest of the world, for the most part, was either "semi-enlightened" or still "unenlightened." Using vivid metaphors from his own society, Yu then described the enlightened countries of the world as "masters" *(chuin)*, the semi-enlightened countries as "honored guests" *(pin'gaek)*, and the unenlightened countries as "slaves" *(noye)*.[8]

But again, as in the Sinitic world, the hierarchy of enlightenment was by no means regarded as static. If the ideal society of the Sinitic world lay in a distant, virtually unrecoverable past, the perfect society of enlightenment lay in an equally distant, almost unimaginable future. In that sense, the West represented only the highest stage of civilization at the moment. Just as China could lose the mantle of civilization, so too could the West forfeit its present exalted position. In the unceasing social Darwinian struggle for existence, masters could become slaves, and slaves could also aspire to be masters. As one of Yu's contemporaries, the Christian reformist Yun Ch'iho, wrote in his diary in 1893 while studying in the United States: "Americans think and say that they are the last effort of the Almighty and that civilization has found her terminus on this continent. This may be, yet it is rather a presumptuous declaration. For the world has not yet reached its last stage or the race, its ultimate development . . . Who knows but that one of those days the nations whom the American condescends to call barbarians and savages will put the cap on the world's civilization."[9]

Yu Kilchun harbored no illusions about what he viewed as the relatively unenlightened state of Chosŏn society. He was also driven by a desperate concern that without reforms, Korea would soon become a "slave" to those countries that had made themselves the "masters" of enlightenment. He pointed proudly to some of Korea's historic accomplishments, including the Koryŏ celadon already mentioned, the armor-plated battleships used against

Hideyoshi, and the invention of metal movable type in the thirteenth century. The problem, he suggested, was that Korea had rested on its laurels rather than building on its past. Nevertheless, Yu never doubted that Korea had the inherent capacity to play a major role in the new civilization. Indeed, he believed that the solution to the country's dilemma lay in "embellishing" *(yunsaek)* a greatness that had existed in the past and was essentially still latent. He was certain that if Koreans only made the effort, such refinement would lead not simply to Korea's becoming an honored guest in the hierarchy of civilization but to its eventually becoming a master, "a model to all nations under heaven." Once again "the glory of the world will *return (kwi)* to our country," he wrote, in a statement that epitomizes the energy and optimism that Yu drew from his sense of Korea's history.[10]

Yu's belief in the potential for Korean greatness in the new world order was a shared understanding that linked the Korean reformists in the last decades of the Chosŏn dynasty, despite factional and policy differences. But, unfortunately, the reformists would not live to see that greatness realized. Indeed, most would die in the bitter knowledge of Korea's colonization by Japan. That their efforts failed in the end was not entirely their fault. The historical forces, both international and domestic, arrayed against them were formidable, and given these circumstances, there may well have been no way for Chosŏn Korea to have escaped its tragic end.

Still, one could also argue that the reformists' fixation on culture may have blinded them to the importance of the economic and military underpinnings of the new world until it was too late. Over and over again they stressed education as the key to "enlightenment," and they envisioned a long, gradual process of development toward mastery of the new civilization. But time was against them. In the ruthless climate of high imperialism in the late nineteenth and early twentieth centuries, the social Darwinian struggle was above all a struggle of economic and military power. By 1905 that struggle, so far as Chosŏn Korea was concerned, was over. Japan had vanquished both China and Russia in two major wars and forced a treaty of "protection" on Korea, which left Koreans only in nominal control of their own affairs. In 1910 even that fig leaf of sovereignty was removed, and the country was formally incorporated into the Japanese empire as a colony.

Korea under Japanese Rule

The harsh thirty-five years of Japanese colonialism left many indelible scars on the Korean peninsula and people. Arrogance and racism, at times blatant, at other times subtle or even unconscious, often colored the policies and pervaded the atmosphere of the occupation. The colonial government-general's explanation for Japan's annexation of Korea reduced Korea's history to one of abject backwardness and dependence on China. It painted the Chosŏn dynasty as utterly stagnant, incapable of regeneration from within, and therefore in need of Japan's protection and guidance. Such rationalizations became the common wisdom of the empire and colony and were integrated into the colonial education system.

This sustained propaganda was not without its effect. Even as late as the 1960s it was difficult to find Koreans who had positive views of their own long history within the Sinitic world order, to say nothing of the Chosŏn dynasty. When Park Chung Hee seized control of the South Korean government in a military coup in 1961, there were many Koreans who were suspicious of his motives and methods. Few if any at the time, however, found anything to criticize in his denunciation of the Chosŏn dynasty for its "criminal history" *(choe'ak sa):* "We brand the history of the Yi [Chosŏn] Dynasty as criminal because of its fourfold partisan strife, servile submission to China, and the complacency of the aristocracy. We blame our present poverty on the evil heritage from the Yi Dynasty. The young generation of today looks back on the past, and the misdeeds of their forebears with wrath and contempt."[11]

The Japanese colonial propaganda was effective in part because it resonated with Korean criticisms of the Chosŏn dynasty that had been developing since the late nineteenth century, and whose correctness had been proved for many Koreans by the dynasty's failure to preserve the country's political autonomy. The early diaries of Yun Ch'iho are replete with such attacks. Later, in the early 1920s, the great essayist and novelist Yi Kwangsu, in a passage that still startles with the depth and scope of its anger and bitterness, condemned the five hundred years of Chosŏn dynasty history as no more than a "record of worthless ideas and empty debates."[12]

Even if many Koreans agreed with the colonial government's negative assessment of the late Chosŏn dynasty, they were not necessarily disposed to accept the government-general's conclusion that colonization by Japan was therefore justified. The will to greatness that had for so long been a part of the Korean psyche did not disappear. In general, the Korean critique of the Chosŏn dynasty was centered on the perceived failings of the ruling *yangban* class rather than on the inherent capacities of the Korean people. Even Yi Kwangsu, who was influenced by the French social psychologist Gustave Le Bon and went much further than anyone else in disparaging the Korean "national character," blamed "bad government" as "directly responsible" for the dynasty's decline. Yi was also careful to distinguish, in the manner of Le Bon, unsatisfactory but correctable "secondary" Korean traits from a "fundamental" Korean national character, which he regarded as a composite of many outstanding qualities. Like Yu Kilchun before him and other Korean intellectuals of his own time and since, he thus never questioned the ability, indeed the destiny, of Koreans, given proper leadership, to achieve greatness as a people in the modern world, to become, as he later wrote in his memoirs, a *yangban* instead of a *sangnom* nation.[13]

The early twentieth century also gave birth to a new school of consciously nationalistic historians, inspired by Sin Ch'aeho. Although Sin and his admirers saw only "subservience to China" *(sadaejuŭi)* in what Yi Hangno and the conservative *yangban* elite had regarded as the greatness of Chosŏn in the Sinitic world order, they nevertheless looked for and discovered that greatness in other aspects of Korea's history. Above all, they held up the image of a long and brilliant Korean military tradition of honor and patriotism going back to the Three Kingdoms period, which they believed had been gradually neglected or deliberately repressed by an effete Confucian elite. The Chosŏn dynasty was for them the nadir of this great tradition, symbolized by the general neglect of the military and the government's shoddy treatment of Admiral Yi Sunsin, the hero of Korea's naval battles against Hideyoshi and the designer of the armor-plated battleships praised by Yu Kilchun. The admiral's dismissal by the court in the middle of the naval campaign against the Japanese forces was seen as a prime example of factional politics at the expense of the national interest.

Ironically, Japanese colonialism worked to reinforce and intensify the Korean will to national greatness in the modern world, at least among many of the educated elite. First, one has to remember that the modernizing trends of the late Chosŏn period did not cease with the advent of Japanese rule. As part of the Japanese empire, Koreans continued to be exposed and subject to all modern developments within Japan itself through newspapers, magazines, radio programs, and films, as well as through the colonial educational system, and study and travel abroad. The colonial regime itself, moreover, became a major agent of modernization in numerous respects, by 1945 transforming the peninsula into the most industrialized region of East Asia outside of Japan.

And Koreans were by no means entirely excluded from this process, especially after weeks of nationwide demonstrations against Japanese rule in

March 1919 helped bring about a more liberal colonial policy. After 1919 the government-general in fact took special care to mollify and court the Korean educated elite in the hope of nullifying, or at least defusing, subversive nationalist sentiment in the most articulate and influential segments of Korean society. The government even allowed a cultural nationalist movement to flourish in the 1920s and 1930s which was centered on the publication of popular and academic Korean-language newspapers and journals. While never overtly posing any political challenge to Japanese rule, such publications preserved an important niche for Koreans to explore, discuss, and participate culturally in the modern world in their own language and in accord with their own interests and sensibilities.

The world of imperial Japan, however, was for Koreans vastly circumscribed in comparison with their historical experience in the Sinitic world order. Despite the modernizing aspects of colonialism and much rhetoric about the universal benevolence of imperial rule and, later, the Greater East Asia Prosperity Sphere, the core ideology of the empire was highly particularistic and rigidly hierarchical, founded on assumptions of Japanese racial superiority and political dominance. In the atmosphere of militarism during the late 1930s and 1940s, these ethnocentric attitudes became particularly intense, but they had in fact been present in Japanese imperialist thinking since the late nineteenth century.

Under such a system there was clearly no room for a separate "Korean" national greatness. Some Koreans, nevertheless, seem to have continued to hope that such an arrangement could be worked out with the empire. Even prior to 1910, members of the Korean Ilchinhoe or "Advance in Unity Society," which actually campaigned for and supported both the protectorate and the annexation, may well have been thinking along these lines, expecting to become part of a new Asian world order in which a modernized Japan assumed the role vis-à-vis Korea that China had played in the premodern past. In the 1920s there was also much talk of "home rule" by various elements in the Korean elite after the March First Movement and change in colonial administration and policy. And during the China and Pacific wars after 1937, many of these same people clung to the hope, abetted by wartime colonial propaganda, that actively supporting the Japanese war effort would give Koreans a special place in the postwar empire. All such dreams came to naught less because of Japan's eventual defeat in the war than because of their inherent improbability given the character of the Japanese imperial system.

Even for those Koreans who eschewed politics and concentrated solely on getting ahead and making their mark in the modern world as members of the Japanese imperial system, the frustrations were many. First of all, there were often unspoken ethnic limits beyond which no Korean, however talented or demonstrably loyal to Japan, could rise in his professional career. Although the government-general had opened the system up considerably at the elite level after 1919, and many Koreans subsequently came to play significant roles in business, law, education, journalism, and even the colonial bureaucracy itself, few could aspire to the very top positions in any field, which for the most part were tacitly reserved for Japanese. All Koreans, even those in the elite who were comfortable in the Japanese language and closely associated with the colonial regime, also carried the psychological burden of being second-class citizens in their own country. In the case of the latter, this burden was particularly onerous, because they found themselves associating on a regular basis with people who, even if they were willing to acknowledge individual exceptions, more often than not tended to regard Koreans in the abstract as racially inferior.

Certain unusual features of Japanese colonial rule also conspired to heighten Korean resentment. In comparison with most if not all of the European colonies, where enormous disparities between the colonizer and colonized in terms of income, educational levels, linguistic and cultural background, and general modes of living tended to intensify feelings of superiority and inferiority, and to limit severely personal and professional interaction, the colonizing Japanese and the colonized Koreans, at least at the elite level, were relatively similar to each other in all these respects. Indeed, Japanese and Koreans shared a premodern Sinitic cultural heritage, and their languages, syntactically so similar as to suggest a common origin in the ancient past, were both rich in Chinese vocabulary and characters. The Japanese colonizers also did not live in strictly isolated or segregated compounds or areas and were not infrequently less well off than some of their wealthy Korean neighbors. Japan's colonization of Korea was in that sense a great anomaly, as if, for example, England had colonized France, or vice versa.

Interaction between Koreans and Japanese in the colony was also enhanced by other factors. One was the geographic proximity of Japan to the peninsula, which facilitated Korean access to the colonial metropole for purposes of education, travel, or commerce. Another was the relatively large number of Japanese colonists in the country—more than twenty times, for example, the number of French residing in colonial Vietnam in the late 1930s. Again, in contrast to many European colonies, here there were no ethnic or religious commercial or professional groups, like the Chinese in the Dutch East Indies or French Indochina, the Sikhs in India, the Asians and Arabs in east Africa, to act as middlemen and reduce contact between colonizers and the natives. Indeed, especially after 1919, Koreans became very active in the commercial economy and continued to be so throughout the next twenty-five years, including during the China and Pacific wars. After 1937, the war itself opened up the colonial system even further, as Japanese were drafted into the army in ever increasing numbers, and as Koreans, who were not formally conscripted until 1944, were often recruited to take their places.

Such special features of Japanese colonialism might have worked over time to diminish Korean resentment had the Japanese authorities been genuinely committed to erasing racial discrimination in the colony and empire, or, to go one step further, been willing to consider a certain degree of political autonomy for Koreans to seek their greatness as a nation within a more loosely constituted empire. But such a commitment, let alone such an idea of empire, foundered on prevailing Japanese notions of racial superiority. While individual Japanese often spoke out and tried to end discrimination where they could, as in the case of the influential colonial banker Aruga Mitsutoyo, who made a point of treating Koreans in his employ on a more equal basis, few Japanese were willing to countenance the idea of some kind of political independence for Korea; it is not clear that Japanese criticisms of discrimination had any substantive impact on general colonial policy and practice.[14]

Some Koreans undoubtedly suffered the psychological effects of colonialism that led to a debilitating sense of inferiority. But generally colonialism intensified rather than diminished the will to national greatness among educated Koreans. Those who had chosen to accommodate themselves in one way or another to the realities of colonialism, by far the majority, and particularly those whose backgrounds and careers had put them into relatively close and frequent contact with the Japanese colonizers, had in many cases developed by 1945 a deep sense of anger and resentment (*han* in Korean) at the ethnic barriers to achievement under Japanese rule. They had also developed a more positive determination to demonstrate their greatness, both as individuals and as Koreans, once the shackles of colonialism had been lifted.

They were encouraged in this resolve by at least two things. One was the historic sense of Korean greatness that had been preserved in modified form by the nationalist historians who had come into prominence in the late Chosŏn period before the annexation and whose ideas had been taken up and developed by others in the colonial period, including many in the cultural nationalist movement. After 1919, and through the late 1930s, the cultural nationalists, whose main patron was the wealthy educator and publishing magnate Kim Sŏngsu, had had a major impact on the literate urban populace through the daily newspaper *Tonga Ilbo* and the monthly magazine *Sindonga,* together the most popular news media of the day. This continuing sense of Korean greatness, which also involved a corresponding sense of Japanese historic inferiority, not only exacerbated Korean bitterness at Japanese discrimination but also suggested that Koreans could equal or surpass whatever level of modern civilization the Japanese might attain.

Koreans were also encouraged by the actual experience of living and working with the Japanese over the course of several decades. In virtually every sphere of modern life, Koreans had taken advantage of the limited opportunities open to them and had often excelled, whether in business, the bureaucracy, education, journalism, law, medicine, science, engineering, the arts, or even the military, where the Japanese considered themselves particularly gifted and accomplished. Such Koreans had few if any doubts about their ability to measure up to Japanese or world standards in fair competition. In 1936, when two Korean marathon runners captured the gold and bronze medals at the Berlin Olympics, they instantly became popular symbols of what Koreans could accomplish if only the Japanese would be more "magnanimous" and allow them full and equal participation in the imperial world. The colonial and imperial authorities, however, not only claimed the marathon victories as "Japanese" Olympic triumphs, which was, of course, their international legal right given Korea's status as a Japanese colony, but also closed down *Tonga Ilbo* temporarily (and *Sindonga* permanently) when the paper carried a photograph of the gold medal winner, Son Kijŏng, with the Japanese emblem on his uniform deliberately erased. These actions were a sign to many Koreans of how determined the Japanese were to deny Korea any sense of national greatness.

Frustrated or outraged by the colonial system, other Koreans sought personal or national greatness by leaving the country for neighboring Manchukuo, where the opportunities and margin for Korean achievement were often more generous, or by working and fighting against the Japanese empire in various ways in Korea and abroad. For many of the militant groups in particular, the bloody March First Movement of 1919 was a watershed event that signified the futility of further attempts at accommodation or peaceful opposition in the hope of securing some kind of Korean political autonomy. In the 1920s, moreover, in the wake of the successful Russian Revolution, the whole range of Western radical thought began to enter and take root in Korea through publications by young Korean intellectuals, including many Korean students recently returned from Japan or from the newly established Soviet Union itself.

In time a new vision of Korean national greatness began to be articulated by Korean Marxist historians, who recast Korea's long history in terms of a glorious struggle of oppressed classes within the Marxist teleology of socioeconomic development. Here Korean intellectuals opposed to colonialism found a new counterhegemonic universal world order and cosmology centered on the Soviet Union that not only provided a rational explanation for Korea's descent into colonialism but also gave promise, indeed, assurance of liberation and of a brilliant role for Korea in the socialist world of the future. Given its uncompromising and optimistic anticolonial stance, as well as its resonance with precolonial notions of Korean greatness, the new radicalism of the 1920s had a profound impact on the best minds of Korea's younger colonial generation that extended well into the postcolonial era.

Korea Divided

Japan's defeat in the Pacific war brought Japanese rule in Korea to an abrupt end, but in less than a month after liberation, the country was divided into two zones of occupation along the thirty-eighth parallel by victorious Soviet and American military forces. Shortly thereafter the onset of the cold war and political and social divisions engendered by colonial rule led to the establishment of two separate and hostile states in the north and south, and, eventually, to a devastating civil conflict that also involved in varying degrees the United States, China, and the Soviet Union, as well as a number of other countries fighting with the United States on the side of the United Nations forces. When it finally ended in a stalemate in 1953, the prewar boundaries of the two states were still largely intact, but millions of Koreans had been displaced, wounded, and killed. The country, moreover, was in ruins, particularly in the north, where sustained bombing by the United States over a three-year period had razed virtually every North Korean city to the ground.

With the war's end, the two Koreas settled down to the work of rebuilding and developing their societies. Koreans, both north and south, were free at last to pursue their visions of national greatness in a now bipolar international order. For South Koreans this meant continuing an involvement with the democratic industrial capitalist civilization of the West, now centered on the United States, but without the political and racial limitations that had characterized the Japanese empire. Like the premodern Sinitic world order, the world of post-1945 Pax Americana was also universalistic. Although the assumption of the new capitalist world order was that the United States would continue indefinitely to play a dominant role politically, militarily, economically, and even culturally, the potential for other less advanced countries within the order to move upward on the ladder of civilization was also acknowledged, as it had been in the late nineteenth century. Indeed, as part of a worldwide effort to "contain" the spread of Soviet power and communism, the United States government actively supported developmental efforts in countries that, like South Korea, were on the front lines of the struggle against communism. American government policies also took shape in a postwar intellectual environment, stimulated and supported to a considerable extent by cold war political priorities, in which the "modernization" of less developed countries came to be regarded not only as a worthy goal in itself, but also as an effective strategy for combating communism and countering Soviet and Chinese influence.

In stark contrast with the premodern Sinitic world order, the American world of postwar "modernization" was focused above all on economic growth, which initially at least, in the 1950s and early 1960s, was seen as the key that opened the door to "modernization" in other areas as well. Economic prowess, of course, combined with military power had always been at the core of the strength of Western industrial capitalist civilization in the world; the Japanese had been quick to recognize and absorb this fact in the early Meiji era. Many Korean modernizing intellectual and political leaders, however, undoubtedly in a reflection of their premodern heritage, continued from the late nineteenth century on to conceptualize greatness in the capitalist world order largely in philosophical and moral terms. Hence, even as late as the 1950s, the problems of slow or unsatisfactory economic development were often seen by social critics less as economic problems per se than as part and parcel of the general moral failure of a political regime that repeatedly violated Western democratic principles. For Syngman Rhee, South Korea's first president, Korea's greatness in the world also seems to have been predicated above all on a political reunification of the peninsula by the South; economic development, though important, was in that sense seen as a secondary national goal.

With the seizure of power by army major general Park Chung Hee in 1961 in the aftermath of a successful student-led revolution against the Rhee government and a brief, chaotic attempt at liberal democracy, "modernization" *(kŭndaehwa)* became the official catchword and policy of the South Korean government for the next eighteen years. For Park, "modernization" meant, first and foremost, economic development, and everything, including democratization of the political system, was subordinated to that overriding objective. Economic development in Park's thinking was directly linked not only to the alleviation of poverty but also to military defense, to eventual reunification of the peninsula on southern terms, and ultimately to national independence and pride.

Park's vision of national greatness stemmed from the various experiences that had shaped his own life: an impoverished peasant childhood, resentment of Japanese colonial discrimination, an attempt to overcome that discrimination by becoming an officer in the imperial Japanese army, and anger and frustration at American interference and South Korean political and economic dependency on the United States after 1945. Meiji Japan's success in building a "rich country, strong army" served as an important historical model for him throughout his life. In 1972, when he restructured the government along more authoritarian lines, Park called his new system "Yusin," adopting the same name and Chinese characters that had been used for the Meiji "Restoration." Like other Koreans who had excelled against great odds in the colonial system, he also had confidence that Koreans, given a fair chance, could do as well as or better than the Japanese in any national undertaking.

From childhood and youth Park had also absorbed many of the ideas of the new nationalist intellectuals such as Sin Ch'aeho and Yi Kwangsu. These writers had attacked what they considered the pedantic scholasticism of the Chosŏn literati and found Korea's true national spirit in such martial heroes as the Koryŏ monk Myoch'ŏng and Admiral Yi Sunsin, whom they saw as asserting Korean independence or resisting foreign domination. As a young man Park had been particularly inspired by Yi Kwangsu's novel about Yi Sunsin, and after 1961 the Chosŏn dynasty admiral became an official icon of national heroism and his birthplace a national shrine. Indeed, throughout his rule Park was critical of many aspects of Western, particularly American, culture which he thought were unsuited to Korea; he deeply resented any

American interference, particularly in the area of domestic politics. Particularly in the 1970s, he used all the resources available to him, including the educational system, to inculcate national pride in Korea's past accomplishments, especially those that in his mind gave evidence of Korean cultural uniqueness and patriotism, and he tried to foster what he believed were the most important Korean traditional values, including such things as harmony and loyalty that also meshed well with his goal of building a powerful and united nation-state.

While welcoming foreign capital and technology in his quest for economic and military self-reliance, Park was also mindful of Korea's colonial past, and foreign investors were subject to a barrage of rules and regulations designed to ensure that Korea would reap maximum benefits from such transactions with minimum loss of economic control. When American economic advisers and funders balked at Park's pet projects such as a national highway system and steel mill as premature or unnecessary, Park ignored their counsel and went ahead on his own, in some cases even turning to Japan for the required funds. To Park such projects were indispensable for Korea, not only in reaching the goal of military self-sufficiency but also in attaining the stature of a great power. He did not take kindly to American suggestions that Korea continue to rely on Japan and other foreign countries for its steel and other heavy goods and chemical products.

Park's ideas and policies were instrumental in bringing spectacular economic growth to South Korea, but his constricted vision of national greatness, obsessively focused on state wealth and power, also became the subject of growing criticism. While most South Koreans appreciated the economic development that Park and his government had wrought, as well as the government's fostering of pride in Korean history and culture, many others, including significant numbers of university students, intellectuals, workers, and even members of a well-educated and increasingly affluent middle class that had prospered under Park's rule, began to question his leadership and legitimacy, especially after the dismantling in 1972 of the existing democratic framework and establishment of the Yusin system, which in effect made Park president for life.

Indeed, despite nearly two decades of successful economically centered "modernization" under Park, many of South Korea's educated elite, including even some who had worked closely with the government, had never fully abandoned the broader vision of modernity that had been the hallmark of Korean reformists in the late nineteenth century such as Yu Kilchun. To them, national greatness was not simply a question of economic and military strength but also a matter of political and social democratization as well as freedom of expression. For Korea to be truly great, it had to have all of these elements, which were identified with the "advanced" nations of the West. In that sense, Park Chung Hee's understanding of national greatness was actually more reminiscent of the imperial Japanese army's chauvinism of the 1930s than either the postwar American "modernization" paradigm or even the more broadly based sensibility of the Meiji era, especially in its earlier decades, when the idea of "rich country, strong army" was only part of a larger vision of universal "civilization and enlightenment."

After Park's assassination in 1979, a younger group of politically oriented military officers led by Chun Doo Hwan and Roh Tae Woo succeeded in taking over the government. But the popular will was against them. Less than seven years after Chun's inauguration as president, which took place under the existing undemocratic Yusin system, massive public protests by Koreans from all walks of life, including the new middle class, forced the government to commit itself to a program of political and cultural liberalization, which eventually culminated in the free and open election of a former dissident politician, Kim Young Sam, in 1992.

Under Kim, the first civilian president since 1960, civil control of the military was reestablished through a series of demotions and forced retirements. Popular revulsion at subsequent revelations concerning Chun's and Roh's accumulation of hundreds of millions of dollars in personal slush funds during their political tenure also led to full-scale official investigations, not only of the two former presidents' finances but also of their illegal seizure of power in 1979–80. These investigations and the trials that followed, extensively covered by the media, served to air and expiate long-standing grievances against three decades of military rule, and to send an unequivocal signal that the country would no longer tolerate military intervention in its politics.

The presidential election of 1997 saw yet another milestone in South Korea's long and tumultuous march toward democracy that has propelled the country into the forefront of democratizing nations throughout the world. Kim Dae Jung, the country's most famous democratic dissident, whom earlier military regimes had tried to silence through kidnapping, attempted murder, torture, and imprisonment, was elected president. His election represented the first peaceful transfer of presidential power to an opposition party candidate since the founding of the republic in 1948. That it occurred

in the midst of the worst economic crisis since the Korean War also seemed
to confirm the depth of South Korea's democratic impulse. Despite the impact of the crisis, the fundamentals of the economy remained strong, and
the Kim Dae Jung government's quick and dramatic efforts at economic restructuring and revitalization once again provided evidence of a determined
sense of national purpose. With such economic potential, a functioning
democratic government, and a society culturally open to the outside world
with a liberalized press, South Korea seems finally to have reached the
threshold of a national greatness in the modern world first envisioned more
than a hundred years earlier.

North Korea

For North Korea the pursuit of national greatness since 1953 has taken a
very different turn. Like the American-centered capitalist world order, the
post-1945 socialist world order also had universalistic aspirations, with
member countries pledging varying degrees of loyalty to an international socialist vision and community originally centered on the Soviet Union. Like
the United States government in its promotion of worldwide "modernization," the Soviet authorities also adopted a global perspective. They saw the
international development of socialism as a way of combating American hegemony, and they conceived of it largely in economic terms, as an alternative to capitalism. Indeed, one of the great appeals of socialism and communism in this period was the promise of economic prosperity and justice.
Fraternal and friendly nations, especially those, like North Korea, on the
front lines of the cold war, thus received Soviet aid and technology just as
"modernizing" nations, such as South Korea, benefited from a similar political and strategic relationship with the United States.

Within this initially Soviet-dominated world, the North Korean leadership, led by Kim Il Sung, an anti-Japanese guerrilla fighter whose rise to
power in North Korea after 1945 had been supported by the Soviet occupying authorities, initially tended to follow a conventional Stalinist approach
to national development, paying due political homage to both Stalin and the
Soviet Union. Nevertheless, just as premodern Korean dynasties had sought
to preserve their own political autonomy and Korean literati operated
within a social and cultural milieu that was both consciously part of the cosmopolitan Sinitic civilization and also distinctively different, Kim rankled
under any sign of foreign political interference, and he tried to find a niche

for North Korea within the Soviet orbit that allowed for maximum national independence and expression. In that sense he was very similar to his South Korean counterparts, most notably Park Chung Hee, with whom he also shared a certain postcolonial mentality that included deep-seated personal feelings of *han*, an acute sensitivity about outside pressure and influence, and an ardor for national greatness. Like Park, he also had a strong military bent and background; his regime placed a similar emphasis in official textbooks and histories on figures and events deemed to demonstrate qualities and examples of patriotic, antiforeign sentiment and military valor.

Kim's search for North Korea's special place in the socialist world was politically facilitated by the death of Joseph Stalin in 1953, and later by the Sino-Soviet ideological rift. Stalin's death removed from the international communist movement the towering autocratic figure who had presided over the Soviet Union through most of its existence and had served as Kim's patron and model, thereby potentially expanding the margin of experimentation and creativity for North Korea as well as opening the door to Kim's own personal ascendancy in the communist world as an established and experienced leader. The subsequent Sino-Soviet rupture also strengthened Kim's hand in this regard, since both of his giant neighbors were eager to keep him from going over to the other side. This allowed Kim to play them off against each other and garner not only material support but also considerable political and ideological independence for North Korea.

The result was communism with a distinctly Korean flavor. Beginning with a now famous speech in 1955, Kim began to articulate a philosophy generally referred to as *chuch'e sasang* (*chuch'e* thought) in Korean, which eventually acquired the status of a reigning state ideology. In English the term *chuch'e* is often rendered as "self-reliance" or "independence," but such a translation is woefully inadequate. Historically the term appears to have meant the "body of the emperor or monarch," and in a general philosophical sense, it refers to the self qua consciousness.[15] In the North Korean context, however, *chuch'e* came to encompass a whole range of political, social, economic, and philosophical-cultural meanings linked to a central notion of self-defined national autonomy. Koreans and Koreans alone were to be the theorists and masters of their own destiny, and all thought and action, whether among Koreans themselves or in interaction with non-Koreans, were to be predicated on subjective national needs and goals. *Chuch'e*, in effect, was a passionate and unrestrained cri de coeur against centuries of perceived incursion or subjugation by external forces that had sought to weaken or destroy the country. It was also, in that sense, an unequivocal re-assertion of Korea's will to national greatness.

In espousing and promoting *chuch'e* thought, the North Korean leadership, of course, never considered breaking off their historic and economically beneficial ties to either the Soviet Union or China. Nor did they ever abandon their commitment to what they regarded as a universally valid ideology of socialism/communism, laid down originally by Marx and Lenin and destined eventually to triumph throughout the world. Gradually, however, images and writings of Soviet leaders, as well as Marx and Lenin, gave way to those of Kim Il Sung. In time, a full-blown national cult of Kim and his family, including his son and eventual political heir, Kim Jong Il, developed to the point that socialism in North Korea became for all practical purposes synonymous with Kimilsungism. Even Korean national history since the late nineteenth century was rewritten to a large extent as a celebration of Kim Il Sung's, his parents', grandparents', and even great-grandparents' patriotic struggles against hostile foreign powers. In this family pantheon of heroes, Kim himself, of course, reigned supreme as the ultimate warrior and savior of the nation, not only in the anticolonial campaign against the Japanese, but also in the anti-imperialist struggle against the United States and its "puppet" Korean state to the south. The capital of Pyongyang, which had been reduced to rubble by American bombs during the Korean War, was rebuilt as a city of monuments to Kim, to his exploits against the Japanese, and to his family. Kim's speeches and writings, as well as the mythicized story of his life, in time became the basis on which the country's entire intellectual and cultural life, as well as its educational system, was organized and developed. In effect, Kimilsungism became a kind of secular religion with Kim himself functioning as a living sage-king or god.

A degree of personal megalomania seems apparent in this deification process. And Kim was undoubtedly inspired to a certain extent by examples of similar, though perhaps less comprehensive, cults of communist leaders in other countries, especially the cults of Stalin, Mao, and Ceausescu in the Soviet Union, China, and Romania, respectively. At the same time, the cult of Kim and his family also served to assert and glorify Korea's special greatness in the communist world order. While all communist countries in a sense shared the legacy of Marx and Lenin, only North Korea possessed the unique legacy of Kim Il Sung.

Such thinking led inevitably to a certain amount of national solipsism, especially as socialism and communism as ideologies became more and more identified with Kimilsungism. If Kimilsungism was the Korean measure of socialist/communist greatness, then North Korea, simply by virtue of being the land of Kim Il Sung, was necessarily great, a "paradise on earth," as North Korean publications so often declared. This kind of tautological thinking was also reinforced by the country's economic recovery and growth after the Korean War, which, at least until the mid-1970s, was more dramatic and impressive than that of the South. Eventually the North Korean government began to hold the country up as a model to other developing countries throughout the world, even taking out full-page ads in the *New York Times* to proclaim its national accomplishments under the "Great Leader" Kim Il Sung.

Myopia on such a scale is not easily corrected. Neither subsequent economic stumbling in the North, combined with a simultaneous economic surge in the South, nor even later the crumbling of the Soviet Union itself, the political birthplace and capital of international communism, has been able to shatter North Korea's exalted sense of itself. Indeed, as Don Oberdorfer, veteran Korea reporter of the *Washington Post,* discovered on a visit to North Korea in June 1991, the opposite was true: the failure of Soviet communism had only reinforced the North Koreans in their belief that their own brand of *chuch'e*-centered socialism was superior: "One might expect . . . to find a regime in a deep funk, fearful of the future and uncertain about which way to go. The greatest surprise to me was that Pyongyang's officialdom was, outwardly at least, undaunted by the revolutionary reversals in their alliances. In the North Korean worldview, the faltering of communism in the Soviet Union and its collapse in Eastern Europe proved the correctness of Kim Il Sung's independent policy of *juche*."[16]

Even today, despite staggering economic problems and virtual international isolation, the North Korean government continues to speak of its state and society matter-of-factly as "the most exemplary system in the world."[17] One cannot help but feel that there is more in this attitude than mere bravado born of desperation. For a historian of Korea, of course, the obvious parallel that leaps to mind is the example of the post-Ming Chosŏn literati, who saw themselves as the last refuge of civilization in an otherwise barbarized world. As Confucius was reported to have said after the death of King Wen of Chou, "With King Wen dead, is Culture not here with me?"[18]

The Power of History

A will to greatness does not by itself guarantee that greatness, however defined, will be achieved or sustained. Looking at South Korea's modern transformation during the past century, still remarkable despite the economic recession of the late 1990s, one must cite numerous other contributing factors besides sheer self-confidence and determination.[19] Here North Korea is a case in point. Despite its first two decades of rapid economic development in the 1950s, the North at the end of the twentieth century was a premier example of the inadequacy of willpower alone to attain national goals.

Nevertheless, it may well be the case that a will to greatness, combined, of course, with a clear vision of the desired national goals, as Thomas Smith once suggested in writing about Meiji Japan, is a necessary if not sufficient element in any successful transition to modernity. One finds such willpower reappearing again and again at different times, in different forms, and with varying degrees of intensity in all the East Asian countries, including Vietnam, throughout the twentieth century, despite periodic national experiences of almost unimaginable destruction and despair. As I have suggested, this orientation is rooted in history. In the case of Korea, its roots can be traced back most directly, perhaps, to the latter half of the Chosŏn dynasty, but in a deeper sense, they can be seen as arising out of more than a millennium of proud and successful dynastic participation in the Sinitic world order. It is impossible to overestimate the residual force of this long history. To quote William James once again: "We learn all our possibilities by the way of experience. When a particular movement, having once occurred in a random, reflex, or involuntary way, has left an image of itself in the memory, then the movement can be desired again, proposed as an end, and deliberately willed. But it is impossible to see how it could be willed before."[20] The more recent experience of Japanese colonialism seems only to have intensified, albeit to a fierce degree, what was already a deep-seated psychocultural disposition. Colonialism also provided a chauvinistic and militaristic Japanese model of national greatness that continued to exert a hold on many Koreans, especially those in positions of power, even after 1945.

This complex legacy of premodern and colonial sensibilities has clearly transcended political and ideological differences between the two post-1945 Korean states on the peninsula. Both Park Chung Hee and Kim Il Sung, each in his own way, were conspicuous and zealous personifications of a postcolonial Korean will to national greatness. In that sense at least, their thinking and goals were more similar than different. If Kim turned the idea of *chuch'e* into a national creed, Park also used the same word in his writings and speeches on "modernization."[21] Both saw in Korean history a capacity for greatness that instilled confidence about the Korean ability to accomplish any national task, however difficult or seemingly improbable. Indeed, during the years of Park's rule, his insistence that whatever the undertaking, Koreans needed only to summon the necessary willpower to succeed *(ha'myŏn toenda)* became a kind of informal national motto. As already noted, both Park and Kim were also profoundly influenced by their colonial experience, and despite the fact that their respective speeches and writings were framed in the dichotomous languages of American "modernization" and Soviet/Chinese communism, their basic underlying conceptions of the nation-state commonly evoked ideas that were strikingly similar to pre-1945 imperial Japanese notions about the *kokutai* or "national essence."[22]

Bitter ideological conflict has also certainly magnified the strength of the common Korean orientation toward greatness, as both North and South have sought to impress each other with their respective national accomplishments and competed for international attention and plaudits. The South Korean government's seven-year-long public countdown frenzy to the 1988 Olympics in Seoul is a case in point. For South Korea, the Olympics were, as Oberdorfer put it, a giant "coming out party,"[23] a signal to the world that South Korea had come of age as a modern nation and a showcase for the country's economic achievements. In that sense, the 1988 games greatly resembled the 1964 Olympics in Tokyo and even the 1936 competition in Berlin. Because the Olympics aspired to be a truly universal event that cut across the ideological boundaries of the cold war, the right to host them also held a special significance for both Koreas in that it implied recognition and approval from countries within the opposing capitalist or communist world orders. For that reason, the North Korean government made every effort first to obtain the Olympic franchise for itself. Failing to do so, it then tried unsuccessfully to dissuade other communist countries, including the Soviet Union, from going to Seoul. Finally, in the apparent hope of scaring people away from the games, it authorized a terrorist bombing of a South Korean airliner that killed all 115 people on board. Although the bombing ultimately did nothing to disrupt the Olympics and even brought considerable international opprobrium on North Korea, that the government in Pyongyang at the highest level—apparently on the personal order of Kim Jong Il himself, then his father's designated successor—resorted to such a frantic and heinous act was an indication of the importance that North Korea attached to the hosting of the Olympics as a symbol of national greatness.

North Korea's bombing of the South Korean plane reminds us, finally, of the inherently mixed nature of the greatness legacy in Korea. When one looks at those things the world most admires in South Korea today, it is difficult to imagine them apart from the intense nationalistic energy generated by that inheritance. In South Korea, too, however, the search for greatness has at times taken on an obsessive character and led to excesses, most notably during the decades of military rule before the popular uprising and reforms of 1987.

A century-long preoccupation on the part of Korea's ruling elites with the themes, problems, and policies of national greatness, moreover, has so dominated the intellectual discourse and political landscape that virtually all ideas, voices, and social groups have been accorded significance and legitimacy only to the extent that they have been seen as contributing to the nation's development and glory. As a result, in South Korea, as well as in the North, though certainly not to the same extent, most non–nation-centered ideas, as well as economic, social, and political agendas, have been overshadowed, marginalized, or deliberately suppressed. Until only recently, for example, literature, especially literary criticism, has been almost completely in the thrall of nationalist paradigms and interpretations. Korean women seeking to explore and express their identities as women or to expand their opportunities and roles in society have also had to struggle not only against still powerful Confucian traditions but also against a tendency on the part of the intellectual and political establishment to regard feminist concerns as secondary, if not irrelevant or even obstructive, to the more crucial issues of national identity and nation-building.[24] In North Korea, of course, one has seen these same patterns taken to an almost pathological extreme and conflated, moreover, with Kimilsungism.

Nevertheless, the historical perspective here does not rule out a cautious optimism. In both the premodern and modern eras, there have always been Koreans who defined and sought greatness for themselves and their country through active participation *within* what they perceived to be a universalistic world order rather than by defiance or isolation. This historic choice of "voice" over "exit," as Albert O. Hirschman might have put it,[25] has allowed South Korea to lay to rest many of the nationalist anxieties that Yu Kilchun and others first expressed in the late nineteenth century, and provided an opportunity for South Koreans to play an important role in the emerging post–cold war world of the twenty-first century. In North Korea, too, one is tempted by history, despite its fundamentally contingent character, at least to hope that there are Koreans who are willing and able to envision and shape their national greatness in terms of international involvement and cooperation, thereby easing the way toward a peaceful and lasting reunification of the peninsula.

Selected Readings

This is only a small sampling of sources, mainly secondary, that have special relevance to this chapter. For the most part, I have included only works in English. The exceptions are a few particularly important primary sources, and secondary works on subjects for which we have little or no work in English.

Amsden, Alice H. *Asia's Next Giant: South Korea and Late Industrialization.* New York: Oxford University Press, 1989.

Anderson, Benedict R. *Imagined Communities: Reflections on the Origins and Spread of Nationalism.* London: Verso, 1991.

Bishop, Isabella Bird. *Korea and Her Neighbors.* New York: Fleming H. Revell, 1897.

Bol, Peter K. *"This Culture of Ours": Intellectual Transitions in T'ang and Sung China.* Stanford: Stanford University Press, 1992.

Buswell, Robert. *The Formation of Chan Ideology in China and Korea: The Vajrasamadhi Sutra, a Buddhist Apocryphon.* Princeton: Princeton University Press, 1989.

Chandra, Vipan. "An Outline Study of the Ilchin-hoe (Advancement Society) of Korea." *Occasional Papers on Korea,* no. 2 (March 1974): 43–72.

——— Imperialism, Resistance, and Reform in Late Nineteenth-Century Korea: Enlightenment and the Independence Club. Berkeley: Institute of East Asian Studies 40, no. 3 (May 1981), pp. 503–523.

Cho Kapche. *Pak Chŏnghŭi: pulman kwa purun ŭi sewŏl, 1917–1960* (Park Chung Hee: the period of discontent and misfortune, 1917–1960). Seoul: Kkach'i, 1992.

Chung, Chai-Sik. *A Korean Confucian Encounter with the Modern World: Yi Hang-no and the West.* Berkeley: Institute of East Asian Studies, University of California, 1995.

Clark, Donald N. *Christianity in Modern Korea.* Lanham, Md.: University Press of America; New York: Asia Society, 1986.

Conroy, Hilary. *The Japanese Seizure of Korea, 1868–1910: A Study of Realism and Idealism in International Relations.* 1960. Philadelphia: University of Pennsylvania Press, 1974.

Cumings, Bruce. "Corporatism in North Korea." *Journal of Korean Studies* 4 (1982–83): 269–294.

——— *The Origins of the Korean War.* Vol. 1. *Liberation and the Emergence of Separate Regimes.* Vol. 2. *The Roaring of the Cataract, 1947–1950.* Princeton: Princeton University Press, 1981, 1990.

de Bary, Wm. Theodore, and JaHyun Kim Haboush, eds. *The Rise of Neo-Confucianism in Korea.* New York: Columbia University Press, 1989.

Deuchler, Martina. *Confucian Gentlemen and Barbarian Envoys: The Opening of Korea, 1875–1885.* Seattle: University of Washington Press, 1977.

———— *The Confucian Transformation of Korea: A Study of Society and Ideology*. Cambridge, Mass.: Harvard University Press, 1992.

Duncan, John Breckenridge. *The Koryŏ Origins of the Chosŏn Dynasty: Kings, Aristocrats, and Confucianism*. Seattle: University of Washington Press, forthcoming.

Duus, Peter. *The Abacus and the Sword: The Japanese Penetration of Korea, 1859–1910*. Berkeley: University of California Press, 1995.

Eckert, Carter J. *Offspring of Empire: The Koch'ang Kims and the Colonial Origins of Korean Capitalism, 1876–1910*. Seattle: University of Washington Press, 1991.

———— "Total War, Industrialization, and Social Change in Late Colonial Korea." In *The Japanese Wartime Empire, 1931–1945*, ed. Peter Duus, Ramon H. Myers, and Mark R. Peattie. Princeton: Princeton University Press, 1996.

———— "Economic Development under Japanese Colonial Rule." In *The Cambridge History of Korea (Modern Volume)*, forthcoming.

Eckert, Carter J., Ki-baik Lee, Young Ick Lew, Michael Robinson, and Edward W. Wagner. *Korea Old and New: A History*. Cambridge, Mass.: Korea Institute, Harvard University, 1990.

Fairbank, John K., ed. *The Chinese World Order*. Cambridge, Mass.: Harvard University Press, 1968.

Fairbank, John K., Edwin O. Reischauer, and Albert Craig. *East Asia: Tradition and Transformation*. Revised edition. Boston: Houghton Mifflin, 1989.

Fukuzawa, Yukichi. *An Outline of a Theory of Civilization*. Trans. David A. Dilworth and G. Cameron Hurst. Tokyo: Sophia University, 1973.

Haboush, JaHyun Kim. *A Heritage of Kings: One Man's Monarchy in the Confucian World*. New York: Columbia University Press, 1988.

———— "Rescoring the Universal in a Korean Mode: Eighteenth-Century Korean Culture." In *Korean Arts of the Eighteenth Century: Splendor and Simplicity*. New York: Asia Society Galleries, 1993.

Han, Sungjoo. *The Failure of Democracy in South Korea*. Berkeley: University of California Press, 1974.

Hirschman, Albert O. *Exit, Voice, and Loyalty: Responses to Decline in Firms, Organizations, and States*. Cambridge, Mass.: Harvard University Press, 1970.

Hwang, Kyung Moon. "Bureaucracy in the Transition to Korean Modernity: Secondary Status Groups and the Transformation of Government and Society, 1880–1930." Ph.D. diss. Harvard University, 1997.

Kim, Chŏngnyŏm. *Han'guk kyŏngje chŏngch'aek 30-nyŏnsa: Kim Chŏngnyŏm hoegorok* (A thirty-year history of Korean economic policy: the memoirs of Kim Chŏngnyŏm). Seoul: Chungang Ilbo Sa, 1995.

Kim, C. I. Eugene, and B. C. Koh, eds. *Journey to North Korea: Personal Perceptions*. Berkeley: Institute of East Asian Studies, University of California Press, 1983.

Kim Il Sung. *Works*. 35 vols. Pyongyang: Foreign Language Publishing House, 1980.

Kim, Key-Hiuk. *The Last Phase of the East Asian World Order: Korea, Japan, and the Chinese Empire, 1860–1882*. Berkeley: University of California Press, 1980.

Kim Se-Jin. *The Politics of Military Revolution in Korea*. Chapel Hill: University of North Carolina Press, 1972.

Kuksa P'yŏnch'an Wiwŏnhoe (National History Compilation Committee, Ministry of Education, Republic of Korea). *Han'guksa* (History of Korea). 25 vols. Seoul: T'amgudang, 1973–1981.

Ledyard, Gari Keith. "Korean Travelers in China over Four Hundred Years, 1488–1887." *Occasional Papers on Korea*, no. 2 (March 1974): 1–42.

——— "Hong Taeyong and His Peking Memoir." *Korean Studies* 6 (1982): 63–103.

Lee, Chong-Sik. *The Politics of Korean Nationalism*. Berkeley: University of California Press, 1963.

Lee Ki-baik. *A New History of Korea*. Trans. Edward W. Wagner. Cambridge, Mass.: Harvard University Press, 1984.

Lew, Young Ick. "The Kabo Reform Movement: Korean and Japanese Reform Efforts in Korea, 1894." Ph.D. diss., Harvard University, 1972.

Memmi, Albert. *The Colonizer and the Colonized*. Boston: Beacon Press, 1967.

Myers, Ramon H., and Mark R. Peattie, eds. *The Japanese Colonial Empire, 1895–1945*. Princeton: Princeton University Press, 1984.

Oberdorfer, Don. *The Two Koreas: A Contemporary History*. Reading, Mass.: Addison-Wesley, 1997.

Palais, James B. *Politics and Policy in Traditional Korea*. Cambridge, Mass.: Harvard University Press, 1975.

——— *Confucian Statecraft and Korean Institutions: Yu Hyŏngwŏn and the Late Chosŏn Dynasty*. Seattle: University of Washington Press, 1996.

Park Chung Hee. *Our Nation's Path*. 1962. Seoul: Hollym Corporation, 1970.

Pusey, James Reeve. *China and Charles Darwin*. Cambridge, Mass.: Council on East Asian Studies, Harvard University, 1983.

Robinson, Michael Edson. "National Identity and the Thought of Sin Ch'aeho: Sadaejuŭi and Chuch'e in History and Politics." *Journal of Korean Studies* 5 (1984): 121–142.

——— *Cultural Nationalism in Colonial Korea, 1920–1925*. Seattle: University of Washington Press, 1988.

Scalapino, Robert A., and Chong-sik Lee. *Communism in Korea*. 2 vols. Berkeley: University of California Press, 1972.

Schaller, Michael. *The American Occupation of Japan: The Origins of the Cold War in Asia*. New York: Oxford University Press, 1985.

Schwartz, Benjamin. *In Search of Wealth and Power: Yen Fu and the West*. Cambridge, Mass.: Belknap Press of Harvard University Press, 1964.

Sin, Ch'aeho. *Tanje Sin Ch'aeho chŏnjip* (The collected works of Tanje Sin Ch'aeho). 1972–1977. 4 vols. Seoul: Tanje Sin Ch'aeho Sŏnsaeng Kinyŏm Saŏphoe, 1982.

Smith, Thomas C. *The Agrarian Origins of Modern Japan*. Stanford: Stanford University Press, 1959.

Spence, Jonathan. *The Search for Modern China*. New York: W. W. Norton, 1990.

Suh, Dae-Sook. *Kim Il Sung: The North Korean Leader*. New York: Columbia University Press, 1988.

Tanaka, Stefan. *Japan's Orient: Rendering Pasts into History*. Berkeley: University of California Press, 1993.

Toby, Ronald P. *State and Diplomacy in Early Modern Japan: Asia in the Development of the Tokugawa Bakufu.* Princeton: Princeton University Press, 1984.

Wagner, Edward Willett. *The Literati Purges: Political Conflict in Early Yi Korea.* Cambridge, Mass.: East Asian Research Center and Harvard University Press, 1974.

———— "The Ladder of Success in Yi Dynasty Korea." *Occasional Papers on Korea,* no. 1 (April 1974): 1–8.

West, James. "Martial Lawlessness: The Legal Aftermath of Kwangju." *Pacific Rim Law and Policy Journal* 6, no. 1 (1997): 1–83.

Woo, Jung-en. *Race to the Swift: State and Finance in Korean Industrialization.* New York: Columbia University Press, 1991.

Yi Kwangsu. *Naŭi kobaek* (My confession). In *Yi Kwangsu chŏnjip.* Vol. 13. Seoul: Samjungdang, 1964.

———— "Minjok kaejoron." In *Minjok kaejoron: Ch'uwŏn ŭimyŏngjak nonmunjip* (National reconstruction: a collection of the master essays of Ch'uwŏn). Seoul: Usinsa, 1981.

Yun Ch'iho. *Yun Ch'iho ilgi* (Diary of Yun Ch'iho). 11 vols. Seoul: Kuksa P'yŏnch'an Wiwŏnhoe/National History Compilation Committee, Ministry of Education, Republic of Korea, 1971–1989.

CHAPTER 5

State and Society in Interwar Japan

SHELDON GARON

The history of Japan between the two world wars has long been written as the tale of two decades. Historians have variously described the 1920s as the "Liberal Twenties," the "era of party rule" (1918–1932), and the period of "Taishō democracy"—the last corresponding roughly to the rule of the Taishō Emperor (1912–1926). Whatever label they apply, scholars generally view the 1920s as an exceptional period in Japanese history. This was a time of rapid political democratization, when governments headed by unelected oligarchs gave way to cabinets formed by parliamentary parties. In short order these "established parties" were themselves challenged by more popular forces, ranging from labor unions to a women's suffrage movement. In cultural terms, the decade witnessed unparalleled artistic expression, new roles for women, changing sexual mores, and the rise of popular entertainments that call to mind America's own "Roaring Twenties."

The attractiveness of the 1920s is all the more understandable in view of what came later. If the 1920s seem a time of possibilities that might have blossomed into a peaceful and democratic Japan, the 1930s have been depicted as a decade when Japanese leaders abruptly changed course and embarked on the disastrous path of authoritarian rule and military expansion that culminated in World War II and defeat. In the wake of Japan's occupation of Manchuria in 1931–32, the country stumbled into a "dark valley," in the words of one Japanese scholar.[1] By most accounts the 1930s were marked by a rollback of the social, political, and cultural progress made during the 1920s. Military-bureaucratic cliques displaced the parties as the organizers of cabinets; popular movements were crushed; and the Westernizing currents of the interwar years were checked in favor of Japanese nativism, patriarchy, and the emperor-centered cult of State Shinto.

Although the wartime regime's repudiation of many of the previous decade's liberal and democratic trends is undeniable, we would do well also to consider the continuities that run through the 1920s and 1930s. The 1920s were not necessarily a decade of liberalism triumphant. Conservatives thwarted several attempts to democratize society, while the bureaucracy helped organize millions of Japanese in state-sponsored federations that often impeded the formation of truly independent popular organizations. Nor should Japanese politics from 1931 to 1941 be dismissed as a revolt against modernity and Westernization pure and simple. The movement toward authoritarian rule attracted many men and women who regarded themselves as progressive and cosmopolitan.

What most distinguishes the *entire* period between 1918 and 1945 from the preceding decades was the increasing involvement of ordinary people in public life. Their participation sometimes promoted democratization, and other times advanced mass-based authoritarianism of the type seen in Nazi Germany or the Soviet Union. In both the 1920s and 1930s, rising popular forces sought influence within society, while the state experimented with new ways of accommodating, managing, and mobilizing the rapidly changing populace. These complex patterns of state-society relations did not disappear in 1945, but continued to shape the contours of postwar Japan.

New Social Forces

Some popular groups had in fact been active long before the end of World War I. Ever since their early formation during the 1880s, the political parties had struggled to wrest governing power from the oligarchs and their military-bureaucratic protégés. Though initially called the "popular parties," the parties were hardly representative of the vast majority of Japanese. Because the franchise was at first limited to adult males who paid more than fifteen yen in direct national taxes, only 1 percent of the populace was eligible to vote in the first parliamentary election of 1890. Most party politicians were prosperous farmers or businessmen, with a smattering of lawyers, journalists, and other professionals. Nonetheless, in challenging the hold of the oligarchy, the parties advanced the democratic principle that the prime minister and his ministers of state should hail from the party that dominated the popularly elected House of Representatives of the Imperial Diet (whereas the upper house, the House of Peers, composed in large part of hereditary nobles and members appointed by the emperor, was not accountable to the electorate). Oligarchic cabinets, for their part, gradually resigned themselves to sharing power with the parties in order to secure the Diet's approval of the government's annual budgets and proposed legislation. In 1900 two of the oligarchs, Marquis Itō Hirobumi and Marquis Saionji Kinmochi, allied with the leading parliamentary faction to found the Seiyūkai, prewar Japan's longest-lived party.

The parties proved remarkably adept at gaining entrée to the halls of power. In imperial Germany, whose political institutions were deeply admired by modern Japan's founding fathers, chancellors resisted appointing members of the largest parliamentary parties to cabinet posts from 1871 to the downfall of the old regime in 1918. In Japan, by contrast, Prime Minister Saionji chose two Seiyūkai politicians to sit in his cabinet as early as 1906, just sixteen years after the establishment of the Diet. Thereafter, in exchange for furnishing parliamentary support, Seiyūkai leaders routinely served as key ministers of state in Saionji's cabinets. In 1913 a second major party, the Dōshikai, coalesced around Saionji's oligarchic rival, bringing a new group of politicians into government. In 1918 the elderly oligarchs appointed Seiyūkai president Hara Kei (Takashi) to be prime minister and organize his own cabinet. For the next fourteen years, excepting an interlude in 1922–1924, the Japanese government alternated between cabinets led by the two big parties, the Seiyūkai and Kenseikai (formerly the Dōshikai and in 1927 renamed the Minseitō).

Other popular groups surfaced between the 1890s and 1918, although few achieved the influence and national organization of the major political parties. Small-business associations may have been the most successful. Frustrated with government policies that favored big business, small manufacturers and merchants joined together in ever larger units as part of the thirty-year campaign to repeal the business tax of 1896. Also, there were individual women and men who advocated voting and other political rights for women. Yet few overtly political associations of women were formed during these years. The state had much to do with this. An 1890 statute, followed by the Police Law of 1900, forbade women to join political parties. The two laws further barred them from sponsoring or even attending meetings at which "political discussion" occurred.

Within the cities, many in the middle and lower classes began to register their dissatisfaction with a government that imposed heavy taxes, conscripted them for war, intruded into their daily lives, yet denied them the right to vote. Compulsory education rapidly took hold in the late nineteenth century, and by 1905 nearly all school-age children attended school. Newspaper readership, even among the working poor, was surprisingly high in the cities, and much of what people read sharply criticized the government. Lacking formal organizations, the urban masses expressed their demands in a series of protest rallies and riots after the turn of the century. Rickshaw drivers, artisans, and small proprietors often joined forces with party politicians and journalists. Together they opposed the actions of the oligarchic cabinets.

In addition, a small but influential labor and socialist movement arose at the turn of the century. During the late 1890s, labor unions developed in Japan's nascent heavy industries, primarily among skilled male workers. These workmen occupied a stronger bargaining position vis-à-vis employers than most female workers, who, although they made up a majority of the early labor force, generally worked for only a short time and in low-skilled positions in the textile mills. During these same years, a sympathetic group of middle-class social reformers, many of them Christian, prepared to organize a European-style socialist party. Neither the early unions nor the socialists fared well, however. Most of the labor unions quickly folded because of unsteady membership and pressure from employers. Others dissolved themselves after the Diet passed the government-sponsored Police Law of 1900, which effectively outlawed most strikes and other labor actions. Pioneer socialists twice founded socialist parties, in 1901 and 1906, only to see the government disband them as a threat to public order. One group of socialists-turned-anarchists was dealt a heavier blow in 1911, when the government executed twelve anarchists on the charge of plotting to kill the emperor. After police arrested organizers of the Tokyo streetcar strike in 1912, little remained of the early labor and socialist movement.

Democratic Challenges

By the 1910s, influential bureaucrats openly boasted of Japan's ability to inoculate itself against the contagion of social unrest and popular movements sweeping the industrializing West. Japan, they insisted, benefited from numerous "beautiful customs" that made it unnecessary to democratize further or create a European-style welfare state. "Paternalistic" employers were said to be compassionate toward their workers, and members of tight-knit Japanese families ostensibly cared for one another rather than depend on welfare.

The elites' confidence in Japan's special attributes was soon shattered by the massive political and social changes that visited the nation at the end of World War I (1914–1918). In a few short years, popular organizations burst on the scene in unprecedented numbers and varieties. Ruling elites quickly recognized the futility of totally excluding the masses from political life.

The rapid democratization of Japanese politics resulted from the coincidence of several developments. World War I may have bled the Europeans literally and financially, but its impact on Japan was a good deal more salutary. Allied with Britain, the Japanese played a bit part in the war itself. Japanese troops forced the surrender of German garrisons in northern China and the South Pacific early in the war but saw little combat during the rest of the conflict. At the same time, the nation's economy grew enormously, fueled by Japan's own arms buildup and vastly increased orders from the Allied powers and the Europeans' former markets in Asia. The number of Japanese factory workers doubled between 1914 and 1919, with much of the expansion occurring in those industries that relied on skilled workmen. If the wartime economy begat a sizable working class, the boom also accelerated the development of an educated "new middle class." Its members included journalists, lawyers, teachers, doctors, and nurses, and its ranks were swelled by salaried employees in large companies, government, and service industries. The expansion of both the blue-collar and white-collar work forces strained a political system dominated by elite bureaucrats, landed interests, and business.

Blue-collar workers most directly challenged the established order. Between 1917 and 1919, Japanese industry was rocked by a record number of strikes. Under the wartime economy large numbers of workers insisted on improved conditions and higher wages, taking advantage of the increased demand for labor while confronting soaring consumer prices that eroded their real wages. Many workers did not simply go on strike but banded together to form enduring labor unions. The number of unions quadrupled between 1918 and 1923 (from 108 to 432). An early workers' organization, the Yūaikai (Friendly Society), transformed itself into the nation's leading federation of labor unions. In 1921 the Yūaikai renamed itself Sōdōmei (Japan General Federation of Labor). Claiming a membership of 30,000 at the end of 1919, the Yūaikai vowed to "rid the world of the evils of capitalism."[2] In addition, many unions took up the political struggle, joining with urban intellectuals and progressive politicians to agitate for universal manhood suffrage and the enactment of laws that would guarantee workers' rights to strike and to organize unions.

Labor's assertiveness placed employers and the government on the defen-

sive, as did the fury of the Rice Riots (July–September 1918). Although Tokyo and other big cities had seen several popular disturbances since 1905,
the scale of the Rice Riots was of a different magnitude. Faced with skyrocketing rice prices, more than a million Japanese took to the streets. In cities
and villages throughout Japan they participated in protest rallies, looted the
warehouses of rice merchants, and battled police. The Rice Riots also revealed the anger of the urban masses at the ineffectual policies of Field Mar-
shal Terauchi Masatake's oligarchic government, which made matters worse
by dispatching 92,000 troops to quash the disturbances. Recognizing that
continued oligarchic rule would only further antagonize the public, the desperate imperial advisers or "elder statesmen" *(genrō)* appointed Hara Kei,
leader of the Seiyūkai Party, to be prime minister in September 1918.

These domestic challenges to the established order occurred against the
backdrop of equally influential international developments. In the eyes of
liberal and left-wing Japanese, the outcome of World War I confirmed the
superiority of "democracy" over autocracy. Britain, France, and the United
States had defeated the antidemocratic monarchies of Austria-Hungary, Tur-
key, and Germany. For its contribution to the Allied victory, Japan was honored at the postwar Paris Peace Conference settlement as the only non-
Western nation among the "Big Five." Accordingly, argued liberal politicians, Japan should cease behaving like a "police state" and prove itself worthy of its new international status; government should tolerate freedom of
expression, permit women to participate in politics, and legally recognize
the workers' right to take collective action.[3] The war against Germany,
moreover, altered the worldview of Japan's powerful bureaucracy. Temporarily cut off from visiting Germany as their elders had routinely done, rising
officials in the authoritative Home Ministry made extensive tours of Britain.
There they discovered the attractions of liberal institutions, responsible trade
unions, and women's suffrage.

No consequence of the war affected Japanese politics more than the
Bolshevik Revolution of 1917. As in many other countries, Russia's revolution stimulated the growth in Japan of Marxism-Leninism as a political and
intellectual movement. An influential generation of student activists quickly
assumed leadership posts in the Yūaikai-Sōdōmei labor federation and in
other popular organizations. Aided by the Communist International, the
Japanese Communist Party formed clandestinely in 1922. Whereas the political opposition of the late nineteenth and early twentieth centuries had
called merely for the replacement of oligarchic ministers of state by elected

representatives, the left in the 1920s demanded the overthrow of capitalism and abolition of rule by the emperor.

Japanese conservatives had long looked to the countryside as a bulwark against the urban currents of liberalism, socialism, and conflict between the classes. Yet agrarian society, too, experienced new movements from below. In 1921 the government reported an unprecedented 1,680 tenancy disputes, pitting some 146,000 tenant farmers against 34,000 landlords. Most of these incidents began when tenants demanded reductions in their rents. The disputes of the 1920s overwhelmingly occurred near big cities in the Tokyo-Yokohama and Osaka-Kyoto-Kobe areas. Industrialization and urban growth created labor shortages in the surrounding countryside and accordingly strengthened tenants' bargaining position vis-à-vis landlords. In the majority of disputes, tenants won either temporary or permanent rent reductions. Like industrial workers, many tenant farmers formed unions. Although few local tenant leaders adopted left-wing ideologies, socialist and labor activists from the cities sometimes had a hand in organizing the tenant unions—especially those affiliated with the Japan Farmers' Union (established in 1922).

Bureaucrats and conservatives also worried about the revolutionary potential of the urban poor after witnessing the explosive force of the Rice Riots. Major slums dotted the landscape of Tokyo, Osaka, and other metropolitan centers, peopled by day laborers, rickshaw drivers, stall keepers, and their families. Unlike skilled workers, few of these marginalized urban dwellers were able to organize among themselves. One exception were the *burakumin,* Japan's outcaste group. Indistinguishable from other Japanese linguistically or racially, *burakumin* constituted a sizable minority, numbering somewhere between 1 and 3 million. They were, moreover, clustered in the southern half of Honshu, northern Kyushu, and Shikoku. Many lived in the poorer areas of big cities. The origins of discrimination against the *burakumin* date back to the Middle Ages and more immediately to the Tokugawa period (1600–1868). After the Meiji Restoration the new regime decreed the legal equality of all Japanese subjects, but de facto discrimination against the *burakumin* continued with little restraint. By the turn of the century, a new generation of activists had emerged from the ranks of propertied *burakumin.* Supported by socially reformist officials in the government, these activists joined local groups that sought to improve material and spiritual conditions within their communities.

Having grown discontented with the limited objectives of the officially sponsored improvement groups, younger *burakumin* in 1922 formed a truly independent organization, the Suiheisha (Levelers' Society). The society claimed nearly 45,000 members in 1926, peaking at 53,600 in 1928. Inspired by liberal and socialist thought after World War I, the Suiheisha championed the causes of equality and improvements in living conditions. The Suiheisha soon became known for its militancy, fueled by ties to left-wing labor, farmers', and socialist groups.

The 1920s were, moreover, a time when women began to take part in politics and public life. The Police Law of 1900, it will be recalled, had excluded women from participating in any activity deemed "political." Government-run secondary schools for girls had further propagated the ideal of the middle-class "good wife and wise mother" who confined her activities to the domestic sphere. By 1920, however, those in power were reconsidering the wisdom of categorically excluding women from public affairs. Rapid increases in the number of girls attending secondary schools gave rise to a new breed of politically aware women in such professions as teaching, medicine, nursing, and journalism. As educational levels rose, large numbers of women read about politics in newspapers and mass-circulation housewives' magazines. International developments further inspired many Japanese to look upon the acquisition of women's political rights as the hallmark of a civilized nation. Following World War I, Britain and the United States enacted women's suffrage at the national level.

During the first half of the 1920s, several new women's organizations demanded gender equality and political rights for women. In 1922, aided by sympathetic party politicians and by the tacit approval of the Home Ministry, organized women persuaded the Diet to eliminate the law banning women from sponsoring and attending "political discussion" meetings. Once able to sponsor political meetings, many women's organizations joined together to lobby for the passage of universal women's suffrage itself.

Bolstering these reformist impulses was the growth of an urban mass culture. On the eve of World War I, Japan was already one of the most literate societies on earth, with 1,500 to 2,000 different magazines and twice as many book titles as were published annually in the United States.[4] By the 1920s, several newspapers had readerships in the hundreds of thousands; the circulation of two Osaka dailies surpassed 1 million each. Widely read magazines such as *Chūō kōron* (Central review) and *Kaizō* (Reconstruction) carried commentary on the leading topics of the day by liberal, feminist, and socialist thinkers. The profusion of so many outlets for expression confounded government efforts to stifle political dissent. At the popular level, city people frequented the newly opened department stores, cafés, dance halls, and cinemas. A more consumerist culture surfaced, frustrating official exhortations to remain frugal and save money for the good of the national economy.

Nevertheless, not all of the emerging mass organizations espoused liberal or left-wing causes. The largest and fastest-growing popular movement of the interwar era may have been the so-called new religions. These tended to be charismatic Shinto and Buddhist groups, which sprang up independently of the officially recognized sects. One Japanese scholar describes them as the other side of the mass awakening following World War I.[5] Whereas intellectuals and skilled workmen were attracted to liberal and socialist movements, the new religions appealed overwhelmingly to small farmers, shopkeepers, day laborers, working women, and others dislocated by urbanization and industrialization. The sects offered this-worldly solutions to their adherents in the form of spiritual healing of disease, guidance in marital problems, and advice in dealing with economic hardships. Most new religions expressed hostility toward the materialistic culture of the cities and toward democratic movements led by labor unions and intellectuals. Some sects yearned to re-create village-like communities.

Nonetheless, in other respects the new religions drew on "modern" messages and organization. Sects such as Ōmotokyō put together nationwide organizations with their own publishing empires and European-style paramilitary bands. Most also accorded prominent roles to women. Like the more cosmopolitan women's groups, they actively introduced housewives to "scientific" and hygienic methods of housekeeping. Some even defied Japan's traditional patterns of patriarchal family relations by preaching the importance of love and partnership between husbands and wives. In so doing, the new religions—no less than other popular movements—challenged the authority of the state.

Contending Elite Responses

Most accounts of the "Taishō democracy" of the 1920s tell the story of missed opportunities. While historians recount the advent of popular movements with enthusiasm, the political elites are invariably found wanting in their response to demands for democratic reform. The major political parties have come in for particularly strong criticism for having failed to enact such reforms as a labor union law and women's suffrage.

To be sure, the Diet did not pass some important pieces of social legislation that, in the judgment of later historians, should have been enacted. But rather than dwell solely on what those in power *failed* to do, we must also examine the ways in which they actively responded to the challenge of democracy. Two points become clear. First, the elites were far from united in their responses; they hotly debated whether to accommodate, ignore, or suppress popular groups. Second, rarely were Japanese leaders inert in the face of the mass awakening. Even those officials and politicians who opposed the liberal solutions of universal suffrage or labor union legislation frequently proposed alternative methods of incorporating the masses into the polity.

Indeed, the elites divided sharply over the thorny question of how to deal with the rise of organized labor and political socialism. Two competing approaches emerged by the early 1920s. The more conservative position was advanced by the Seiyūkai, which governed through its party cabinets from 1918 to 1922 and again from 1927 to 1929. The Seiyūkai formulated its policies in tandem with conservative bureaucrats in the Ministry of Justice and pro-business officials in the Ministry of Agriculture and Commerce (reorganized into the Ministry of Commerce and Industry in 1925). Completing the conservative coalition were organizations representing large-scale industrialists, which vehemently opposed the labor movement's demands for political and economic rights.

Not that the Seiyūkai rejected all efforts to democratize Japanese politics. Under Hara Kei's government (1918–1921), the Seiyūkai forcefully asserted the principle that cabinets should be organized by the dominant party in the popularly elected House of Representatives. Also, in 1919 the Hara cabinet significantly expanded the Seiyūkai's popular base by extending the vote to adult males who paid the relatively minor sum of three yen or more in direct national taxes. Large numbers of small landholders in the countryside became enfranchised as a result.

Yet the Seiyūkai's vision of democracy accorded little place to the working and middle classes of the cities. Hara preferred to cultivate a political base among local notables, independent farmers, and businessmen that would counter those politicians "who win elections by instigating workers and other poor people."[6] During the early 1920s, the Seiyūkai repeatedly opposed the enactment of labor union legislation that would have recognized and protected the right of workers to organize. Seiyūkai-led governments, moreover, took a hard line against collective labor actions and socialism. In 1920 and 1921, Prime Minister Hara ordered authorities to arrest hundreds of striking workers and organizers on the basis of the Police Law of 1900, which prohibited anyone from "instigating" or "inciting" others to strike and form unions. The following year the Seiyūkai government sponsored a "bill to control radical social movements." The measure failed in the Diet because moderate parliamentarians feared that its open-ended provisions would be enforced against even academics, advocates of universal suffrage, and the opposition parties. At the ideological level, Seiyūkai leaders and allied bureaucrats remained convinced that Japan's "beautiful customs" of harmony among the classes obviated the need for Western-style democracy and social policies.

The Seiyūkai camp's conservatism did not go uncontested. The party's chief rival, the Kenseikai/Minseitō, offered a coherent liberal alternative in the debate over how to manage the social and political challenges of the era. Just as the Seiyūkai allied with other elites, the Kenseikai was at the center of a socially reformist coalition that encompassed innovative officials in the Home Ministry as well as smaller-scale employers. Small-business associations were more inclined than the powerful industrialists to recognize labor unions. In the course of the 1920s, Kenseikai politicians and the Home Ministry's socially minded bureaucrats arrived at a firm consensus on behalf of reform measures. Both groups embraced the need to enact universal manhood suffrage and labor laws. If the Seiyūkai justified its resistance in terms of Japan's "beautiful customs," the Kenseikai and Home Ministry insisted the nation adopt democratic reforms in keeping with the "trends of the world" and Japan's newly acquired status as a "civilized" power. The reformers were particularly guided by Britain's historical success in mollifying the lower classes by enfranchising the masses, legally recognizing labor unions, and introducing health insurance and other welfare measures.

To Home Ministry officials, who were responsible for both social welfare and the centralized police force, suffrage and trade unionism offered effective means of staving off a Bolshevik-style revolution in Japan. Workers would be less likely to succumb to political radicalism, reasoned the bureaucrats, if they gained the right to vote for parliamentary representatives and if their unions could bargain collectively with employers in an orderly fashion.

Similarly, Kenseikai leaders envisioned manhood suffrage and labor unions as a "safety valve" for lower-class discontent. Political considerations further motivated party members. Although the Kenseikai resembled the Seiyūkai in the preponderance of landlords and entrepreneurs among its parliamentary delegation, a much greater proportion of the Kenseikai's influential members represented urban districts or closely identified with the concerns of the cities. These politicians championed labor policies and universal suffrage in part to win the votes of the soon-to-be-enfranchised masses. Some Kenseikai mavericks went further to help organize labor unions. The result was a cordial alliance between the Kenseikai/Minseitō and the moderate wing of the labor and social democratic movement, whose support in turn strengthened the party's commitment to democratization.

The elite proponents of reform gained their first opportunity to act on their proposals during the mid-1920s, when the Kenseikai came to power in a series of cabinets. Sponsored by a Kenseikai-led coalition government, universal manhood suffrage was enacted in 1925. The enfranchisement of nearly all adult males was a crowning achievement for a parliamentary system that was only thirty-five years old. Britain, it should be noted, extended voting rights to males more gradually between 1832 and 1918. Having acquired the right to vote, intellectuals, workers, and tenant farmers speedily organized the nation's first viable socialist parties. In 1926 a Kenseikai cabinet and the Home Ministry successfully sponsored several pieces of labor legislation, which they billed as "universal suffrage for industry." One measure significantly liberalized the workers' right to strike by repealing provisions of the Police Law of 1900, which had prohibited "instigation or incitement" in collective labor actions. Another, the Labor Disputes Conciliation Law, emulated the policies of various Western nations in establishing a legal mechanism for government, labor, and management to settle industrial disputes. The cabinet also activated Japan's first workers' health insurance law, whose enforcement had earlier been blocked by conservative and business forces. The Kenseikai's two attempts to enact a labor union law failed twice, however, in 1926 and 1927, when the Seiyūkai marshaled opposition within the Diet.

The Seiyūkai's success in blocking the Kenseikai's labor union legislation was a harbinger of the growing polarization among political elites during the latter half of the 1920s. The debate over Japan's destiny was not limited to domestic affairs. If anything, the nation's leaders divided more bitterly over matters of foreign policy. This division was new to the late 1920s. In the half decade following World War I, both parties—together with diplomats and military leaders—had embraced the new international order of multilateral cooperation embodied in the League of Nations. Japan eagerly participated in the naval limitation conference at Washington (1921–22), and it placed a premium on maintaining good relations with the greatest powers of the day,

Britain and the United States. The practice of "cooperative diplomacy" became personified in Shidehara Kijūrō, who served as foreign minister in every cabinet headed by the Kenseikai in the mid-1920s and again under the Minseitō governments of 1929–1931. Shidehara further enunciated that it was not in Japan's interests to interfere in the internal affairs of neighboring China—particularly in the civil strife brought on by the Guomindang (Nationalist Party) campaign to reunite China in 1926–27.

The bipartisan consensus behind cooperative diplomacy proved to be short-lived. In 1925 the Seiyūkai began attacking Shidehara and the Kenseikai for doing little to protect Japanese interests in Manchuria and China. The Seiyūkai did so in alliance with prominent army officers, right-wing organizations, and conservatives in the Privy Council and House of Peers. Unaccountable to the electorate, the Privy Council was composed of imperially appointed advisers and held the power to ratify treaties and decide on important matters of legislation. After opponents of Shidehara diplomacy toppled the last Kenseikai government in 1927, a Seiyūkai cabinet was formed by the retired general Tanaka Giichi. Prime Minister Tanaka and other Seiyūkai leaders became obsessed with stamping out communism in both Japan and China. Reversing Shidehara's policies, Tanaka in 1927 and 1928 dispatched three military expeditions to China. There the Japanese army stopped the sometimes left-leaning Guomindang from reuniting northern China and Manchuria with the rest of China.

At home, rather than endeavoring to give workers and tenant farmers a stake in the established order by means of positive social policies, the Seiyūkai government stepped up the repression of popular organizations. The authorities staged massive raids on alleged members of the illegal Communist Party in March 1928. They followed up by disbanding several *legal* socialist organizations as well. These included the leading socialist party, the Japan Farmers' Union, and one of the two major labor federations. The Tanaka cabinet thereupon revised the already draconian Peace Preservation Law of 1925, granting the state the additional power to *execute* anyone who formed an association aimed at "radically altering the national polity." The term "national polity" *(kokutai)* was not clearly defined, although most Japanese leaders understood it to refer to the emperor's sovereignty under the Meiji Constitution.

It is noteworthy that the Minseitō, in alliance with the newly elected socialist deputies to the Diet, opposed the Seiyūkai's efforts to toughen the Peace Preservation Law in 1928. The Minseitō's predecessor, the Kenseikai, had, it is true, cosponsored the original Peace Preservation Law in 1925 as part of the coalition government with the Seiyūkai. At the time, however, the Kenseikai and Home Ministry officials had intended the law to apply only to those deemed truly subversive of the economic and political order—that is, to anarchists and Communist Party members. Few in the Kenseikai/Minseitō and Home Ministry wished to suppress the masses of workers, tenant farmers, and others who chose to participate in the established order and who accepted the legitimacy of the monarchy. From the perspective of the Minseitō and its allies, the Seiyūkai's indiscriminate repression of the left threatened to drive the populace into the arms of the enemies of the state.

The reactionary policies of the Seiyūkai cabinet set back the efforts of those elites who wished to integrate the masses into a more broadly based political system. But they did not deter reformers from trying once again after the Tanaka government fell in 1929. Under Hamaguchi Osachi, the Minseitō formed what many contemporary observers regarded as the most liberal cabinet of the interwar years. Known as the "lion," Prime Minister Hamaguchi stood out among the era's party leaders in his determination to improve the lives of ordinary people and wrest control of government from the unelected elites in the military, House of Peers, and Privy Council. No other party government did as much to reach out to labor unions, women's groups, intellectuals, and social democrats.

The Hamaguchi cabinet quickly committed itself to enacting a labor union law and a tenancy law, the latter of which would guarantee the rights of tenant farmers to remain on tenanted land and to negotiate rent reductions at times of poor harvests. In addition, the Minseitō cabinet became the first Japanese government to support voting rights for women. A "women's civic rights bill" was formulated that would grant adult women the right to vote and hold office at the municipal level. Seeking to shift some of the nation's resources from military spending to domestic programs, Hamaguchi and Foreign Minister Shidehara also negotiated the London Naval Treaty, a major arms-limitations accord, in 1930. The Minseitō's policies were unusually popular with the voters, and in the election of February 1930 the ruling party won a sizable parliamentary majority.

Historians often criticize the interwar parties for having done too little to advance democracy. Hamaguchi's problem, as it turned out, was that he promoted reforms too *boldly* in the face of entrenched antidemocratic opposition. By spring 1931, his progressive agenda was in shambles, beset by foes on several fronts. Rallying conservative forces in the military, Privy Council, and House of Peers, the rival Seiyūkai accused the Minseitō cabinet of compromising Japanese security in its negotiation of the London Naval Treaty. In November 1930, Hamaguchi himself was mortally wounded by a right-wing youth irate over the naval treaty. The Minseitō hung on to power for another year, but, shorn of its dynamic leader, it proved no match for the conservative forces.

The Minseitō's caretaker cabinet presented the party's ambitious reform legislation to the Diet in early 1931, only to see every measure go down to defeat. The labor union bill fell victim to a nationwide opposition campaign by the united business community. Legislative attempts to recognize unions had got as far as they had in the past because leading associations of smaller-scale employers favored placing labor-management relations within a legal framework—in contrast to the vehemently antiunion stance taken by the large industrialists. But that was before the worldwide depression struck Japan in 1930. Plagued by declining profits, companies attempted to cut wages and lay off employees. Workers responded by striking in record numbers. Small-business organizations suddenly turned against trade unionism in any form. In 1931 the Minseitō succeeded in passing a weakened version of the labor union bill in the House of Representatives over Seiyūkai opposition. The measure, however, died in the House of Peers, where prominent industrialists enjoyed considerable influence. Similarly a bastion of wealthy landlords, the House of Peers shelved the long-anticipated tenancy bill at the same time.

Likewise, the government's local women's suffrage bill of 1931 fell victim to the deep divisions within the Japanese polity. In this case the fault line lay not between the Minseitō and Seiyūkai, for both parties had come to endorse the rights of women to vote and hold office at the municipal and prefectural levels (though not at the national level). Rather the debate hinged on two competing representations of gender and politics. In addition to the two parties, supporters of women's political rights included leading women's organizations and Home Ministry bureaucrats. Although supporters differed among themselves over details, they fundamentally agreed that women officeholders and voters would significantly improve *local* politics; they believed that women, by nature, would act as "good wives and wise mothers" close to home. In the words of one bureaucrat-turned-politician, "cities, towns, and villages are to a certain degree extensions of the household when it comes to, say, schools, sewers, or public toilets."[7]

Ranged against the advocates of women's suffrage was an older generation of Japanese elites, which rejected the prospect of women undertaking any political or civic role outside the home. Like the labor union and tenancy bills, the women's civic rights bills were ultimately defeated in the House of Peers. The upper house's titled nobles and retired bureaucrats and military men adhered to an extremely conservative view of gender roles. If women were granted the vote, predicted one baron, they would leave their homes, take on the same jobs as men, and "go beyond birth control and refuse to bear children at all." The era of "making humans in test tubes is at hand," he warned.[8]

The demise of the Minseitō's progressive agenda in spring 1931 marked the beginning of the end for interwar Japan's experiment with liberal democracy. That September the Japanese army occupied southern Manchuria in defiance of Foreign Minister Shidehara and the Minseitō cabinet. When infighting over how to handle the Manchurian incident forced the Minseitō cabinet to resign in December, with it fell the last hope for liberal reform. Not until 1945, in the wake of the nation's defeat in World War II, would a Japanese government again sponsor women's suffrage, labor union, and tenancy legislation. Party-led cabinets themselves disappeared in May 1932, following the five-month rule of the conservative Seiyūkai. For all the promise of manhood suffrage and social legislation, the era of "Taishō democracy" did not see substantial improvements in the political position of most workers, tenant farmers, and other lower-income Japanese.

The nation's middle classes, by contrast, made significant political gains during the interwar years. Although elites divided over whether to accommodate the masses, they firmly agreed that the nation would benefit from the participation in public affairs of those who stood between the rich and poor. Some members of the educated new middle class became active in the major parties and socialist parties. Indeed, the Kenseikai's reform programs were closely identified with a vocal group of university-educated journalists, lawyers, and professors. Of the various middle-class elements, the most politically effective were those who owned small businesses. Unlike most industrial workers, shopkeepers and petty manufacturers successfully organized themselves into neighborhood associations and regional federations, some with tens of thousands of members. In 1926 their political clout persuaded the major parties and the Kenseikai cabinet to repeal the Business Tax and replace it with a business earnings tax deemed more favorable to small businesses. Likewise, in 1937, nationwide campaigns by neighborhood retailers forced the government to sponsor the Department Store Law, which restricted the operations of the rival department stores and impeded their establishment.

Yet, by and large, the middle classes acquired power and influence not by joining in partisan politics, but by assuming public roles in alliance with the state bureaucracy. Following World War I, the Japanese government confronted a bewildering set of social and economic problems, from labor and tenancy disputes to unmanageable cities. Its small corps of civil servants necessarily turned for help and expertise to educators, social workers, academic specialists, physicians, nurses, and other middle-class professionals. Tokyo authorities, for example, relied heavily on Christian social reformers to work with juvenile delinquents, run soup kitchens, and establish day nurseries for children of the working poor. Public-minded members of the new middle class came to influence policy making itself. Increasingly they served on a number of authoritative government commissions and nongovernmental study groups, which brought together bureaucrats, party politicians, outside experts, and leaders of private organizations.

Women, it should be mentioned, were among the many middle-class Japanese who assumed prominent roles in cooperation with the state. Lacking the vote and the right to hold office, women's leaders who wished to advance programs for women and children were more likely to work directly with sympathetic bureaucrats than with party politicians. Women educators assisted officials in seeking to persuade the populace to adopt healthier diets and "improve daily life." National and local women's groups enthusiastically participated in the state's periodic campaigns to encourage households to save more money for economic development.

At the grassroots level, the 1920s also saw new public roles for tens of thousands of activists from the "old middle classes"—that is, artisans, petty merchants, and workshop owners. Prior to World War I, the Home Ministry relied on wealthy local notables to help administer urban neighborhoods. The outbreak of the Rice Riots and the growing gap between rich and poor prompted interwar officials to recruit local agents from the broader middle classes, for small proprietors more commonly came in daily contact with lower-income residents. One successful innovation was the "district commissioner system." Appointed by the authorities, neighborhood merchants and others served as unpaid social workers who assisted and monitored poor households. Although it might appear that the state simply mobilized a docile middle class, the relationship between officials and community volunteers was very much a two-way street. A great many shopkeepers and small manufacturers came forward on their own to form associations designed to restore order and harmony to their neighborhoods (and also to elevate their own status within the community). These organizations included youth associations, sanitation associations, and "moral suasion groups"—the last of which might do charity work, seek to reduce consumption of alcohol, or teach residents how to spend their money wisely.

Local women's associations, which emerged as a nationwide phenomenon during the 1920s, were especially active in efforts to improve daily life. Because the government encouraged their formation, critics commonly dismiss these neighborhood groups as mere handmaids of the state. But a growing body of scholarship demonstrates that the local women's associations were not always tightly controlled by the government. They frequently took independent stands in support of women's suffrage or opposed the government's system of licensed prostitution. The participation in public life of middle-class women and men during the interwar years may be regarded as the beginning of a long-term development that would continue under various political orders in twentieth-century Japan.

The 1930s: Fascism, Japanism, or Democracy without Liberalism?

Although historians of Japan generally consider the developments of 1931–32 as a critical turning point, recent scholarship questions whether a rupture occurred in the early 1930s. If we are to understand the historical flow from the 1920s to the 1930s, we must be precise about what changed and what did not. The era of liberal experimentation had ended, without question. Between 1919 and 1931, the Kenseikai/Minseitō had sought to contain social conflict by granting the powerless some voice in the political and economic marketplace. Thus, lower-income Japanese were permitted to elect representatives to legislative bodies. Had the full liberal agenda been enacted, the rights of workers and tenant farmers to form unions and bargain would have been guaranteed; women would have been able to join political parties, and to vote and hold office at the local level. Moreover, the liberalizing elites of the interwar years had consciously tolerated greater freedom of expression, believing it prudent to accommodate—rather than suppress—most forms of political dissent.

The tumult of the early 1930s eviscerated these attempts at liberal reform. As it did in other industrial societies, the Depression discredited the liberal suppositions of the Minseitō government in the eyes of many Japanese. Faced with destitution in the countryside and rising unemployment, the Minseitō cabinet responded much as classically liberal and fiscally orthodox governments did in the United States, Britain, and Germany. It refused to expend large sums on relief projects out of fear of incurring massive budgetary deficits. Against the backdrop of Japan's occupation of Manchuria and military incursions into northern China, officials and the media declared the nation to be in a "state of emergency." In the face of crises at home and abroad, few Japanese remained confident that a liberal system of freely competing groups—whether political parties, labor unions, or employers' associations—would ultimately bring about what was best for the country. Critics disparaged competition of any type, preferring rule by military men and technocrats. These "officials of the emperor" were thought to transcend partisan wrangling and operate in the true interests of the Japanese people. Matsuoka Yōsuke, a former Seiyūkai member of parliament and future foreign minister, denounced party politics as "blind to everything but party interests." Referring to organized labor and socialism, he called on his countrymen to "renounce consciousness of class war, halt rivalry among economic units and, in short, wipe out antagonism of every sort in favor of cooperation."[9] Impassioned military officers took antiparty sentiment one step further. In 1931 one clique of army officers stopped just short of staging coups d'état on two separate occasions. During the first months of the following year, young naval and army officers assassinated the previous Minseitō cabinet's finance minister, a prominent business leader, and the Seiyūkai prime minister, Inukai Tsuyoshi.

The crisis mentality affected liberal politics in all its forms. With the fall of the Inukai cabinet, no party leader was again appointed to lead the government until after Japan's defeat in World War II. Cabinets gradually became dominated by military officers and higher civil servants. As disillusionment with Western-style parliamentary democracy set in, political leaders questioned whether universal *manhood* suffrage, not to mention proposals for women's suffrage, had been a good idea. In addition, officials steadily narrowed the boundaries of acceptable political expression. Whereas in the 1920s the state had reserved its worst suppression for the far left, during the 1930s the authorities increasingly arrested professors, liberal thinkers, and leaders of religious groups for espousing beliefs that allegedly ran contrary to the "national polity." In 1935 the Home Ministry launched a massive campaign to "eradicate the evil cults," by which it meant the burgeoning new religions. Although none of these sects posed a threat to domestic peace, the authorities feared the new religions' "unscientific" methods of healing, their mass followings, and their very existence as a spiritual alternative to the cult of the emperor, or State Shinto. Over the next several years, police made sweeping raids on several new religions. Sacred shrines were gutted and even dynamited. The religious groups themselves were forced to dissolve, and their leaders went to jail—often for having violated the Peace Preservation Law, which had theretofore been applied only to Communists and anarchists.

This erosion of liberties reversed a key trend of the 1920s, but one should not exaggerate the degree of overall change during the first half of the 1930s. From our perspective today, the illiberal developments of those years appear as the first step in the inevitable drift toward the authoritarianism and militarism that became evident at the height of World War II. At the time, however, it was by no means clear that Japan would jettison all aspects of Taishō liberalism and Westernization.

It was not obvious in 1935, for instance, that party rule was dead. Many regarded the two so-called national unity cabinets of 1932–1936 not as repudiations of the principle of party cabinets, but as interim governments that would guide Japan through its state of emergency. Party men in fact held nearly half of the portfolios in each cabinet. The Seiyūkai, which enjoyed a large majority in the House of Representatives, expected to return to power once the initial emergency subsided. The Minseitō, for its part, hoped to exploit its influence within the national unity cabinets to become the governing party following the next parliamentary elections in 1936. Indeed, the ostensibly nonparty governments became closely identified with the Minseitō after the Seiyūkai refused to furnish members to the newly formed cabinet of Okada Keisuke in 1934. Although the national unity cabinets substantially increased military budgets and recognized the army's expansion into Manchuria and northern China, these coalitions of party elders, businessmen, and elite bureaucrats resisted the more radical efforts to alter the foreign and domestic policies of the 1920s. Headed by moderate retired admirals, the two cabinets checked the army's attempts to mobilize the domestic economy for "total war," and endeavored to maintain good relations with Britain and the United States.

In social and cultural terms as well, the first half of the 1930s witnessed the continuation of previous trends associated with urbanization and industrialization. Officials might trumpet the virtues of the countryside and traditional values, but in reality more and more Japanese were migrating to the cities and joining the industrial work force. Not only did rapid armament after the Manchurian incident produce new factory jobs, but also the Japanese economy experienced a boom in the export of manufactured goods following the devaluation of the yen in late 1931. Far from coming to a halt, the urban culture of the 1920s became a greater part of everyday life. Readership of family and housewives' magazines such as *Kingu* (King) and *Shufu no tomo* (Housewife's friend) steadily expanded. What is more, rural households now read about urban lifestyles in these publications or in the agricultural cooperative movement's glossy magazine *Ie no hikari* (Light of the home), which reported 1 million subscribers in 1935. Even Marxist writings became a commodity for mass consumption, ironically at the very time when the authorities were stamping out what remained of the Japanese Communist Party. The continued appeal of Marxism lay in part in the widespread disillusionment with the workings of capitalism amid the dislocations of the depression. Along with several other Marxist tracts, the translated complete works of Marx and Engels were published in thirty-two attractively priced volumes between 1928 and 1934.[10] And for all the talk of recovering the "Japanese spirit," Parisian-style cafés exploded on the urban and provincial scenes during the first half of the 1930s. Motion pictures, both Japanese and Western, attracted large audiences, even in remote villages. Ordinary people flocked to Hollywood films throughout the 1930s, despite growing antiforeignism within the leadership.[11]

While long-term socioeconomic trends continued, the political order nonetheless began to experience profound changes in the mid-1930s. Opponents of parliamentary liberalism went beyond earlier criticisms of the parties to propose new authoritarian mechanisms that would give the state greater powers to mobilize and control society. Few had pressed for radical changes at home when Japan's military actions were confined to Manchuria and involved relatively small numbers of casualties. By 1935, however, the media were filled with predictions of war with a host of world powers—ranging from the Soviet Union and China to Britain and the United States. Japanese representatives had already stormed out of the League of Nations in 1933 after an international commission censured its takeover of Manchuria. Japan further isolated itself between 1934 and 1936, withdrawing from the Washington and London naval disarmament treaties. Anxieties over impending war made both the Japanese state and the general public far less tolerant of conflict and disunity on the home front—whether it took the form of workers' strikes or heterodox new religions.

Reinforcing these illiberal tendencies was the growing influence of the army in domestic politics. The high command became alarmed about threats to Japan's position in northeastern Asia coming from the Soviets, Chinese nationalists, and Chinese Communist Party. Army planners increasingly spoke of the need for a "national defense state," in which the economy and decision-making apparatus would be placed in the service of the military. On February 26, 1936, one faction of army officers staged a nearly successful coup d'état. Their troops killed finance minister Takahashi Korekiyo, former prime minister Saitō Makoto, and several other moderate leaders who had tried to curb the army's insatiable demands for expanded budgets. The mutiny was put down, but the succeeding cabinet of Hirota Kōki generally did the bidding of the army. High-ranking officers took direct aim at the core institutions of parliamentary democracy. Some even recommended restricting suffrage to household heads instead of all adult males, and they made plans to absorb all existing political parties into a single mass party that would unconditionally support the military. Allied with the army were many higher civil servants or "renovationist bureaucrats." They, too, disdained party rule and wished to strengthen the state's controls over industry, labor, the media, and daily life.

The outbreak of a full-fledged war with China in 1937 accelerated the regime's drive to manage society. In 1938 the cabinet of Konoe Fumimaro cajoled the reluctant Diet into passing the National General Mobilization Law. The measure granted the bureaucracy unprecedented powers to control the economy and society on behalf of the war effort. Meanwhile, Prime Minister Konoe—together with a curious coalition of progressive younger politicians, socialists, academic specialists, and army officers—advanced plans to form a single mass party on the model of Hitler's Nazi Party. They achieved their goal in 1940, when Konoe returned to power. The nation's political parties and labor unions dissolved themselves, some willingly but many under various degrees of coercion. In short order, they and myriad groups—from farmers' organizations to writers' guilds—lost their autonomy and were absorbed into the newly created Imperial Rule Assistance Association. A vast hierarchical structure, the IRAA was in reality administered by the bureaucratic state. The authoritarian consolidation of Japanese society was thus well under way by the time of Pearl Harbor in December 1941, although the desperate war against the United States and other Western powers prompted the regime to step up its interventions into everyday life.

How do we understand the chain of events that led to Japan's authoritarian transformation in the 1930s? Some at the time and since have likened it to the rise of fascism in contemporary Italy and Germany. Japanese leaders vehemently denied the resemblance, insisting that their nation was pursuing its own course under the incomparable rule of the Japanese emperor. Indeed, a majority of scholars in the West today are uncomfortable about applying the term "fascism" to Japan. They prefer to highlight the indigenous and conservative traits of Japanese authoritarianism: the cult of the emperor, agrarianism, and rule by a military-bureaucratic elite. In contrast to Fascist Italy and Nazi Germany, they note, Japan had neither a genuine mass party nor a charismatic leader, nor did an outside group seize power. Moreover, the Imperial Rule Assistance Association was, at best, a pale imitation of the Nazi Party. Within its unwieldy confines politicians from the former parties continued to contend, rival ministries vied for control, and big business commonly stood up to meddling bureaucrats. To the eminent thinker Maruyama Masao, European-style fascism did not develop in Japan because the nation had not sufficiently democratized during the 1920s and previous decades. In Germany, he argued, the Nazi Party's mass organization and appeal ironically owed much to democratic developments occurring under the Weimar Republic, whereas wartime Japan remained ruled by much the same elites that had dominated since the early Meiji period.[12]

The contrasts with Nazism are apparent, but it would be wrong to conclude that Japanese authoritarianism was simply a retreat to the nativism and oligarchy of the past. There was much that was new, even "modern," about Japan's New Political Order. Moreover, contrary to Maruyama, there was much that was "democratic" in the sense that Japanese authoritarianism would not have taken the shape it did in the absence of the "Taishō democracy" of the 1920s. To be precise, the authoritarian programs of the 1930s recognized the advent of mass participation in political and public life, regardless of age, gender, and class. The evolving organization of women, youth, and petty proprietors—albeit under state control by the late 1930s— was a far cry from the political order of the late nineteenth century, when a few notables or family patriarchs monopolized public life at the local level. Taishō democracy need not have resulted in mass-based authoritarianism; yet interwar democratization was a necessary precondition for the authoritarian structure that followed. As one Japanese scholar astutely observes, the 1930s witnessed the rise of "democracy without liberalism."[13]

How the masses fared under the new system of forced participation varied considerably. Officials regarded some groups as irredeemably subversive, and these elements were categorically excluded from mobilization efforts.

The authorities continued to hammer away not only at the Communists and their sympathizers but also at the new religions, despite the latter's general conservatism and reverence for the emperor.

Other popular organizations attempted to expand their public roles under the new order yet ultimately were unsuccessful. Weakened by employers' onslaughts and the Diet's rejection of labor union legislation, many labor and socialist leaders allied with sympathetic bureaucrats. These officials seemed inclined to grant workers at least some collective voice in the workplace. Guided by the desire to achieve social harmony and maintain wartime production, the bureaucrats constructed a national hierarchy of plant-level "industrial patriotic units," bringing together employers, workers, and white-collar employees. In 1940 the state-supervised Industrial Patriotic Association was established on the order of Nazi Germany's Labor Front. Oddly enough, many labor leaders eagerly dissolved their unions and joined the new labor front. They actively supported the Industrial Patriotic Movement, calculating that workers, now protected by the state, would strengthen their position vis-à-vis employers at the plant and national levels. Employers' associations and more conservative officials, however, were not about to permit workers to participate in industrial relations on an equal basis. The plant-level units were stripped of the power to discuss working conditions, and few met regularly for the duration of the war.

Although the democratic potential of the Industrial Patriotic Association was hardly realized during World War II, the idealism underlying its creation may have contributed to postwar democracy. The bureaucrats rhetorically emphasized the equality of manual labor and management, as well as the workers' full membership in the enterprise community. Postwar unions often exploited this ideology to achieve guarantees of long-term employment and to secure benefits equal to those of white-collar employees.

For small business owners, participation in the wartime structure brought mixed results. Having emerged in the interwar years as leaders of urban communities, petty entrepreneurs continued to accrue power and prestige as the wartime state's local intermediaries. The regime elevated their political status further by vastly expanding the various neighborhood associations that were charged with law enforcement, extracting savings for the war, and mobilizing the populace. In the economic arena, by contrast, small businesses were forced to participate in wartime "control associations," the compulsory cartels which in most cases promoted the interests of large firms at the expense of smaller enterprises. Nonetheless, in the years following defeat in 1945, small-business associations built upon their interwar and wartime strengths in having organized themselves and asserted their interests. Postwar associations successfully lobbied for numerous laws and policies that protected small and medium-sized enterprises against competition from larger companies.

In the countryside, the authoritarian revolution piggybacked on previous democratic trends, perhaps more than in any other area of society. As in the cities, local power had been gradually passing from wealthy landlords to the middling strata of farmers who owned and cultivated small parcels of land while commonly renting other plots as tenants. The social status of middling farmers rose as they benefited from universal education and served in the armed forces. At the same time, the large landlords became detached from village society as they shifted their attention to more profitable investments in commerce and industry. Middling farmers often led tenant unions during the 1920s. With the onset of the depression, however, they typically spearheaded campaigns to secure government relief and improve conditions for the village as a whole. Just as the state deputized the old middle classes in urban neighborhoods, bureaucrats bolstered the local power of the middling farmers by relying on them to promote the "economic rehabilitation" of the villages during the 1930s. Owner-cultivators became the mainstay of the newly expanded semiofficial organizations—notably agricultural cooperatives, mutual aid associations, and hamlet associations. The middling farmers' cooperation with the wartime regime paid economic dividends as well. To secure ample supplies of rice in 1942, the Ministry of Agriculture and Forestry purchased rice at a substantial premium from those who actually cultivated the crop, snubbing the big landlords in the process. Even before the Allied occupation mandated land reform in 1946, rural democratization and authoritarian mobilization paved the way for the emergence of small owner-cultivators as an assertive force in the postwar political order.

Much the same argument may be made in the case of women's participation in wartime mobilization. As they had since the 1920s, officials steadily recognized the value of bringing women into public life, while organized women regarded cooperation with the state as the best means of advancing the interests of women and children. The country's best-known suffragist, Ichikawa Fusae, greeted the war with China in 1937 as a grand opportunity for Japanese women to prove their worth in mobilization efforts and thus elevate their position.[14] Leaders of interwar women's groups formally took part in the wartime regime in unprecedented numbers. Some served on mobilization councils or worked for government ministries. Many others officially exhorted women's groups throughout the nation to increase household savings or recycle materials for the war effort. With most adult males in the military, ordinary women by the tens of thousands became the de facto civic leaders of their communities through their activities in the ubiquitous state-sponsored women's associations. In their newly recognized identities as the guardians of public morality, women also played central roles in official campaigns to stamp out cafés, dance halls, and that notorious Western hairstyle, the permanent wave. Although women's leaders after World War II sought to dissociate themselves from the pre-surrender regime, their wartime activism undoubtedly contributed to the rapid formation of large women's organizations in the postwar era.

For intellectuals who criticized or refused to support the war effort, life under authoritarianism was unpleasant at best and horrific at its worst. Liberal professors lost their jobs, and government censors were on the lookout for even the mildest forms of dissent in periodicals and books. Most feared were the Special Higher Police, or "thought police," who monitored, arrested, and sometimes tortured prominent progressives and publishers. As has been true elsewhere, however, imperialism and war also opened up opportunities for countless graduates of Japan's burgeoning institutions of higher learning. The educated new middle classes had already gained considerable influence within the state apparatus during the 1920s. Ironically, the extreme statism and militarism of the 1930s accelerated the regime's incorporation of the intelligentsia.

As the state assumed new responsibilities to manage society and govern occupied territories, it employed veritable armies of specialists. Economists, political scientists, and labor experts served in a series of cabinet-level research bureaus or in semiofficial think tanks. Several looked to the European models of fascism and national socialism, radically proposing the formation of mass organizations that would link state and society. In the puppet state of Manchukuo (Manchuria), left-leaning specialists worked with army officers to devise an authoritarian system of government controls over the economy and daily life. Other recent graduates went off to Manchuria and elsewhere to manage native workers or, in the case of many women, to teach. Yet others were employed in Japan's extensive surveys of land tenure and rural society in China. Those with a knowledge of English or other foreign languages were pressed into service as civilian administrators and propagandists, particularly after Japan occupied the Southeast Asian colonies of the Western powers in 1941–42. Some of the educated performed their overseas duties with reluctance, but a great many saw themselves as warriors in Japan's grand struggle to liberate fellow Asians from the yoke of Western imperialism.

In the wake of Japan's defeat in 1945, the active role played by women and intellectuals in the war effort raised uncomfortable questions over the extent to which they had "collaborated" with the militaristic regime. Many, to be sure, became opponents of postwar conservative governments. One might further argue, as many Japanese have done, that the military and civilian elites would have committed their nation to authoritarianism and war with or without the cooperation of popular elements. Nevertheless, the spirited participation of women's groups, middling farmers, and the old and new middle classes made the regime's mobilization of its people much more effective than if an autocratic state had simply imposed control from above.

At the height of the Pacific war (1941–1945), relations between state and society were considerably more elaborate than they had been in 1918. If we judge these relations by the measure of liberal democracy, Japan had unquestionably regressed from the era of "Taishō democracy." Civil liberties had been severely curtailed, and the evisceration of parliamentary democracy made it extremely difficult for popular groups to weigh in on the great issues of the day.

The picture looks somewhat different if we consider the roles that people played in lower-level arenas of power. The authoritarian and war years continued and even accelerated the rise of new social forces in Japanese public life. There was, however, at least one disturbing legacy of this historical process. Large numbers of Japanese emerged from World War II intensely active in civic life, yet unaccustomed to taking initiatives outside the supervision of the state. Leading women's organizations, for example, remained based on hierarchically structured federations of neighborhood women's associations, and they continued after 1945 to serve as the state's local agents in various campaigns to promote household savings and mold popular behavior. This interesting mix of democracy and state management of society persisted well into the postwar era and, in some respects, endures to this day.

Selected Readings

Barnhart, Michael A. *Japan Prepares for Total War: The Search for Economic Security, 1919–1941*. Ithaca, N.Y.: Cornell University Press, 1987.

Barshay, Andrew E. *State and Intellectual in Imperial Japan: The Public Man in Crisis.* Berkeley: University of California Press, 1988.

Berger, Gordon Mark. *Parties out of Power in Japan, 1931–1941.* Princeton: Princeton University Press, 1977.

Bernstein, Gail Lee, ed. *Recreating Japanese Women, 1600–1945.* Berkeley: University of California Press, 1991.

Cook, Haruko Taya, and Theodore F. Cook. *Japan at War: An Oral History.* New York: New Press, 1992.

Duus, Peter. *Party Rivalry and Political Change in Taishō Japan.* Cambridge, Mass.: Harvard University Press, 1968.

Fletcher, William Miles III. *The Search for a New Order: Intellectuals and Fascism in Prewar Japan.* Chapel Hill: University of North Carolina Press, 1982.

Garon, Sheldon. *Molding Japanese Minds: The State in Everyday Life.* Princeton: Princeton University Press, 1997.

———— *State and Labor in Modern Japan.* Berkeley: University of California Press, 1987.

Gordon, Andrew. *The Evolution of Labor Relations in Japan: Heavy Industry, 1853–1955.* Cambridge, Mass.: Council on East Asian Studies, Harvard University, 1985.

———— *Labor and Imperial Democracy in Prewar Japan.* Berkeley: University of California Press, 1991.

Havens, Thomas R. H. *Valley of Darkness: The Japanese People and World War Two.* New York: Norton, 1978.

Kasza, Gregory James. *The Conscription Society: Administered Mass Organizations.* New Haven: Yale University Press, 1995.

Lewis, Michael. *Rioters and Citizens: Mass Protest in Imperial Japan.* Berkeley: University of California Press, 1990.

Neary, Ian. *Political Protest and Social Control in Prewar Japan: The Origins of Buraku Liberation.* Atlantic Highlands, N.J.: Humanities Press International, 1989.

Smethurst, Richard J. *Agricultural Development and Tenancy Disputes in Japan, 1870–1940.* Princeton: Princeton University Press, 1986.

Tipton, Elise K., ed. *Society and the State in Interwar Japan.* London: Routledge, 1997.

Waswo, Ann. "The Transformation of Rural Society, 1900–1950." In *The Cambridge History of Japan,* ed. Peter Duus. Vol. 6. *The Twentieth Century.* Cambridge: Cambridge University Press, 1988.

Young, Louise. *Japan's Total Empire: Manchuria and the Culture of Wartime Imperialism.* Berkeley: University of California Press, 1998.

CHAPTER 6

China in the Early Twentieth Century: Tasks for a New World

ERNEST P. YOUNG

Living in today's China, one faces three unavoidable tasks: against authority from above one has to challenge the erroneous ideas and beliefs of a tradition that has lasted 2,000 years; domestically one has to fight the habits and inertia of 400 million illiterates; internationally one has to confront all other nations in the world that threaten us with either outright aggression or insidious manipulation. Without an utmost broad mind and unparalleled courage, how could one even think of breaking through in this desperate situation and leading the nation into the new world?!

—Liang Qichao, 1900

The prominent author of these remarks, at age twenty-seven, succinctly outlined an agenda that was to preoccupy more than one generation of Chinese in the first decades of the twentieth century.[1] How was one to cope with China's weighty political and cultural heritage, apparently ill adapted to present problems? How to mold China's vast population into proper citizens? How to fend off predatory nations in their rivalrous but co-ordinated attack on China's autonomy? In the years that followed, Liang Qichao was the intellectual guide for many educated Chinese in exploring these pressing questions, which still echo a hundred years later.

Liang Qichao had been a leading associate of Kang Youwei in the mobilization of reform sentiment after the Sino-Japanese War of 1894–95. In the dramatic summer of 1898, the young Guangxu Emperor issued a series of reform decrees that sought to move the country in directions that Kang Youwei had advocated. As the summer ended, however, the empress dowager Cixi, who from the 1860s had carved out for herself a dominant position in court politics, conscripted key allies in officialdom to take power away

from the emperor—without dethroning him. She sent other leading participants in this reform episode to their deaths or into exile. Liang Qichao, like
Kang Youwei, escaped abroad. Reform appeared thwarted.

There was much cause for gloom. Since the defeat by Japan in 1895,
China lay ever more vulnerable before the world. In a "scramble for concessions," various European countries had taken options on parts of China's
land and resources. They had added to their colonial footholds on Chinese
soil—including a ninety-nine–year lease on an expansion of British Hong
Kong (to expire in 1997). Then in 1900 armies of a coalition of eight countries temporarily occupied major parts of north China in retribution for attacks on foreigners and Chinese Christians in the Boxer affair. These countries—the world's leading powers of that time—extracted a promise of huge
indemnities and the establishment of a multinational military presence near
China's capital for the indefinite future. To these and other indignities was
added the unhappy fate (dismissal, suicide, execution) of officials who had
indulged their anger at Christian missionaries and representatives of the
foreign powers during the 1900 upheaval. These happenings demoralized
an already insecure officialdom. The dynasty's mere survival seemed to
owe more to foreign convenience than to any remaining strength in the old
order.

Out of these degrading events, surprisingly, a new, determined reformist
mood emerged among leaders in and out of the government. China in the
last years of the Qing dynasty experienced the beginnings of a major transformation.

The broadly based enthusiasm for reform in the first decade of the twentieth century can be attributed to the spread of nationalist attitudes among
important parts of the Chinese population. The term "nationalism" has no
sure boundaries, nor is there any one term in modern Chinese that exclusively translates the English word. In the debates of the late Qing, at least
three expressions were used to refer to important aspects of the notion:
guojia ("nation" or "country," with emphasis on the state), *aiguo* ("love of
country," pointing to the sentiment), and *minzu* ("nation," with emphasis
on the people and with connotations ranging from nationality to ethnicity
or race). Together, these words were used to express the idea that state and
people should join with each other in compelling ways, including the formation of identities derived from the relationship. In the ideal espoused by
nationalism, the people see themselves in the state, and the state is defined
by the people and territory it administers. Unlike the traditional approach,

whereby, in only one of his roles, the ruler cares for the people and measures his virtue by their contentment, this new conception locates the raison d'être of the state entirely in its people. Much of the excitement of the last years of the Qing arose from efforts to apply this ideal to Chinese circumstances.

The need to do something drastic had been brought home by the catastrophic ending of the nineteenth century. The emergence of new forms of power wielded by a number of foreign countries had been obvious since the middle of the nineteenth century. A growing body of Chinese intellectuals had traced the sources of that power to the internal organization of those countries. The lesson they learned from China's defeat by Japan in 1895 was that the adoption of Western material military technology, in which China had not been inferior to Japan as the war began, was not a sufficient answer. The subsequent Boxer fiasco showed that facile alliances with popular sentiment (in this case the peasant Boxer movement) were no solution when "the people" were themselves unreformed. Liang Qichao insisted that ordinary Chinese could not even *name* their country properly but referred to it only by the title of the reigning dynasty![2]

There was never any single, authentic Chinese nationalism. The ideas to which the term is applied here were always in the process of being formulated, argued over, and redefined. The two common threads that link the various strategies of the time as nationalist were the reconceptualization of China's place in the world as one nation among many, no longer a civilization unto itself; and a readiness to see the country undergo serious transformation to achieve a dignified and secure place in the "new world," as Liang Qichao characterized it.[3] After 1900 this understanding dominated all major political arenas.

The New Reform Program

One such arena, although perhaps the most resistant, was the imperial court. When the empress dowager had seized control of the imperial institution in September 1898, she appeared to reject the sort of reform prescribed by the nationalist outlook. During the Boxer affair, she endorsed a narrow, reactive, xenophobic policy. In the first years of the new century, however, she turned around. Until her death in 1908, she presided over the conspicuous dismantling of some core institutions of the Qing state. Her regime planned to replace them with a broad range of new structures—administrative, educational, military, judicial, representative—that borrowed liberally from recent Western and Japanese models. These changes, known as the New Policies *(xinzheng),* were well under way before the dynasty was overthrown by the 1911 revolution.

The empress dowager heralded the turn toward thoroughgoing reform by an imperial decree in January 1901 in which she called on high officials in the capital and the provinces

> to reflect carefully on our present sad state of affairs, and to scrutinize Chinese and Western governmental systems with regard to all dynastic regulations, national administration, official affairs, matters related to people's livelihood, modern schools, systems of examination, military organization, and financial administration. Duly weigh what should be kept and what abolished, what new methods should be adopted and what old ones retained. By every available means of knowledge and observation, seek out how to renew our national strength.[4]

The follow-through was impressive. Officials responded to the call. Those who took the lead, such as Yuan Shikai (later president of the Republic), gained more power from the success of the reforms. In contrast to earlier reform efforts, this one was coordinated on a national level. Reforms in the period of Self-Strengthening, from the 1860s to the early 1890s, were episodic and scattered, often depending on the initiative and support of particular province-level officials, whose tenures were limited. Moreover, high regional officials, such as provincial governors-general, tended to dominate the country's politics more than officials serving in the capital. In the dynasty's last decade, however, planning groups formed at the top of the government structure and sought to coordinate changes throughout China. Indeed, an important aim of the court's reforms was to increase the centralization of authority in the empire.

Change came most swiftly and deeply in the realm of education. Following study missions abroad and the proposals of high officials, the government issued regulations for a national school system in 1904. New schools with new curricula proliferated. The next year the government abolished the venerable civil service examinations, which tested command of a specific literature of classics and commentary.

The implications were immense. Book learning was at the core of Confucian ways of securing proper political leadership and social harmony. To change the content of education and the mode of access to it was to tamper with basic assumptions. The educational reforms of the late Qing meant that the established canon of texts, sanctioned by centuries of reverence and study, no longer defined learning. Science, math, world geography, and modern history joined the Chinese classics as the substance of education. The end of the examination system deprived the dominant social class, the gentry, of its primary instrument of certification, both for government office and for local prestige and privilege. Although no revolution was intended, to plan education for all was to imply a citizenly role for all. Citizenship meant political participation and changes in the legitimation of authority.

A number of limitations to the educational reforms, however, constrained their social impact. In practice, the goal of universal education was nowhere near attained. The new schools, which were often instant creations out of converted academies and requisitioned temples, and were overwhelmingly (though not exclusively) for males, served only an upper fraction of society, including the same families that had done well under the old examination system. The change would gradually sap the legitimacy and solidarity of the gentry. In the short run, however, elite adjustment to new definitions of education was rapid and smooth. Although officials and educational associations planned to bring some sort of education to all through spare-time, literacy, and vocational schooling, the common folk were more often struck by the higher taxes that went to establish schools beyond the reach of their children. The last years of the Qing were marked by frequent local protests, sometimes violent, against the reforms.[5]

Study abroad was a major component of the government's forced-draft program to create an educational system at all levels. The purpose was to bring back "new knowledge" to China and supply teachers for the burgeoning schools. Provinces granted scholarships; many students went at their own expense. The numbers going to Japan far outstripped those studying elsewhere, for reasons of propinquity, economy, cultural closeness (including the relative accessibility of the Japanese written language through its use of Chinese characters), and a Japanese effort to attract and accommodate them. In the peak years of 1905–1907, 7,000 to 13,000 Chinese students each year attended schools in Japan.[6] The Qing government attempted, but was unable, to supervise at a distance the large community of Chinese students abroad. Radicalism and political dissidence developed in Tokyo and among smaller groups in Europe.

Nurturing a political opposition was one of the unintended consequences of the reforms. The court sought to remold the Chinese to be useful, responsible citizens in a nation headed by the Qing monarch. The constituents of the nation had to be taught the contents and importance of their national identity. The specific content of the identity, however, was vigorously contested. The Qing state could not control its definition. This was certainly the case with those who went abroad in pursuit of "Western learning." They often became schoolteachers when they returned. Or they became the journalists and essayists most widely read by the educated classes. Many among them discerned no necessary connection between a Chinese nation and the Qing. To some the relationship seemed contradictory. Indeed, because the throne and various other key positions in the state were restricted to Manchus—a small minority among the overwhelmingly Han Chinese population—the government's effort to conscript nationalism to its purposes was deeply problematic.

Similar ambivalence marked military reform, and here the risk for the dynasty was even more conspicuous. The Qing had experimented with new versions of military training in the late nineteenth century, but it was only after 1900 that a major effort was undertaken to create an army based on contemporary military science. Without actually disbanding all the military forces on which the regime had relied in the previous century, the government at considerable expense created a New Army *(lujun)*, which reached about 200,000 before the Qing was overthrown. As an instrument of central authority it was imperfect. Although six divisions—about a third of the total force—were located near Beijing and were centrally financed, much of the New Army's development was left to provincial administrations, primarily for fiscal reasons. These troops sometimes acquired a local coloration or a spirit of autonomy from central authority. Moreover, in keeping with the patriotic mood of the time, a portion, notably some of the officers, joined out of a sense of national service. Their political ideas were open to persuasion by critics of the regime. Accordingly, major elements of the New Army took the lead in bringing down the Qing during the 1911 revolution.

Why, then, did the government continue to encourage reforms that sowed the seeds of its own demise? Officials were not unaware of the disaffection in schools and the army. The last years of the Qing witnessed an abundance of uncovered plots, dissident publications, and military mutinies. Of course, the government could hope that its repressive mechanisms would suffice, that some gestures toward reducing Manchu privilege would mollify ethnic resentments, and that its aim of binding people and government more firmly together in a centralized polity would gradually be achieved.

Aside from that hope, however, the nationalist impulse left no choice but to stay the course. The desire to preserve the regime was always present and explains the many hesitations, especially in the last three years of the Qing. But it was too late to call off the reforms, and there was no serious effort to do so.

For many reformers in and out of government, the keystone of reform was constitutionalism, that is, the shaping of representative institutions. Two broad models of relations between state and people marked the discourse of the time. One was the old paternalistic ideal of a nurturing ruler who recognized that the welfare of the people was the foundation of good order. If the people did not remain politically passive, it indicated the ruler's failure. This view was supported by an ancient tradition of Confucian thought, with special reference to Mencius. The other model embodied the ideal of integration of state and people through political participation. The success of government depended on people's capacity for undertaking active political roles and their opportunity to do so. The inspiration for this model was not all foreign. It drew on another strand of equally Confucian thought, under the designation *fengjian,* which called for dispersal of power to the localities. It cited Chinese critics of autocracy from previous centuries. But its particular programs—representative institutions—as well as much of its rationale, came from the political example of leading Western countries and Meiji Japan.[7]

The late nineteenth and early twentieth centuries witnessed the growing displacement of the first model by the second. Advocates of the second model within the framework of a continuing Qing monarchy were loosely grouped as "constitutionalists." They were a vigorous voice in some of the leading journals and newspapers of the late Qing.[8] They were also an important presence within the Qing government. In the belief that national strength and hence Qing survival required some sort of representative institutions, the government adopted a constitutional course, albeit with a misplaced confidence that it would fortify the policy of centralization. After further missions abroad, commissions at home, training of local leaders, and small-scale trial runs, the regime launched an array of elections for deliberative bodies at the provincial and local levels.

The official architects of these moves did not intend to institute democracy. They were impressed by Japan's Meiji Constitution, which combined representative bodies with the retention of sovereignty in the emperor and a tightly centralized administration. When provincial assemblies were elected in 1909, the ascribed powers of the assemblies were limited and the electorate was small (less than half a percent of the population).[9] The formation of county and sub-county councils, although originally scheduled for 1912 and beyond, began earlier, and they soon numbered in the several thousands. While these local bodies apparently were chosen by a somewhat larger proportion of the population, like the provincial assemblies they were predominantly gentry in social complexion.[10] A national assembly was promised for 1917. The government's emphasis was on gradualism and the enlistment of provincial and local elites in support of official reform programs.

It did not work out that way. The provincial assemblies immediately became assertive, not only with provincial officials but also with the central government. Key leaders in the assemblies had already accumulated considerable political experience. They had been active in campaigns to recover economic concessions granted by the Qing to foreign firms or governments, notably options to build more railway trunk lines and open more mines. In this "rights-recovery movement" the nonofficial provincial leaders had sometimes worked with Qing authorities and had sometimes forced the government's hand. Out of such campaigns emerged provincial railway companies, dedicated to building trunk lines without foreign participation, with purely Chinese financing and control. These efforts at securing Chinese economic rights against foreign encroachment often evoked a high-pitched patriotism and widespread popular enthusiasm.[11] The experience of provincial elites in political mobilization was transferred to the provincial assemblies, which were soon in serious confrontation with Beijing.

Three times in 1910 representatives of the provincial assemblies carried petitions to the capital, asking for the opening of a national assembly within one year. The third visit was accompanied by large demonstrations. The central government lopped three years off the timetable for a national assembly but otherwise rejected the petitions.

The mood in the country turned sour. In the next months some constitutionalists gave up on the Qing, or at least on the feckless court leadership that came to power after Empress Dowager Cixi's death in 1908.[12] The disaffection deepened with the successive announcements in May 1911 of a Manchu-dominated cabinet (a new institution) and of the central government's takeover of the provincial railway projects. Beijing proceeded to negotiate a huge loan from a foreign consortium of banks to build the railways. Outrage at this betrayal of the patriotic impulses of the provincial railway companies—which had fought to keep new trunk lines out of the foreign hands into which Beijing now appeared to be delivering these strategic projects—was widespread. It became insurrectionary in Sichuan, a province where considerable financial loss accompanied the insult. The legitimacy of the Qing regime hung by a thread. Still, it took a revolutionary act to cut the thread.

The foregoing activities highlight two major developments. One is the prominence of political activity based in the gentry elite. The government suppressed attempts to create political parties. Nevertheless, newspapers and journals (despite press laws), as well as schools, officially endorsed chambers of commerce, the railway companies, and the representative assemblies, provided proxies for open political organization. This politicization of the gentry class—its coming together outside the government for broad purposes, beyond localities and across regions—was foreshadowed by the organization of relief and other welfare efforts in the aftermath of the Taiping Rebellion.[13] By the last decade of the Qing, gentry coalescence enabled mobilization around issues concerning the fate of the nation. While the Qing regime attempted to channel this gentry energy into reform programs supportive of the central state, it could not contain the augmented political assertiveness of this self-confident class.

A second development in gentry politics is the growing importance of the province as a focus for action. As a unit of territorial administration, the province had long had great salience and marked the identity of its inhabitants, especially when they sojourned elsewhere in the country. When groups outside officialdom became more active around issues of national import, they often organized themselves at the provincial level. The resistance to the foreign construction of railway trunk lines across several provinces, for example, took the form of provincially based railway companies, usually led by high gentry from the respective province. The fact that the first elected representative institutions were provincial assemblies reinforced and accelerated this tendency. Before the end of the dynasty, gentry aggregations of political clout at the provincial level reached a point in several provinces where the centrally appointed officials became its instruments. The upshot was a dramatic face-off between provincial and central authority.

In this conflict, both sides claimed to be motivated by the good of the nation. From Beijing's perspective, the obstreperousness of the provinces damaged national strength. Those engaged in organization at the provincial level, however, argued that the central authorities had brought China to its present plight and that further centralization would only exacerbate the country's weakness. The provinces, they maintained, held the key to national strength and recovery of independence. China's immense size lent plausibility to such arguments. The provincial unit had already shown itself able to mobilize against foreign encroachment in the railway battles. From this perspective, the center had sold out and lacked patriotism. The political focus on the province was more than a transformation of old local loyalties into a modern politics. It was a species of nationalism, no less politically sophisticated than the centralizing version. The 1911 revolution reflected these developments.

The Revolution against the Qing

The first Chinese to lead a rebellion in the name of a republic was Sun Yat-sen in 1895. Although of peasant stock, he had been educated in his teens in Hawaii and then in Hong Kong. He relied heavily on overseas Chinese for talent and funds in his political organizing. Meanwhile, after the turn of the century, radical sentiment flourished among the mostly upper-class Chinese students in Tokyo and Shanghai, for some of whom constitutionalism under a continuing monarchy was not enough. Interest in revolution surged in 1903, when the Qing government rebuffed students who offered to fight against a prolonged Russian occupation of Manchuria. In 1905 Sun joined his forces with student-based revolutionary groups in Tokyo to form the first revolutionary organization that could claim participation from almost every Chinese province. The resulting Revolutionary Alliance (Tongmeng-hui) spread the republican revolutionary message across the country.

Yet the Revolutionary Alliance suffered from factional infighting and lost its coherence well before 1911. The republican revolutionary movement was at best a loose federation of different groups without effective central direction. Local revolutionary conspirators often spun their plots with little reference to those planning national strategies.[14] The 1911 revolution itself began as a locally initiated action in a provincial capital (Wuchang, in the province of Hubei, on October 10), and was taken up in many other provinces in much the same way. Interprovincial coordination came only after the revolution had spread quite widely, and even then the national leaders of the movement, including Sun Yat-sen, enjoyed only tenuous influence over the whole.

Revolutionaries shared the objective of overthrowing the Qing and replacing it with a republic. Beyond this basic agreement, however, there were important divergences. Some, like Sun Yat-sen, saw in China's secret societies a potent link to popular discontent and therefore likely allies in revolution. Others rejected reliance on the unruly lower classes and looked to the more socially reliable New Army for revolutionary muscle.

While agreeing on ending the Qing dynasty, the revolutionaries differed with regard to their understanding of why it had to go. Sun Yat-sen faulted the Qing for blocking the beneficent influences of the West and thereby stifling China's modernization. From his point of view, the Qing was hopelessly backward, and China could not advance until the dynasty had been overthrown. He regularly sought foreign assistance for his revolution. By contrast, the student revolutionaries (many of whom were no longer youths and entered various professions upon returning to China) pointed precisely to the Qing's subordination to foreign power as the principal reason for revolution. In this view, China was imperiled by foreign aggression. Since the Qing had permitted the country to sink into this quagmire, the rulers could not be trusted to lead the people out of it and into nationhood.[15]

One way that revolutionaries submerged their differences was through adoption of a racial vocabulary. From the end of the nineteenth century, Chinese intellectuals strove to incorporate into their understanding of China's predicament the racial view of the world so prominent in Western discourse at the time. Racial definitions of human difference and of struggle among groups provided the revolutionaries with another reason to oppose the Qing. The regime could be described as the rule of one race (the Manchus) over another (the Han). There was much to work with: early critiques of the Qing conquest, accounts of Qing brutality, the anti-Qing tradition of the secret societies, and the anti-Manchuism of the mid–nineteenth-century rebellions (stereotyping of the Other was hardly new to Chinese attitudes). The revolutionaries refurbished this history with the gloss of Western "scientific racism" and used it against the Qing.[16] Their propaganda was replete with racial vilification of the Manchus. One need not specify whether the Manchus' crime was their poor relations with the West or their willingness to accommodate Western encroachment. That they were Manchus sufficed to justify revolution.

As Manchu leaders sustained a Manchu distinctiveness and revolutionaries expounded a racial definition of China's politics, the anti-Manchu dimension to the revolution was conspicuous.[17] When the revolution did occur in the fall of 1911, Manchu communities, strategically spotted around the country as part of Qing security, were brutally assaulted in some places. The largest slaughter was in the northwestern city of Xi'an, where secret society assailants wiped out some twenty thousand Manchus.[18]

Nevertheless, the racial attack on the Manchus was not general and subsided quickly.[19] The racial diatribes of the revolutionary ideologues in the years preceding the revolution carried more propagandistic than analytic weight.[20] In the social Darwinian frame that dominated the discourse, race was too confusing, unstable, and self-defeating a category. How was one to sort out the racial world of East Asia?[21] How comfortable could a Chinese ever be with the idea of the racial survival of the fittest, which apparently doomed the weakened Chinese to extinction?

One of the revolutionary spokespersons, Chen Tianhua, who propagated the racial definition of sides in the fight against the Qing, accompanied such fulmination with appeals to the Manchus to join with the Han against the imperialist predators.[22] The trouble, he wrote, was that the Qing had become puppets of the foreign powers:

> You say that today China still belongs to the Manchus? For some time now it has belonged to the various [foreign] countries . . . So, if we think of making any sort of move, the governments of the various nations send an order and have the Manchu government send out telegraphic edicts to the provincial governors, who send notes to local officials, who immediately do away with us with great thoroughness on behalf of the foreign countries . . . Consequently, if we wish to oppose the foreigner, all we can do is preach revolution and independence.[23]

The author of these remarks, just before his death in December 1905, wrote that for him politics had always been more important than *minzu-zhuyi*—nationalism of the ethnic or racial sort—and he bore no hatred for the Manchus.[24]

Although revolutionaries were a diverse lot, the events of the revolution rendered the differences inconsequential. From October 10, 1911, as one province after another declared its independence of the Qing and its adherence to the idea of a republic, the revolutionaries, even the local ones, lost control. Action by elements from the New Army was commonly decisive. Sometimes officers with little or no revolutionary record were conscripted to head the provincial revolutionary governments. Leaders of the provincial assemblies—up to that point constitutionalists, not revolutionaries—adjusted rapidly and endorsed the break with the Qing. In most provinces they gained a considerable share of the power. The result was that committed revolutionaries were often no more than a part of the emerging structure of authority. In only three of the fourteen revolutionary provinces did a veteran revolutionary head the provincial government through the first year of the Republic. In a curious way, the revolutionaries were deluged by the great success of their project.

The turbulence of the revolution was sufficient to make the socially privileged anxious, but it did not unseat the inherited social hierarchy. The constitutionalists and the New Army officers were generally from elite families. Most members of the revolutionary organizations were hardly less privileged in social background. In some provinces, secret society participation in the revolution contributed to the overthrow of Qing authority and dramatized the possibility of social upheaval, as in Shaanxi, in whose capital city of Xi'an many Manchus were killed. Some revolutionaries tentatively encouraged this infusion of popular energy, but most joined with constitutionalists and New Army officers to contain and to smash aggregations of secret society force.[25] The revolution was kept in elite hands.

The revolutionary provinces federated for purposes of negotiation with the Qing government. Their representatives chose Sun Yat-sen as provisional revolutionary president upon his return from abroad at the end of December 1911. The prominent reformist official Yuan Shikai negotiated for the Qing, whose administration now reached only a minority of the country's provinces. By the beginning of February 1912, the two sides had reached agreement. In return for the abdication of the emperor and the replacement of the Qing with a republic, the emperor was allowed to remain in his palace at public expense, the Manchu military families of the Qing banner system were pensioned, and Yuan Shikai (of Han ethnicity) was given the provisional presidency of the Republic. As the price of a prompt restoration of peace and unity to the country, Sun Yat-sen resigned his revolutionary presidency. In April 1912 a republican national government was in place in Beijing, under a constitution drawn up by Sun Yat-sen's revolutionary government before its dissolution.

The effects of the revolution were mixed. It had certainly not been a social revolution, aside from the removal of the thin layer of Manchus at the top of the political order and some prominent Han officials who would not adapt to the new republican order. The political impact was nonetheless of great consequence. For two millennia Chinese political theory and practice had been constructed around the imperial figure, which embodied many layers of meaning. Could another central principle take its place, or would the imperial role, by whatever name, turn out to be an ineluctable feature of the Chinese political order? Much of subsequent Chinese politics has taken place in the shadow of this question.

Another effect of the revolution was to unleash the forces of provincial politics. The form of the revolution, in which one province after another declared independence, shaped the postrevolutionary order. Despite the formal unification of the country under the new republican government in Beijing, most of the provincial governments retained their autonomy. They collected and disposed of taxes independently, which had the practical effect of starving Beijing of funds. They retained their own armies, with hardly a nod toward any central command (although Yuan Shikai as president had at his disposal some of the best of the New Army divisions, which had remained under Beijing's command right through the revolution). Moreover, most offices in the provinces were reassigned to natives of the province, thereby reversing the Qing system of forbidding official service in one's home area. In short, the centralized structure of the Qing, as well as its monarchy, was largely subverted.

The Republic under Yuan Shikai

The de facto federalist organization of the Republic in its first year facilitated the liberal enthusiasms of the moment. The press proliferated and was relatively free. Radical notions received respectful hearings. A socialist party established itself around the country. Advocates of women's rights aggressively lobbied political leaders. Women were for a time members of the provincial assembly in Guangdong. Continuing a program of the late Qing, most provincial authorities zealously suppressed domestic opium production. Reform was uppermost on many agendas.

The prospect of deciding the big political questions through elections, as provided in the new constitution, stimulated the formation of political parties. Those who had formed the Revolutionary Alliance in 1905 and had subsequently conspired to overthrow the Qing reconstituted themselves as an open parliamentary party, called the Guomindang (Nationalist Party). Liang Qichao, returned from exile after the Qing's fall, set to work at building a party out of his national network of reformers. Many lesser parties emerged. National elections were held in the winter of 1912–13, with a much larger electorate than in the late Qing elections for provincial and local bodies. The Guomindang, despite its administrative weakness in most provinces, prevailed over the other parties. It was, after all, the party of the revolution. At the same time, it ran on a moderate program, dropping earlier calls for social reform, and included an openness to provincial autonomy.

Few of these developments of the first year of the Republic were to Yuan Shikai's taste. As provisional president of the new Republic, he could not be expected to appreciate the autonomy of the provinces. He fondly recalled the administrative coherence and authority of Qing officialdom. He had no sympathy for the liberal enthusiasms of the time and believed that many official posts were occupied by incompetents, selected for their revolutionary credentials rather than relevant skills. He saw the national elections as a threat to his continuing at the pinnacle of the polity.[26]

On this last point, at least, he was no doubt right. The Guomindang's electoral victory had been managed by the youthful Song Jiaoren, an important revolutionary leader in the late Qing and enthusiast for parliamentary government. After the elections, Song added to his advocacy of the political supremacy of the national assembly the aim of restricting the powers of the president, or even replacing him. The instrumentality was at hand in the constitution, of which Song Jiaoren had been a primary drafter. It stipulated that the national assembly would choose the president, an office only provisionally occupied by Yuan Shikai. Song's party could look forward to a preeminent voice in this matter. As usual, Yuan acted decisively. He arranged for Song's assassination. On March 20, 1913, Song was shot at the Shanghai railway station as he boarded to go to Beijing to participate in the organization of the national assembly. It was soon apparent that his death had aborted the emergence of a liberal national politics.

Other revolutionary leaders, like Sun Yat-sen, who had not shared Song's parliamentary focus or who had been willing to work with Yuan Shikai, were enraged by Song's murder. They turned decisively against the president. Additional issues further embittered the atmosphere. Yuan contracted a large foreign loan without the constitutionally specified ratification by the national assembly, which began functioning in April 1913. In June Yuan dismissed from office the only three provincial chiefs who had revolutionary credentials. His strength derived from the foreign loan and from the army divisions, known as the Beiyang Army, which he had taken the lead in developing under the Qing and which he had inherited as a result of the 1911 revolution (After his death, some of the officers became prominent warlords—a phenomenon described later in this chapter.) In early July, fighting began between Yuan's divisions and such provincially based military forces as the revolutionaries could muster. This event is sometimes called the Second Revolution. Yuan's forces quickly prevailed. The most prominent of the revolutionary leaders escaped abroad.

In October 1913 Yuan intimidated the remnants of the national assembly into electing him regular president. He then proceeded to centralize power in himself while consolidating his administrative authority over the great majority of the provinces.

The result looked like a dictatorship. Yuan abolished elected bodies at all levels, from the national assembly to sub-county councils, including the politically lively provincial assemblies. Military forces responsive to Beijing's orders occupied a number of northern and central provinces that had enjoyed autonomy since the 1911 revolution. For a while repression was at a high pitch. Thousands were executed in 1913 and 1914 by the military and a bloated secret police for real or imagined ties to Guomindang conspiracies. Yuan replaced the 1912 constitution with an authoritarian version. (In this he was assisted by, among others, his American constitutional adviser, Frank J. Goodnow, soon to become president of Johns Hopkins University.) His new regime censored the press and outlawed the nascent women's movement. The exuberant liberal politics of the first republican year expired, as did provincial autonomy. Yuan's fearsome aggregation of administrative power over the whole country was unsurpassed until the Chinese Communist ascent to national power in 1949.

Yuan has one of the most malodorous historical reputations among prominent political figures in twentieth-century Chinese history. His career can be reduced to a series of betrayals with only one purpose in view: self-aggrandizement. Yet his government's programs still require explanation. His guiding principle was bureaucratic order in a centralized polity. His experience with the liberal Republic of the first year had made him nostalgic for his time as imperial governor-general. The late Qing aim of greater administrative centralization was one he shared. While sweeping out of office (or, more drastically, imprisoning or executing) those who had used provincial posts to defy the center after the 1911 revolution, he put in place civil officials from the reforming bureaucracy of the late Qing. He reimposed a rough-hewn version of the Qing avoidance rule—that one not serve in one's native province. Although his assertion of control over the country depended on his authority over armies (another heritage from the late Qing), he worked to bring the military under civilian control in the manner of the old empire. He was heir to the reform agenda of the late Qing, but his emphasis on bureaucratic order and fiscal responsibility meant that the ambitious Qing reforms could not be sustained. Retrenchment, instead, was the order of the day.

Liang Qichao, the reforming intellectual, joined with Yuan against the Guomindang in the early stages of the dictatorship. He accepted high office in Yuan's administrations in 1913 and 1914. Though motivated in part by a decade of antagonism toward the republican revolutionaries, Liang represented the attitudes of an important part of the Chinese elite in sharing Yuan's belief in the importance of a strong central government as a basis for reform and national strength. When Liang broke with Yuan in 1915, he criticized him, not for his dictatorship but for his lack of vision and his inability to plan for the long-term future of the country.[27]

Liang's actual break with Yuan, however, like the disaffection of many others, was precipitated by Yuan's infamous attempt to make himself the new emperor of China when he found that his centralization of power had not elicited positive support from the country at large. Nor had it shielded the country from foreign importunity. He looked for ways to reach the country and strengthen his government, without the "disorder" of the first year of the Republic. He sponsored a range of traditional retrievals, such as ceremonies for Confucius and Heaven, adding some modern touches. Then, in 1915, reeling from Japan's Twenty-one Demands for augmented privileges in China, to all but the most extreme of which Yuan ultimately acceded before an outraged nation, he launched a campaign to elevate himself to the Dragon Throne. He proposed to update the monarchy: airbrushing out its unmodern features, such as ceremonial prostrations and eunuch servitors, and linking it to a new (as yet undrafted) constitution. Even the reign title he adopted (Hongxian) was a reference to constitutionalism. Nonetheless, it was to be a monarchy, and even many of his close allies and longtime protégés were dismayed. These actions betrayed the republican promises of 1912 and claimed too large a reward for too little accomplishment.

For the third time since 1911, provinces rebelled against the center. The "National Protection Movement" against Yuan's monarchy started in December 1915 in Yunnan, one of four southern provinces which had not been occupied by Yuan's own military forces. Elements of the small Yunnan army invaded neighboring Sichuan Province and held their own against Yuan's larger forces. As other opponents of Yuan became emboldened, more

provinces joined the revolt. Some of Yuan's own generals defected or refused to act vigorously on his behalf. Yuan's public abandonment of his monarchical ambitions in March 1916 did not stem the tide of disaffection. In
early June 1916, while contemplating flight abroad, he died of natural
causes. His career ended amidst the dire consequences of an enormous political miscalculation.

Had the Chinese people, then, already internalized a republican version of
national identity? Contemporary observers were not so persuaded. The opposition to Yuan's monarchical attempt could be attributed not only to a rejection of monarchy but also to an opposite sentiment: emperor was too elevated and august a position for the likes of Yuan Shikai. Some intellectuals
saw in Yuan's monarchism not just a personal betrayal of a republican oath
but a sign of the unregenerate traditionalism of the country at large. They
began a campaign of attack on China's cultural inheritance, broadly conceived. Their efforts would swell into the May Fourth Movement.

Warlords and the Politics of the Province

After Yuan Shikai's demise, his successors temporarily revived the political
forms of the first year of the Republic. The national assembly that Yuan had
dissolved reconvened, as did the provincial assemblies. Yet the government
in Beijing, though recognized internationally, did not regain administrative
control over the country.

Commanders of local military forces, including units of Yuan's Beiyang
Army, increasingly decided local affairs. Alliances and factions among military leaders, often cutting across provincial borders, determined the political
map of China. Civil war became endemic in the jockeying for territory and
sources of revenue. An internal arms race ensued. The number of men under arms escalated. People caught in the path of war or by the extortionate
tax collectors suffered grievously. These conditions, generally referred to as
warlordism, extended over the next decade and more. China's storied talent
for order and political management was reduced to the maneuvers and esca-
pades of devious if clever generals.

There was no concerted campaign by a military class to seize the reins of
power. Rather, repeated disagreements among important political groups resulted in invitations to military men to join the fray.[28] Both the 1911 revolution and the Second Revolution of 1913 had been steps in this direction.
Yuan Shikai had accelerated the process when, in an effort to save his un-

popular monarchical effort, he reversed his policy of reducing the political salience of his generals and instead bribed them with enhanced powers. Similarly, the armed movement against Yuan's monarchy left generals more firmly in charge in a number of southern and central provinces.

Among the unresolved issues around which these national contests were waged was one left over from the late Qing: centralization versus provincial autonomy. The Qing court fell, in part, because its centralizing version of reform led to conflict with a patriotism focused on the province. In the Second Revolution, veteran revolutionaries resisted President Yuan's authority by mobilizing provincial resentment against Beijing's claim to appoint and rule directly in the provinces. At that time centralization won, but when some provinces rose up against Yuan's central authority in the National Protection Movement in 1915–16, Beijing as national capital did not recover. Liang Qichao was a leader in that revolt. Though a champion of centralization, he observed that he might as well make the most of the fact that "the province has long been the basic unit in Chinese politics."[29] Much use was made of it in bringing down Yuan's national regime.

Despite the breakdown of national unity and the attendant turbulence, the warlord era was marked by a good deal of provincial patriotism and reform.[30] From the 1920s, the two main revolutionary parties, the Guomindang and the Chinese Communist Party, established in 1921, adopted centralization as the proper nationalist posture. They condemned as window dressing for warlordism initiatives toward provincial autonomy or federalism, including efforts to formalize provincial constitutions. A convinced federalist, however, might interpret their pejorative and indiscriminate use of "warlord" and "feudal" as rationalization for their unease with provincial autonomy, self-government, and federalism.

A provocative sample of provincial patriotism comes from Mao Zedong, who would become the greatest centralizer in all Chinese history. As a young man in Hunan in 1920 and not yet a Communist, he campaigned for a provincial constitution. Arguing against the idea that large countries could better defend themselves against imperialist aggression, he asserted that, to the contrary, China would fare better if divided into a number of self-governing countries, from which at some future time a federation might naturally result.

What about Hunan? As for this Hunan of ours, every one of its 30 million people must wake up right now. There is no other way for the people of

Hunan. The only method for us is to pursue self-determination and self-government and create a "Republic of Hunan" on the territory of Hunan. I have thought it over time and again, and I have come to realize that only by so doing can we save Hunan, save China, and stand hand in hand with all the liberated nations of the earth. If the people of Hunan themselves lack the determination and courage to build Hunan into a country, then in the end there will be no hope for Hunan.[31]

In this passage Mao slips effortlessly from province to China to the international arena and then back to province, without appearing to change the subject or the definition of the problem. At the time, the field of play for nationalism and the proper focus of patriotic energy and devotion were open to debate. Much of the debate, however, was soon cut off by the energetic construction of a centralizing ideology by the revolutionary parties. Advocates of a decentralized federal polity either abandoned the position, like Mao Zedong, or were politically marginalized, like Chen Jiongming, the reformer and "warlord" of Guangdong Province, who fell out with Sun Yat-sen over this issue in 1922.

The May Fourth Movement and the People

Someone tracking progress on the "three unavoidable tasks" specified by Liang Qichao in the 1900 quotation that begins this chapter—challenging China's two thousand–year-old tradition, overcoming the backwardness of the masses, and confronting foreign aggression—would have had hopes raised only to see them repeatedly dashed. China's political traditions had indeed been challenged by both constitutionalists and revolutionaries, and the monarchy had been exchanged for a republic. Yet the fledgling public school system and the modern press served only an elite. The mass of the people were unreached and "unenlightened." And, despite patriotic protests, foreign intrusions into China had not been stemmed. On the contrary, the imperialists had abetted the removal of Outer Mongolia and Tibet from Beijing's hegemony at the time of the 1911 revolution, had secured more railway concessions, and had imposed foreign management on China's official salt monopoly—an important source of government revenue. Yuan's dictatorship had succumbed to most of Japan's Twenty-one Demands in 1915, and his successors in Beijing were even more vulnerable to foreign manipulation. Although the country had escaped the division into colonies that threatened at the end of the nineteenth century, the recovery of dignity and autonomy remained a distant prospect.

In this context prominent intellectuals again faulted the tradition and launched a full attack. This time, however, instead of political structures, they targeted social values and social practice and judged Chinese culture culpable. In 1915 Chen Duxiu, soon to be dean of letters at Peking University and later first head of the Chinese Communist Party, sounded the keynote:

All men are equal. Each has his right to be independent, but absolutely no right to enslave others nor any obligation to make himself servile . . . For once the independent personality is recognized, all matters of conduct, all rights and privileges, and all belief should be left to the natural ability of each person; there is definitely no reason why one should blindly follow others. On the other hand, loyalty, filial piety, chastity and righteousness are a slavish morality . . .

Now our country still has not awakened from its long dream, and isolates itself by going down the old rut . . . All our traditional ethics, law, scholarship, rites and customs are survivals of feudalism.[32]

At issue, in other words, were the inscribed values of the old order, summed up as Confucianism. The new cultural critique attracted the attention of educated classes across the country and became a powerful tide of thought—the intellectual component of what became known as the May Fourth Movement. It called for the use of the vernacular language to replace the classical in serious written discourse, for realism in literature, and for concern with social problems. It decried the Chinese family as a stifling institution. It spoke predominantly in the tones of liberalism, and evoked the purgatives of "science and democracy" as the cure for what ailed the Chinese.

Disparagement of one aspect or another of Chinese society, including complaints about the family system and the special oppressions of women, had been appearing since at least the end of the nineteenth century. The intellectual attack of the late 1910s, therefore, was a summation of critiques of old ways. The May Fourth climax, however, was a more total rejection of the past. Its openness to foreign ideas—whether anarchist or liberal, socialist or individualist—was less cautious, more enthusiastic. Its appeal extended to an enlarged population of students at the secondary and university level.

The extraordinary ferment turned political with an incident that gave to the mobilizations of the preceding and subsequent years the name of the May Fourth Movement. The background was that the Allied leaders, meeting in Paris in 1919, left in Japanese hands the special position in China's Shandong Province that Germany had acquired in the 1890s but that Japan had seized during World War I. Some Chinese officials had secretly committed their government to accepting Japan's claims in Shandong for considerations that looked like bribes. When word of the Allied decision reached Beijing, students marched, attacked the residences and persons of Chinese officials suspected of conspiring with Japan on the matter, and were arrested in some numbers. The day was May 4, 1919.

Demonstrations and arrests continued for several weeks, spreading to other Chinese cities. Students took the lead, working with different elements of the population, notably educational leaders, shopkeepers, and, especially in Shanghai, workers. The resulting coalitions organized various activities—school strikes, boycotts of Japanese goods, street corner speeches, dramatic performances, commercial and industrial strikes, and petitions to the government calling for release of imprisoned students and for rejection of the Allied agreements in Paris. In June, arrested students were released and the government announced that China would not sign the peace treaty. Nevertheless, Japan was still in possession of the former German holdings, and the warlord-dominated government persisted in Beijing. Only a few compromised officials were dismissed.

Although the surrounding intellectual ferment might seem a quite different phenomenon from this patriotic political moment in 1919, many at the time felt them to be intimately linked. Certainly Chen Duxiu's exhortation to independence of mind, for example, helped prepare the way for protest against constituted authority. Chen himself entered the struggle in 1919 and was arrested while distributing leaflets. The intellectuals who had led the attack on the tradition became advisers and mentors to the radical students. The connection, then, was partly inspirational and personal.

There were also conceptual links: political reinvigoration and cultural transformation shared an agenda. The demonstrations of 1919 were directed against the two antagonists of warlordism (embodied in traitorous officials) and imperialism (in this instance, Japan, supported by the Allied powers). These domestic and foreign forces became a single enemy through the corruption by Japan of a Chinese government dominated by warlords. In the thinking of the time, the domestic component—warlordism—was an expression of China's social and cultural backwardness, that is, of the "feudalism" of Chen Duxiu's critique. In this way, the demonstrations of 1919 and the intellectual movement were a common project. The May Fourth Movement, broadly understood, joined cultural revolution and nationalism as parts to a whole.

Not all were sympathetic to this combination, then or subsequently. To cultural conservatives it even seemed contradictory: how else could a worthy Chinese nation be constructed than by drawing upon its great cultural heritage? Nonetheless, the moment left a legacy for later decades. The image of militant marching students, representing the highest aspirations of the country, was particularly indelible.[33]

The May Fourth Movement spoke to another preoccupation of those devoted to national construction: the quality of the Chinese people. When Liang Qichao wrote in 1900 of the need to fight "the habits and inertia of 400 million illiterates," he was highlighting what he and others saw as the benighted backwardness of China's masses. In his essays of the time, Liang dwelt on the servility, passivity, stupidity, mendacity, and cowardice of the Chinese.[34] Initially looking to "liberty" to remedy these deficiencies, he came to doubt that full representative government would be viable under Chinese conditions and talked of intermediary regimes of "enlightened despotism."[35] Hesitation about democracy in the face of the perceived "ignorance" and "superstition" of the mass of the Chinese people was common among politicians and political thinkers.[36] Even the revolutionary Sun Yat-sen applied the metaphor of "a sheet of loose sand" to the Chinese people, in disparagement of their readiness for self-rule. His revolutionary program provided for a period of transition ("tutelage") while the people were readied for democracy. He faulted the rush to parliamentarianism after the 1911 revolution.

Prominent May Fourth Movement intellectuals, too, were unsparing in their criticism of "the habits and inertia" of the populace. It followed from their scathing view of the tradition that, after so many centuries of immersion in Confucian society, the people would be morally and psychologically stunted. Critics charged these intellectuals with reproducing the belittlement of Chinese national character common among foreigners.[37] Lu Xun, the eminent May Fourth writer and pioneer in China's literary revolution, may indeed have drawn from foreign missionary discourse on "Chinese characteristics" when, in his famous novella "The True Story of Ah Q," he pilloried Chinese self-delusion, willing victimization, passivity, and resignation.[38] Whatever their sources, such discouraging portraits of the human raw material for nationhood provided no grounds for easy optimism about China's emancipatory future.

Just as nationalism, in its assertions of shared identities between state and people, led to a newly critical stance toward the Qing (and subsequent governments), it also required a fresh look at the people. When intellectuals measured the Chinese masses against their new role as citizens—integral and active parts of the nation-state—they tended to judge the people inadequate, another impediment to China's fulfilling its modern destiny.

Yet there were other possibilities and other voices emerging from the May Fourth experience. Shanghai's workers had shown their patriotism in 1919 with political strikes in support of the marching students. Guided at first by ideas of anarcho-syndicalism, intellectuals took notice.[39] Li Dazhao, a leading May Fourth intellectual and later a founder of the Chinese Communist Party, called for "uniting with the laboring classes" and urged urban youth to carry ideas of liberation to the peasant villages in order to help dissolve the encrustation of centuries of oppression and ignorance.[40] Mao Zedong in Hunan, following the urban demonstrations of 1919 and before any commitment to Marxism, wrote a rousing appeal for a cross-class reform coalition. Acknowledging the issue of the Chinese people's capacity for collective action, he optimistically concluded that a corner had been turned and the people were ready:

> Our Chinese people possess great inherent capacities! . . . I venture to make a singular assertion: one day, the reform of the Chinese people will be more profound than that of any other people, and the society of the Chinese people will be more radiant than that of any other people . . . Our golden age, our age of glory and splendor, lies before us![41]

In the next decades, social mobilization on behalf of revolution would occupy a central place in Chinese politics. The issue of the people's backwardness, however, was not fully laid to rest. Some post-Mao intellectuals have questioned whether the Communist-led revolution based on peasant energies might not have absorbed what was retrograde in Chinese society instead of fully transforming it. Even the vast increase in popular literacy achieved in the postrevolutionary years did not resolve concerns about "feudal" contaminants in the populace. The persistence of these problems on the Chinese agenda underlines the cogency of Liang Qichao's call to broad-mindedness and courage at the beginning of the century.

Yet the twentieth century was certainly a time of profound transformation. The first two decades of the century contributed a great deal to putting the country on new tracks. The reforms of the last decade of Qing rule, the revolution of 1911, and the May Fourth Movement were major moments of both destruction and construction. The reforms displaced key parts of the inherited system of government, even before the last dynasty was toppled. A start was made in replacing them with institutions that had been developed out of previous reforms in the West or Japan, some of which, such as a school system and representative institutions, implied a new relationship between state and people. The 1911 revolution extended these changes to ending the monarchy, and released a flood of political and social experiments. The new republican order, however, could not consolidate itself. Differences about the desirability of the new liberalism and a decentralized polity soon led to further conflicts. President Yuan Shikai in 1913 and 1914 brutally suppressed these tendencies and imposed a dictatorship. Yuan's conservative and despotic ways and his monarchical ambitions, in turn, ignited political opposition and, more significantly, a ruthless questioning of China's social and cultural inheritances. In the May Fourth Movement at the end of the second decade of the century, patriotism and cultural revolution interacted to set a more radical agenda for the country.

Selected Readings

Bailey, Paul F. *Reform the People: Changing Attitudes towards Popular Education in Early Twentieth-Century China.* Vancouver: University of British Columbia Press, 1990.

Bergère, Marie-Claire. *Sun Yat-sen.* Stanford: Stanford University Press, 1998.

Chang, Hao. *Liang Ch'i-ch'ao and Intellectual Transition in China, 1890–1907.* Cambridge, Mass.: Harvard University Press, 1971.

Chang, P'eng-yüan. "The Constitutionalists." In *China in Revolution: The First Phase, 1900–1913,* ed. Mary Clabaugh Wright. New Haven: Yale University Press, 1968.

Chen, Leslie H. "Chen Jiongming (1878–1933) and the Chinese Federalist Movement." *Republican China* 17, no. 1 (November 1991): 21–37.

Chen Duxiu. "Call to Youth." In Ssu-yü Teng and John K. Fairbank, *China's Response to the West: A Documentary Survey, 1939–1923.* Cambridge, Mass.: Harvard University Press, 1954.

Dikötter, Frank. *The Discourse of Race in Modern China.* Stanford: Stanford University Press, 1992.

Dirlik, Arif. *Anarchism in the Chinese Revolution.* Berkeley: University of California Press, 1991.

——— *The Origins of Chinese Communism*. New York: Oxford University Press, 1989.

Duara, Presenjit. *Rescuing History from the Nation: Questioning Narratives of Modern China*. Chicago: University of Chicago Press, 1995.

Esherick, Joseph W. *The Origins of the Boxer Uprising*. Berkeley: University of California Press, 1987.

——— *Reform and Revolution in China: The 1911 Revolution in Hunan and Hubei*. Berkeley: University of California Press, 1976.

Fincher, John H. *Chinese Democracy: The Self-Government Movement in Local, Provincial, and National Politics, 1905–1914*. Canberra: Australian National University Press, 1981.

Fitzgerald, John. *Awakening China: Politics, Culture, and Class in the Nationalist Revolution*. Stanford: Stanford University Press, 1996.

Fogel, Joshua A., and Peter G. Zarrow, eds. *Imagining the People: Chinese Intellectuals and the Concept of Citizenship, 1890–1920*. Armonk, N.Y.: M. E. Sharpe, 1997.

Fung, Edmund. *The Military Dimension of the Chinese Revolution*. Vancouver: University of British Columbia Press, 1980.

Gasster, Michael. *Chinese Intellectuals and the Revolution of 1911: The Birth of Modern Chinese Radicalism*. Seattle: University of Washington Press, 1969.

Gillin, Donald G. *Warlord: Yen Hsi-shan in Shansi Province, 1911–1949*. Stanford: Stanford University Press, 1967.

Harrell, Paula. *Sowing the Seeds of Change: Chinese Students, Japanese Teachers, 1895–1905*. Stanford: Stanford University Press, 1992.

Hsieh, Winston. "The Ideas and Ideals of a Warlord: Ch'en Chiung-ming (1878–1933)." *Papers on China* (Cambridge, Mass.: East Asia Research Center, Harvard University), vol. 16 (1962): 198–252.

Judge, Joan. *Print and Politics: "Shibao" and the Culture of Reform in Late Qing China*. Stanford: Stanford University Press, 1996.

Krebs, Edward S. *Shifu, Soul of Chinese Anarchism*. Lanham, Md.: Rowan and Littlefield, 1998.

Laitinen, Kauko. *Chinese Nationalism in the Late Qing Dynasty: Zhang Binglin as an Anti-Manchu Propagandist*. London: Curzon Press, 1990.

Lary, Diana. *Region and Nation: The Kwangsi Clique in Chinese Politics, 1925–1937*. London: Cambridge University Press, 1974.

Levich, Eugene William. *The Kwangsi Way in Kuomintang China*. Armonk, N.Y.: M. E. Sharpe, 1993.

Liang Qichao. *Yinbingshi wenji* (Collected essays from the Ice Drinker's Studio). 16 vols. Taibei: Taiwan Zhonghua shuqu, 1960.

Liu, Lydia H. *Translingual Practice: Literature, National Culture, and Translated Modernity: China, 1900–1937*. Stanford: Stanford University Press, 1995.

MacKinnon, Stephen R. *Power and Politics in Late Imperial China: Yuan Shi-kai in Beijing and Tianjin, 1901–1908*. Berkeley: University of California Press, 1980.

McCord, Edward A. *The Power of the Gun: The Emergence of Modern Chinese Warlordism*. Berkeley: University of California Press, 1993.

Meisner, Maurice. *Li Ta-chao and the Origins of Chinese Marxism.* Cambridge, Mass.: Harvard University Press, 1967.

Min Tu-ki. *National Polity and Local Power: The Transformation of Late Imperial China.* Cambridge, Mass.: Council on East Asian Studies, Harvard University, 1989.

Nathan, Andrew. *Chinese Democracy.* Berkeley: University of California Press, 1985.

Pusey, James. *China and Charles Darwin.* Cambridge, Mass.: Harvard University Press, 1983.

Rankin, Mary Backus. *Elite Activism and Political Transformation in China: Zhejiang Province, 1865–1911.* Stanford: Stanford University Press, 1986.

Reynolds, Douglas R. *China, 1898–1912: The Xinzheng Revolution and Japan.* Cambridge, Mass.: Council on East Asian Studies, Harvard University, 1993.

Schiffrin, Harold Z. "The Enigma of Sun Yat-sen." In *China in Revolution: The First Phase, 1900–1913,* ed. Mary Clabaugh Wright. New Haven: Yale University Press, 1968.

Schiffrin, Harold, and Eto Shinkichi, eds. *China's Republican Revolution.* Tokyo: University of Tokyo Press, 1994.

Schoppa, R. Keith. *Chinese Elites and Political Change: Zhejiang Province in the Early Twentieth Century.* Cambridge, Mass.: Harvard University Press, 1982.

——— "Province and Nation: The Chekiang Provincial Autonomy Movement, 1917–1927." *Journal of Asian Studies* 36, no. 4 (August 1977): 661–674.

Schram, Stuart R., ed. *Mao's Road to Power: Revolutionary Writings, 1912–1949.* Vol. 1. *The Pre-Marxist Period, 1912–1920.* Armonk, N.Y.: M. E. Sharpe, 1992.

Schrecker, John. *The Chinese Revolution in Historical Perspective.* New York: Praeger, 1991.

Schwarcz, Vera. *The Chinese Enlightenment: Intellectuals and the Legacy of the May Fourth Movement of 1919.* Berkeley: University of California Press, 1986.

Sutton, Donald. *Provincial Militarism and the Chinese Republic: The Yunnan Army, 1905–1925.* Ann Arbor: University of Michigan Press, 1980.

Tang, Xiaobing. *Global Space and the Nationalist Discourse of Modernity: The Historical Thinking of Liang Qichao.* Stanford: Stanford University Press, 1996.

Thompson, Roger R. *China's Local Councils in the Age of Constitutional Reform, 1898–1911.* Cambridge, Mass.: Council on East Asian Studies, Harvard University, 1995.

Tsou Jung (Zou Rong). *The Revolutionary Army: A Chinese Nationalist Tract of 1903.* Trans. John Lust. The Hague: Mouton, 1968.

Wasserstrom, Jeffrey N. *Student Protests in Twentieth-Century China: The View from Shanghai.* Stanford: Stanford University Press, 1991.

Young, Ernest P. "Politics in the Aftermath of Revolution: The Era of Yuan Shih-k'ai, 1912–1916." In *Cambridge History of China,* vol. 12, ed. John K. Fairbank. Cambridge: Cambridge University Press, 1983.

——— *The Presidency of Yuan Shih-k'ai: Liberalism and Dictatorship in Early Republican China.* Ann Arbor: University of Michigan Press, 1977.

——— "Problems of a Late Ch'ing Revolutionary: Ch'en T'ien-hua." In *Revolutionary Leaders of Modern China,* ed. Chün-tu Hsüeh. New York: Oxford University Press, 1971.

———— "The Reformer as a Conspirator: Liang Ch'i-ch'ao and the 1911 Revolution." In *Approaches to Modern Chinese History,* ed. Albert Feuerwerker et al. Berkeley: University of California Press, 1967.

Zarrow, Peter G. *Anarchism and Chinese Political Culture.* New York: Columbia University Press, 1991.

CHAPTER 7

The Nationalist Regime and
the Chinese Party-State, 1928–1958

WILLIAM C. KIRBY

When the People's Republic of China (PRC) was inaugurated by the Chinese Communist Party (CCP) in 1949, it offered "liberation" from the past. There were few specifics about the nature of the state that Mao Zedong and his colleagues were founding. China was to practice something called New Democracy, without ever having experienced the old, "bourgeois" variant. Yet the Chinese Communist Party was to rule in coalition with China's small, officially designated "democratic" parties, thereby confirming its own nondemocratic nature. Meanwhile, China was divided into military commanderies in a manner more fitting to the early stages of a dynastic transition than to a Communist revolution. Mostly the new People's Republic of China was simply new: "New China" *(xin Zhongguo)*. It defined itself by what had come before: "Old China." Politically, this meant the total repudiation of the dictatorship of the Nationalist party-state that had immediately preceded it.

In practical political terms, this repudiation was extraordinarily successful. Like the Qing after 1912, the Nationalists disappeared as a political force on the mainland virtually overnight. Whatever the cause—recent memories of Nationalist corruption, incompetence, or "anti-counterrevolutionary" terror in the PRC's first years, or all three—the rapid and thorough delegitimization of the predecessor regime was surely an important component of the new government's strong grasp on nationwide power.

Yet from the historian's perspective the Nationalist state did not disappear so quickly or completely. It was an essential, if unacknowledged, foundation of the Communist party-state, which inherited concepts, institutions, and policies that had been part of Chinese political life for nearly three decades. It would survive to lead Taiwan to prosperity and—in a final transformation that is beyond the scope of this discussion—electoral democracy. In the Nationalist regime of the 1920s, 1930s, and 1940s, we find the roots of both contemporary Chinese regimes.

For all Chinese concerned with politics in the republican era, the fundamental questions were both simple and daunting: What political form, what kind of economy and society, what relationship between state and society would replace those that had distinguished the old empire? The Qing, or Manchu, empire had conquered China in 1644 and then built upon—in some areas improved upon—a two thousand–year-old imperial tradition. Although it passed unlamented from the political scene in 1912, its achievements in conquest, government, and civilization had made it one of the most powerful and sophisticated states in world history.

As to what would follow it, as Ernest Young (Chapter 6) and Keith Schoppa (Chapter 8) show, there has been no shortage of answers in our century of experimentation. Within China, as Schoppa suggests, its twentieth-century revolutions were in part a search for social cohesion. In external relations, the states that emerged from revolution had grander ambitions still. They sought to defend the far-flung borders that the Chinese Republic inherited from the Great Qing, to regain the foreign "concessions" and privileges that had been wrested from the Manchus, and to become a full, indeed major, participant in the affairs of nations.

This nationalist agenda helped to propel the Guomindang (GMD), or Nationalist Party, to power in 1927. As it strove to reunify the nation and to defend its sovereignty, it undertook domestic initiatives unlike those of any Chinese government before it. Its leaders aimed to develop the national economy at a furious pace, summoning the resources of modern science and technology quite literally to "engineer" a new China. To these ends the Nationalist regime endeavored to mobilize, industrialize, militarize, and above all nationalize the resources of the nation. It attempted all this through a revolutionary political construct, the party-state, which is the focus of this essay.

Birth of the Chinese Party-State

The question of postimperial China's political form was answered by Sun Yat-sen in 1924, when he reorganized his Guomindang as a Leninist party, including in it the young Communist Party, which had been founded in 1921. This he did on the basis of Soviet advice, and in anticipation of assistance from the "General Staff of the World Revolution,"[1] the Soviet-led

Communist International, or Comintern. Even before the Comintern catalyzed, energized, and reorganized the Guomindang, it had actually founded the Chinese Communist Party,[2] which would not have existed without it. But if, as Hans van de Ven has suggested, the CCP was not truly a Leninist organization until 1927,[3] then the Guomindang must be considered China's first Leninist party, adapting both the political and military lessons of the Soviet experience. Indeed, nothing was more Bolshevik than the splitting and "purification" of the party in April 1927 as the Guomindang purged its Communist allies and went on to establish China's first party-state.

Although Sun Yat-sen had died in 1925, his principle of *yi dang zhi guo* (government by the party) meant that China under Nationalist rule would not be a parliamentary republic, like the first short-lived post-Qing regime; nor would it be a presidential regime on the model of Yuan Shikai's reign. It would be a party-state, that is, a *one*-party state. A new national flag was modeled on the party banner. A stirring national anthem set to new music the hymn of "our party." The Nationalist Party (Guomindang) committed itself to "tutor" both the National Government *(Guomin zhengfu)* and the nation at large until China was prepared to enter an era of constitutional democracy. A parallel system of party and state organizations was set up nationwide, from the central government down to the provinces. Moreover, the party procreated its "cells" within state administrative organs. In theory, the government existed to execute the policies dictated by the party.[4]

The party-state thus became the central arena of Chinese politics. When the National Government was formally established in 1928, the Guomindang was the ruling party *(zhengdang)*. All other political parties were banned. "Tutelage" was to last six years. For Chinese under Guomindang rule on the mainland and on Taiwan, it lasted sixty. And when the Guomindang was ousted from the mainland in 1949, it was replaced by the other Chinese party-state, that of the resurgent Communists, in a continuation—indeed, an intensification—of *zhengdang* political culture that has survived until the present day.

The Marxist scholar Su Shaozhi has used non-Marxist terminology to describe this form: "party-cracy with Chinese characteristics." Its main features, he argues, included the centralizing tendency of Leninist political direction (including orchestrated mass mobilization), the relentless politicization of public life, a high degree of militarization, and a central role for a leading political idol, or leadership cult.[5]

Certainly Guomindang rule presumed centralization: an extraordinary number of party and government institutions founded after 1927–28 began with the term *zhongyang*, or "central." The Central Executive Committee managed the Central Party Office *(Zhongyang dangbu)*, which oversaw party and state, communicating to China and the world through the *Central Daily News (Zhongyang Ribao)*. Students studied at the Central University *(Zhongyang daxue)*, while scholars advised the government from the Central Research Institute *(Zhongyang yanjiuyuan)*, better known abroad as the Academia Sinica. There was a Central Legislative Council, Central Military Academy, Central Organization Department, Central Planning Board, Central Political Academy, Central Statistical Bureau, Central Supervisory Committee, Central Training Corps, and on and on.[6] This was a regime with ambitions for overpowering control.

For this the ruling party was supposed to be the essential instrument. The Guomindang adopted the Leninist principles of "democratic centralism," in which central party leaders commanded a nationwide hierarchy of party organizations. Political power was concentrated in a small group of one to two dozen figures, normally members of the Political Council of the party Central Executive Committee. The highest-ranking party members served on the standing committees of these bodies and were often in charge of powerful party committees, such as the Organization Department, which controlled party appointments and patronage. Such individuals also held leading government positions. Even the highest organs of the government were subordinate to party rule.

The party existed not only to lead the government but also to remake the people. The "party-ization" *(danghua)* of cultural and political life was taken very seriously even before the establishment of the Nanjing government in 1928: the GMD-controlled Sun Yat-sen University in Canton, for example, was "purified" of the politically incorrect by its Office of Political Education as early as 1926.[7] The party's cultural role extended further in the first decade of Nationalist rule, as evidenced in the growth of press and film censorship and the ubiquity of weekly political study meetings in schools, businesses, and government offices. As a self-styled "revolutionary" party, the GMD aimed to revolutionize public conduct by a revolution in morality, to give "new life" to an ancient people. Chiang Kai-shek's New Life Movement of the mid-1930s was a nationwide educational campaign that linked the cultural virtues of propriety, justice, integrity, and self-respect with the military discipline its followers believed was needed in a modern citizenry. The aim of all this was not to create the Chinese equivalent of the New Soviet

Man, but rather to discipline an undisciplined populace, to give it a sense of obligation to the nation. This was the Chinese party-state's first crack at cultural revolution.

The party-state was also a military state. It seized power, and when necessary held it, by force. In 1926–27, the Nationalists conquered China south of the Yangzi and tried to extend military control over the rest. The chairman of the Military Affairs Commission (normally also the party chief), not the head of government, was invariably the most powerful man in the realm. Military expenditures accounted for at least half of the government budget in *every* year of Nationalist rule of the mainland. Throughout the Nationalist period, China had more men under arms than any other nation on earth. And those outside the military—the common man rallied to "new life"— were to be militarized as well *(junshihua)* in their outlook and deportment.

The party-state had a Leader. The formal titles given first to Sun Yat-sen, the "General Manager," or *zongli,* to Chiang Kai-shek, the "General Director," or *zongcai* of the Guomindang, or for that matter to Mao Zedong as Communist Party "Chairman" *(zhuxi),* hardly capture the spirit and scope of their domination over their followers. Slighting the "democratic" aspect of democratic centralism, the Guomindang (like the Communist Party after it) was led by a series of leadership cliques that are perhaps understood better as conspiratorial brotherhoods rather than as political factions. All were bound to a central individual. In the case of Sun Yat-sen's leadership, this was true even after death: when the *zongli* passed prematurely from this world in 1925, GMD elders decreed that all party meetings thereafter would begin with members standing for the reading of the Leader's Testament.[8] To his closest circle, Chiang Kai-shek was known less as *zongcai* than as *lingshou,* or Leader with a capital *L.* These were Leaders in a reverential, charismatic, and perhaps fearsome sense, at least to their immediate followers. Whether as a continuation of monarchical political culture or as an example of Soviet and fascist influence, the Chinese party-state demanded a single head, a *yuanshou*—as the term *Führer* used to be translated into Chinese—and always found one.

Although these traits of the Chinese party-state would endure, none of them automatically defined the policies or priorities of a regime. As noted earlier, the party-state came into existence with two overriding and interrelated missions: in external relations to defend China's sovereignty and reassert China's importance in an unstable world; and internally to *jianguo,* literally, to build the nation, or as the term was officially translated, to "reconstruct" a powerful industrial China. Having won its revolutionary wars and attained international recognition as the government of all China, the early Nationalist regime devoted its first years to China's industrial transformation.

Engineering China: The Developmental State, 1927–1933

Although the political dominance of the Leninist party was unchallengeable, it was not by itself sufficient to govern, let alone to "reconstruct" the country. Nor could it alone unify the nation militarily or defend its borders. For the latter goal it needed a strong military. For the former it needed a professional civilian elite in government committed to the physical transformation of China.

After 1927 this was the National Government of China. No one can say that it had unambitious goals. It planned a gleaming capital rising out of the mud alleys of Nanjing, a city that had been destroyed not once but twice in the previous century. Its cities would be industrialized, the countryside electrified, and the provinces joined by networks of railroads, motorways, and—most exciting of all—air routes to get the "stagnant race" of Chinese (Sun Yat-sen's phrase)[9] on the move. The mission of modern government was to transform China's landscape and to plan China's future "scientifically" in cooperation with advanced industrial nations.

To some degree this transformation had already begun in the 1910s, when China experienced what Thomas Rawski has called a "dynamic and robust"[10] industrial boom, particularly in light and consumer industries, as European competition vanished during the First World War. By the early 1920s, China's greatest cities (Shanghai, Beijing, and Canton) were engaging in rudimentary urban planning. Connecting at least some of these cities was an embryonic rail network, created with foreign capital. The National Government arrived with an agenda to do more. Its late leader, Sun Yat-sen, had proposed a "second industrial revolution" in which 100,000 miles of rail would be laid, the Yangzi tamed and its Three Gorges dammed, and automobiles manufactured so inexpensively that "everyone who wishes it, may have one."[11]

Sun Yat-sen's *Industrial Plan (Shiye Jihua)*, published first in English as *The International Development of China* six years before the establishment of the Nationalist regime, was the first attempt to plot out the integrated economic development of modern China. It remains the most audacious and—even today, many three-, four-, five-, and ten-year plans later—the most memorable of national development programs. On the broadest level, Sun's faith that international capital could be mobilized to construct Chinese socialism would be shared widely by later Nationalist and Communist leaders.[12]

Sun's more concrete plans also left their mark. For example, his sketch of a national Chinese rail network, which emphasized political unity (for example, linking provincial capitals) over economic relationships, provided the framework for Nationalist and, to an even greater degree, early Communist routing plans.[13] His two-paragraph proposal to "improve the upper Yangzi"[14] with an enormous dam spawned seventy-five years of effort and debate until its construction finally began in 1994. Revered by his disciples as the nation's founding father, or Guofu, Sun was more precisely the father of the Chinese developmental state, the high priest in China of the secular religion that James Scott has termed "authoritarian high modernism."[15]

The academies, commissions, and ministries created to reconstruct China did much to define the purpose of the new party-state. The state would be the leading agent of economic development and industrialization. First in the Nationalist and then in the Communist years, economic planning and bureaucratic goal-setting became a national obsession.

The New National Capital

The National Government's transformative ambitions can be discerned in its plans for its seat of government, Nanjing. With a population about one-third of what it had been in early Ming times, when it was last the capital, this sad and frequently ransacked city hardly seemed up to the part. Within a year of the founding of the regime, the Office of Technical Experts for Planning the National Capital had developed a detailed and beautifully illustrated design for a reconstructed Nanjing.[16] The city's boundaries were expanded to house the government and a much larger population. Rail connections were to be enhanced and a huge airport built. Plans were drawn for modern sewage, drinking water, and electric power systems. A new government district of ten square kilometers was to be erected on the site just west of the old Ming palace, south of the Ming tombs and an imposing Sun Yat-sen Mausoleum. At its center would be a modern palace complex, on a north-south axis, dominated at its northern end by a massive Guomindang headquarters (Zhongyang dangbu), an architectural marvel combining features of Beijing's

Temple of Heaven and the U.S. Capitol in Washington, D.C. Fitting the theory of the party-state, the site of the National Government was on a smaller, subservient scale. An Olympic stadium would adorn Wu Tai Mountain. Parks, tree-lined avenues, and electric streetlights in the shape of Chinese lanterns would beautify the downtown. "Obnoxious and dangerous industries" would be located away from the city center, on the opposite bank of the Yangzi. A "comprehensive system of parkways and main arteries" was conceived, dominated by the grand six-lane Sun Yat-sen Road. A "ring boulevard" would encircle the new capital, but not, as later in Communist Beijing, at the expense of the city wall. The wall would be retained, perhaps with the thought—times being what they were—that it might be needed. Nanjing's ring road would run *on top* of the old wall—a republican parkway atop a Ming fortification.[17]

Any visitor to contemporary Nanjing, which again looks more a provincial than a national capital, knows that most of these projects were never built. A few were, in dramatic fashion: Sun Yat-sen Road was bulldozed forty meters wide through the city center in time for Sun's interment in his stately mausoleum in June 1929. Xinjiekou, where Sun Yat-sen Road converged with other main arteries, became the new center of the city. The central buildings of the party-state were located near an old palace—but in rather more modest quarters in the old Taiping palace grounds. And massive numbers of trees were planted: seedlings imported from France would shade a Communist Nanjing.

What matters historically about Nanjing's facelift was that it was *planned* "reconstruction." Nanjing was the first Chinese city to employ comprehensive zoning and planning regulations based on international standards. If Nanjing today can lay claim to being "one of the most beautiful, clean, and well-planned cities in China,"[18] it is thanks in part to the blueprints of Nationalist engineers and public works officials—and perhaps also to the fact that their most pompous schemes were unrealized.

"Reconstruction"

This pattern of grandiose dreams and much less grand achievement marked the National Government throughout its tenure on the mainland. Yet the regime's ambitious planning for the entire country, based on an international technological standard, was relentless. A Reconstruction Ministry (Jianshebu) was created in January 1928, fittingly enough with Sun Yat-sen's son, Sun Ke, as minister. He developed a *fifty-year* plan to construct the railways, harbors, and industries that Sun Yat-sen had envisioned. This work was then taken up by a National Reconstruction Commission *(Jianshe weiyuanhui)*, which focused initially on electrification. It drafted a grandiose Soviet-style plan for lighting up the country. But as in Lenin's Russia, where the unveiling of the national electrification plan in the form of an enormous map dotted with lightbulbs took enough of Moscow's meager power supply that the rest of the city had to be blacked out,[19] the National Reconstruction Commission had its hands full just illuminating the capital city. Coordinated economic development work then fell to a National Economic Council *(Quanguo jingji weiyuanhui)*, with nominal authority over all publicly financed projects for economic development but with particular attention to public health and flood control; finally, in the mid-1930s, it passed to a National Resources Commission *(Ziyuan weiyuanhui)*, charged with exploiting China's mineral and fuel resources and establishing a state-owned heavy industrial sector. These projects had barely begun when the Sino-Japanese War broke out in 1937.

The activities of the National Economic Council (NEC) were considered internationally to be models of economic development. They evolved out of programs of technical and intellectual cooperation with the League of Nations. The League was not a World Bank capable of financing industrial infrastructure. Its work in China was defined by the three main League organizations represented in the founding of the NEC: those for health, economics and finance, and communications and transit. They provided advice, technical training, and (to a small degree) loans for experimental projects. In addition, the League's Committee on Intellectual Cooperation supported educational and scholarly exchanges. As a group, however, these were categories broad enough to support programs of Chinese-foreign cooperation on matters ranging from silkworms to highways to higher education.[20]

The League's economic and finance section was employed by the NEC to promote fundamental reform of sericulture in order to revive one of China's most important export industries. In Japan a centralized system of "scientific breeding control," government subsidy, and export promotion had overcome China's former dominance in the world market and made Japanese silk of a standard quality that was both cheaper and better than the best Zhejiangese. As the Great Depression took hold in the West between 1928 and 1933, exports of the inferior Chinese product fell by two thirds. The National Government had promoted reform in the industry since 1927, and had worked with provincial officials to establish a Commission for the Standardization of Sericulture in Jiangsu and Zhejiang provinces. In 1932 the national and provincial governments worked with the Silk Reform Association of private industrialists to set national quality standards for silk manufacture, with government funding for research, agricultural extension, and inspection. To control a blight affecting Chinese silk larvae and to standardize quality, only silk certified by a Silk Control Bureau could be sold.

The government also intruded into the industry in three new ways: it sprayed with disinfectant the homes used in silk production; it collectivized silkworm maturation in temperature-controlled sheds; and as in Japan it banned privately grown silkworm eggs (eggs grown on government-licensed sericultural farms were to be used instead). While these regulations were highly unpopular with farmers, who made their feelings known in the Zhejiang Silk Riots of 1933, they were highly effective in improving yield and quality in the counties where they were carried out with determination. As Terry M. Weidner has noted, the regulation of the silk industry "went a long way toward righting a troubled industry desperately in need of reform."[21]

The most publicized aspect of the National Economic Council was its cooperation with the League of Nations Engineering Mission to China in flood control and water conservancy. After Yangzi River floods resulted in the deaths of 600,000 Chinese in 1931, the NEC and the League moved toward greater centralization and government control of all aspects of water conservancy. Initial work in flood relief and epidemic prevention (70 percent of deaths were due to disease and starvation) evolved into an integrated approach to national hydraulic engineering under a centralized Water Conservancy Administration, which trained two generations of Chinese hydraulic engineers. Dikes were restored on the Yangzi and its tributaries, and engineering plans were set out for the management of the Huai River Valley.[22]

The most visible result of the NEC's work was in road building. Sun Yat-sen's vision of "one million miles of road built in a very short time as if by a magic wand"[23] did not come to pass, but whereas in 1920 perhaps as little as 100 miles of improved road (theoretically passable by motor vehicle) existed in the entire country outside the foreign concessions, over 40,000 miles had been built by 1932, and 60,000 by 1937. The NEC funded the majority of its road building through provincial Reconstruction Bureaus: in Zhejiang, for example, the Nanjing era saw the construction of a system of all-weather roads "linking every major political and economic center in the province."[24]

And, as in everything it did, the government tried to centralize and standardize. Road engineering standards, road signs, and traffic laws varied enormously from province to province, often from locality to locality. Until 1932 cars licensed in one province could not be driven in another. It was with great fanfare, therefore, when the first multi-lane Chinese "highway," built to the best international standards, opened on October 10, 1932. The Shanghai-Hangzhou Motor Road was part of a seven-province, eleven trunk-line project of about 14,000 miles. Some two hundred automobiles motored that day the seven hours from Shanghai to Hangzhou, some completing the return trip the same day. It was characteristic of the National Government that the road was in fact not quite finished (ready or not, it *had* to open on National Day). Typical, too, were the protests: by farmers who lost their land, and so built a stone wall across the road; and on behalf of pedestrians who were accidentally run down by the minister of finance as his car raced to Hangzhou. Nonetheless, provincial boundaries had been crossed and economic development and political integration had been served: from these standpoints, it was a triumph.[25]

Economic development led by other government agencies and ministries had less ambiguous successes. The Ministry of Finance carried out reform that for the first time gave China a national (and fully convertible) currency. The Ministry of Communications expanded the rail network (adding 50 percent, or 2,300 miles, to China's rail mileage), and introduced civil aviation, linking the major cities on regular schedules. The National Resources Commission surveyed and began the development of oil fields and mines as a means of financing China's first producer industries. The developmental ethos of the center was emulated nationwide in the Reconstruction Bureau (*Jianshe ting*) of every province.

The state's role in education grew steadily in order to promote this developmental agenda. The worldwide reputation of Chinese in science and engineering dates from this period. In 1932 the National Government—here again advised by the League of Nations—restructured higher education to limit enrollment in the humanities and social sciences in favor of science and engineering. From 1931 to 1936, the percentage of students in the fields of science and engineering doubled in government-funded institutions. For the decade of the 1930s as a whole (including the early war years), engineering enrollments trebled. Simultaneously, the numbers of students enrolled in the arts fell by one third and those in law and political science by one half. As Wang Shijie, the minister of education, argued, knowledge was to be "harnessed to produce results in connection with the economic development of the country."[26]

Sun Yat-sen had conceived a national scientific academy in the service of the state. Borrowing serially from British, French, American, and Soviet models of sponsored research, the Academia Sinica became in fact as well as in name the nation's "central research institute" *(Zhongyang yanjiuyuan);* its descendants on the Chinese mainland and Taiwan would play the same role. Every ministry, too, recruited academic expertise into government, favoring top Chinese graduates of domestic or international universities. The ministries of railroads and finance were particularly distinguished for a high degree of technical professionalism. All Nanjing's ministries in the mid-1930s stressed the "scientificization" *(kexuehua)* of administration and the professionalization of civil service.[27]

Specialized bureaucracies emerged in part because professional and scientific associations had preceded them and now signed on to the nation-building project. After the establishment of the National Government, the Chinese Society of Engineers took as its central purpose the development of the engineering industry and the realization of Sun's *Industrial Plan.* Over time the society's work (and indeed the careers of many of its members) would be incorporated in and become indistinguishable from that of the National Resources Commission, which became a form of "national service" for Chinese engineers.

This increasing specialization had potentially powerful implications for the nature of the Chinese party-state. If government officials were to be chosen on the basis of competence rather than political loyalty or service, where would this leave those GMD cadres and officers who had devoted their lives to the party? What was now the purpose of the party in the party-state? The first years of Nationalist rule already witnessed a growing divide, evident in official terminology, between political generalists *(wenguan, zhengwuguan)* and technical or functional specialists *(gongzhi renyuan, shiwu renyuan).*[28] To the degree that the purpose of government was defined as economic development, the propagandists and mobilizers of party activity were hardpressed even to supervise the work of their better-educated, internationally certified colleagues in the various ministries, commissions, and bureaus concerned with "reconstruction." At a lower level, engineers in public enterprises were allowed to pursue their work in isolation from GMD "partyization" campaigns.

Since Sun Yat-sen had intended that party tutelage be temporary, it made sense—as he also prescribed—that China regularize the recruitment of talent into government by returning to and improving on the ideal of the old imperial examination system. Unlike the imperial mandarinate, this would be a technocratic civil service chosen on the basis of standard, rational measures of competence. To that end the Examination Yuan, one of the five equal branches of government proposed by Sun Yat-sen, was created in 1930, with its Ministry of Personnel responsible for reviewing the qualifications of all officials.

Like much of Nationalist developmental planning, however, this effort ended in frustration. What then did it all amount to? While the Nanjing regime may be considered an embryonic "developmental state," no single or coherent developmental strategy existed in its early years, save for the desire (eventually) to realize Sun Yat-sen's plan. China received useful international development advice but—in part because of the worldwide economic depression of the 1930s—very little in foreign investment. Many important domestic social and economic issues, not the least of which was land reform, were never really addressed. Over forty years ago Douglas Paauw summed up, quite accurately, the Nationalist approach as one limited to "some aspects of the technological preconditions for economic growth."[29]

Still, an ethos of optimism existed, not describable or even rational in economic terms, that China could be remade physically by the application of scientific planning and international technology under the leadership of the state. The Nanjing government's very partial success in economic development should not conceal the fact that the purpose and makeup of China's central government had undergone a significant change. The government was responsible for national economic development, and its ministries had to be staffed accordingly.

National defense was another responsibility of government. Here the challenges were even greater. By the end of the 1930s, China was involved in a life-or-death struggle with Japan and engaged in a military-economic mobilization that would transform the modern Chinese "developmental" state into something quite different.

Defending China: The National Security State, 1933–1949

Military agendas were never far removed from the economic plans of the late Qing and early Republic. In retrospect, what is surprising is that they were almost entirely absent as the rationale for Sun Yat-sen's *Industrial Plan* and very understated in early Nanjing-era reconstruction efforts. To be sure, programs for road building, railroad development, and electrification had implicit military dimensions; the concept of a massive hydroelectric power station in the Yangzi Gorges received its first scientific survey under the Defense Planning Commission in 1932. Yet despite continued domestic campaigns against residual militarists, there was an expectation in the first Nanjing years of a gradual demobilization from the incessant warfare and continuous militarization of the early and mid-1920s.

But less than five years after the establishment of the National Government, the Japanese army seized control of China's northeastern provinces and presided over the establishment of the puppet state of Manchuguo in 1932. Perhaps the Japanese militarists did not expect Chinese to fight over what had been, after all, the original homeland of the deposed Manchus, into which Han Chinese settlement had been illegal until the twentieth century. Yet because the loss of Manchuria in 1931–32 was a national humiliation, its recovery became a national obsession. While Nationalist China was in no position then to challenge Japan militarily, it fought on the battlegrounds of economic warfare (boycotts) and international public opinion and gradually began to prepare for the war that broke out in July 1937. That war lasted for eight years and cost the lives of 15 to 20 million Chinese. It was followed almost immediately by a bloody civil war with the Chinese Communists that led to the founding of the People's Republic and the expulsion of the Nationalists from China's mainland.

From 1933 on, the Nationalist regime carried out a gradual but steady remilitarization. In the five years before full-scale war broke out with Japan, domestic warfare, in the form of attacks on the renewed Communist insurgency, increased; eradication of the CCP was declared to be a prerequisite to fighting Japan. Chiang Kai-shek launched a series of "encirclement and extermination" campaigns against the CCP's "soviet republic" in Jiangxi. After victory in that province in 1934, his armies pursued the Communists along their "long march" (more accurately a long retreat) to the less accessible province of Shaanxi, in north-central China. Only the greater threat of war with Japan brought Chiang and the Communists to a temporary truce, in a "second united front" of the two party-states in the mid-1930s.

Foreign relations also became consumed with military matters. The League of Nations, so involved in economic and technical assistance, proved of no help whatsoever in the diplomatic field, as Japan ignored its condemnations and sanctions on the Manchurian issue. Multilateralism in foreign policy gave way to a series of bilateral searches for patrons or allies that could help China confront Japan. An existing German military advisory mission was reorganized and strengthened in 1933–34; it would be followed in turn by Soviet and American missions during the war. The government imported machinery and armaments as well as advisers, at any one time primarily from the nation with which it had the closest military advisory relationship. China channeled foreign investment toward its own war industries, and paid for this through the export of strategically important metals. Thus there developed a certain symbiotic relationship between the war economies of China and of its foreign partners. Above all, China's security needs sparked a search for a military alliance with any nation willing to fight Japan. For the first time, China joined the international system as a full participant in the diplomacy of alliances and alignments that would culminate in global struggle between the Allied and Tripartite powers, better known as World War II.

Domestic economic policy increasingly followed these military imperatives. The establishment of a Central Steel Works in Xiangtan, Hunan, which had been under discussion almost from the start of the Nanjing regime, became the focus of a 1935 three-year plan to develop the industrial capacity for modern warfare. Government planning and resources were devoted to the concept of a defensible military-industrial bastion in the interior provinces of Jiangxi, Hunan, and Sichuan, away from vulnerable coastal regions. Arsenals were modernized and expanded. Construction began on China's first truck and aircraft assembly plants, and the national rail network was expanded to serve this "new economic center."

This remilitarization had political consequences. Without question, the threat of war strengthened authoritarian tendencies in the party-state. It ended any thought of a timely end of GMD tutelage and a transition to constitutional rule. A series of constitutional documents was drafted from 1932 to 1935, each more authoritarian than the last. Ultimately none was adopted. Lloyd Eastman has summed up the prevailing view of GMD leaders: "The people should be sovereign, but should not interfere with the actual governance of the nation."[30] As for the rights of citizens, even Sun Ke, the son of Sun Yat-sen and a political figure in his own right who had been a vocal proponent of constitutionalism, now saw these in a minimalist light: "Freedom is a tool . . . so that [the individual] may strive for society . . . It goes without saying that it should be subject to many forms of restriction."[31]

Such attitudes were reinforced in the 1930s by the growing international prestige of fascism, which was openly admired by the self-styled "Blue Shirt" organizations within the army, who urged Chiang Kai-shek to act like "China's Hitler."

No organized "Chinese fascism" emerged, as the various factions of the regime could not agree on its meaning, let alone on the utility of this European phenomenon for China. But the party-state continued unimpeded by constitutional restraint with Chiang Kai-shek as its indispensable man. He ruled now less as party chief (he would not be anointed *zongcai* until 1938), or as head of government, the position which he resigned in late 1931, than as "Chairman" Chiang, that is, as chairman *(weiyuanzhang)* of the Military Affairs Commission. As such he had full military powers and far-reaching civilian authority. In the many provinces in which the Communists were active, he established "bandit suppression" administrations in which he had full control of government, party, and military authorities. Indeed it frequently appeared that the seat of power was not Nanjing but Nanchang, Wuchang, Chongqing, or wherever Chairman Chiang had his military headquarters. As the army trained to fight internal and external enemies, its work of internal pacification took place in tandem with the expansion and professionalization of the police and secret services.[32] Unofficially but unmistakably, the military was again the third leg on which the party-state stood.

In the government, the promise of the new Examination Yuan and a technocratic civil service was another casualty of the sense of impending crisis in the mid-1930s. The top political and military leadership created a series of ad hoc agencies (some of them secret) to circumvent existing bureaucracies, over which the Examination Yuan had no power. At best, the Ministry of Personnel could exert moral encouragement on behalf of those it examined. While scientific and technical elites continued to serve in government, they served at the whim of the party-state. It was not by examinations but through Chiang Kai-shek's personal recruitment that such Academia Sinica scholars as Jiang Tingfu (T. F. Tsiang) and Weng Wen-hao staffed the famous "Cabinet of Talent" of 1935.

The militarization of economic policy expanded the scope of state planning. Developmental efforts were devoted almost entirely to the creation of a "national defense economy," which was to be entirely state-owned and state-managed. It was the first step toward a "controlled" economy in which private and foreign investment would be regulated according to national priorities. Paradoxically, the autonomy of civilian experts managing this economy—cohabiting, as it were, with party and military for the nation's salvation—could be legitimized on patriotic grounds. It was in any event essential if China were to fight and survive a modern war.

For China, as for all the major participants, World War II reinforced its tendencies toward a stronger state, not least by raising the manpower, revenue, and armaments production needed for war. Manpower was the easiest to mobilize through the mass requisitioning of soldiers and laborers. To pay military costs, taxes were increased on income, consumption, and transit; the land tax, which had been the preserve of provincial governments since 1928, was claimed in 1941 by the central government, which collected it in kind; and the government created state monopolies for tobacco, matches, sugar, and salt. In addition, the state engaged in "compulsory borrowings," especially of grain to feed the armies. Once hostilities broke out, the task of mobilizing the nation for "total war" fell to a new Ministry of Economic Affairs, which included the National Resources Commission and replaced the moribund National Reconstruction Commission and National Economic Council. Charged with the "economic administration of the whole nation," the Ministry of Economic Affairs became "the largest organization dealing with economic administration that China had ever seen."[33] Its prerogatives grew further through the National General Mobilization Act of March 29, 1942, which subjected "every person and every means of production" to government economic control. Above all the ministry oversaw the enormous growth of state enterprises, indeed of state socialism. By 1942 over half of the industry of "free China," that is, the area under direct Nationalist control, was in government hands. By that time the economic agencies associated with the Ministry of Economic Affairs had become the largest bureaucracy in terms of numbers of employees. Even though it ruled but half of its former territory, the National Government grew substantially during the war.

The spreading power of the economic bureaucracy in the wartime state provoked open division between the professional "pragmatists" in government and true-blue Guomindang "ideologists," who resented the "usurpation" of authority by non-party professionals.[34] But at the highest levels, the wartime emergency blurred formal distinctions between party and state, as Chiang Kai-shek's political authority became ever more dictatorial and militarized. Anointed *zongcai* in 1938, with full powers over the party and an unlimited tenure, in his government capacity as chairman of the Military Commission he assumed broad powers "to direct the people of the whole nation for the purpose of national defense."[35] During the war, party and state merged ultimately in the Supreme National Defense Council, which replaced both the Political Council of the GMD Central Executive Committee and, for all practical purposes, the government cabinet. Headed by the *zongcai*, the standing committee of the Supreme National Defense Council brought together the leading figures of party, government, and army. It was inclusive, if not formally representative, of the leading forces in the GMD party-state.[36]

The Nationalist regime's original commitment to economic development and planning found expression after 1940 in a Central Planning Board—also chaired by Chiang Kai-shek—whose task it was to integrate all political, economic, and military activity in comprehensive government plans. Its plans for China's postwar future foresaw continued government controls, growth of state power, and broad militarization of economic development at an even faster pace. The defeat of Japan would not end the need to maintain national sovereignty through military strength. As one of the "great powers" of the Allied coalition, China was to earn its great power status through the development of state enterprises in an economy that was no longer simply "controlled" but fully "planned." While this recalled the faith in scientific planning of the 1920s, the vision of the 1940s foresaw an industrialized, militarized China quite different from that conceived by Sun Yat-sen. While China's postwar five- and ten-year plans, with their detailed designs of thousands of enterprises, transportation networks, and electrical grids,[37] shared the ambitious spirit of Sun's *Industrial Plan*, in substance they more closely resembled the first five-year plan of the People's Republic.

Thus the victory over Japan in August 1945 signaled no demobilization—political, economic, or military—of the hybrid structure of the national security state. In postwar politics, the Nationalists finally promulgated a constitution in 1946–47, but one meant to ensure their monopoly on political power. Political opponents could still be gunned down—as they were in the thousands in Taiwan in the February 28, 1947, "incident"—while Chiang Kai-shek added the title of President of the Republic to his calling card. In economic reconstruction, several thousand engineers, who had been trained in America during the war, returned to lead the postwar national defense economy. Through relentless expropriation and nationalization, particularly of Japanese- and "puppet"-owned enterprises, the state's postwar industrial empire included nearly 70 percent of China's total industrial capital. And in military affairs, the Nationalist armies, far from demobilizing, re-armed for the final showdown with the Communists. In 1946 they started a civil war that they could not finish.

Two Party-States, 1949–1958

Throughout the civil war of 1946–1949, the promise of a "New China" under the leadership of the Chinese Communist Party was linked to the concept of New Democracy. Communism, Mao Zedong and other leaders proclaimed, was a very distant goal. Until it could be realized, the CCP would lead a coalition government of all "democratic" forces. As Mao reported to the party congress of 1945, "throughout the stage of New Democracy China cannot possibly have a one-class dictatorship and a one-party government, and therefore should not attempt it." The New Democratic system would preside over a mixed economy, setting clear limits to state power. New Democracy would continue "for a long time to come."[38]

New Democracy was a useful slogan during the civil war. A few CCP leaders may even have believed in it. But for most, and particularly for Mao Zedong, it was not the "real stuff" for which the party-state was made.[39] It was abandoned in fact well before it was renounced publicly in 1953. Ultimately the Chinese civil war had offered no fundamental choice to the Chinese people, no alternative to the party-state. There occurred instead an exchange of *zhengdang,* or ruling parties, as first the Nationalist and then the Communist dictatorships ensured that there would be no "third way."[40]

In fact, the CCP had already created its party-state, first in its Jiangxi Soviet Republic, and then in the territories ruled from Yan'an. It had all the distinguishing characteristics of "party-cracy" practiced by its Nationalist adversary: the theory of democratic centralism, party tutelage, the centrality of the Leader and the small group of men around him, and the overwhelming militarization of political and economic priorities.

It is no accident that a textbook description of the PRC's formal governing system could just as well be applied to that of Nationalist China.[41] Of course, both parties took directly from the Soviet model. But the commonalities and shared experiences go deeper than that. The CCP was, to be sure, the offspring of the Comintern. But it grew up as a political-economic-military force first by joining and then by confronting the Guomindang, itself transformed by Soviet tutelage. From 1924 to 1927 the Guomindang was its unwitting political mentor, as CCP members joined the GMD in a united front.

Thereafter the CCP matured under the shadow of the Guomindang party-state that sought to exterminate it. It would be unusual if the political, economic, and military culture of the period of Nationalist rule had no influence on the developing CCP party-state. To be more blunt: one did not need to learn directly from the Soviet Union (although the CCP continued to do that, too) to understand the workings of party dictatorship, organized political murder and terror, censorship, statist economic controls, and the militarization of political and civic life. These features were part of the Chinese scene under the Guomindang party-state, and many of them would continue under the relocated GMD regime on Taiwan in its early years. What distinguished the Communist party-state, and indeed ultimately set it apart from its predecessor, was its attempt to take these trends—political, economic, and military—to the most extreme conclusions.

Politics

As a political form, then, the Chinese party-state proved powerful and enduring. It may be correct but also an understatement to see in the CCP's rule, as Robert Bedeski has described it, "a postwar refinement of [Guomindang] political tutelage."[42] But the CCP, unlike the GMD, never promised to end its guardianship. In comparison with the GMD, its political dictatorship was much wider in geographic terms, deeper in its dominance over society, and broader in terms of the powers it arrogated to itself. It was also more relentless in its persecution of its opponents. The Terror of the PRC's first years has never been adequately researched, but it is certain that several million landlords and "counterrevolutionaries," real and imagined, lost their lives.

For its first eight years in power, the ruling group in the CCP party-state was more united internally and even more dependent on its central figure than had been its predecessor. No study of the PRC political system can ignore the overwhelming dominance of Mao Zedong. His position was "the backbone" of the PRC regime. However much his colleagues might disagree with him on policy, they dared not undermine him.[43] Thus his harebrained scheme for sudden economic development, the calamitous "Great Leap Forward" of 1958–1960, was allowed to continue even after senior leaders knew it to be ruinous. Thirty million Chinese perished. For even within a leadership group of hardened revolutionaries, the Chinese Communist Party was inconceivable without Mao Zedong. With their help, Mao became the "great helmsman," the "red sun," whose personality cult knew no bounds: it was even written into the PRC constitution. Although after his death in 1976 the Chinese Communist Party would admit of Mao's "mistakes," the PRC's legitimacy became so entwined with the person of Mao Zedong that more than two decades after his death, no comprehensive critical scholarly inquiry into the disasters of his rule was possible in China.

On Taiwan, Chiang Kai-shek continued his personal rule until his death in 1975, and his family's dominance persisted until his son and successor, Chiang Ching-kuo, died in 1988. The elder Chiang's appreciation for party dictatorship only grew following his expulsion from the mainland. One of the lessons he took from that "great shame" was that the CCP had proved an even better, tighter organization than his GMD. Reasserting the basic principles of Leninist governance in 1950–1952, Chiang carried out a far-reaching reform and purge of the GMD on Taiwan. While he called the new GMD a "democratic" party because it held elections, albeit as the only important legal party, above all it was a revolutionary party. As such it "should strengthen the organization, maintain strict discipline, arouse revolutionary spirit, and accumulate revolutionary strength in order to stage a life-and-death struggle with the Communist bandits."[44]

Both party-states continued the mission of remaking the Chinese people under their control. In the PRC this would culminate with Mao's Cultural Revolution. For the GMD party-state, ruling as a "national" government of which Taiwan was but one province, the cultural front was also central to its politics. The first Nationalist governor of Taiwan wrote even before the island's return to China in 1945 that the political and linguistic "reeducation" of the Taiwanese people—the teaching of Sun Yat-sen's Three People's Principles and the speaking of Mandarin Chinese—was the "most important area" for postwar Taiwan's development.[45] Mirroring the Communist domination of society on the mainland, the GMD in the 1950s "penetrated virtually the entire social fabric" of Taiwan as it refounded the party-state on that island. It penetrated and dominated all important social, educational, and media organizations, ranging from youth groups to trade unions to farmers' associations.[46]

The most striking difference in the political realm between the two party-states in the 1950s was that the GMD's political domination had limits. Outright political dissent was suppressed harshly. Unlike in the People's Republic, however, where early on a relentless politicization permeated private lives, on Taiwan it was possible to remain apolitical, out of the whirlwinds of political campaigns. When Hu Shih, a leading intellectual who relocated to

Taiwan, left his Beijing home on the eve of the Communist takeover, he told
a Nationalist official, "The only reason why liberal elements like us still prefer to string along with you people is that under your regime we at least enjoy the freedom of silence."[47]

Economic Development

Hu Shih's comment would have special meaning in the realm of economic
development by the end of the 1950s. Before then, however, both party-
states married the developmental ambitions of the early Nanjing period to
the national security priorities of the later 1930s and 1940s. Both proposed
enormous programs of economic development, and both skewed state investment to military purposes. Both emphasized central economic planning,
the PRC more totalistically than Taiwan. In agriculture, both went well beyond the pre-1949 state in enacting revolutionary land reforms (albeit in
quite different ways). In either case, their purpose was to finance the state-
led, heavy industrial, import-substituting path to national development that
both still favored. As for industry, the Nationalists had already nationalized
most of it, sparing the Communists no small task. The Nationalist accumulation of state capital was the foundation for the PRC state sector in the same
way that the eighteen state corporations on Taiwan provided the industrial
base of Nationalist rule. The Nationalists even bequeathed to their mainland
foes a model of industrial organization. This was the *danwei,* the comprehensive "work unit" in state enterprises, in which housing, dining, recreation,
and health facilities were provided for engineers and workers alike. Within
its first decade, the PRC would apply this model to all urban Chinese.

   While nationalist economic leaders of the 1940s had talked of "following
the socialist road,"[48] their successors followed that road to its terminus in
Moscow. They engaged in the largest planned transfer of technology in
world history. With 250 industrial projects constructed, thousands of industrial designs transferred, and with 10,000 Soviet specialists visiting China
and over 50,000 Chinese engineers, trainees, and students visiting the Soviet Union, this was at least partial fulfillment of Sun Yat-sen's dream of
China's international development. Beyond this, the Sino-Soviet exchange
was but one part of a larger web of cooperative relationships with the
planned economies of all the "socialist brother countries." Yet even this remarkable relationship had been foreshadowed, if hardly forecast, by a series
of Sino-Soviet agreements in the Nationalist era for joint industrial ventures

and barter-credit exchanges, which were miniature models of what was to follow. Even for the Nationalists, the Soviet Union had been a logical, if not politically compatible, economic partner. And for the 200,000 employees of the Nationalist industrial and planning bureaucracies, almost all of whom remained on the mainland in the service of the PRC, the heyday of Sino-Soviet economic cooperation in the mid-1950s would be, for most, the high point of their careers.

It was also the end of their careers. Where Nationalists and Communists differed fundamentally in the 1950s was in their treatment of the scientific and technological talent that both inherited. On the mainland as on Taiwan, personnel from the pre-1949 bureaucracy formed the core of early economic planning bodies. On both sides of the strait, this personnel continuity contributed to the policy continuity that continued to stress defense-related heavy industrial growth until the late 1950s. And both the PRC and Taiwan faced a set of economic decisions in 1958 that would make that year, much more than 1949, an important divide in the economic and political history of the Chinese party-state.

The comparatively small cadre of economic planners on Taiwan were on that island not so much because of diehard loyalty to the GMD but because they had been assigned there after 1946 to take part in postwar reconstruction plans. They were in place—indeed, could not leave!—when the refugee regime arrived to stay in 1949, and provided an important portion of what the economist Simon Kuznets called the "experience and human capital" needed for Taiwan's subsequent progress.[49] By the late 1950s, it had become clear that the attempt to practice on Taiwan a set of industrial policies designed for the mainland was untenable given Taiwan's size, its meager natural resources, and the free market agenda of its foreign partner and protector, the United States. As in earlier periods of the GMD party-state, economic policies on Taiwan were largely determined by a well-credentialed technocratic elite that still found it possible, if at times distasteful, to serve in the shadow of the GMD dictatorship. Chiang Kai-shek gave planners such as K. Y. Yin and K. T. Li considerable administrative autonomy as they put in place what were, for the time, rather unpopular policies of economic liberalization. The reorientation of 1958–1960 set Taiwan's path toward "export-led" growth and economic "miracle."[50] In time the great success of these policies and the stable stewardship of Taiwan's economy raised the glass ceiling that had kept China's intellectual/technological elite mere servants of the GMD party-state, as several of their members would rise to positions of real eminence within it, Premier Y. S. Sun (Sun Yunxuan) and President Lee Teng-hui (Li Denghui) among them.

That, by contrast, became simply inconceivable on the mainland, particularly after its own economic turning point of the late 1950s. The PRC, too, faced the economic limitations of the national security state and concluded in 1957–58 that even with Soviet aid it could not replicate the successes of its first five-year plan (1953–1957). At the same time it determined for ideological reasons to dispense with the services of the several hundred thousand intellectuals who were found to harbor "rightist" views. In 1958, as Taiwan began to leap outward for economic growth, Mao Zedong began his Great Leap Forward into communism unencumbered by either Nationalist holdovers or Soviet advice. For the first time since the founding of the Nationalist regime, a Chinese government repudiated the services of its most highly trained citizens. The ethos of the early developmental state was now dead, not to be resurrected until the Maoist era was over and "modernization" and "reconstruction" returned to the top of the national agenda.

Lost to the PRC after 1958 was that faith in the transformative power of science and engineering in the service of the state that would continue to mark Taiwan's ruling system well into the 1980s. Lost, too, was an ideal of professionalism *(zhiye zhuyi)* in government that the Nationalists had always espoused, if not practiced, but the CCP would not tolerate. The one realm in which the PRC's technical intelligentsia was permitted to work as professionals, free from political interference, was in building an atomic bomb.[51] Its results after nine years of work—the culmination of the national security state—were visible in the mushroom cloud over Xinjiang on October 16, 1964.

The Military

For the CCP as for the GMD, the military remained an inseparable part of the Chinese party-state. This is no surprise when one recalls that the CCP fought for power for three decades before conquering China. Mao's famous dictum, "Power grows from the barrel of a gun," was the result of being outgunned by Chiang Kai-shek's Guomindang in 1927. The party-state of the Jiangxi Soviet Republic, unlike earlier CCP organizations, was based on its military foundation. Ultimately the CCP would come to national power not by speeches or majority resolutions, nor on the basis of mass mobilization or popular revolution, but by armed rebellion in which hundreds of thousands died. CCP armies decimated Nationalist forces in the Northeast, won a series of major battles in north and central China, and then marched through the south as the Nationalists collapsed and fled. Upon its founding, the new regime ruled through a form of martial law. Soldier-politicians played central roles in CCP and PRC governance in an interlocking directorate; military values crowded out others and became the source of political campaigns.[52] Whereas Chiang Kai-shek had tried to militarize the common man in his New Life Movement of the 1930s, the CCP really did it, as Chinese farmers engaged in the Great Leap were organized into "brigades," which marched in step to their day's work.

For their part the Nationalists did not demilitarize upon decamping to Taiwan. Nationalist Taiwan, too, had to be pacified militarily in the bloody suppression of 1947 before it could be governed successfully. It too would be ruled on the basis of martial law, which was declared when the Nationalist regime retreated to Taiwan in 1949 and which remained formally in effect until 1987. In the years 1950–1958 its military, like the party, would be purged and reformed to create an efficient, loyal, and formidable force capable of defending the island.

It was on the mainland, however, that militarization, like the other central traits of the party-state, would be taken furthest. The history of the CCP, Kenneth Lieberthal has argued, witnessed "an almost unique, symbiotic relationship between the party and the military."[53] The Military Affairs Commission through which Chiang Kai-shek ruled in the 1930s and 1940s was a government body; the PRC military was and is governed by the *Party* Military Affairs Commission that reports to no government authority. Whereas the Nationalist military took oaths to defend the nation, the People's Liberation Army swore to uphold the rule of the Chinese Communist Party. Finally, in the post-Mao PRC, a significant part of the state sector of the economy (no one knows for sure how much) became owned and operated by the military, outside the control of government industrial and planning ministries, until such practices were supposedly stopped in 1999. The military's independence from governmental authority in the PRC was thus also economic: the People's Liberation Army, Incorporated, became a state within the party-state.

Like the Nationalist party-state that preceded it (and the Manchu conquerors that preceded *it*), the PRC was a military conquest regime. Unlike the Manchus and other successful ruling houses in Chinese history, by the end of the twentieth century the CCP conquerors had yet to show that their power could be transferred to civilian political and legal institutions with enduring legitimacy. Civilians could serve the party-state but could not govern separate from it. The Nationalists, by contrast, at least demonstrated an ability to cohabit with several generations of technical and managerial elites, from those who dreamed of physically "reconstructing" China in the 1920s to the more sober-minded authoritarian technocrats who guided Taiwan's economic miracle. But even these elites never exercised political power independent of the party-state and never fundamentally challenged it. Pressures for Taiwan's eventual democratization would come from other quarters. Even after the end of party "tutelage" on Taiwan in 1987, certain habits of the party-state died hard. From an external perspective Taiwan may have democratized, but internally, the Guomindang had not. Only with the emergence of a "reform" movement which split the Guomindang into two factions in the presidential elections of March 2000 did the Guomindang finally lose its position of overwhelming dominance. The victory of the Democratic Progressive Party candidate, Chen Shui-bian, may have signaled the end of the era of the party-state, at least on Taiwan.

On the Chinese mainland, the other party-state still clung to power at the beginning of the twenty-first century. As the twentieth-century successor to the old empire, the Chinese party-state has shown that it can do many things better. It can organize. It can industrialize. It can militarize. And it can terrorize. But unlike the system that disappeared in 1912, it has not yet shown that it can *civilize*. One may use that term in two senses: first, to reestablish a lasting system of *civil* service, and indeed to institutionalize civilian rule, using the great talent of the Chinese people; and, second, to stand for something enduring in human values, for a civilization that goes beyond political control, material development, and martial strength. Perhaps this will be the quest of political structures still unformed, once the Chinese party-state has finally had its day.

Selected Readings

Bergère, Marie-Claire. *Sun Yat-sen.* Trans. Janet Lloyd. Stanford: Stanford University Press, 1998.

Cheek, Timothy, and Tony Saich, eds. *New Perspectives on State Socialism in China.* Armonk, N.Y.: M. E. Sharpe, 1997.

Ch'ien, Tuan-sheng. *The Government and Politics of China, 1912–1949.* Stanford: Stanford University Press, [1950] 1970.

Domes, Jürgen. *Vertagte Revolution: Die Politik der Kuomintang in China, 1923–1937.* Berlin: Walter De Gruyter & Co., 1969.

Eastman, Lloyd E. *The Abortive Revolution: China under Nationalist Rule, 1927–1937.* Cambridge, Mass.: Harvard University Press, 1974.

——— *Seeds of Destruction: Nationalist China in War and Revolution, 1937–1949.* Stanford: Stanford University Press, 1984.

Fitzgerald, John. *Awakening China: Politics, Culture, and Class in the Nationalist Revolution.* Stanford: Stanford University Press, 1996.

Gold, Thomas B. *State and Society in the Taiwan Miracle.* Armonk, N.Y.: M. E. Sharpe, 1986.

Hsiung, James C., and Steven I. Levine, eds. *China's Bitter Victory: The War with Japan, 1937–1945.* New York: M. E. Sharpe, 1992.

Jeans, Roger, ed. *Roads Not Taken: The Struggle of Opposition Parties in Twentieth-Century China.* Boulder, Colo.: Westview, 1992.

Kirby, William. "Engineering China: Birth of the Developmental State, 1928–37." In *Becoming Chinese: Passages to Modernity and Beyond, 1900–1950,* ed. Wen-hsin Yeh. Berkeley: University of California Press, 2000.

——— *Germany and Republican China.* Stanford: Stanford University Press, 1984.

Kuo Heng-yü. *Die Komintern und die chinesische Revolution.* Paderborn: Schöningh, 1979.

Rawski, Thomas G. *Economic Growth in Prewar China.* Berkeley: University of California Press, 1989.

Strauss, Julia C. *Strong Institutions in Weak Polities: State Building in Republican China, 1927–1940.* Oxford: Oxford University Press, 1998.

Sun Yat-sen. *The International Development of China.* New York: Putnam, 1922.

Tien, Hung-mao. *Government and Politics in Kuomintang China, 1927–1937.* Stanford: Stanford University Press, 1972.

van de Ven, Hans J. *From Friend to Comrade: The Founding of the Chinese Communist Party, 1920–1927.* Berkeley: University of California Press, 1991.

Wakeman, Frederic, Jr. *Policing Shanghai, 1927–1937.* Berkeley: University of California Press, 1995.

Wilbur, C. Martin. *Sun Yat-sen, Frustrated Patriot.* New York: Columbia University Press, 1976.

Yeh, Wen-hsin. *The Alienated Academy: Culture and Politics in Republican China, 1919–1937.* Cambridge, Mass.: Council on East Asian Studies, Harvard University, 1990.

CHAPTER **8**

The Search for Social Cohesion in China, 1921–1958

R. KEITH SCHOPPA

Traditional Chinese society was fragmented by particularistic loyalties to family, personal networks, and native-place. Several powerful ideological and political glues, however, had held Chinese state and society together: Confucianism, the state monarchy and bureaucracy, and the common classical language. With their demise in the early twentieth century, social and political fragmentation created a Chinese society that Sun Yat-sen described as a "sheet of loose sand." Rapid modern changes only exacerbated this fragmentation, not just in particular communities, but especially between communities that experienced change at different rates: urban and rural, core and periphery, eastern seaboard and hinterland. As the search for the modern identity of China intensified, the emergence of new social groups marked by their own self-conscious identities—military, youth, women, urban laborers—accentuated the pluralistic nature of early republican society and culture. Even the vaunted values of the May Fourth period—science and democracy—promoted analysis, differentiation, and diversity, not synthesis, similarity, and uniformity. With imperialist powers continuing to hover vulture-like, ready to take advantage of China's weakness, many came to believe that in its fragmented state, China could never fend off, much less compete with, aggressive outsiders.

The problem was, then, to construct a modern state bolstered by institutions and approaches that could engender the cohesion necessary for sociopolitical stability. This chapter focuses on the wide-ranging experimentation with sociopolitical forms and strategies that shaped and drove the Chinese revolution. In it I argue that Chinese policy makers embarked on a multipronged search for the sociopolitical groupings, patterns, and approaches (the means) that might provide the new glue to cohere a nation-state (the end). Like the struggle to define a modern Chinese nation-state itself, this is

238

an account of a search, not of the realization of sociopolitical cohesion. Indeed, along the way, many of the experiments to create that cohesion spawned instead greater fragmentation and disharmony. The period under consideration stretches from 1921, when the first important sociopolitical grouping, the Chinese Communist Party, was founded, to 1958, when the establishment of communes during the Great Leap Forward offered to some the fantasy that the search for social cohesion had at last been realized. Instead that particular experiment led to disarray, chaos, and ultimately the tragedy of the Cultural Revolution.[1] Like any search and experimentation, the revolution was uneven, developing in a myriad of different contexts, with many different actors, patterns, and dynamics.

New Institutions and Approaches: The First Phase

The Nationalist revolution of the 1920s brought onto the public stage mass political parties, new goal-directed collective actors bound together by ideology and personal networks. In 1924 the Guomindang discarded its earlier incarnations to be reborn, with Michael Borodin, the Comintern representative, serving as midwife. Its large ideological umbrella covered progressive intellectuals and students, elements of the bourgeoisie, and stalwarts from the 1911 revolution. While personal networks were essential in the Guomindang's composition, the Chinese Communist Party evolved more organically from personal networks to cells in a number of Chinese and European cities to its formal Leninist establishment in 1921 also with the assistance of Comintern agents. Its initial appeal was primarily to intellectuals and students. Both parties saw themselves as building blocks for the nation, collective units that would provide the new nation's essential organization, personnel, and direction for the struggle against warlords and imperialists. In 1924 and 1925 the revolutionary institutional base offered by the parties was outwardly broadened by the united front which brought Communists into the Guomindang in joint revolutionary efforts in cities and countryside. But it was a facade of cohesion: for while most in the Guomindang sought social cohesion by championing visions of social harmony, the Communist Party strove for what it considered a more fundamental social coherence by passing first through the fires of class struggle.

Another new institution, the party army, promised to bring organizational cohesion to the immense task of halting the military fragmentation of the warlord years. Given the military chaos of the period, parties with any pretension to *national* unification knew that the task required military means—a reality indicative of the growing militarization of Chinese society. The Guomindang army's core, the graduates of Whampoa Military Academy, organized with Comintern assistance, gained cohesion and direction through ideological indoctrination, theoretically differentiating this army from warlord forces that were predominantly marked by the personal dynamics of networks and hierarchical status. That the commandant of the academy, Chiang Kai-shek, continued to rely on Whampoa cadets throughout the Republic in a personalized fashion, however, points to the persistence of longtime cultural patterns. Whether through ideology, personal ties, or both, the army provided an institution that could first make possible and then enhance party power as it attempted national unification.

Contingencies within three months of each other in the spring of 1925 changed the parties, the army, and the sociopolitical landscape. The March death of Sun Yat-sen factionalized the Guomindang openly along the lines of personal networks and ideology. The impact of this development on the Communist Party was equally traumatic, gradually isolating the party from its Guomindang host from which it had gained sustenance. In addition, since Sun's death occurred so relatively close to the time of military readiness to unify the nation, it raised the political stature of Commandant Chiang, linking him perhaps more integrally with unification than other party leaders. The second contingency was the May Thirtieth massacre in Shanghai, where Chinese demonstrators were gunned down on orders of a British inspector. It ignited a firestorm of national feelings expressed in meetings, demonstrations, and boycotts which tended to build a sense of national community interests against the imperialist powers. The nationalistic zeal ironically hastened the destruction of the united front, the initial Communist Party and the Guomindang's apparent unity.

When Chinese began to make revolution in the 1920s, inclusivity was a watchword; the "bloc within," for example, enabled individual members of either the Guomindang or the Communist Party to join the other party as well. But as the revolution caught fire in the mid-1920s, its dynamics propelled its proponents toward the exclusivity of ever greater revolutionary purity, a tendency that would reappear in later revolutionary phases when they neared what seemed to be imminent success. Both parties tried to take advantage of the upsurge in national feeling to build their power at the grass roots. Communists who were also Guomindang members traveled to core zone cities and towns and to inner peripheral county seats to proselytize and to establish partisan party branch bureaus.[2] Networks within parties, such as the generally conservative Western Hills group within the Guomindang, set out to establish their own local branch bureaus. The Guomindang repeatedly reregistered party members to sift out those who did not fit the current ordained line. The reregistrations underscored the apparent inability and unwillingness of the new parties' leaders to compromise. The revolution in the 1920s splintered the cohesion of the new nation's supposed political party building blocks even as it gave ever more importance to the army as an institution of state.

In the midst of May Thirtieth nationalism and the military campaign of the Northern Expedition in late 1926 and 1927, Communists and progressive Guomindang cadres created another revolutionary collectivity, the mass organization, framed by occupational and gender parameters. Whereas the parties were built from personal relations and networks and then structured in Leninist forms, mass organizations attempted to go beyond personalism and link all those in a particular locale who shared particular social attributes—women, peasants, workers, and merchants. As identity became more generic, the frameworks of personal relations and networks, while still obviously a part of the associations, were transcended. The mass organizations were thus more potentially revolutionary. This mass mobilization of social forces followed sporadic efforts earlier in the decade to form unions and peasant associations and to raise the social position of women. In 1922 Communist organizers in Hunan formed the first "workers' clubs," the numbers of which grew in cities around the country. Communists in May 1925 organized the National General Labor Union, whose membership in one year reportedly skyrocketed from 540,000 to 1,241,000.[3] It was opposed in some cities by labor "federations" with ties to Guomindang conservatives. Though strikes had become quite commonplace in the years after World War I, in the aftermath of May Thirtieth, widespread and lengthy strikes erupted with nationalistic content proclaimed by workers sporting a new identity of class.

Guomindang–Communist Party figures Shen Dingyi and Peng Pai first organized peasant associations, in 1921 and 1925, respectively, to grapple with a variety of socioeconomic grievances. In keeping with Sun Yat-sen's imagery of the power of collective action, Shen spoke of peasant-worker solidarity, arguing that what was needed was to construct a "big stone," not a "pile of loose sand."[4] The Guomindang's Peasant Movement Training Institute in Guangdong prepared association organizers beginning in 1924; although the number of associations increased in the province, growth was substantial only in areas held by the Guomindang army. Peasant associations became involved in sometimes bloody struggles with landlords, officials, merchants, and local militia. Between the May Thirtieth massacre and the Northern Expedition, many peasant associations, such as unions, were driven in part by revolutionary nationalism. Women's associations were also prompted by the dual dynamics of self-interest and nationalism. The first Woman's Day, calling for "gender equality in wages, educational opportunities, and the law," was celebrated in Guangzhou in March 1924, the same year the Guomindang set up a Central Women's Department.[5] Most women's associations, however, developed in the May Thirtieth aftermath, when anti-imperialistic nationalism became an energizing force. Although the number of associations in several provinces grew, they remained subsidiary to the establishment of nationalistic organs and proletarian organizing.

The Northern Expedition, promising the military unification of the nation, stimulated intensive organizing of peasant, labor, and women's associations. The National Revolutionary Army forces seized Wuhan in September 1926, where frenzied unionizing by Communist cadres led to the establishment of more than 70 unions with over 80,000 members.[6] Labor unions became key players in Shanghai and Hangzhou, among other cities. But it was in the mushrooming peasant associations that the revolutionary potential of mass mobilization was most evident. In areas that had been liberated from warlord control, Communists and progressive Guomindang operatives openly organized these associations. Whereas before the Northern Expedition there had reportedly been 161 peasant associations in Hunan, Jiangxi, and Hubei with over 43,000 members, reports in November 1926 showed almost 6,900 local associations in Hunan alone with over 1.2 million members. Even if the latter figures are inflated, they suggest an astonishing escalation of revolutionary zeal. Many associations turned violent in disputes with landlords, "local bullies and evil gentry," and corrupt officials. Landlords fought back, forming their own associations and hiring their own militia. Although it looked like the beginning of a bloody revolution in the countryside, the political and military course of national unification moved in a different direction.

In April 1927, after reaching Shanghai on the eastern route of the military campaign, Chiang Kai-shek, upset by the mass organizations and turn to the left in Wuhan, violently attacked Communists and Guomindang leftists in the beginning of a bloody nationwide purge that lasted well into 1928. Its impact was incalculable. First, it eliminated the progressives in both the

Guomindang's leadership and rank and file. Chiang's Nanjing regime generally lacked a cohort of progressive reformers or even gadflies; their absence meant that the nature and direction of his government's rule differed substantially from what they might have been. Second, the White Terror generally destroyed the Communist Party as it had existed. The sinologist Simon Leys asserts, "History might have been very different if the original leaders of the Chinese Communist party" had not been killed or later expelled. "They were civilized and sophisticated urban intellectuals, holding humanistic values, with cosmopolitan and open minds, attuned to the modern world . . . Their sudden elimination marked an abrupt turn in the Chinese revolution."[7] Although this view of the original leaders may be over-romanticized, it is true that when the party reemerged, its personnel and its agenda were sharply different.

Chiang also halted all mass mobilization. The Guomindang imposed its own organizational framework on labor unions. Peasant associations were forbidden; women's associations were abandoned. The first phase of the revolution ended with the collectivities devised to build the nation abolished (mass organizations), destroyed (the Communist Party), and factionalized (the Guomindang). Only the military as an essential vehicle to modern nationhood was generally victorious. Mass organizations were too unpredictable for Chiang; based on general social attributes, they tended to dilute and diminish the social boundaries that offered conservative cultural meaning: family, personal networks, native place. The power of these traditional webs of relationships (and the relative hollowness of existing institutions), however, were clearly evident in both the factionalized fate of the Guomindang and the personalized loyalty and disposition of the army.

Searching for the Sociopolitical Keys for Nation-Building, 1928–1937

For both the Guomindang and the Communist Party, the decade before the eruption of war with Japan was a period of experimentation with new approaches in an effort to find nation-building's elusive cohesive social base. The Communists, driven underground in the cities and to mountainous areas in the southeast, had nothing to lose by trying new strategies to build their power. Assuming control of the national government, the Guomindang, with all the obvious advantages over its rivals, had the opportunity to establish new institutions on a nationwide basis; the regime had dynamic and capable civil servants who could effectively plan China's "reconstruc-tion." But the advantages were more apparent than real. Even apart from the economic difficulties (the worldwide depression, the insufficient and poorly structured tax base, serious currency issues), there were critical polit-ical problems. The party was not unified. Disaffected party members aligned themselves with the remaining warlords and continued to make trouble. The relationship between the party and the state apparatus was muddied; the two institutions were often controlled by opposing factions that fre-quently worked at cross purposes. The relationship between the state and society, while not continuously antagonistic, was seldom amicable. Some historians have seen little relationship between state and society other than state policies of extraction and control. At times and in different locales, sup-port came from the bourgeoisie, the professions, the bureaucracy, intellectu-als, and landlords; yet at other times in these and different locales, these same groups were hostile opponents of the regime. In the myriad local are-nas of China, there was, as the scholar Christian Henriot has said, "no single, all-embracing scheme [that] can suffice to take account of [the] multihued reality" of state-society relations.[8]

Culture, ideology, and history made the relationship between the center and the localities a crucial challenge. With cultural emphasis on family and ancestors, personal networks, native-place, and local gods, the natural focus of Chinese civilization was the local. Studies have shown that local loyal-ties and identities (such as native-place) were not always particularistic but might be transformed to higher-level loyalties and identities (such as nation-alism).[9] Nevertheless, these local foci always had the potential to remain pri-marily local and parochial. The locality had played an important role in Sun Yat-sen's nation-building ideas to which the Guomindang had sworn alle-giance. As Ernest Young has noted (see Chapter 6), Sun had argued that without previous experience in the ideals and institutions of constitutional and democratic government, the Chinese had to be trained in the forms and practices of self-government, first built on a firm foundation at the lower levels of the polity. Clouding the vision of self-government was Sun's belief that the masses had to be guided by a modernized elite. The ambivalence, even contradiction, between the ideas of local self-governance and state control of the self-governors was one that the Nanjing government—and its Communist successors—were never able to resolve.

Historical developments also complicated the state's dealing with local so-ciety. With a weakened center during the late Qing and continuing into the politically and socially fragmented Republic, local elites in institutions such as self-government bodies and professional associations had played increasingly important and blatantly political roles on the local stage, undirected and undeterred by the center (when it even existed). It was thus difficult for a new centralizing regime to exert greater general control on the localities and to restrict local elites. But that was the challenge Chiang's regime set for itself at the party's plenum at the end of the Northern Expedition. In its view, considerable local autonomy was not conducive to rapid nation-building and might further exacerbate sociopolitical fragmentation. Nanjing was determined to penetrate more deeply into society than had the imperial state. According to a 1928 law, counties were divided into wards which contained from ten to fifty townships; under the wards were villages *(cun)* and urban neighborhoods *(li)*. Beneath these groupings was a resurrected *baojia* system of group mutual surveillance. These groupings, based on families and community collectivities, theoretically could have served as the smallest building blocks in the erection of the nation. But despite much tinkering in county-level structures and below, the emphasis was on increased bureaucratic control with the vision of nation-building remaining top-down.

Another approach during the Nanjing decade that provided the possibility for bottom-up social transformation was the experimental use of the locality as a potential model for the nation. Models of rural reconstruction were initially begun by private citizens. In 1928 Shen Dingyi set up his East Township Self-Government Association, using as a base the mass organizations of farmers, women, merchants, and three workers' unions. It was a holistic attempt to transform a township: conservation projects, educational and sericultural reform, the introduction of credit and retail cooperatives, road construction, insect control, and the establishment of various social service institutions. Shen noted that his effort followed Sun's legacy and asserted that he "was constructing the foundation of our country."[10] Although the experiment had some marked successes, Shen's assassination in August 1928, most likely because of his potential threat to the Guomindang, in effect ended the effort.

Two better-known efforts at rural reconstruction focused on education as the key to remaking China. Jimmy Yen's Mass Education Association in Ding County market towns and villages set up "people's schools" to offer some practical education with an emphasis on public ethics. Liang Shuming's Shandong Rural Reconstruction Institute in Zouping County was recognized by the Nanjing regime, which gave it considerable leeway to administer several counties (more than seventy were under the direction of the institute). Liang was openly anti-Western and self-consciously espoused Confucian values and methods in the training of youths for rural work. The Nanjing government also became involved in setting up experimental counties as models of bureaucratic reform in Lanxi (Zhejiang) and Jiangning (Jiangsu) counties. Although in the end efforts under the Nanjing regime to build models for the nation were stillborn, and were destroyed completely by the war with Japan, the structuring and promotion of models were also a traditional strategy frequently employed by the Communists.

One other collectivity endorsed by the Nanjing regime in 1930 was the economic cooperative. Established to bring farmers together to provide a better method for marketing and obtaining credit, cooperatives began in the 1920s under the sponsorship of the China International Famine Relief Commission and the University of Nanjing. In succeeding years other universities and, after 1927, provincial governments initiated a wide range of cooperatives—credit, supply, production, marketing, insurance, and consumption—bringing farmers into economic cooperation. Cooperatives, like the native-place tie, stemmed from the important impetus of self-interest. Located primarily in Hebei, Zhejiang, and Jiangsu, many cooperatives in the beginning were successful, but the economic exigencies of the depression had bankrupted most of them by the mid-1930s. Relative to the farming population of China, the numbers of members were insignificant; in 1932, nationwide there were almost 2,700 cooperatives with almost 102,000 members. Nevertheless, the official sponsorship of joint rural economic cooperation was a harbinger of more widespread activity in the future.[11] In sum, the Nanjing government envisioned reform but accomplished very little; it is important to note, however, that some of the approaches initiated or supported by the Guomindang regime would later in another context come to fruition.

In the aftermath of Chiang's purge, the Communist Party began its long march from decimation to new life. The standard party (Maoist) version of this rebirth carries us from the founding of the Jiangxi Soviet through Chiang's extermination campaigns which forced the Long March to the establishment of a revolutionary base in Yan'an as the launching site for the eventual seizure of national power. Recent studies have pointed out that the Communist movement was much more diverse and polycentric, with Communist bases and activity in the mid-1930s in Hebei, Henan, Shandong, Jiangsu, Anhui, Zhejiang, Jiangxi, Fujian, Guangdong, Hunan, Hubei, Shanxi, and Hainan as well as in Shaanxi.[12]

In the aftermath of the 1927 party debacle, Mao Zedong retreated to Jinggangshan on the border between Hunan and Jiangxi, where in early 1928 he and the military commander Zhu De established the first base area in the countryside. In some ways the base areas that proliferated across China during the 1930s and 1940s were analogous to the experimental model efforts undertaken by Guomindang reformers. They provided local arenas for experimental policies in order to devise the best strategies for revolution. They were also, as Mao called them, "the buttocks of the revolution," the foundation on which the body of the Communist Party rested. As such, they provided a home for party and army and the human and material resources for revolutionary activity.[13] Following the earlier example of the Guomindang but building on the Soviet model, the party also established its own army under Zhu De, who had directed a Guomindang regiment and had considerable military expertise. Composed mostly of illiterate peasants and workers, the Red Army gave political training priority, a policy that necessitated parallel organizations to handle political work and military command. In late 1928, continuous Guomindang military pressure forced abandonment of the Jinggangshan base and led to the Red Army seizure of Ruijin, Jiangxi, where there had been little Communist activity. There on the Jiangxi-Fujian border Mao began to organize and expand his control, establishing the Chinese Soviet Republic (Jiangxi or Central Soviet) in November 1931. After 1927 the Party Center had remained underground in Shanghai under Li Lisan and the Soviet-trained "returned Bolsheviks" (Chinese students dispatched by Moscow) with party policy still in thrall to the Comintern. Beginning in 1931, some Shanghai leaders started to join Mao because of growing Guomindang pressure in the city, and the Party Center merged with the Central Soviet in January 1933. At its largest, the soviet included eleven counties in southern Jiangxi and ten in western Fujian.

During the Jiangxi period, the Communist leadership first wrestled with the process of land revolution, an effort that utilized bold new social groupings involved in class struggle supposedly to achieve a new type of social cohesion. In the mid-1920s period of social inclusiveness, the party had called for the formation of *peasant* associations to combat their landlords and evil gentry enemies. But already by the time of Mao's 1927 "Report on an Investigation of the Peasant Movement in Hunan," the party had made clear that the peasantry was not a unified group with common interests. Since class struggle was presumably based on the common economic interests of strata of peasants vis-à-vis those of other strata, it was necessary to define class categories, a process that further fragmented Chinese society in the name of an ultimate greater social cohesion and revolutionary direction. Basing his categories on a scheme developed by Soviet Communists, Mao divided the peasants into three groups: rich, middle, and poor.

In such categorizations, the identity of a particular stratum and of those so grouped was relative to others based on attributes that might vary according to the arena and the categorizers. In particular contexts, such social relativity and fluidity at a minimum produced chaotic policies and at worst considerable social disarray and ultimately violence. A case in point is the treatment of rich peasants. Although the party declared in 1928 that the "rich peasants will inevitably join the counterrevolutionary camp," the party strategy was to try to "absorb" those who continued to struggle against warlords, landlords, and gentry.[14] At Jinggangshan, Mao pulled back from more radical policies because they antagonized rich peasants. But in the summer of 1929, the Comintern ordered the CCP to radicalize its stance on rich peasants; it did so in the land law of February 1930, which announced the confiscation of the land belonging to landlords and rich peasants. While Mao was more pragmatic on the issue, the "returned Bolsheviks" hewed to the Comintern line. From June 1933 to October 1934, the Jiangxi Soviet launched a land investigation campaign, a main function of which was to re-classify peasants. In ordering the investigation Mao wrote, "We should take the working class in the countryside as the leaders, rely on the poor peasants, firmly ally with the middle peasants, and resolutely attack the feudal and semifeudal forces. Weed out all landlords and rich peasants who falsely call themselves 'middle peasants' or 'poor peasants.'"[15]

Thus, social and political policy was here continually in flux. A major issue became the demarcation between the rich peasant and the rich middle peasant. Mao's definition of rich peasant was complex, filled with a range of possible factors that might conceivably contribute to such classification. The result was considerable confusion when investigators attempted to implement the definition. Thereupon the People's Commissariat redefined the rich peasant by specifying that it was one whose total income included no more than 15 percent from exploitation. This definition required yet another investigation and yet another categorization. As a result, in one county, out of 3,125 households, 1,512 (48 percent) were reclassified from landlords or rich peasants to middle or poor peasants![16] Such slipperiness of definition and categorization could hardly give rise to stable policy that might be conducive to political development and in part led to the abandonment of radical land reform in this period.

In addition to class issues in the years in Jiangxi, Mao addressed gender in his efforts to mobilize women. A purpose of the CCP government as included in the "Outline of the Constitution of the Chinese Soviet Republic" in November 1931 was "to guarantee the thorough emancipation of women." A new marriage law was announced in December 1931, outlawing arranged marriage, forbidding marriage through purchase and sale, and making divorce easy. But the historical record shows that Red Army soldiers and party cadres often took advantage of women against their will and that CCP authorities even connived in prostitution for those groups.[17] In Jiangxi, as it later became even clearer at Yan'an, the "emancipation" of women was not for purposes of gender equity but for mobilizing for the national revolution. Already in 1928 the party had noted that one of its main tasks was "to recognize peasant women as extremely active participants in the revolution."[18]

Although the Jiangxi Soviet was the CCP center of power and governance, it was not the only base area that existed in the early 1930s, and its policies were not necessarily carried out in other bases. The Eyuwan (Hubei-Henan-Anhui) Soviet, led by Zhang Guotao, reportedly emphasized the emancipation of women more than in Jiangxi; and in instituting the mass line of revolutionary mobilization, Zhang relied on the Red Army to carry out mass mobilization rather than engage the masses through land reform. Zhang was a strong supporter of the anti–rich peasant line. The Xiang'exi (west Hubei and Hunan) base controlled by He Long apparently developed more rapidly and in more arenas of action than the Jiangxi base; with more highly developed mass associations, the base leadership undertook campaigns for land reclamation and production and against opium, gambling, and superstition. But its campaign against rich peasants was lackluster.

Fearful of the expanding power and organization of the Communists, Chiang had launched two campaigns against the Jiangxi base, in December 1930 and May–June 1931, utilizing old warlord forces to wear the Red Army down. In both cases Guomindang armies were lured into the base area, overextending themselves without proper defensive preparations; the Communists' mobilization paid off as the masses denied Guomindang troops intelligence, destroyed bridges to prevent them from retreating, and attacked them from behind. Though Guomindang forces ground deeply into the base area in the third campaign in July–October 1931, the Manchurian crisis with Japan forced Chiang to withdraw. The fourth campaign in early 1933 once again failed. The fifth and successful campaign was launched in October 1933, with Chiang's forces moving slowly, constructing road systems, building blockhouses, and undertaking political mobilizational work with masses along the military routes, gradually tightening the noose around the soviet. The Communists tried with various tactics to blunt the attack, but an August meeting of CCP leaders and Comintern agent Otto Braun began to plan the evacuation. In mid-October about 86,000 (including thirty-five women) broke out of the base to the southwest and thus launched the fabled Long March, a year-long trek of about 6,000 miles over snow-covered mountain ranges and marshlands whose bogs swallowed people alive. Roughly 10,000 survived to reach Yan'an in Shaanxi Province. Along the way at a momentous January 1935 meeting in Zunyi in Guizhou Province, Mao Zedong emerged as leader of the party, shaking off the challenge of the "returned Bolsheviks" who had taken leadership of the Soviet on their arrival from Shanghai and who were now blamed for its military defeat. It was thus Mao and his leadership who profited most from the development and perpetuation of the Long March legend. The social bonding of survivorship produced by the march created a longtime cohesion among the leadership that itself was legendary.

When the Jiangxi base was evacuated, about 42,000 troops were left as guerrillas to harass and pin down Chiang's troops and to maintain a foothold and networks of support in the area. Over the next three years they continued guerrilla activity—the Three-Year War—in eighteen bases mostly along the borders of eight provinces. For many, the hardships of leading a primitive existence in the mountains brought a bonding almost as intense as for the Long March veterans. Guerrillas tried to build power in an area by strategies such as subverting and seizing control of *baojia* units and utilizing kinship ties. Here individual manipulation rather than mass mobilization was the important strategy. Since each locale was different, the appropriate approach demanded flexibility, sensitivity to local realities, and willingness to learn from the locals. The approach might be called "localization": the guerrillas sought to gain power, "living on society's margins, stretching out tendrils into it, learning its ways, and studying its social arrangements not to change it but to strike deals with it"—a sharp contrast to the bureaucratic-centralist style of the Jiangxi Soviet and at Yan'an, and ultimately a more successful revolutionary strategy.[19] In the end, bases founded by locals and least subject to central demands were the most successfully organized. There were important similarities between the roles of these guerrillas in their relations with local society and those the party would play in south China during the war against Japan and the civil war.

Guerrilla policies toward the people living in the base areas ranged from carrying on with land reform to pressing for reductions in rents and interest, resisting the government's military and labor conscription, and confiscating grain and dispensing it to peasants. The Long March led to what one historian has called the "feminization of the party" in the bases with the exodus of so many males.[20] Women as a result played important roles in intelligence gathering, fighting, arranging for supplies, and nursing. They provided Communist continuity in the area after the Long March and again in 1937, when many of the remaining male cadres left as members of the New Fourth Army. On the whole, even though there are no direct lines between this guerrilla struggle and the revolution's denouement, the struggle contributed to the revolution by diverting the forces that Chiang could apply to the main Red Army. It also underscored the weakness of the Nationalist regime, emphasized the Communist claim that it was a nationwide movement, and provided bases from which the party could move into all of eastern China during the war against Japan.

The Period of the Resistance War: Crucible of Revolution

Like today's more polycentric picture of the Communist movement in the early 1930s, the "standard" historical version of the years of the resistance war against Japan—that Yan'an was *the* important controller of the Communist war effort—has been challenged. The alternative view does not deny the importance of Yan'an in the Shaan-Gan-Ning base as the party and government center: that capital center, after all, was the destination of an estimated 100,000 immigrants—likely up to 50 percent of them students, teachers, journalists, and intellectuals in general—from 1937 to 1940. It seeks rather to put the Shaan-Gan-Ning base into fuller perspective, for there were other bases that also played important roles in the expansion of Communist power during the war years. In north China, the Jin-Cha-Ji base in the Shanxi-Chahar-Hebei border region was established in January 1938 under the auspices of the Eighth Route Army's 115th division; the Jin-Sui (Shanxi-Suiyuan) base was set up at the same time by the 120th division; and the 129th division in July 1941 formed the Jin-Ji-Lu-Yu base (Shanxi-Shandong-Hebei-Henan). In central China by late 1942, at least nine additional bases had been developed.

The bases shared various initial aspects: establishment of centralized political and military power; seizure of existing political structures by party cadres; and co-optation of existing military units and mass organizations. But the variability of natural environment, social and economic institutions, and the war itself meant sharp differences in base developments. Shaan-Gan-Ning, for example, was the only base that did not have to defend against military attacks and was not forced to move; its greater stability meant that socioeconomic reforms and administrative development could advance more quickly. Of the other bases, Jin-Cha-Ji and Jin-Ji-Lu-Yu sponsored and carried out the most extensive reforms in reducing rents, taxes, and interest. Not all policies set in motion in Shaan-Gan-Ning were operative in other bases. Fiscal systems and tax burdens differed in each base, with each attempting to achieve self-sufficiency and issuing its own currency. But it is not just variability among the bases but within the bases as well that is significant: differences in local ecology in Shaan-Gan-Ning itself, for example, meant that certain policies that might succeed in one area would likely not in another area.[21] To speak of the "Yan'an Way" as the blueprint for subsequent policies and developments is to accept the "official" genealogical version and vastly oversimplify the reality of the revolution.

In addition to the development of base areas as models and geographic units for the expression of political cohesion, the war years saw renewed emphasis on the institution of the party itself. Party strategies seem on first glance to head in opposite directions. The party in Yan'an became more focused on its identity, coherence, and even purity. In part this stemmed from the wartime immigration that poured into Yan'an. Attracted by Communist idealism, many joined the party: membership, recorded as 40,000 in 1937, skyrocketed to some 800,000 by 1940.[22] Certainly many were not properly ideologically imbued; some were undoubtedly opportunists, trying to save their own economic and political skins; some partisans still owed primary loyalty to Liu Zhidan, the region's indigenous Communist leader. Facing questions of quality control and a threatened diminution of party cohesion and direction, the party leadership adopted or, in some cases, continued earlier strategies of exclusivity to deal with the diversity of personnel by setting a firm "line" and using it to sift out dissenters. The second strategy, in contrast, was the rapid outward expansion of party presence and power through party-led mass mobilization and the formation of mass associations.

Several policies reveal the party's efforts to maintain its control over the revolution and to protect its revolutionary purity; in basic concern and approach, they are analogous to approaches to control in Chiang's regime. The party continued its Jiangxi strategy of centralized control from Yan'an, a policy on its face at odds with the mass line. Part of the concern about the relationship between locality and center was that government structures did not extend beneath the township level; villages remained politically unpenetrated. Centralization would in addition allow more administrative control over the enormous variation in party-controlled regions. A July 1941 party Central Committee decision declared that "the spirit of unity in the party, party centralization, and the importance of submission to central leadership" must hold sway.[23] Soon the traditional hallmarks of centralization—a growing civil and military bureaucracy, increasing routinization, and an emphasis on hierarchy—began to appear.

But very quickly the Communist Party broke from the Nanjing mold. Beginning in winter 1941, the party made efforts to slow the rush to bureaucracy by reducing its size and instituting a "to the villages" *(xiaxiang)* program—which would remain a staple of its state policies for many years to come. Higher-level cadres were sent to the countryside to learn from peasants and to help decentralize various party and government functions. Later, intellectuals were sent to break down the barriers between city-reared elites and peasants; in this way the *xiaxiang* policy was a strategy to encourage greater social cohesion—even as it illustrated Mao's distrust of and distaste for intellectuals and bureaucrats. Despite these "corrective" policies, a 1943 report noted that the number of full-time bureaucrats actually increased after 1941.[24] Further, in the 1945 party constitution (the first since 1928), centralization in the party and at its top was enshrined as policy. As with the Guomindang regime's dilemma, determining the most appropriate relationship between center and locality, between statism and local initiative, remained one of the party's greatest tensions and most intractable problems.

Yet another policy to ensure greater uniformity was the use of a model for emulation. Often before the widespread initiation of a policy, a model district conducted an experimental demonstration. It generally followed long-term, focused preparations with the assistance of well-prepared personnel. The usual success (even if self-proclaimed) recommended the introduction of the policy on a more general level. Examples were the Yancheng (Jiangsu) model of mass mobilization, which "heralded a general CCP policy shift throughout central China," and the Nanniwan model project, in which an Eighth Route Army brigade was given the task of becoming as self-sufficient as possible, producing its food and even its industrial needs.[25] In the Nanniwan model—as in the fervent centralization—the seeds of later Maoist policies are visible: the stress on self-sufficiency and the joint agricultural-industrial functions that would emerge in communes during the Great Leap Forward fifteen years later. In general, Communist models, like the Guomindang models of the 1920s and 1930s, used the locality to provide potential blueprints for the making of the nation.

An extraordinarily important strategy used to attain party cohesion was the rectification campaign, the first of many in the history of the Communist Party and its political regime. By late 1940 and early 1941, the situation at Yan'an had become tense and troubled. Unfavorable weather had led to two poor harvests. But it was military developments that provided the greatest threat and that had seemingly heightened the lack of coherence in the party. By 1940, the Nationalists had 400,000 soldiers blockading Shaan-Gan-Ning to their south and west. After a promising beginning, the Hundred Regiments Campaign (August–December 1940)—the Eighth Route Army's most extensive offensive of the war—went down to defeat. In turn, it set off the brutal Japanese search-and-destroy backlash (1941–1944) against both Communist forces and civilians known as the "Three All" campaign: kill all, burn all, loot all. Then, in the January 1941 New Fourth Army incident in central China, Nationalist forces ambushed part of that army and killed over 3,000 men, ending, if not in name, any effective functioning of an anti-Japanese united front formed in the mid-1930s.

Amid such crises, Mao launched the rectification campaign in February 1942 to ensure that cadres and intellectuals were unified in their focus on the party's mission and to indoctrinate thousands of young people coming from coastal cities. Cadres were to participate in small group sessions studying selected documents, undertake self-criticisms, be criticized in mass meetings, and confess their errors. In the end, they were often sent to the countryside for menial work and ostracism. As in the reregistrations of the young parties in the 1920s, revolutionaries became increasingly concerned with exclusivity rather than inclusivity. In part this was a function of the perceived health and promise of the revolutionary movement (where the party could afford to dismiss and destroy members in the name of doctrinal purity), in part the radical logic of those certain they possessed the Truth. By 1944, central China bases were also involved in rectification activities.

For intellectuals, the other target of rectification, Mao expanded his thoughts on the functions of art and literature in a socialist society in May 1942. Art and literature were "powerful weapons for uniting and educating the people . . . as well as to help the people wage the struggle against the enemy with one heart and one mind."[26] The twin themes of the militarization of society and politics and of the striving for social cohesion and unity are noteworthy. Just as in many of the strategies in the search for cohesion that emerged at Yan'an, so Mao's points in this speech and party decisions in spring 1942 presage the future relationships of state to society, here specifically to intellectuals and artists. Art, Mao posited, did not exist apart from social class and could not be independent of politics. Art and literature serve the "people"—workers, peasants, soldiers—not the petty bourgeoisie, students, or intellectuals, and, above all, serve the revolutionary cause. When the author Ding Ling criticized the party for its sexism, she was sent to the countryside. Writer Wang Shiwei pointed out the inequalities between lifestyles of the ruling Yan'an elite and non-elites and in the name of "unity" and the dissolution of non-elite resentment wrote, "Men with a heavier responsibility ought to share the life-style of lower level cadres (a national virtue that truly ought to be fostered) and by doing so, the lower levels will feel heartfelt affection for them. Only this can weld an ironclad unity."[27] For this, party cadres attacked him, put him on "quasi-trial," and executed him in 1947. While Wang called for unity by breaking down walls between elites and non-elites, the Yan'an leaders' call for "unity" was to be imposed by controls and an exclusivist orthodoxy.

Yet the motive force of the revolution during the resistance war was party-directed mass mobilization and associations. The most important strategy of mass mobilization and class struggle appeared both in base areas and in guerrilla zones—not in the form of radical land reform from which the party had retreated after Jiangxi, but in reducing rents, taxes, and interest. Work teams were dispatched to villages to mobilize against landlords, officials, and the "usurious" bourgeoisie. Since much of the north had few landlords and thus few problems with tenancy and rent, in many areas the key resentment among the masses was over heavy taxes. In some bases of north China, mobilizational efforts were well under way by 1939–40; in others they did not begin until 1943–44. In central China bases, reforms began only in 1941. Big landlords, more a problem in central and south China, were not generally demonized until 1943. Another technique, capsulizing class struggle and making it tangible, was the struggle meeting, the "most intense, condensed form of peasant mobilization."[28] These meetings were launched in the north against local despots by 1942 and were infrequent in central China until autumn 1943. Encouraged and facilitated by party cadres who chose the targets, struggle meetings often turned violent with the eruption of latent peasant anger against village bosses and landlords. These staged events were pivotal in shaking up mass apathy and passivity and disrupting erstwhile solidarity among targets and community. As with class categories, a new social commonality and identity emerged from the sense of being first victims and then enemies of local tyrants.

There were other strategies of mass mobilization, many of them base-specific.[29] For at least two in central China—the Yuwansu base (Henan-Anhui-Jiangsu border) and the Rivereast in eastern Henan—the war against Japan and the consequent necessary collective defense based on local kin and community organs were the keys to mobilizing the people. In the Suwan base of northern Jiangsu, rural reconstruction, especially land reclamation, hydraulic engineering, and an emphasis on agricultural production, provided the most potent mobilizational tools. In the Taihang guerrilla base, part of the Jin-Ji-Lu-Yu base area, famine relief, revival of the silk industry, and production drives were most significant. As the last two cases indicate, production campaigns became important parts of the Communist mobilizational repertoire, especially in consolidated central base areas.

Most significant is that the secret of Communist revolutionary success varied from place to place, from time to time, and from tactic to tactic. To discover the secret for any particular site, Communist mobilizers had to understand the locale—the natural environment, the social, economic, and political structures, and particular needs and grievances—then build coalitions with local leaders, mobilize the local masses, and carry out pragmatic policies. For such strategies, the Three-Year War approaches were a better precedent than many in the Jiangxi-Yan'an years. These efforts were not always or even often successful; leftist excesses and rightist treachery were common; many times contingencies rather than strategies gave the Communists their success. In the Rivereast base, for example, the balance of power between the Communists and their enemies changed to the benefit of the Communists only when the Japanese withdrew their troops from the area after the beginning of the war in the Pacific in late 1941.

Mass associations were also a key to the Communist revolutionary successes. Although the Guomindang regime had outlawed such associations in the mid-1920s, the war provided the Communists with the opportunity to revive them with the Communist imprimatur. Cadre work teams first helped organize peasant associations primarily as bodies for economic assistance. At least in central China, most peasant association officers at the district *(qu)* level or higher were Communist cadres; but grassroots leaders were usually poor peasants or hired hands. Peasant associations helped lead rent, interest, and tax reduction efforts, made decisions about struggle meetings, and often, at least in the beginning, were in charge of the militia. Because peasant associations in the villages carried out Communist economic policies, they directly challenged the village elites. It is no exaggeration to argue that the "rise of the peasant associations fundamentally changed rural power relations."[30] The second wave of mass organizing focused on women and workers. The difficulty of mobilizing women in women's associations came from men's attitudes. Many women came into the association, however, when it emphasized production issues, sponsoring, for example, cotton weaving—to which men did not object because it brought extra money. Women also became members through the association's mediation of family disputes.

Another "community building" movement the party sponsored in some wartime base areas was consumer and producer cooperatives, a harbinger of future policies. In the 1940s the movement did not yet envision moving toward collectivization, "but pointed towards the ideal of the 'cooperative village'—a community whose members all invested in the local co-op, and whose co-op coordinated the village's 'all-round economic and cultural reconstruction.'"[31] Since they were a mixture of government sponsorship (undertaken with government initiative and in the beginning with government shares) and populism (community self-help, village democracy, and local economic initiative), their considerable success in areas of Shaan-Gan-Ning and in the Taihang Mountains of northern Henan was often talked about as the model of a working democratic centralism, but not frequently practiced. As had become customary in the search for models, Mao named the South District co-op near Yan'an city as the model cooperative to be emulated. In any case, cooperatives represented, as they did under Guomindang sponsorship, yet another attempt to find appropriate organizations to foster a community's economic cohesion.

Revolutionary Tidal Waves: Land Reform

The goals of land reform and collectivization were, in the words of the party leader Liu Shaoqi, "to free the rural productive forces from the shackles of the landlords' feudal land-ownership system, so as to develop agricultural production and open the way for new China's industrialization."[32] It was to be a two-stage effort: destruction (breaking the shackles of the old system) and construction (developing a new system of collective rural production with the ultimate goal of building a strong nation). The task of land reform, the heart of the first stage, was enormous. Most difficult was to apply the concept of class struggle to the immense ecological and social differences in the vastness of China. In areas of the north, the peasant was often a managerial farmer, tilling land that he owned; landlordism was not a major problem. In Hebei and Shandong, for example, the tenancy rates in the 1930s were about 12 percent. In the south and southwest, where tenancy rates were much higher (56 percent in Sichuan), absentee landlords exploited tenants. The social and political culture of various areas was starkly different: the south was marked by the power of lineage groups, the north by secret organizations such as the Red Spears and the Elder Brothers' Society. Within the regions themselves, there were also vast differences: in the Shaan-Gan-Ning base area, the subregion of Yanshu (where Yan'an was located) was "sparsely populated, bandit-ridden badlands," while in the Suide subregion directly to its north, the population was highly concentrated, farming was intensive, tenancy rates were high, and commerce was more developed.[33]

The variety of regional wartime experiences further created immense differences in people's attitudes and expectations. The long savage warfare of much of the north contrasted with the relatively peaceful Shaan-Gan-Ning base. Some parts of central and southern China had been controlled by the Japanese for varying lengths of time, other parts not at all. Manchuria had experienced a lengthy Japanese colonial rule. The southwest had been the Guomindang base, subject to Japanese bombing but not ground warfare. The party had taken control in the north in the midst of war, but in east, central, south, and southwest China the Communist armies came in after the Guomindang withdrawal, picking up large chunks of territory with relatively little military action. Land reform in the north thus took place mostly before and during the civil war, while in the south it happened after the establishment of the new national government. Therefore the party's approach and even the *meaning* of land reform varied according to the time when it occurred.

Land reform in north China was often marked by a substantial degree of populism demonstrated in the violent settling of old scores with village elites. The often non-class violence of the anti-traitor "settling of accounts" had erupted in the last months of 1945, spreading to even middle and poor peasants who had collaborated with the Japanese. A directive of May 1946 called on cadres not to interfere with the process in villages and to give free rein to poor peasant leagues and peasant associations, which were in charge of expropriating and redistributing land and property. This directive actually encouraged extremism among the masses. As the *People's Daily* explained: "For the masses to take action themselves, even if they become disorderly, is better than for us to lead them. If the disorder leads to injustice, it may cause them to want to organize themselves."[34]

The timing of the more radical phase of the land reform effort with the Guomindang's unexpectedly strong 1946 military offensive was not coincidental. Party leaders claimed that land reform, using the poor peasant leagues and peasant associations, was a key for mobilizing the population against attacks by Chiang's forces. In this view land reform fulfilled the immediate needs of the party in its military struggle for power: "the rural revolution became . . . the Communists' supply train and recruiting station."[35] Several thousand men per county formed militia units; local self-defense corps took charge of transporting supplies and ammunition; women's associations managed sentry-post surveillance systems; youth association members did service work in rear areas; cultural teams were involved in propaganda work; and peasant associations, in addition to managing land reform, spearheaded army recruiting drives. The connection between land reform, recruitment, and military mobilization was continually stressed, underscoring the ever closer linkage between militarization and the search for the social keys to the revolution.

In late 1947–early 1948 the party moderated the "leftist excesses" of the land reform–mobilizational effort—misclassifying residents' class status, killing landlords and rich peasants, attacking commercial and industrial enterprises, taking land from middle peasants, and distributing no land to landlords. It pointed out, for example, that miscategorizing class status "did not isolate the enemy; it isolated us," and that middle peasants must not be targeted, "otherwise we will isolate ourselves and lead the revolution to defeat."[36] Fear of losing that social-connectedness to classes and mass organizations that was necessary for the revolution to succeed led the party to undertake a rectification movement to purify the party and to silence political opposition among intellectuals and cadres. This rectification movement of the late 1940s was much more intense than the Yan'an movement of the early 1940s. Opposition voiced in literary or ideological terms had turned overtly political in the writings of intellectuals such as Xiao Jun.[37]

In this campaign the rectification process for the first time was opened to the masses so that party meetings merged with mass meetings in which peasants could provide information and opinion on party cadres. This rectification thus bridged another social gulf. Liu Shaoqi described it as a "precious experience of mobilizing the masses" when "land reform integrated with the democratic movement of party rectification."[38] The years 1948 to 1950 saw a moderation in land reform policy, partly as a result of the rectification, partly in preparation for more constructive goals as the end of the civil war neared. The uncontrolled class struggle that was meant to enhance military effectiveness in 1947 through rapid mass mobilization was now seen as a detriment. An August 1948 announcement ordered that land reform would be suspended in newly liberated areas of the Central Plains region until control of the area was established, peasants were politically indoctrinated, and more cadres were trained.

The secret of Communist success in the civil war, as during the anti-Japanese struggle, was understanding the particular situation and acting pragmatically. In the larger military struggle, commanders of the People's Liberation Army "appl[ied] a strategy that elevated flexibility in the field to the highest art of defensive warfare."[39] Another reason for the Communist victory was the Guomindang's weaknesses, among them political corruption, neglect of or inability to undertake social and economic reforms, failures of military strategy, and runaway inflation that led to loss of the people's confidence. On the eve of liberation, the cost of one *grain* of rice in Xiaoshan County—Zhejiang, for example—was estimated to be 2,500 yuan.[40] In many ways the unification of the nation under Communist control in 1949 was the realization of the goal of political cohesion. Underwritten by a sense that the humiliations of the past were gone forever, that national sense of cohesion offered the victors an opportunity to move toward political and social inclusivity. But their ideological drive to realize their vision of a Communist society moved them instead toward more social division in the land reform effort.

The areas of the south and east coast liberated at the end of the civil war were taken by conquest in the cities first, then the countryside, the obverse from the north. The Communist regime faced daunting challenges: maintaining control and undertaking land reform in a vast area where there had been no advance work and where there was thus little, if any, structural readiness for great social change. Even before political mobilization could begin, public administration had to be established, open opposition dealt with, and reconstruction undertaken. The mobilizational pattern used in the north was imitated elsewhere, beginning with efforts to target local tyrants and introduce the struggle meeting, followed by a rent reduction campaign. Because of the shortage of cadres and trained personnel, however, confusion often reigned. Moreover, the cadres who led the efforts were often commandist in style, making decisions and issuing orders on their own authority and paying little heed to the mass line.

After the party came to power in 1949 and the agrarian reform law was promulgated in June 1950, massive land reform began. Four provinces (Guangxi, Sichuan, Yunnan, and Guizhou), however, were not targeted to begin the process until the winter of 1951–52. Work teams played a much greater role in land reform after 1949 than in the north in the 1940s, when the local party organization, poor peasant leagues, and peasant associations had already gained adequate power to force the landlords to submit. In the newly liberated areas, work teams faced formidable problems. Class sentiments were not developed. In many areas of the south and east, tenancy itself was linked to lineage and to village membership. Given all-important kin and native place networks, it was difficult for villagers to understand what "feudal" class structures were or what exploitation meant exactly. Whereas the party had sometimes wrestled with the tension between state-making and democratic populism in the north as it struggled for power, in the south the necessity of state-making and holding onto power already won pushed it squarely into statist actions.

Initially the work teams maintained stricter control over the struggle process than in the north, in large part to prevent hampering agricultural production. But because many landlords were apparently able to manipulate the situation to their advantage, the party adopted a more radical line in November and December 1950. Though work teams still generally maintained control, in some places violent outbreaks flared up and an estimated 1 to 2 million landlords were executed. Work teams traveled from place to place, but to ensure that landlords and other elites did not reemerge, different work teams returned periodically. Over a period of eighteen months of land reform, it is reported that at least four different work teams visited most villages under the Central-South Military and Administrative Committee, which controlled Henan, Hubei, Hunan, Jiangxi, Guangxi, and Guangdong. To preclude rightist or leftist errors, village property was generally not redistributed until at least the third work team visit.[41] Although revolutionary change was uneven, an estimated 88 percent of households in the countryside had completed the "land to the tiller" movement by summer 1952.

As in other developments in the revolution, events far from the locality sometimes shaped the temper and timing of land reform; in Guangdong, for example, disagreements over the pace of reform led to political struggles between provincial leaders and the Central-South Bureau. Nevertheless, some six years after it had begun, land reform had produced new ways of thinking. The social and political horizons of countless poor and middle peasants "had been broadened by the class-oriented perspective of the CCP."[42] Land reform had created new functional associations which displaced old kinship, religious, and voluntary associations, providing new social identities and new personal networks. The common experiences of class struggle fostered a stronger social cohesion among those struggling against landlords and village tyrants and also produced a new demarcation of the "us" from the "them." While in the old society the "them" for any local community was most likely the outsider, the person from a different native-place, now the "Other," the "enemy," was in the community itself, where his status as class alien could be resurrected at will.

As in land reform, the urban phase of the revolution targeted and attacked class enemies. It also produced tensions between state-making and populism. In the campaign to suppress counterrevolutionaries (1951–53), and especially the Three-Anti Campaign (targeting urban party cadres) and the Five-Anti Campaign (against the national bourgeoisie) in 1951–52, the party went into battle against non-Communist bourgeois values rife in cities. Since these groups had not yet been subject to constraints, the campaigns seemed to many brutally intense. Like the land reform campaigns, they created a sense of an enemy presence and a distrust that fractured old relationships and created new commonalities and identities.

Like the Guomindang regime in the late 1920s and early 1930s, the Communist regime sought to sink its roots deeply into the Chinese political landscape. The Guomindang's wards, townships, villages, urban neighborhoods, and *baojia* units never succeeded in serving as the territorial-administrative national building blocks. The Communist government formalized the work, education, and residence unit *(danwei)* to enforce surveillance, control, political conformity, and ideological correctness at the lowest level of the polity. As an arm of the state, the *danwei* was most effective. Nevertheless, it flew in the face of the revolution's general search for ways to broaden social identities into larger constructs that could contribute to building the nation. Far from fostering social cohesion, the *danwei* promoted social isolation.

Over time, contacts between these units became structurally more difficult "to the point where major units maintained 'foreign affairs offices' to manage their contacts with other Chinese units."[43]

Whereas the *danwei* illustrates the commitment to statism, the burgeoning mass organizations, based on shared interests or sometimes specific objectives, provided the balancing social framework to enlarge the masses' horizons; they joined together the whole country across provincial and regional lines. In 1953, for example, trade union membership had climbed to 12 million; there were 9 million in the New Democratic Youth League (the pre-1957 name of the Communist Youth League); and no fewer than 76 million women joined the Women's Federation. They were especially significant forces in the parade of mass campaigns repeatedly launched against "class enemies" of the People's Republic, providing another framework for implementing the party's directives and a venue for mass mobilization. Mao argued that these organizations "changed the Chinese condition of 'being like loose sand,'" helping to forge a "national unity."[44]

Revolutionary Tidal Waves: Collectivization

In the midst of land reform, the party leadership began a new revolutionary movement to attain the other goal necessary for building the state: the expansion of agricultural production through collectivization so as to serve as a base for China's industrialization. Not only was collectivization more ideologically compatible than the "land to the tiller" program, but also, more important, it facilitated agricultural mechanization, greater efficiencies, and state extraction of resources. By mid-1950, when the northern wartime bases completed land reform, it is estimated that a third of northern peasant households were already members of mutual aid teams (MATs). MATs were formalized versions of traditional practices of peasant cooperation in the sharing of labor, farm animals, and tools. The party had first introduced MATs in the Jiangxi Soviet after land reform was undertaken, and then in the northern base areas during the resistance war. The first MATs in the 1950s operated only in peak season; but they were soon made permanent. The number of cooperating households was generally ten or fewer, and in many areas they were members of the same kinship group. Other than the cooperatives of the 1930s and 1940s, it was the first purely economic functional grouping in the revolutionary repertoire. Estimates assert that by the end of 1952, 40 percent of all peasant households were MAT members, a number that reached about 92 percent in 1956. Analysts have seen them as an important preparatory stage in the movement to collectivization.[45]

The MAT became the building block of the lower-level agricultural producers' cooperatives (APC), the next stage of collectivization. The state's push for more advanced stages of cooperativization was not only to produce socioeconomic change but also to create larger socioeconomic groupings to give the government greater control in rural areas. Approximately three to five MATs (thirty to fifty households) were joined to create this semisocialist unit: members contributed land, draft animals, and equipment as capital shares to the cooperative and received payment, after wages were deducted, for their contributions. Under the watchword of "central management but private ownership," the lower-level APCs in many areas of south and east China were still composed of kinship groupings. But even if an APC was composed of agnates, its being formalized and recognized by the state made it a new institutional hybrid on the local scene.

The pace of the establishment of lower-level APCs varied. They began in some areas in 1951, but areas in southeast China did not establish their first APC until 1954 or 1955. By that time, local resistance had arisen against the movement. With pressure from the government to keep up the pace of developing APCs, cadres reacted either by ignoring the supposed principles of cooperativization—voluntary participation and mutual benefit—or by compelling peasants to participate even if they objected. Peasant recalcitrance and discontent arose in locales where MATs had been slow to develop and cadres had moved from private ownership to the lower-level APC. Early in the movement for revolutionary rural organization, the party-state displayed a "great leap" mentality. For collectivization to move gradually— through seasonal MATs, permanent MATs, lower-level APCs, and eventually upper-level APCs—to become solidly rooted in the local socioeconomic terrain would take a substantial amount of time. Although in early 1955 party leadership was arguing about the pace of cooperativization, an October party plenum, with Mao leading the way, decided to push full steam ahead to upper-level APCs, at the very time when only 15 percent of peasant households were members of lower-level APCs. Frenetic organizing in the last months of 1955 led to the skyrocketing—at least on paper—of membership in lower-level APCs to over 80 percent of peasant households in January 1956. A remarkably ironic and tragic aspect of these revolutionary developments is that the party leadership abandoned its strategy of pragmatically developing cohesive socioeconomic units that had brought them political and military victory. As a result, they destroyed what they had tried to build.

Higher-level APCs were substantially more revolutionary than their lower-level predecessors. Much larger, they comprised two hundred to three hundred households; private ownership was abolished and land was owned by the collective; and payments for contributions of land and other assets were ended. By the end of 1956, almost 88 percent of peasant households were reported as already in higher-level APCs. If true, the pace was breathtaking. In Xinhui County, Guangdong, for example, from June to November 1956, 1,210 MATs and lower APCs were reportedly "upgraded and restructured"; 925 cooperatives became 534 collectives, only 11 of which had under 50 households, 307 of which had 100 to 300 households, and 24 of which were whole townships. A farmer who had earlier helped set up a lower APC in a county township remarked: "It was awful. All households were made to join the collective like a swarm of buzzing bees. There was no prior experimental model or experience. Work teams made up of provincial and prefectural cadres came to supervise us. We had to deliver. We cadres spent every day calculating work-points for bickering households. We hardly ever saw the fields or the crops."[46] Many peasants in the area considered the establishment of the higher APC or collective as a turning point in their relationship to both the party-state and the rural cadres. As marketing restraints, quotas, and rations hemmed them in and local cadres as agents of the state daily assumed more authority, peasants lost control over their lives. In the name of ever-larger socioeconomic groups, the rural world became "cellularized" by the demands of the party-state, which directed and manipulated mass organizations rather than respond to them.

Then, in 1958, with the launching of the Great Leap Forward, the Maoist visionary ideal of the organizational key to building China into a strong nation-state culminated in the people's communes. This movement militarized Chinese society. A Politburo resolution in August 1958 called the people's communes "the basic social units of Communist society"; it specified that "we should actively use the form of people's communes to explore the practical road to transition to communism."[47] On average about 5,500 households initially constituted the commune, which became the locality's main governmental unit and socioeconomic organization. It was in charge of agricultural production, industry, commerce, health, social services, and education. Private plots and private ownership of livestock were ended. Whereas in higher APCs income had been distributed on the basis of labor performed, in communes most of the earnings were paid on a per capita basis; thus differences between incomes on communes were greatly reduced.

Perhaps no change made a greater difference than community mess halls. Gone were meals around a family table, the daily comings together, long a traditional centerpiece of farm life. Though not a direct blow against kinship, communal meals perhaps subtly undermined the closeness of the kin unit. From the perspective of agricultural production, the mess halls in Henan, according to the *People's Daily,* "meant that each commune member had three extra hours for work or study, labor productivity had been raised by about 30 percent, and six million units of female labor power had been released from domestic chores."[48] Familial closeness was further undermined by commune nurseries and kindergartens. Grandparents no longer needed to care for their grandchildren; instead they could now spend their time at "happiness homes" for the elderly. Boarding primary schools and even boarding kindergartens took some children from parents' control at an early age. The state thus was impinging far more deeply into the grass roots than ever before, primarily into the family, where it began to replace traditional practices with government services.

These revolutionary changes improved the status of women. The Marriage Law of 1950 (going beyond that of the Jiangxi period) had abolished the traditional family system "based on arbitrary and compulsory arrangements and the superiority of man over woman." The new system was based "on equal rights for both sexes, and on the protection of the lawful interests of women and children." The Marriage Law gave women the right to own land in their names, thus permitting them to benefit from land reform. Communization freed women from daily kitchen responsibilities and child care for labor on the land. From one perspective this further equalized the status of men and women. For the first time rural women achieved an economic identity; an estimated 90 percent performed farm labor in 1958–59. From another perspective, however, this shift redefined women primarily as workers who labored with men outside the home. The *proper* woman served the state, not simply the family. This policy extended the Yan'an period's emphasis on the "national woman," whose status was defined for purposes of the party-state, not for purposes of gender equity.[49]

The militarization of Chinese society, which had gradually been developing since the first years of the century, culminated with the communes. Collectives were organized into military units and renamed brigades (sometimes companies). They in turn were divided into production teams or platoons. Overseeing the brigades were management districts, often termed battalions. The choice of military terminology suggests the degree of regimentation imposed on the masses by the party-state and the militarization of labor. The military ethos also penetrated the rhetoric. In speaking of competing with other areas for productive output, cadres in one Guangdong commune declared: "In order to promote the leap forward, we shall compete with other districts in the entire county. Our soldiers and horses are strong, our generals brave and numerous . . . We dare to be challenged. Clad in our armor and ready in our formations, we await the battle cry."[50]

The establishment of the commune militia further militarized the commune. Every able-bodied citizen between the ages of fifteen and fifty was in the ordinary militia and those aged sixteen to thirty were in the "hard-core" militia. By January 1959, 220 million men and women had become militia members. Although even most hard-core militia members never fired a gun, they were "psychologically mobilized" by training two to three hours per day. Leaders insisted that militia members adhere to "rising, eating, sleeping, setting out to work, and returning from work" at the same times: "This greatly strengthened the collectivization of life and organizational discipline, and nurtured the fighting style in production and work." The use of military terminology was to induce peasants to work even harder. They became "fighters" on the "agricultural front"; the countryside became the "battlefield"; and nature itself became an "enemy" to be overcome.[51] It is no coincidence that the party had thrived most in the past when it had an enemy that could be demonized.

Through the communization movement, the party-state appropriated the ethos and dynamics of its past military victories and linked them to the functioning of the new organization—the commune—for the supposed building of a strong nation. The commune had purposely been created large; as a slogan of the time put it, "First Big, Second Selflessness," suggesting that, through the contributions of the masses, communes could be expanded until all the nation would become one mammoth commune—and communism would have been achieved. Land reform, collectivization, and the communes were the tragic culmination of the Maoist vision and the Communist Party's experimentation with various social approaches, strategies, categories, and institutions. The terrible irony and tragedy was that the communization and other policies of the Great Leap, which a visionary Mao had seen as the culmination of the search for a social base on which a modern nation-state could be firmly built, far from bringing social cohesion, brought greater social and political disruption and the largest human-induced famine in world history.

In the 1920s and 1930s, the revolutionary search for social cohesion moved through several strategies. First came specific macro-institutions, the parties and armies, in which identity was generally specific: one was a member of the GMD, the CCP, or (during the united front) both. In the mobilized mass organizations identity became more generic: peasant, woman, worker, student. With the coming of land revolution, artificial and relative noninstitutional groupings—rich, middle, and poor peasants—were drawn up for class struggle. Here identity itself might change at any time; indeed, a major role of the leadership was devising and revising those identities. As the revolution moved forward, personal identities tended to become less specific and increasingly relative to social structures and strategies.

Throughout the revolutionary search, the party used two fundamental methods for establishing social cohesion: the structuring of social units and categories of various sorts and sizes (e.g., mass associations, middle peasants) and the mobilization of the masses *through action* in the process of revolution (struggle meetings). At Jiangxi and the other soviets, the objective had been mass mobilization through the conscious structuring of associations, the creating of class strata that could be used politically, and the common experience of class struggle. The Long March, undertaken in the face of an enormous Communist military defeat, demonstrates as well that social cohesion grew not only from the self-conscious orderings of society and social forms but also directly out of existential experience. For the survivors of the Long March who continued to govern China until the late 1990s, the traumatic experience created a remarkable sociopolitical cohesion at the top: to have survived in the face of overwhelming odds brought to the work of completing the revolution an almost tangible sense of destiny.

The content and direction of the revolution in its various phases took shape from particular historical moments, rising out of specific historical problems and locales. The Jiangxi Soviet and the Long March both underscored the increasing militarization of revolutionary politics and society. The encirclement campaigns created of necessity a military response, whereby "military imperatives were often at odds with the needs of social revolution and nearly always overrode them."[52] The Long March was a military affair. Twenty months after the marchers reached Yan'an, China was at war with

Japan and the Communists were allied with Chiang Kai-shek's government in a militarily defensive united front. Although base areas attempted to carry on with the imperatives of the revolution, the reality remained largely military.

In retrospect, the war was an enormous boon for the Communist Party; by war's end, it had sunk widespread roots in both northern and central China, having established nominal control over large areas and increased the number of its supporters. While the war transformed (and made possible the continuation of) the revolution, it also helped to determine the development of policies and political strategies that shaped the contours of revolution. In the late 1940s the linking of military action with land reform underscored the reality that revolution and militarization were unified strategies, the culmination of which came with the militarization of commune life during the Great Leap Forward.

In 1927 Mao had written that there "must be a revolutionary tidal wave in the countryside in order to mobilize tens of thousands of peasants and weld them into this great force."[53] The wartime mobilization from 1937 to 1945, however violent the struggle meetings might have become, had avoided destroying the structures of rural property relations. In stark contrast, from 1945 until 1958 the Chinese countryside was swept by revolutionary tidal waves, as ever greater numbers of the Chinese masses were mobilized directly through the action of land reform and collectivization to destroy the power of the landlords. During these years, when the often violent tidal waves destroyed societal structures, making social cohesion less possible than ever, a central question remained: Could the destructive power unleashed and fostered by class struggle ever constructively "weld" masses into one "great force"?

In the history of the search to find the appropriate social institutions and approaches both for revolution and for building a modern state, the party-state was able to penetrate more deeply into Chinese society than had likely been imaginable early in the century. The Guomindang efforts to establish sub-county administrative units and resurrect the traditional *baojia* pale when viewed against the *danwei* and its control over the lives of the masses. Those units, though discrete in themselves, were instrumental in prompting the mass mobilizations that became so important a part of the revolutionary landscape. Finally, strategies of the party and later the party-state left a legacy of social suspicion and a continuing sense of the presence of social and political enemies in a community's midst. The idea of class struggle out of which a greater cohesion was theoretically to come produced instead peasant economic categories, struggle meetings, rectifications, and enemies of the people. The introduction of an enemy ethos into society was the sowing of an ill wind that would contribute to the reaping of a Cultural Revolution whirlwind and to a continuing demonization of state critics and dissidents.

Selected Readings

Benton, Gregor. *Mountain Fires: The Red Army's Three-Year War in South China, 1934–1938*. Berkeley: University of California Press, 1992. An almost encyclopedic account of the sporadic warfare waged by Communist forces left behind at the evacuation of the Jiangxi Soviet. It is a crucial work in decentering the standard Jiangxi–Long March–Yan'an version of Chinese Communist history.

Ch'en Yung-fa. *Making Revolution: The Communist Movement in Eastern and Central China, 1937–1945*. Berkeley: University of California Press, 1986. Ch'en's work is indispensable in revealing the complexity and diversity of the Communist revolution during the Sino-Japanese War. Marked by rich detail on revolution in localities, it is a model of careful and compelling analysis.

Fei Xiaotong. *From the Soil*. Trans. Gary G. Hamilton and Wang Zheng. Berkeley: University of California Press, 1992. First published in 1947, this work, a translation of *Xiangtu Zhongguo*, has been called by a reviewer "the Rosetta Stone of Chinese society, Chinese culture, and the human relationships which form their foundation." It is essential reading.

Gilmartin, Christina K., Gail Hershatter, Lisa Rofel, and Tyrene White, eds. *Engendering China: Women, Culture, and the State*. Cambridge, Mass.: Harvard University Press, 1994. In addition to being a pathbreaking contribution to studies of gender in China, these sixteen essays contribute significantly to our understanding of revolution and state-society relationships, among other issues.

Goodman, Bryna. *Native Place, City, and Nation: Regional Networks and Identities in Shanghai, 1853–1937*. Berkeley: University of California Press, 1995. This work argues cogently that the particularistic value of native-place need not be fragmenting but in actuality facilitated the development of nationalism.

Henriot, Christian. *Shanghai, 1927–1937: Municipal Power, Locality, and Modernization*. Trans. Noel Castelino. Berkeley: University of California Press, 1993. This work presents a compelling picture of the complexity of relationships among power holders in state and society as it raises significant questions about our understanding of state-society relationships during the Nanjing decade.

Hinton, William. *Fanshen: A Documentary of Revolution in a Chinese Village*. New York: Random House, 1966. Several decades since its appearance, this book still offers an important depiction of the process of rural revolution in Long Bow village, Shanxi Province.

Lieberthal, Kenneth. *Governing China: From Revolution through Reform*. New York: W. W. Norton, 1995. In its detailing of the legacies of imperial China, its description of the revolution, and especially its treatment of the issues and developments in the People's Republic, this book is a model of clarity and compelling analysis.

Saich, Tony, ed. *The Rise to Power of the Chinese Communist Party: Documents and Analysis.* Armonk, N.Y.: M. E. Sharpe, 1996. The most important documents of the party from 1920 to 1949 are given enlightening context and analysis in this essential volume of almost 1,400 pages. It is indispensable for understanding the party and its revolution.

Saich, Tony, and Hans van de Ven, eds. *New Perspectives on the Chinese Communist Revolution.* Armonk, N.Y.: M. E. Sharpe, 1995. The twelve essays in this volume contribute substantially to our understanding of the diversity and complexity of the revolution.

Schoppa, R. Keith. *Blood Road: The Mystery of Shen Dingyi in Revolutionary China.* Berkeley: University of California Press, 1995. This study of the Nationalist revolution in the 1920s focuses on personal networks, the nature of revolutionary identity, and the importance of place as essential components in understanding the process of social and political revolution in China.

Wou, Odoric Y. K. *Mobilizing the Masses: Building Revolution in Henan.* Stanford: Stanford University Press, 1994. A very important work on the revolution in Henan. Its empirical richness, its analytical care, and its continual awareness of the complex and diverse possibilities of revolutionary change make it essential reading.

CHAPTER 9

Society and Politics from Transwar through Postwar Japan

ANDREW GORDON

On August 15, 1945, the emperor of Japan stunned his subjects with a radio broadcast announcing the nation's surrender to the Allied forces. The most destructive war in history was over, and Japan had been utterly defeated. The combination of firebombing and the detonation of two atomic bombs left urban Japan in ruins. At home and overseas roughly 3 million Japanese had died, out of a population of 70 million. For eight years, since Japan launched a full-scale war in China, the Japanese people had been exhorted by their leaders to sacrifice for the sake of a great and certain victory to liberate Asia from the tyranny of the "British and American devils." Small wonder, then, that Emperor Hirohito's apparently sudden broadcast marked a traumatic rupture in the minds of most listeners. Like "zero hour" in Germany in 1945, many people later recalled that August as the instant of "rebirth," a moment when past experience and values were rendered illegitimate, and a totally new course, both personal and national, was charted. To be sure, not every Japanese person repudiated the experience of the immediate past, and to this day it remains a matter of profound controversy to assign blame and assess the causes and legacies of World War II. But however they judged the war and its aftermath, people agreed that its end marked a decisive turning point.

The occupying forces swiftly imposed a blizzard of reforms upon the nation, which reinforced the sense of 1945 as a sudden instant of rupture in Japan's historical experience. Formally conducted by the wartime allies, Japan's occupation was in fact an American operation. An organization called SCAP (Supreme Commander of Allied Powers), referring to both the commanding person of General Douglas MacArthur and the bureaucracy that implemented occupation policy, oversaw far-reaching transformations of the Japanese political and economic systems, as well as social and cultural life.

Both the inner experience of August 1945 and the external force of the occupation reforms make "postwar Japan" too obviously a coherent historical era with a precise beginning. Simply to accept Japanese memories of "rebirth" and an America-centered narrative of revolution from above as frames for analysis limits understanding of the experience of postwar Japanese history. In many ways, Japanese society of the late 1940s and 1950s changed little compared to the prewar and wartime eras. In the hindsight of one half century, the new social patterns of postwar Japan did not actually emerge until the late 1950s and 1960s. The midcentury decades stretching across the war appear as a different, "transwar" phase of history, prelude to what people usually identify as a truly "postwar" condition. It would be foolish to deny that profound changes began with the end of the war; but the fascination of the decade after 1945 lies precisely in the overlap of a transformed political system and cultural world with a relatively unchanged transwar society.

Transwar Society through the 1950s

One enduring image of the early postwar era is the dusty, stooped migrant from a rural village in northern Japan disembarking at Ueno terminal in Tokyo, household possessions in a huge sack on her shoulders. After a temporary outflow of population owing to wartime evacuations and the starvation conditions in cities immediately after the surrender, the flow of migrants from countryside to city that had been under way since the nineteenth century resumed. The population of Japan's six major cities rose by 50 percent in the 1950s. But these were also years of the baby boom. At its peak, over 8 million children were born in just three years, from 1947 to 1949. Even though millions moved to the cities, the sharp overall increase in population allowed the rural population to remain high as well. Thus, one important social link across transwar Japan is the centrality of the experience of rural life and agriculture. Japan's agricultural population at the end of World War II accounted for roughly 50 percent of the populace, or 36 million people, a level little changed from the 1920s or 1930s. A decade later in 1955 this absolute number stood unchanged, an agricultural population of 36 million, and the proportion of the population in rural areas had fallen just slightly. Not until later did the migration from country to city, and the outward growth of city into former countryside, combine to make a metropolitan middle-class lifestyle the majority and the defining experience of "modern" postwar society.

Beyond numbers, the material conditions of rural living were little changed in the first postwar decade. The technology of Japanese agriculture in the 1950s was much closer to that of the 1930s than the 1970s. The modern technologies of the 1950s had already entered most villages to some extent in the 1920s and 1930s: electricity, simple kerosene-powered motors, chemical fertilizers. A simple way to make the point is to note that photographs of village life in the 1950s resemble those of the 1930s more than those of the 1970s. People wore sandals and kimono-style everyday clothing. Houses still had thatched roofs, roads were unpaved, and working cattle plowed fields. The "necessities" of life in the 1970s were as yet great luxuries or entirely out of reach: motorcycles, cars, electric fans, refrigerators, or television sets.[1] And the cultural life of the village continued much as it had, centered on festivals, ancestor-based religious observances, funerals, and weddings, the last usually still held at home or in the neighborhood.

While there was a dramatic change from a curriculum exalting military values and the emperor to one teaching the virtues of peace and democracy, the hierarchic structure of the education system continued. In prewar Japan, education was compulsory through "higher elementary school," sixth grade in American terms. Formal schooling for a majority of the population ended at this point. The occupation reforms extended compulsory education through middle school, or ninth grade. But for the first decade after the war, it was still a relative privilege to study beyond compulsory education. Roughly half of Japan's middle school graduates, both young boys and girls, ended their schooling with middle school in the 1950s, going directly to work in agriculture, manufacturing jobs, or the large service sector of the economy. Such a path was in no sense regarded as "dropping out" of school. Manufacturing industries in particular were eager to hire middle school graduates as regular workers for long-term employment, although such youths were unlikely to advance past low-level supervisory posts.

A high school diploma thus remained a proud achievement in Japan of the occupation era and the 1950s, and a male high school graduate would enter a company in a relatively privileged status, expecting to reach at least the level of supervisor, though not upper management. Going to college was still the privilege of a small, if expanding, minority. Rates of university attendance (including public and private universities, as well as two-year colleges mainly for women) stood at less than 20 percent throughout the 1950s. Roughly speaking, the transwar school system ran along two tracks: a basic education that expanded from six to nine years in 1946 and prepared youths for working-class careers, and a higher education that offered the possibility or the promise of a secure middle-class existence to those able to pursue it.

Transwar continuities are also profound in the realms of family structure and a gender-based division of work roles at home and outside it. Again, as with agricultural processes, this transwar continuity refers to the early postwar persistence of a certain kind of prewar modernity rather than a continuation of ancient tradition. For example, to judge from relatively scarce statistical data, already by the 1920s as many as 54 percent of families in Japan, especially in urban areas, were "nuclear" in form: just two generations, parents and their unmarried children, living under a single roof. This also meant, of course, that nearly half of all families were "extended," with three generations in some combination together, or parents and married children together. The proportion of nuclear families stood basically unchanged from 1920 through 1960.[2] The transwar era, then, was a time of the ongoing coexistence of multiple family types, and extended families remained quite typical.

A related feature of the socioeconomic structure of the 1950s stands at the intersection of family and work life and constitutes another link to the prewar past: self-employment or family employment was a more common experience than paid employment outside the family. For all the impressive growth of Japanese industry from the 1880s through the 1930s, to world power status in textiles and a substantial and sophisticated presence in shipbuilding and machine industries and even aircraft production, the majority of the nation's labor force through the 1950s consisted of family members working on a family farm or fishing boat or in a small family-owned retail, wholesale, or manufacturing shop in a village or city. The husband would be counted as the business owner. The wife, on a farm or in a vegetable market, a sandal "factory," or a barbershop, would work alongside him, counted as "family labor." Government statisticians did not classify these women as "employees," and typically they received no wages. From the 1930s through the 1950s, well over two thirds of women workers were so-called family workers. This, too, was part of the transwar character of society for at least fifteen years after the war.

In the significant minority of workplaces outside the home, a prewar-style division of labor between men and women continued in place through the 1950s, and even into the 1960s with a slight but interesting shift. Again, prewar does not mean premodern. It certainly does not mean a division between wage-earning men and homemaking women. From the 1880s into the early twentieth century, women by the hundreds of thousands, especially young women, were recruited as factory workers. They accepted these jobs in part because the alternatives in their home villages were equally harsh or even more grueling. These working women nonetheless endured oppressive conditions, cut off from whatever immediate support their native communities might have offered. Their labor made possible the takeoff of industrial capitalism in Japan. By the 1920s, and continuing through the 1950s, women made up a little over one third of the total Japanese work force (36 to 38 percent). Over half of these women worked in agriculture. Of the substantial proportion in manufacturing, the great majority in the prewar decades were textile operatives; about two thirds of female factory workers labored in textile mills in the 1920s. And in the early 1950s, as many as 55 percent of women in manufacturing jobs still worked in textile factories. The transwar gender division of the wage labor force thus placed women in light industries, especially textiles, while men were concentrated in mining, machine, and metal work, so-called "heavy industries," as they had been since early in the century.

Beginning in the mid-1950s, the Japanese economy began its twenty-year "miracle"; GNP surged at an average annual growth rate in excess of 10 percent from 1955 to 1973. Although sites of women's factory work began to change dramatically as a result, the shift in the substance of this work was more apparent than real. As the mass production factories of electronic equipment makers boomed, they hired thousands of young women, so that the proportion of women employed in textiles plummeted from over half in 1955 to just 18 percent of female manufacturing labor by 1965. But the labor-intensive substance of work on a television set assembly line was not very different from that of a textile operative. From the mid-1950s into the 1960s, women on assembly lines producing transistor radios, and then television sets, became international symbols of the emerging Japanese economic miracle. The characteristics of these workers were precisely those of the textile operatives of years past: teenage girls hired directly upon completing compulsory middle school, living in company housing, and enjoying the very constraining benefits of paternalistic management policies.

The structure of daily life, and the life cycles of Japanese people, also had a certain transwar continuity. One can see this in small facts with large implications. Social surveys reveal that in Japan in 1950, a full two hours of a woman's average day—every day—were devoted to sewing.[3] This datum reveals first that homemaker remained a time-consuming occupation demanding considerable skill. It also shows that a commercialized consumer society, which had first emerged in urban Japan as far back as the late 1600s, still coexisted with a significant realm of home-based, noncommercial productive activity. Women bought cloth in stores, but they fashioned it into new clothes at home, and they repaired and altered old clothing. Ready-to-wear was still a novelty and a luxury, out of reach of the daily life of even middle-class families of transwar Japan.

In other ways as well, individuals were as yet not wholly integrated into or overtaken by mass, bureaucratized, profit-seeking institutions. The world of leisure through the 1950s, as before the war, remained tied to local community events such as shrine or temple festivals, or holiday visits to nearby sites or to ancestral villages, rather than the group tours to distant places organized by travel agencies that emerged in full force in later decades. Most people in Japan until the late 1950s were born at home, not in hospitals, attended by midwives, not doctors. They died at home as well. Funerals and weddings took place at home (especially in the countryside) or at temples and shrines, rather than the commercial establishments of later years, dedicated to providing lavish weddings in fancy halls.[4] One must not romanticize these home-based transwar experiences. Home birth in the 1950s in Japan was dangerous in ways that medically attended hospital births of later decades were not, and infant mortality remained high. But despite these risks, there was also a certain comfort in a society where the great milestones of individual and family life—birth, marriage, death—continued to be marked in relatively intimate settings.

A Newly Divided Political Culture

In manifold ways, from the routines and the turning points of daily life to the composition of the labor force, the importance of rural, agrarian society, the structure of families, and the system of education, the experience of Japan through the 1950s thus remained part of a transwar social system. What nonetheless gives these years a particular texture setting them off from the past is the new, and newly contentious, character of political life in Japan.

Democratic activism and ideologies had been a significant part of Japanese political culture since the Movement for Freedom and People's Rights began in the 1870s. The Diet was an important institution from the time of its founding in 1890, and cabinets formed by elected party politicians had been the norm for most of the period from 1918 to 1932. But before 1945 the legitimacy of democratic institutions and ideas was tenuous. They were readily bypassed, co-opted, or suppressed by the rulers in the "dark valley" of fascism, militarism, and war from 1932 to 1945. Against this background, the many reforms imposed by the American occupiers from 1945 to 1947 gave unprecedented legal protection and socioeconomic grounding to values and institutions of democracy, equality, and international cooperation.

Japan's new postwar constitution was drafted by a committee of American occupation officials in the winter of 1946, discussed in the Imperial Diet (still in existence until the new constitution replaced the Meiji document), and adopted that November, to take effect in May 1947. The new constitution transformed the emperor from absolute monarch to "symbol of the State and of the unity of the people." It granted to the people of Japan an array of "fundamental human rights" that included the civil liberties of the American Bill of Rights such as freedoms of speech, assembly, and religion. It then boldly extended the concept of rights into the social realm. The new constitution guaranteed rights to education "correspondent to ability" and to "minimum standards of wholesome and cultured living." It assured the right (and obligation) to work, to organize, and to bargain collectively. It outlawed discrimination based on sex, race, creed, social status, or family origin (referring implicitly to the former outcastes, so-called *burakumin*), and it gave women explicit guarantees of equality in marriage, divorce, property, inheritance, and "other matters pertaining to marriage and the family." Finally, its Article 9 committed the Japanese people to "forever renounce war as a sovereign right of the nation and the threat or use of force as a means of settling international disputes."[5]

Japanese elites were initially stunned by these sweeping guarantees, imposed by Americans who insisted the Japanese government present them to the people as the government's own recommendation, but the draft document met an enthusiastic popular response. Many of the social rights, in particular, ran far in advance of social experience and practice, and continue to do so. And Article 9 has not prevented the buildup of a huge, well-trained and well-armed "Self-Defense Force." But the constitution has not once been amended in its half century and more of life. As officially sanctioned goals or ideals, its ambitious provisions have framed and continue to frame postwar discourse and shape institutions in important ways.

SCAP reformers went well beyond designing this new basic law of the land. They disbanded the oppressive "thought police" and decentralized the national police force. They disestablished the official State Shinto religion.

They freed Communist Party members from jail and allowed a greater range of political expression than was possible in the United States at the time. They attacked the sprawling business empires of the *zaibatsu*, taking away ownership and control from holding companies dominated by the *zaibatsu* families (Mitsui, Sumitomo, Yasuda, Iwasaki) and breaking up some of the larger firms. They encouraged unions and tolerated an extraordinary surge of organizing and strikes. They imposed a program of land reform that revolutionized the distribution of social and economic power in rural Japan, essentially expropriating the holdings of landlords and creating a countryside of small family farms. As the Americans had hoped, these sweeping measures changed the climate of ideas and the distribution of economic and social power. The reforms reinforced and expanded existing constituencies, from intellectuals and the press to factory laborers, tenant farmers, and newly enfranchised women, who supported the newly egalitarian and democratic political system.

In response to these reforms, a virtual fever of "democratization" swept Japan in the late 1940s and 1950s. Democracy and equality were understood in extremely expansive terms by their advocates; the terms meant far more than voting and land reform. They implied to many—and this was both promise and threat—a remaking of the human soul. Talk of renovating and transforming was everywhere in the Japan of these years. Excitement over remaking the nation affected not only villages, workplaces, and organizations expected to embrace change, such as the Japan Socialist Party or the Japan Communist Party, but also that citadel of the establishment, the national civil bureaucracy.

Thus, the ministries of agriculture, of welfare, and of education all participated in a campaign called the New Life Movement in the 1950s, promoted by agencies of the national and local government, some organizations of women, and some corporations. While it sought some of the same goals of the similarly named New Life Movement of the Guomindang in China in the 1930s—better hygiene, better nutrition, birth control, and improved civic morality—it also set forth goals of democratizing social relations. Representatives from the various ministries (social workers or extension officers modeled after American predecessors) made the rounds of villages and organized women into small groups that met to talk about redesigning kitchens, cooking nutritious meals, and improving sanitation (for example, disposing of garbage so as not to attract flies). In addition, the leaders and local participants spoke continually of democratizing the family. What people meant by a "democratic family" was more egalitarian family relationships, such as rotating the order in which family members took their baths instead of always letting father go first. They meant giving girls and boys equal portions of food, and changing mealtime seating order so the father was not always given pride of place. They also meant giving married women, who had the greatest interest in limiting family size, the means to order condoms by mail.

It is impossible to measure the actual implementation of these changes. Many families did not change their daily routines as urged; some men complained bitterly that easy access to contraceptives would make loose women of their wives and destroy the family. Nevertheless, birthrates quickly and dramatically declined in the 1950s owing in large measure to new legal access to both abortion and contraception. Bureaucrats, local activists, and residents engaged in unprecedented discussions of the need for change in the nitty-gritty of daily life. To the extent that the state and corporations were its major promoters, the New Life Movement combined impulses to manage and contain change as well as to empower its grassroots advocates. But the common postwar saying "The only things stronger since the war are women and [nylon] stockings" reflects not only male anxiety but also new practices in the realms of discourse and behavior.

In addition to an extraordinary desire to democratize the nation, Japanese people in the late 1940s and 1950s, and beyond, enthusiastically talked about fostering "culture" and science. The meaning ascribed to these terms, especially to culture, was not always clear or consistent, and the enthusiasm was not wholly new. Both "cultured living" and science had been favored goals of reformers and middle-class Japanese in prewar cities and villages. But the postwar scope and intensity of interest in these notions were unprecedented. The New Life Movement, for example, was often described as a campaign to realize a modern "cultural life." The expression implied many things: a life open to change, progress through technological innovation, more rational, scientific, Western, pacifistic, and democratic ways of doing things. The difficulty of translating this term "culture" *(bunka)* into meaningful English has sometimes led people to drop it from translations altogether, thus obscuring to outsiders the importance of the concept. One lodging house, library, and meeting place for foreign and Japanese students and academics in postwar Tokyo is called, in English, the International House of Japan. A literal translation of the Japanese name for this institution *(kokusai bunka kaikan)* would actually be the International Culture Hall. The label invokes a sense of cosmopolitan, liberal, and democratic values. It suggests the possibilities of progressive and successful modernization. Given this positive postwar connotation of the word "culture," it pops up in unexpected places in the commercial realm as well. One major producer of windows, doors, and shutters in postwar Japan is the Cultural Shutter Corporation, whose products are by this label associated with modern home design and progressive living.

The positive value attached to science and rationality in early postwar Japan was also great. Among scientists, intellectuals, and the public at large, the Japanese wartime regime was seen to have overstressed the efficacy of the Japanese spirit as a weapon of war and undervalued Western science and the power of technology. The greatest symbol of the fearsome power of Western technology was certainly the atomic bomb. But the postwar awe of science is apparent in attitudes toward more commonplace inventions as well. One Japanese woman looked back on 1946, when her husband was an American prisoner in the Philippines accused of war crimes, and recalled that "his letters from Manila were written on light blue letter paper like airletters today. The thing that surprised me most about them was the Scotch tape. I'd never seen that before. That's what truly convinced me Japan had lost the war."[6] One important institution whose founders in the late 1940s were moved by a profound commitment to modern science was the Japan Union of Scientists and Engineers (JUSE). In later years JUSE became a leader in the campaign to introduce quality control to Japanese industry; the body gained international recognition for these efforts by the 1980s. Its founders saw the promotion and application of science as vital not only to reviving the nation's industrial output and raising productivity, but also to the success of democracy and improvement of Japanese society.

Together with democracy, culture, and science, peace was embraced as essential to Japan's postwar reforms. A commitment to make Japan a nation of peace has been a defining social value of the postwar era, as well as a controversial one. This commitment did not emerge gradually; it erupted suddenly as the exaltation of military institutions and militaristic values vanished with extraordinary speed in August 1945. This sharp change shows how dangerous it is to assume that any group of people is imbued with immutable cultural traits. For fifteen years, Japan's leaders had exalted war as the mother of creativity, the means to a glorious future. Death in battle had been presented as the most admirable sacrifice possible, and most Japanese people at least acted as if they believed this profoundly. Yet in an instant, it seems, this certainty dissolved. It was destroyed by revulsion at the devastation inflicted on Japan by atomic bombs and firebombs more than by reflection or contrition at the devastation Japanese people had inflicted on others. Postwar pacifism seems to have sprung primarily from a determination never again to be horribly victimized by war. Whatever its source, the commitment to making Japan a nation of peace mobilized a powerful constituency against the U.S.-Japan security alliance established in 1952, and made this the most contentious foreign policy issue in Japan for at least twenty years.

Large numbers of Japanese people, across boundaries of class and region, and including some in the old elites of bureaucracy, business, and political parties, thus embraced the occupation reforms and looked forward to a future characterized by terms such as democracy, culture, science, and peace. The precise proportion who did so shifted over time and with the issue at stake. By the early 1950s these concepts, especially peace and democracy, had taken on a clear political meaning, and allegiance to them defined one as a member of the "opposition" or "progressive" forces.[7] Advocates of peace and democracy could be rigidly orthodox in their adherence to a vision of a social revolution led by a vanguard party, but they could be creative and flexible in both tactics and objectives as well. Labor unions mobilized both their members and local communities in some important campaigns for higher wages and greater control of the workplace in the 1950s. Support for causes such as a ban on nuclear weapons testing in the 1950s, opposition to American involvement in the Vietnam War in the 1960s, or tighter controls on environmental pollution in the 1970s gained broad support well beyond the formal membership of the Socialist or Communist parties. In the divided political culture of early postwar Japan, these voices constituted an important force seeking to give meaning to the postwar reforms through grassroots activism.

Not everyone shared this enthusiasm. Members of the prewar and wartime ruling elite, especially those in the bureaucracy and in the Liberal and Democratic parties, which had formed cabinets in the 1920s and continued to dominate the Diet in the 1920s, managed to preserve their positions of power. Until 1954 their most important leader was Yoshida Shigeru. He had served as a diplomat of modest importance in the 1920s and 1930s, and had managed to build a reputation as a pro-American liberal. This helped him become president of the Liberal Party and prime minister from May 1946 to May 1947, and then again from October 1948 through the end of 1954. After that, prewar politician Hatoyama Ichirō and top wartime bureaucrat (and briefly an accused "Class A" war criminal) Kishi Nobusuke took up the cause of reaction. They railed against the "excesses" of American reformers, condemned "irresponsible" Japanese agitators, and bided their time in the expectation that once the Americans departed, they could easily turn back the tide of reform and restore the old order of things, minus the military establishment, whom they blamed for the disaster of war.[8]

Japan's old guard was bolstered in its efforts by the Americans in two ways, one ironically unintended and one quite intentional. The most important source of continuity in the ruling structure of postwar Japan was the bureaucracy, whose personnel and organization were scarcely modified by the American occupiers. SCAP did purge some top bureaucrats and abolish the Home Ministry, with its notorious apparatus of domestic censorship and repression. But SCAP otherwise ruled Japan indirectly, through existing state bureaus. It did so in order to implement occupation reforms efficiently, certainly with no intent to bolster the status quo. Yet by fostering bureaucratic continuity in this way, SCAP unintentionally helped maintain important characteristics of the old order.

Bureaucratic continuity also allowed state officials to learn from prewar and wartime experience and devise more effective means to manage society and economy. The most important such continuity was arguably the survival of the officials of the 1920s Ministry of Commerce and Industry bureaucrats, through the wartime "economic general staff" of the Munitions Ministry, into the postwar Ministry of International Trade and Industry (MITI). That ministry became the proud and influential superintendent of Japan's industrial policy of the high-growth era and beyond.[9]

Old guard elites seeking to protect elements of the prewar system received intentional help in the form of the so-called reverse course in American occupation policy. The onset of the cold war in Europe, the increasing strength and then the victory of the Communist revolution in China, and the considerable power of the left in Japan, in labor unions and among intellectuals as much as at the polls, changed the balance among American policy makers. These men had been divided from the outset over the extent to which Japan was a potential enemy needing fundamental reform or a potential ally needing slight adjustment. Beginning in 1947, the Americans downplayed some policies to democratize Japan and repudiated others. They focused more on rebuilding Japan as the revived capitalist workshop of Asia and cold war ally. The Americans abandoned the program of *zaibatsu* dissolution. They also encouraged a willing Japanese government to revise labor laws to restrict public sector unions in particular, purge thirteen thousand members of the Japan Communist Party from positions in public and private sector workplaces and unions, and form a national police force, then a Self-Defense Force.

The Japanese leaders who supported these changes did their best to continue the reverse course when the occupation ended. They sought to roll back institutional reforms at home, revive Japan's military power and open the way to an independent foreign policy, and restore the imperial symbol to something closer to its prewar perch at the apex of the social and political hierarchy. They proved unable to realize all these ambitious goals, but they did enjoy some noteworthy successes. They reconcentrated economic power under the banks of the old *zaibatsu* and restored centralized control over education policy and the police force. They even built a new military, the Self-Defense Force, albeit with no prospect of projecting power beyond Japanese borders. Business consistently confronted and defeated labor unions engaged in militant actions in the 1950s, and the government overrode a huge protest movement to renew the U.S.-Japan Security Treaty in 1960.

The architects of these programs of reaction had significant popular support. Some of it was passive; so long as the economy was booming, many people were willing to vote for the Liberal Democratic Party, formed through a merger of the Liberal and Democratic parties in 1955. In addition, a significant constituency of activists on the right mobilized support through the same political tools, such as demonstrating and lobbying, available to the progressive forces. In particular, the Association of Bereaved Families (of soldiers killed in the war) and the association of Shinto shrine priests roused their supporters on behalf of a variety of conservative causes, such as revival in 1967 of a national holiday to commemorate the mythical founding of Japan by the Sun Goddess, progenitrix of the imperial line.[10]

But the reactionary drive of the 1950s fell short of its most cherished goal to amend the constitution by eliminating Article 9 and banishing its democratic "excesses." Over the next two decades, the ruling elites shifted to a strategy of accommodating and co-opting the new order rather than dismantling it.

The early postwar years from 1945 to approximately 1960 were thus marked off from the era which preceded it by several dramatic changes: the occupation reforms; a new emphasis on the modern, the progressive, the cultural, and the scientific; the disappearance of overt expression of military values; and a gut-level pacifism among many. At the same time, substantial popular and elite resistance to these changes continued. Although a "transwar" socioeconomic structure changed relatively little, this era was characterized by a peculiar postwar condition of political and cultural diversity and contention.

Social Transformations from the 1960s

Beginning in the late 1950s, the social patterns of transwar Japan began to change dramatically. First, the countryside began to shrink. Both the number and the proportion of full-time farmers began a sharp and steady decline, from 2.1 million full-time farm households in 1955 to well under half that number (830,000) in 1970. The proportion of the labor force employed in agriculture fell below 20 percent in 1970, and continued falling to less than 10 percent in 1985, and roughly 4 percent today. In extreme cases this demographic shift created entirely empty ghost villages. But the evacuation of the countryside was not as profound as these numbers suggest, because in many ways both the city and new forms of employment moved out to the country. With improved roads and the ability to afford motorcycles and cars, postwar Japanese were increasingly able to live in the village and commute to work in the city or suburb, and with new farm machinery, they could till fields on the weekend. The decline in full-time farming was thus balanced by a sharp increase in part-time farm households, from 1.6 million in 1955 to almost double (2.7 million) in 1980. Only the grandparents and grandchildren were left on the farms during the working day.[11]

The patterns and experience of education in Japan likewise changed dramatically over these years. In the late 1940s and early 1950s, increased numbers of youths began advancing to high school, though the proportion did not pass 50 percent until 1955. Then, from the end of the 1950s and into the 1960s attendance rates soared, reaching 82 percent in 1970 and 94 percent by 1980. Large proportions also entered two- or four-year colleges. By 1975, 35 percent of high school graduates entered college each year, a rate exceeding that of most European societies and approaching that of the United States.

Higher education in Japan thus changed from a mechanism regulating entry into a small ruling elite of men and their relatively well educated wives, as it had been since Meiji times, to a sorting machine for the masses. The Ministry of Education and the leaders of corporate Japan observed and managed this transformation with care. Advisory committees of businessmen in the early 1960s joined with education bureaucrats to call for exam-focused public schooling that would impart basic skills to an expanded pool of new workers, blue- and white-collar, able to adapt to rapidly changing production and office technologies, and would allocate a hierarchy of credentials, from high school to junior college to college degrees, to help slot young men and women into appropriate levels and roles in the workplace. The expansion of Japan's notorious "examination hell" must be seen in this light. Against the wishes of many teachers who wanted to emphasize other modes of learning, the examination-centered school curriculum was designed both to sort young people and to discipline them. It prepared them, boys especially, for a demanding, competitive working routine by requiring repetitive cramming for dull exams.

Ironically, the spread of mass higher education also turned college into the only moment of respite that a young man or woman could look forward to. For the men, college by the 1960s was a break between an exhausting regime of exam cramming and the grind of a fast-track, or even a routine, career. For the women, college was a time of freedom between exams and the likewise demanding job of a full-time homemaker who was often a part-time wage worker as well. Japanese universities since the 1960s through the present have not been places where young people go to be educated. They go to make friends, learn to drink and be social, perhaps become political (especially in the 1960s). If they are serious about academic learning, they are free to pursue it in informal study groups as well as in the classroom, but they are hardly required to study to graduate.

One important feature of mass higher education in the first decade of rapid growth sharply sets this period off from both the era before the war and the period of the 1970s through the present: access was remarkably egalitarian. In the case of the public universities, which were (and are) the most prestigious ports of entry to elite positions, students from the most economically privileged families who entered public universities in the 1960s were only slightly overrepresented, and the children of the poorest families in the nation were represented almost precisely in proportion to their numbers in the overall population. Of students in national universities in 1961, 19.7 percent came from the poorest 20 percent of families, and 20.2 percent were from the next quintile, roughly speaking the lower-middle class.[12] This remarkably egalitarian profile of student backgrounds was testimony to the standardized quality of public schools across the nation as the economic miracle began. Equality then eroded gradually in the 1960s and more quickly after 1970, as attending expensive private after-school examination-prep schools became a virtual prerequisite for passing university entrance exams.

A related characteristic of the postwar social condition of the high-growth era was the emergence of the nuclear family as the norm, both in practice and in the reigning cultural image of typical and desirable family life. As young adults migrated from rural to urban Japan, became more affluent, and aspired to independence from what many saw as the oppressive hierarchy of the extended family, the proportion of nuclear families rose steadily through the 1960s and 1970s, from 54 percent in 1960 to nearly two thirds of all families (64 percent) in 1975.

Such families constituted what commentators in the late 1950s began to call Japan's "new middle class."[13] The adjective "new" marks a contrast to the families of the urban middle class of the prewar and transwar era, primarily shopkeepers, small traders, and small manufacturers who had been the dominant presence in the neighborhoods of Japanese cities from early in the century (and before) through the 1950s. Just as village life was transformed but not destroyed in the high-growth era, these older urban families did not disappear. Indeed, they remain numerous and a source of the vitality of city life in Japan to this day.[14] The new social phenomenon of middle-class "salary man" families did not obliterate old social forms. It instead coexisted with the old forms in social practice but overwhelmed them in social discourse, eventually provoking a reaction of nostalgia and yearning for the "authentic" social roots of Japanese city and country life.

The new middle class took up residence in the growing suburbs of Tokyo, Yokohama, Nagoya, Osaka, and other cities. In the booming decades of the 1960s through the 1980s, huge apartment blocks sprouted in what had been rice or vegetable fields, and developers put up single-family homes sprawling in all directions out of these cities. In the typical nuclear families of these years, the husband commuted by train to a demanding full-time job in an office or a factory, and the wife devoted herself primarily to the care of their children, rarely more than two in number, and she perhaps took on a part-time job.

The world of official Japan, leaders in the bureaucracy, politicians, and corporations, did not observe these trends passively. A variety of programs did not simply encourage the emergence and sustenance of the nuclear family, but supported a particular version of it. Japan's postwar social security system, put into place from the 1950s through the 1970s and reinforced thereafter, was premised on the "standard" nuclear family with a strictly gendered division of labor. Tax policy built in strong disincentives to women's working more than part-time: a spouse's income under approximately $10,000 was untaxed, but over that it was taxed at the primary earner's much higher rate. And the officially sponsored New Life Movement took on a new dimension in the mid-1950s when major companies started extensive programs to teach employee wives to be "professional" household managers.

Japanese workplaces also took on new "postwar" social characteristics. The proportion of family workers in the labor force dropped steadily from two thirds of all workers in the late 1950s to under half by the end of the 1960s. As high school education came to be the norm, it lost value as a job credential. In the 1940s and 1950s, one found an education-based hierarchy in the workplace, with roots in the prewar era. Male and female middle school graduates worked as blue-collar operatives with relatively limited future prospects. High school boys could take on skilled production or clerical jobs with a reasonable expectation of rising at least to foreman, in some cases beyond, while girls with high school degrees could move into secretarial office jobs in relatively prestigious companies. And university graduates entered the elite managerial positions in corporate and bureaucratic offices. Then, as almost everyone went on to high school in the 1960s and 1970s, the degree came to define a floor rather than a privileged middle point of entry.

A better-educated and better-disciplined work force was one result. Another was a significant closing of the gap between white- and blue-collar work, at least among men. When technicians and managers with college degrees had managed production workers with a middle school education, the differences in experience and expectations were vast. But when virtually all employees had gone to school through age eighteen, and college education itself imparted relatively little new knowledge or skill, the gap was much smaller.

The postwar society of high-growth Japan was marked by a range of cultural changes related to these shifts in rural life, education, family structure, and the workplace. A spread and increase in the power of the mass media marked a new departure of the late 1950s that reflected the takeoff of television set ownership. Prodded by electronic and print advertising for the new products flooding from Japanese factories, a heightened fever of consumerism permeated society. Of course, a consumerist commercial culture had existed in prewar Japan, especially among middle-class city dwellers, but it is fair to say that Japan moved in these years from a society in which the majority of inhabitants worked most of the time to satisfy their relatively basic needs for food, clothing, and shelter to one whose members were "liberated" to pursue their wants and desires as shaped and manipulated by mass advertising.

New forms of desire emerged in human relationships as well. In upper-class and middle-class Japan of the early twentieth century, marriages were typically arranged, although a minority and somewhat subversive ideal of love as the basis of marriage had appeared. Through the 1950s the arranged marriage, in which the partners were introduced by parents, friends, or relatives and met several times for a brief "look-see" (the *omiai*), was still quite common in the new middle class of white-collar salaried workers.[15] But the ideal of the "love marriage" was no longer regarded as subversive. The custom of dating became popular among college youths and young workers in the 1950s, and the word for date *(deeto)* was imported from English. Gradually but steadily, the proportion of marriages defined by the couples as "love matches" rose.

Japan in the postwar era also became for the first time a society in which large-scale bureaucratic *and* commercial institutions were omnipresent in the lives of most people. Hospitals became the almost universal sites for birth and death: in 1955, 82 percent of childbirths took place at home; by 1975, the proportion was a mere 1.2 percent![16] Weddings were transformed into lavish and costly spectacles, aggressively marketed and expertly performed in thousands of hotels and wedding halls nationwide.[17] Funerals and the various anniversary memorial services of Buddhist observance were also increasingly provided by such institutions. As bullet trains, automobiles, and jet travel came within reach of the middle class, mass tourism at home and, increasingly, abroad surged from the 1960s through the 1990s.

Finally, new ideas about what it meant to be Japanese began to spread widely. The only constant in the identity of being "Japanese," one might say, is the popular conviction dating back at least to the late Tokugawa era that such an identity exists or ought to exist. But the defining experiences and attitudes of this imagined community of "the Japanese" changed as the shared experiences of people changed. The nation of the Japanese people in the postwar era came to be knit together by new images of what it meant to be Japanese. When Crown Prince Akihito (Emperor Hirohito's son) broke with tradition and married the daughter of a wealthy industrialist, nonetheless a commoner, in 1959, their union symbolized a modern postwar ideal of love marriage and nuclear family. Only a fraction of the population saw the parade, but a desire to watch the event reportedly sparked a boom in sales of television sets, as the wedding took place just as the industry was taking off.

The mass media provided the means to share this experience; their producers and announcers defined the event's meaning for viewers. Five years later, Japan hosted the 1964 Olympics in Tokyo, signaling the nation's reentry into international society. Again, of course, only a small minority could actually attend the games. But everyone could share by watching on television, this time in color. In cultural terms, the everyday and the ceremonial experiences of middle-class, educated urban Japanese families thus came to define a new image of contemporary "Japanese-ness," reflected in the eye of the TV camera and beamed into homes proudly adorned with Sanyos or Sonys.

These postwar social patterns coalesced in the high-growth era from the late 1950s through the early 1970s. They consisted of a package of more or less related parts. The new experience of being a mother in Japan during these years encapsulates this package. Married women with children in the 1960s and after did much less sewing than before. They relied increasingly on purchased, finished goods. Automation of housework and commercialization of various services, such as food preparation, freed some of their time. Yet these changes did not necessarily lead women to seek work outside the home. Working for wages was indeed one choice made by married women, and from the mid-1960s on, part-time employment among married women with children became very common. But large numbers also committed themselves to remaining full-time homemakers. And this home-based role was defined as much by what mothers did for their children's education as by housework. The very possibility of the so-called "education mother" of postwar and contemporary Japan was premised on a host of other changes, from increased ability to afford consumer goods and household appliances, to living in nuclear families where care of the in-laws was not a major task, to raising fewer children in the first place.

Political Accommodation and a Transformed Conservative Hegemony

As Japanese social and economic conditions took on this postwar character in the 1960s and beyond, the political alignments of the 1950s, both institutional and ideological, were transformed as well. Lines of influence and causation ran two ways. Politics and policies of growth promotion hastened the shift from a transwar to a postwar socioeconomic system, while an increasingly middle-class Japan in turn eroded support for the harsh early postwar agenda of the reactionary right as well as the politics of the activist left. The result from the 1960s through the 1980s was a politics of the status quo. The rhetorical gestures of left and right still clashed angrily at times in both foreign and domestic policy debates. But the Liberal Democratic Party (LDP) came to accept and effectively manipulate the basic structures of the new constitutional order, while the left changed from a political force talking of revolution to a dissenting gadfly. It even became conservative in a way, as it sought to defend the increasingly entrenched status quo of pacifism and democratic ideals inscribed in the postwar constitution.

One key moment in the transformation of the right-wing forces in the Liberal Democratic Party and the bureaucracy came in 1960. The new prime minister, Ikeda Hayato, learned from the bitter experience of his predecessor, Kishi Nobusuke, who had used force to renew the U.S.-Japan Security Treaty in the face of mass protests outside the Diet and fistfights within it. He adopted a much more conciliatory and commoner-friendly stance. He shelved plans to revise the constitution, and he announced a fundamental goal of doubling real national income by 1970.[18] This would have required real annual growth rates of 7.8 percent for ten years, which would have been extraordinary enough. In fact, the Japanese economy grew at a rate of 10 percent per year; the national income doubled three years ahead of schedule! Although critics complained with much validity that social welfare was being ignored in the rush to produce goods for industry and for export, and that growing national wealth, much of which was reinvested by corporations, outpaced the gains for individual Japanese people, enough voters perceived benefit in high-speed growth to sustain LDP political hegemony throughout the decade.

Toward the end of the 1960s, critics of the ruling triumvirate of LDP, bureaucracy, and big business mounted a vigorous movement of protest against the increasing environmental costs of a growth-above-all policy. They focused most of their attention not so much on damage to the natural environment itself as on the human tragedy of diseases such as those caused by mercury or cadmium poisoning suffered by residents in the vicinity of several major chemical producing plants in southern, central, and northern Japan. At first, bureaucrats and corporate executives denied any problems and suppressed evidence of links between unexplained diseases and factory wastes. But as public protests spread, the state eventually shifted to a more accommodating policy. It established and strengthened major laws to control pollution in 1967, 1968, and 1970, including some of the strictest air pollution standards in the world, and set up an Environmental Agency in 1971. It offered modest financial compensation to victims in the most notorious pollution cases. Consequently, the government effectively contained the energy of the broad-based citizens' movements that had led the protests. At the same time, it carefully supported industry and continued its pro-growth policies. Enforcement of the new standards was not as stringent as the standards themselves, and some were subsequently lowered in response to business pressures.

In these same years the Liberal Democrats and their bureaucratic allies also engaged in a creative project to co-opt the political opposition in the realm of social welfare policies. Urban voters in the high-growth era included a relatively large percentage of labor union members. They supported the Japan Socialist and Japan Communist parties more generously than their rural counterparts, and the late 1960s and 1970s were a time of so-called progressive local government. Socialist or Communist Party mayors and governors were elected in most major cities; at the peak in 1971, progressive mayors were in office in over 160 cities, including Tokyo, Yokohama, Osaka, and Kyoto. Among their most popular initiatives were generous new programs of health insurance and social welfare. The national government headed by the LDP came late to these causes, but it eventually addressed and controlled the issues effectively. It significantly expanded the scope and generosity of national health and old-age welfare programs in 1973, dubbed "Year One of the Welfare Era." But again, as with pollution controls, the government later moved to scale back some commitments, especially in the area of old-age pensions, which it deemed too expensive.

As conservative elites thus moved to capture a growing political center by co-opting programs of citizens' movements or left-wing parties, the local bases and some national leaders of the progressive forces likewise moved to the center. In the wake of a series of failed strikes led by unions seeking to promote grassroots activism and workplace control by employees, a new breed of leaders, until this time a defensive minority in the labor movement, took charge of the union movement. With a center of gravity located in enterprise-based rather than industrial unions, they consolidated control first in private sector workplaces in the 1960s, and gradually in the public sector in the 1970s and 1980s. They argued that cooperation with management and short-term moderation in wage and other demands would guarantee the long-range prosperity of corporations and their employees. Beginning in the 1970s, they joined ongoing forums for tripartite consultation with business leadership and state officials over wage and employment policies, and strikes diminished sharply in frequency and intensity.

In this context of economic boom, social change, and political accommodation, the parties of the left were sharply divided among and within themselves. They ultimately failed to attract consistent popular support. In 1960 the right wing of the Japan Socialist Party (JSP), supported by the cooperative wing of the labor movement and willing to accept the U.S.-Japan military alliance, split off to form the reformist, decidedly antirevolutionary Democratic Socialist Party (DSP). In subsequent elections the DSP never won at the polls as many seats as it had at the moment of its founding. The majority who remained in the JSP then argued for more than two decades over the extent to which the party should modify or abandon support for a revolutionary transformation of capitalism. In place of such a radical position, in the early 1960s some in the party articulated a vision of a pacifist Japan and a parliamentary democracy whose government would offer extensive social security and welfare and gradually modify the capitalist economy to benefit common people. At the time, this might have been a fresh and attractive program for many voters, but the majority in the party condemned it as an excessively moderate betrayal of the party's ideals. When the Socialist Party in fact adopted even less ambitious positions in the 1980s and 1990s, the Liberal Democratic Party's politics of social accommodation had given it a plausible claim to be the champion of similar goals. Such halting moves to the center from both sides made it possible, if still astonishing, for these once bitter rivals to join in a coalition government in 1994.

By the 1980s, a politics of accommodation seemed firmly in place in Japan. Peace movements, left-wing parties, grassroots labor union activism, citizens' movements, and environmental protests had forced some important policy changes, but they had generally lost their vitality. Feminism had become increasingly vigorous and visible, but it remained a relatively marginal ideology and movement. At the same time, the reactionary push from above and at the grass roots to turn the clock back and revive the symbols and the structure of the prewar past had won hollow victories at best. The imperial institution had survived, and for several months in late 1989 the long illness and death of the Shōwa Emperor (Hirohito) indeed cast a coercive net of "self-restraint" over the nation, as people everywhere heeded official prodding and curtailed their year-end celebrations. But the media treatment of his funeral, the subsequent imperial rituals inaugurating the new Heisei era, and especially the 1993 marriage of Hirohito's grandson, Crown Prince Naruhito, to Masako Owada, a young diplomat educated at Harvard, rendered the throne a somewhat banal, Disneyesque source of spectacle and entertainment. The institution's sacred aura and once literally awesome disciplining power seemed a relic of a distant age.[19]

For most of the 1980s, then, the population of an ever more affluent Japan seemed increasingly apolitical and complacent. As the Japanese economy continued to outperform its advanced capitalist competitors in North America and Europe, and as the financial as well as productive power of Japanese corporations reached dizzying heights between 1985 and 1990, complacence gave way to arrogance in some quarters. Companies listed on the Tokyo stock exchange accounted for more than 40 percent of the total value of the entire world's stock markets. The aggregate value of real estate in Tokyo reportedly exceeded that of the entire United States.

The benefits and the costs of this boom were not evenly shared. One sign of discontent erupted with the confluence of LDP scandal and a regressive new consumption tax imposed in 1989. These sparked a brief moment of apparent political mobilization, in which "floating" voters of the middle class, especially women, drifted from the LDP to the Socialists. The Socialist revival proved short-lived, and the LDP retained its lower-house majority in the election of February 1990. But 1990 (conveniently for those who like to mark eras by the decades of the Christian calendar) turned out to be the year the financial bubble burst. The Tokyo stock market lost well over half its value in a single year. As the market crash turned into a recession, commercial land prices fell by as much as 80 percent over the next several years, and banks which had lent vast sums to poorly scrutinized development schemes and businesses found themselves holding nearly worthless mortgage paper. By some estimates, Japanese lenders held as much as $1 trillion of bad debt by 1998.

In this context, respected pundits such as Morita Akio, the founder of the Sony Corporation, issued calls for the total restructuring of the Japanese economic system. When the Liberal Democratic Party split and fell from power for the first time in its history in 1993, a political restructuring seemed imminent as well. But despite various major steps toward deregulation, the government and certainly the private sector were unwilling to deal openly and quickly with the massive debt that paralyzed the financial system, and no viable alternative to the Liberal Democrats emerged either.

The recession continued through the end of the 1990s. And in 1995 both complacence and arrogance gave way to a widespread sense of despair when a devastating earthquake struck Kobe and a lethal rush-hour nerve gas attack, apparently the work of one of the many small evangelical religious organizations that had mushroomed in the 1980s, killed twelve commuters and injured thousands in Tokyo.

By early 1997 the economy was showing signs of recovery, at which point the government imposed a 2 percent increase in the consumption tax, first introduced against huge opposition in 1989. This slowed consumer spending, and when the Asian financial crisis exploded in the summer and fall of 1997, exposing already weak Japanese lenders to further losses overseas, signs of recovery vanished, the gross national product began to contract, and an even deeper recession returned. Japan's economy at the end of the twentieth century was caught between a rock and a hard place. The financial crisis seemed to require painful steps to close failed enterprises or sharply reduce their size and retire bad loans. But economic recovery depended on consumers, who would be even more reluctant to spend money if business were failing and their jobs seemed likely to vanish.

In addition, the society faced serious long-range problems. The burden of caring for a rapidly aging population appeared likely to fall on individuals and families with relatively little community or state support, although the government in 1998 did introduce a major new program of long-term care insurance. Japan in the 1990s was a much less egalitarian place than it had been a generation earlier, in both access to education and distribution of assets. People recognized these problems and were unhappy about them, and they were certainly troubled by the extended, deep recession. But in the ongoing process of political restructuring, it was not clear whether new alignments would offer significant alternatives.

In 1998, the newly formed Democratic Party showed surprising strength in a Diet election which saw the LDP suffer a major defeat. The Democratic Party consisted of relatively liberal politicians who had left the LDP, and others from the socialist parties and the labor movement. If it proved able to articulate an alternative vision of consumer-friendly and economically viable policies, it stood to emerge as a serious contender for power, but its leaders lacked experience, and it faced significant internal divisions. As the century drew to a close, masses of Japanese remained frustrated at their inability to influence public affairs, which, for better or worse, were still being managed by the superintendents of huge organizations, whether state bureaucrats or corporate executives.

Selected Readings

Bestor, Theodore C. *Neighborhood Tokyo*. Stanford: Stanford University Press, 1989.

Brinton, Mary. *Women and the Japanese Miracle*. Berkeley: University of California Press, 1993.

Dore, Ronald. *British Factory–Japanese Factory*. Berkeley: University of California Press, 1973.

———— *City Life in Japan: A Study of a Tokyo Ward*. Berkeley: University of California Press, 1958.

———— *Shinohata: Portrait of a Japanese Village*. New York: Pantheon, 1978.

Dower, John W. *Embracing Defeat: Japan after World War II*. New York: W. W. Norton, 1999.

Garon, Sheldon. *Molding Japanese Minds*. Princeton: Princeton University Press, 1997.

Gordon, Andrew. *The Wages of Affluence: Labor and Management in Postwar Japan*. Cambridge, Mass.: Harvard University Press, 1998.

Gordon, Andrew, ed. *Postwar Japan as History*. Berkeley: University of California Press, 1993.

Johnson, Chalmers. *MITI and the Japanese Miracle: The Growth of Industrial Policy, 1925–1975*. Stanford: Stanford University Press, 1982.

Robertson, Jennifer. *Native and Newcomer*. Berkeley: University of California Press, 1991.

Rohlen, Thomas. *For Harmony and Strength: Japanese White-Collar Organization in Anthropological Perspective*. Berkeley: University of California Press, 1974.

Smith, Robert J. *Kurusu: The Price of Progress in a Japanese Village, 1951–1975*. Stanford: Stanford University Press, 1978.

Vogel, Ezra. *Japan's New Middle Class: The Salary Man and His Family in a Tokyo Suburb*. Berkeley: University of California Press, 1963.

CHAPTER 10

Searching for the Appropriate Model for the People's Republic of China

MERLE GOLDMAN AND ANDREW J. NATHAN

Soon after the Chinese Communist Party announced the establishment of the People's Republic of China on October 1, 1949, the new regime resumed the effort to achieve "wealth and power" *(fu qiang)*, the national goals that had eluded Chinese reformers since the late nineteenth century. China's slow, tortuous development and military disasters in the first half of the twentieth century had left it further than ever behind the advanced countries. Only by modernizing its economy and military in the shortest possible time and revolutionizing Chinese society, party leaders believed, could the regime make good on Mao Zedong's bold promise announced a week before the PRC's founding that "China has stood up."

In this effort, party leaders during the next half century experimented with a number of different developmental models. Yet it was not until the post-Mao era, when they followed a course that resonated with China's own history and experience and responded to the changing realities of East Asia, that they finally appeared to have found the path to prosperity and world influence.

The Mao Era, 1949–1976

The Soviet Model

Most of China's population welcomed the Chinese Communist Party's assumption of power and unification of the country in 1949 in the belief that at long last, warfare would end and order would be restored.

Although party leaders initially sounded a note of moderation while they consolidated their position and revived the economy, it was clear from the very beginning that they intended to carry out a sweeping revolution. Evidence for that already existed in the countryside, where wholesale execution of landlords began in areas under party control during the later stages of the civil war with the Guomindang and continued into the early 1950s. Using the violent methods that the Soviets had used against the kulaks (landholding Russian peasants) in the late 1920s, the party presided over millions of summary executions and even larger numbers of beatings and imprisonments of landlords throughout the country. Whether friend or enemy, soon everyone received the message that a revolution was under way and that, as Mao had said, "Power grows out of the barrel of a gun."

After putting party cadres in the leadership positions vacated by the executed and purged rural landlords, redistributing the land to the peasants, rebuilding the economic infrastructure, and quelling the inflation left from the Guomindang era, Mao and the party were ready by the mid-1950s to emulate the Soviet model of development fashioned by Stalin. Their choice was shaped by two historical legacies, one intellectual and one economic, and was also influenced by China's position in the international arena after the 1949 revolution.[1]

The intellectual legacy was based on the conviction among Chinese elites, Communists and non-Communists alike, that the Soviet model offered the best path to rapid industrialization. Most Chinese intellectuals in the late 1940s regarded capitalism as a corrupt and unstable form of political economy, characterized by wasteful boom and bust cycles, diversion of resources needed for investment to luxury consumption, widening economic inequalities, social injustice, political disorder, and international aggression. In Chinese eyes the Soviet, specifically the Stalinist, model provided a proven path to rapid, rational growth. The Chinese understood Stalinism to consist of state mobilization of the rural surplus ("primitive accumulation") and the rational allocation of this surplus to high-priority industrial investments (the "planned economy"). Hence, without much internal debate, China's new leaders, starting in 1954, moved to establish a state planning apparatus, nationalize commerce and industry, and, in 1955, collectivize agriculture.

China's economic legacy was an economy that was more rural than Russia's. About 80 percent of China's population lived on the land, engaged in intensive agriculture, and produced little surplus above subsistence. The main obstacle to China's rapid industrialization, the party leaders argued, was not the lack of technology or urban manpower, but the small size of the surplus produced by China's densely populated agrarian sector and the landlord class's misuse of what surplus there was in luxury consumption. Therefore, China's leaders believed that the most effective way to increase and get control over that surplus for industrialization was through collectivization of agriculture.

China's use of the Soviet model was also impelled by its international situation. When the party came to power, it faced a hostile anticommunist America. Nevertheless, since it was in actual control of the Chinese mainland, the State Department had intended to move toward diplomatic recognition of the new regime. This policy was reversed in 1950, however, when North Korea invaded South Korea with Stalin's and Mao's permission to try to reunify the divided peninsula, thus starting the Korean War. With the outbreak of the war, the United States not only led the military effort to stop the North Korean advance, but also interposed the Seventh Fleet in the Taiwan Strait to protect the Republic of China (ROC) on Taiwan from mainland attack. Four years later, the United States signed a Mutual Defense Treaty with the ROC. These events introduced over two decades of American-led Western containment and isolation of China. The possibility of Chinese diplomatic links with both East and West was foreclosed. Through most of the 1950s, China "leaned to one side," as Mao called it, by signing a Treaty of Friendship, Alliance, and Mutual Assistance with the Soviet Union in 1950 that specified Soviet assistance in case of war with Japan or the United States.

Although China's huge size and its international isolation dictated that it had to be self-reliant for most of the capital and technology needed to build modern industry, during the 1950s it received crucial even if limited development aid from its Soviet ally. Soviet experts helped set up a system of economic planning and administration and assisted in constructing 156 infrastructural and industrial projects. Soviet financial assistance was neither large nor free; it consisted of loans worth $430 million. Nevertheless, these funds and the accompanying transfer of technology were crucial to the success of China's First Five-Year Plan (1953–1957),[2] which built on and expanded the industrial foundation begun by the Guomindang, as described by William Kirby in Chapter 7.

The Chinese Communists also followed the Soviet model in politics. They established a Leninist-style single-party dictatorship, the party-state. It was built around a vanguard party that controlled the careers of both party members and nonmembers via a Soviet-style nomenklatura, a list of jobs to be filled by party appointment. The Chinese Communist Party penetrated even further into society and into the local areas than either the Soviet party or the Guomindang, which had also emulated the Leninist party-state. Because of its low level of differentiation from other power structures, the party not only reigned but also ruled, not only led society but also controlled it. At the top, party power was concentrated in thirty to forty persons who had the authority to make major decisions. Among them, authority was personalized, uninstitutionalized, and fluid.

Personalities and private relationships exerted a major influence on policy. Psychological pathologies of power flourished in an atmosphere of court politics, as was also the case in Stalinist Russia. Although Mao was the dominant leader and was made the subject of a cult of personality, his power was intermittently checked or challenged by his Long March colleagues. Suspicious and alert, Mao constantly balanced the power of his followers and played on their jealousies and rivalries. As in other Leninist party-states, the army had a commissar system and a system of party organizations, but it was not the party as an institution but rather Mao personally who "controlled the gun." The military reported to him through the Military Affairs Commission, which he chaired.

Yet soon after agricultural collectivization began in 1955, the leadership confronted a series of setbacks. Despite collectivization, the proceeds from forced grain sales and the grain tax were disappointing. Agriculture did not grow as fast as the leaders had expected; they suspected that the peasants were not delivering the full surplus. Also expecting faster industrial growth, they were disappointed by the inability of Soviet-type planning to resolve bottlenecks in transport, energy, and construction materials that accompanied the rapid development. Peasants in search of a better life began to migrate into the cities, where they could not find work and became a drain on urban resources.

With increasing misgivings about the Soviet economic model, Mao began searching for a new approach to economic development. In 1956 and the first half of 1957, he launched a campaign which he called "One Hundred Flowers Bloom; One Hundred Schools Contend," during which he encouraged intellectuals to come forth with new proposals and to criticize the party cadres for problems encountered in following the Soviet model. But when some intellectuals went beyond criticism of local party cadres for abusive treatment and incompetence to criticism of the leadership and its policies, especially its repression of intellectuals, Mao in June 1957 launched the "anti-rightist" campaign against the critics. An estimated 750,000 people were labeled "rightists" and received punishments ranging from demotions to twenty years in labor camps. Most rightists were read out of society for almost two decades and not rehabilitated until after Mao's death in September 1976.

The anti-rightist campaign was just one in a series of movements that Mao had launched, beginning in Yan'an in the early 1940s, in the Northeast in 1948 and in a 1955 nationwide purge of literary intellectuals, who he believed were undermining both him and the party. After the Hundred Flowers period, Mao's distrust of intellectuals intensified, culminating in the Cultural Revolution (1966–1976), a campaign against virtually all intellectuals. Most party cadres also turned against the intellectuals during the Mao era. They regarded them as a potential alternate source of legitimacy because of their specialist and professional training and the Confucian tradition of rule by a literati elite.

Maoist Models

THE GREAT LEAP FORWARD, 1958–1961 Rejecting the proposals offered by the intellectuals as well as by the Soviet model, beginning in the late 1950s Mao prescribed his own remedies for China's developmental problems.[3] He first prescribed the Great Leap Forward, a program that was supposed to achieve a totally modernized society virtually overnight. In the Great Leap, Mao experimented with a number of different institutions drawn from several different sources, including the Taiping Rebellion of the mid-nineteenth century, which had attempted to establish a heavenly kingdom on earth. As a whole, however, Mao devised a new and unique economic, social, and political program for China.

The most representative of the Maoist institutions were the rural communes. With populations ranging from around ten thousand to over sixty thousand, these communes were meant to be able to take care of all the needs of their members. In reality, they were a larger, more regimented version of the earlier rural collectives. Commune residents were obligated to deliver fixed amounts of grain to the government regardless of the size of the harvest. Initially the communes succeeded in squeezing the maximum surplus out of the countryside to be used for industrial development. In addition, they mobilized peasant labor to build extensive rural modernization projects. Yet the communes ultimately stifled productive growth because of the disincentives intrinsic in their tight controls over virtually all rural enterprises and peasant activities.

Other parts of the Maoist ensemble were mobilizational "Leap"-style assaults on bottlenecks to economic growth: establishment of enormous vertically integrated industrial enterprises, repression of consumption, enforcement of social and political controls through the all-encompassing "work unit" *(danwei)*, and segregation of rural and urban residents. These practices began with the implementation in the mid-1950s of a household registration *(hukou)* system which forbade citizens to change their place of residence or work without permission. Such permission was rarely given. Consequently, peasants were virtually tied to the land in order to prevent the rural population from flooding the cities.

Through the *danwei*, the regime further tied rural and urban residents to their work or residential units. Because assignment to a unit was for life, the unit's party authorities had all but complete control over an individual's and his or her family's daily life, including work, dwelling, marriage, births, health care, educational opportunities, vacations, and retirement benefits. Favorable treatment depended on personal relations with the leaders, political activism, and especially a family's class background *(jieji chushen)*, of which there were two large categories—"good" and "bad." The *hukou, danwei*, and *chushen* together created a virtual caste system which marked the major social boundaries and an individual's fate throughout the Mao era.

Unlike in the Soviet Union, where the police primarily controlled the population, these systems, particularly the *danwei*, exercised political control, whereby the party secretary had nearly unchecked power to make one a class enemy. Therefore, whereas the Soviets created physical and psychological terror through specialized institutions such as political police and labor camps, Mao's China dehumanized class enemies within the institutions of everyday life. In addition, China also had a large labor camp system for the supposedly worst offenders. The threat of terror was always implicit.

Despite the uniqueness of the Great Leap Forward, Maoist institutions still retained some resemblance to the Soviet model: capital for development was drawn predominantly from the autarkic domestic economy, with little capital input from foreign aid or trade; a high rate of accumulation (forced savings) of GNP was achieved by repressing consumption; and investment flowed from agriculture to industry, further perpetuating the urban-rural social gap. Forced rapid industrialization was concentrated in a small number of huge, inefficient state-owned factories, in which major inputs were set at low prices to encourage enterprise growth. The sacrifice of rural and urban living standards in favor of extensive growth through increasing investment became the regime's largest political liability.

China's "command" or administered economy, however, was not coordinated either by a well-developed plan as in the Soviet Union or by market mechanisms as in the West. The lack of both plan and market created village and enterprise "cellularization" (extensive local autarky), so enterprises coordinated their activities informally through bureaucratic and personal networks. The system left no alternative to breakthrough development, or what Mao called "creative imbalances." Consequently, to fulfill the unrealistic production targets that had been set in the Great Leap Forward, the agricultural population was organized on military lines to undertake specific infrastructure projects and to send food to the cities to help increase industrial production. By virtue of this set of institutions, the government was able to invest a staggering 30-plus percent of GNP annually in economic development to build a self-sufficient industrial economy.

This achievement, however, came at enormous costs. The high levels of accumulation required strong political coercion, and the absence of either markets or well-developed planning mechanisms led to vast waste. While it did produce spurts of growth in certain industrial sectors and infrastructure projects, the Great Leap Forward's harsh exploitation of the rural population for industrial growth devastated and starved the agricultural sector. Though the grain warehouses were full and the cities well fed, the diversion of agricultural production to the cities and to international trade caused the worst famine in world history in 1958–1961, with a death toll estimated at over 30 million people.

The Maoist model was characterized by a distinctive mentality, involving the personality cult of Mao, asceticism and self-denial, the definition of human value in political terms, and the valorization of cruelty in the service of class struggle. Ideological mobilization was carried out through political campaigns, study groups, criticism and self-criticism sessions, and a massive propaganda system. In the Great Leap Forward, Maoism took on a utopian cast as Mao prophesied that through its unique institutions China would reach communism before the Soviet Union and would catch up economically with Great Britain within fifteen years. Yet the closer one came to the center of power, the more one found ideology being wielded primarily for power purposes rather than as a real guide to political goals.[4]

Maoism also resembled the classic concept of totalitarianism in the broad scope of the regime's elimination of civil society, the imposition of the party's authority over all social groups, the monolithic nature of the political system, the extreme centralization of political authority in an all-powerful leader, the use of ideological indoctrination and terror as means of control, the aspiration to remake nature and human nature, and the aim not just to control the population totally but to mobilize it for specific purposes. But Maoism was neither classless nor changeless, as early theories of totalitarianism would have predicted.

Among totalitarian systems, Maoism closely resembled Stalinism and also exhibited features of fascism. There were, however, some important differences. Since terror in China was created through the work unit, the police and labor camps played a less important role than in Stalin's Soviet Union or in the concentration camps of Hitler's Germany. The military was a more important factor in inner-party politics, serving as a trump card in Mao's hands, whereas Hitler and Stalin relied on their secret police to buttress their rule and kept the military for the most part out of politics. Although power was centralized in the top leader, local party officials were left relatively unchecked within their units so long as they implemented Mao's orders and did not resist the changing ideological winds emanating from the party center.

Fooled initially by inflated statistics of great leaps in grain production in 1958, Mao and other party leaders truly believed that communism was around the corner and China was on the verge of achieving it before its elder brother, the Soviet Union. But as the intensifying mobilization and regimentation of the peasants in the communes tore apart the whole fabric of life in the countryside and they were pushed beyond physical endurance, the peasants engaged in passive resistance. By the early 1960s, China's rural realities forced the regime to discontinue the Great Leap Forward and revise its policies. Mao had to defer to his more pragmatic colleagues to lead an economic recovery. The communes remained as political units, but the villages (now called the production brigades) were reinstated as the basic level of agricultural production, and the management of industry was recentralized. Nevertheless, the major institutional innovations Mao had promoted in the great leap were left in place.

Another reason for Mao's move away from the Soviet model was that Soviet and Chinese priorities diverged in the late 1950s. The Soviets advised against the Great Leap Forward; they had tried communes early in their revolution and they had failed. The new Soviet Communist Party general secretary, Nikita Khrushchev, pursued peaceful coexistence rather than confrontation with the West. The Soviets gave only weak support to China's efforts to challenge the U.S.-Taiwan relationship, and canceled an agreement to help China acquire nuclear weapons. At the same time, Washington remained adamantly anti-China, hoping to drive a wedge between the two Communist powers.[5]

The break with the Soviet Union became public in 1960, when Soviet advisers abruptly left China, withdrawing their nationals, funds, and plans, and the Chinese party purged officials with close ties to Moscow. Mao personally directed a series of polemics excoriating Moscow's "revision" of Marxism-Leninism and labeling the Soviet Union's attempt to dominate its alliance partners as "hegemonism." When Khrushchev and President John F. Kennedy signed the limited nuclear test-ban treaty in 1963, China charged that the two superpowers were colluding to deny nonnuclear states the means to defend their national sovereignty. In October 1964, China's 1958 decision to continue its nuclear weapons program without Soviet support was vindicated by the successful testing of a nuclear device.

Consequently, in the 1960s China faced encirclement by both superpowers. The United States maintained its Asian alliance system stretching from South Korea and Japan in the northeast to the Philippines, South Vietnam, and Thailand in the southeast. The new Soviet leader in 1963, Leonid Brezhnev, doubled the number of forces in the Soviet Far East and Siberia from about twelve divisions in 1961 to twenty-five by 1969. Soviet probing of Chinese defenses sparked frequent border incidents. Chinese anxiety reached a new peak after the Soviet-led Warsaw Pact armies invaded Czechoslovakia in August 1968 to terminate Prague's experiment with democratizing communism. The Soviet party secretary enunciated the Brezhnev Doctrine, which asserted Moscow's right to intervene militarily in the internal affairs of other socialist states in order to defend the Soviet version of socialism. Mao regarded this doctrine as a direct threat to his version of socialism, to Chinese sovereignty, and to himself.

THE CULTURAL REVOLUTION, 1966–1976   At the same time that Mao was orchestrating and intensifying the polemics with the Soviet Union, he became engaged in a power struggle at home. During the retreat from the Great Leap Forward, Mao's party colleagues and Long March survivors began to question his judgment. They no longer regarded him as infallible. In the early 1960s a number of their associates published indirect criticisms of Mao's policies in the major party media. When Mao became aware of these criticisms in the mid-1960s, he tried to get his party colleagues to stop them and purge his critics. His colleagues, however, no longer responded to his orders as they had in the past. In addition to their disillusionment with Mao and his policies, they feared engaging in any more peremptory actions and campaigns that could lead to another disaster.[6] In the belief that his colleagues were conspiring against him and that the revolution for which he had worked so hard was becoming bureaucratized, as had happened in the Soviet Union, Mao launched the Cultural Revolution in 1966. Bypassing the unresponsive party apparatus, he mobilized young people in groups, called Red Guards, to attack his suspected party rivals and the remnant class enemies from the old regime, particularly the intellectuals.

The Cultural Revolution began as a purge of Mao's supposed enemies, in which the youth at first enthusiastically participated in the belief that the removal of party leaders and intellectual authorities would provide more freedom and opportunities for advancement. But the movement quickly turned into an uncontrolled massive persecution not only of party leaders and intellectuals but also of millions of party officials, bureaucrats, professionals, and skilled workers, who were accused of resisting Mao's revolutionary ideology. While the cases of top party officials were handled by "special case examination groups," the movement spread broadly in urban society as Red Guards and Mao loyalists manipulated and coerced colleagues, friends, and even relatives in neighborhoods and work units to turn on one another with humiliations, beatings, imprisonments, and killings. The Red Guards sacked households, destroyed private possessions, and terrorized anyone they deemed to be a "class enemy."

As the movement became totally out of control, Red Guards broke into factions which fought among themselves and with rival groups of "revolutionary rebels" composed chiefly of mobilized factory workers and, in the summer of 1967, with units of the People's Liberation Army (PLA). When their uncontrolled actions led to further violence against party officials and intellectuals, disrupted the urban economy, and brought the country close to civil war in some places, Mao finally ordered the army to restore order in 1968. There are no comprehensive figures indicating how many were killed or committed suicide, but it is estimated that millions of people were persecuted by rampaging Red Guards during the Cultural Revolution.

Once the most chaotic phase of the Cultural Revolution ended in 1969 when the military was brought in, further real and imaginary opposition continued to be suppressed by the military and also by ideological campaigns launched by Mao's wife, Jiang Jing, and her ideological allies, called "the Gang of Four." Some of the campaigns in the late years of Mao's life included one against a shadowy alleged ultra-left organization called the

May 16 Group (1972); the "Campaign to Criticize Lin Biao and Confucius" (1973–74), directed at discrediting Mao's onetime designated successor Lin Biao, whom Mao accused of planning a coup in 1971, and indirectly against Zhou Enlai, who had sought to limit the excesses of the Cultural Revolution; and the 1975 campaign to criticize the classic Chinese novel *Water Margin* because of its supposed advocacy of class compromise.

Facing the enmity of both the Soviet Union and the United States during the Cultural Revolution, China also mobilized for a "people's war" against any invader. As military clashes with the Soviets broke out along the eastern sector of the Sino-Soviet border in March 1969, and along the western border in August, Moscow threatened nuclear attack. Mao then ordered four retired marshals to analyze the changing global situation. Their report concluded that Moscow was bent on war with China and that the Soviet Union, not the United States, posed the greater threat to Chinese security.[7] Subsequently, Mao authorized contacts with the United States that led ultimately to Richard Nixon's historic visit to China in 1972 and the start of a tacit alliance between the United States and China against the Soviet Union.

By the time of Mao's death on September 9, 1976, it was clear to many Chinese that the Maoist regime had enacted a political tragedy. It had designed its component institutions piecemeal, some for a good purpose. A classic example was the cradle-to-grave delivery of welfare, universal health care, and education through the work unit. But this pattern of organization, put into place in the early 1950s, evolved under the system of one-party control into a form of totalitarian power that trapped individuals for life, cutting off people's alternatives.[8] Rather than engendering a better life for the people, such a system enhanced the power of the leaders, who defined right and wrong and whose utterances became the license for mass violence.

Perhaps the most fundamental question to be asked about the politics of the Mao era is one that also applies to Stalin's Soviet Union, Hitler's Germany, Kim Il Sung's North Korea, and other dictatorships throughout history: Why did so many citizens go along for so long with a system that caused them and their loved ones so much suffering? Since the Maoist system built its power on social cleavages, by classifying one social group as politically advanced and another as backward, and leaving the bulk of individuals unsure of their status, the regime divided people from one another and demanded criticism of others and of oneself as the path to redemption. Class enemies, a fungible designation, were portrayed as scheming and evil, less than human. Many harbored a secret fear of sliding into that category. The only salvation from being cast among the victims was to side with the abusers. Even the victims in such a system waited for a chance to prove their loyalty by participating in and victimizing others. The distinguished journalist Liu Binyan recalls, "When I saw so many people who had done much less and said much less than I being labeled rightists, I began to convince myself: between Mao and myself, there could only be one wrong, and since he was beyond wrong, it could only be me."[9]

Post-Mao Reforms with Chinese Characteristics, 1978 to the Present

The Deng Xiaoping–Jiang Zemin Reforms

When Mao's Long March colleague Deng Xiaoping became China's paramount leader shortly after Mao's death and, in late 1978, launched a series of reforms, China finally seemed to find the elusive road to "wealth and power" which its leaders had been searching for since the late nineteenth century. Deng reached the road by relying on China's own history, experience, and strengths and by emulating the economic achievements of its post-Confucian and ethnic neighbors—South Korea, Taiwan, Japan, and Singapore.

Mao had left a legacy of both possibilities and weaknesses. He had managed to deter first the American and then the Soviet threat, to establish China as a nuclear power, and to engineer a rapprochement with the West in the early 1970s that gave his successors the option of a Western-leaning diplomatic and economic strategy. Though productivity was low and declining and the overwhelming majority of the population was poor and still lived in deprivation, under Mao's leadership China had begun to establish an industrial economy, provide literacy for about 70 percent of the population, grant more equality for women, and increase life expectancy equivalent to that of developed countries. But Mao's utopian policies of the Great Leap Forward in the late 1950s and the Cultural Revolution in the 1960s greatly damaged and undermined the fragile modern infrastructure he had started to build.

At the time of Mao's death, widespread popular disaffection, failed policies, a bankrupt ideology, international isolation, economic stagnation, and political chaos had weakened the party's legitimacy. Yet, though the party-state apparatus had been decimated, it still retained the ability to suppress any organized political opposition. Nevertheless, because of the persecution its members had suffered during the Cultural Revolution, the party leadership as well as the party rank and file yearned for a different approach to development and for more freedom in their personal lives. Mao's system had generated a "crisis of faith" perhaps wider and deeper than that suffered in the Soviet Union after the Brezhnev era, thus providing the impetus for further opening to the West and far-reaching reforms.

Deng Xiaoping defined a global role for China that combined engagement in the normal institutions of world politics with a historical sense of special mission. He portrayed China as a great power but not a superpower; a spokesperson for the Third World yet a member of the Big Five club of the UN Security Council's permanent members; an advocate of "peace and development" representing other countries' interests as well as its own; and an independent actor on the world scene. As China cut its ties with revolutionary movements in Asia and Africa, it became a status quo power. It no longer regarded the United States as a threat, except in the case of Taiwan, where it continued to suspect the United States of encouraging de facto independence. After Mikhail Gorbachev came to power in the Soviet Union in 1985, embarking on domestic reforms and ending the cold war, China's leaders regarded the Soviet threat as also receding.

At the same time, Deng Xiaoping announced that China would strengthen its economic position at home and abroad. He ended the siege mentality which had cut China off from the markets, capital, technology, education, and culture of the international community and declared an "open policy" in the early 1980s. For the first time, the People's Republic tailored its development strategy to its comparative advantage, joining the world economy as a low-cost supplier of labor to manufacture products for international consumer markets. In this way Deng to some extent reoriented the Chinese economy away from the Stalinist and Maoist models of heavy industrial autarky and toward the "East Asian model" of its consumer export–oriented neighbors. China's foreign trade soared so that by 1997, China enjoyed a trade surplus of over $40 billion.[10] During the first two decades after Mao's death (1977–1997), foreign direct investment in China, nonexistent under Mao except for Soviet aid, amounted to over $360 billion.[11]

Because of China's vast size, its economy remained more self-sufficient than the smaller economies of its neighbors; yet the impact of its involvement in world trade and its improving economic position had already be-

come evident by the late 1980s in the high-rise skylines of formerly somno-
lent Beijing, Shanghai, and other cities, in the smokestacks and freeways of
the formerly rural coastal countryside, and in the frenetic consumerism of
the formerly ascetic Chinese people. China's opening up and move to the
market were also felt in the spread of crime and corruption, the decline of
ideology, and, in the eyes of those nostalgic for the Mao era, the loss of economic security, equality, and socialist ideals.

Although influenced by the reforms that gave China's East Asian neighbors increasing prosperity, many of the post-Mao economic reforms, unlike
the developmental models imposed during the Mao era, were initiated from
below. With the economy in a state of stagnation, peasants in the poorest areas of Anhui Province shortly after Mao's death began to take their lands out
of the commune and work them as family farms, as their ancestors had done
until the 1949 revolution. When these events were reported to Deng, instead of stopping such actions, as Mao had done when a similar revival of
family farms occurred after the Great Leap Forward, Deng let them continue. As this revival showed increased productivity, Deng then allowed the
"family responsibility system" of landholding to become national policy. In
just a few years in the early 1980s, China was virtually decollectivized.

On most economic issues Deng's policies embodied the pragmatism en-
capsulated in the words negatively attributed to him during the Cultural
Revolution: "It does not matter whether the cat is black or white, so long as
it catches mice." He began the reforms without blueprints or models; his approach was described as "feeling for the stones while crossing the river." As
the family responsibility system became the norm, the regime dismantled
the communes, leased land to peasant households for up to thirty-year
terms, and in effect restored traditional household agriculture. As in pre-
1949 China, peasants were allowed to sell much of their crops in free markets. With an accompanying increase in the state procurement prices for
grain, the peasants' living standards quickly rose in the 1980s. In the early
reform years this virtual land reform led to more than a doubling and in
some areas a tripling of agricultural production.

Another reform that percolated up from below was the establishment of
small and medium-sized collective enterprises, called township and village
enterprises (TVEs). Their development was confirmed as national policy by
Deng in the mid-1980s, when he praised their unexpectedly high rates of
growth. Run by local governments, often with the help of private entrepreneurs, TVEs became the fastest-growing sector of the economy. They not

only filled the needs of the peasants but also became an engine driving China's export boom. While these enterprises increased the incomes of entrepreneurs as well as those of their workers, they especially enriched local officials, who had ultimate control, because they were essential in acquiring inputs and markets for the goods produced. In some respects these alliances resembled the late Qing enterprise structure, "Officials supervise, merchants manage" *(guandu shangban)*.

By the mid-1980s, the economic loosening and the beginnings of markets had spread to the urban areas. In part the regime was again responding to what was already happening. Another Deng slogan, "To get rich is glorious," allowed the growth of private enterprises *(getihu)*, which were similar to the family-run and small-scale retail and service enterprises of the pre-1949 period. As 16 million "sent-down" youth, whose education had been suspended in the Cultural Revolution, returned to the cities from exile in the countryside, they sought to support themselves in these small-scale, nonstate enterprises.

Deng's policies also gradually broke down the sharp divisions of the Mao era between the rural and urban sectors by allowing peasants to migrate to the cities or coastal provinces to look for work, mostly in construction and export-oriented factories. By the late 1990s, it was estimated that over 100 million internal migrants were on the move in search of better livelihoods. Although peasants were still forbidden to move permanently into cities, they were encouraged to move to small rural towns to work in factory jobs, and they were allowed to look for temporary work in big cities, usually in export manufacturing for women and in construction for men.[12]

In some respects it was as if China were resuming the economic pattern of development begun in the late nineteenth century. Even the Special Economic Zones and foreign joint ventures along China's southeast coast and the Yangzi River were reminiscent of the treaty ports established in the nineteenth century. In the late twentieth century, however, these zones were controlled not by foreigners but by Chinese. At the same time, Deng invited overseas Chinese who had left China to make their fortunes as the middle classes in other parts of Asia and elsewhere to invest in and provide entrepreneurial savvy for China's new enterprises and joint ventures with state industries. Whereas Mao had rejected the help offered by overseas Chinese, Deng encouraged it. Their capital and business acumen became another driving force of China's economic growth.

As a result of pressure from below and policy confirmation from above, therefore, Maoist policies and institutions were reversed. The "unit" system was virtually dissolved in the rural areas with the demise of the communes, and the *danwei* was weakened in the cities with the development of non-state enterprises and the rise of an embryonic labor and real estate market. As the regime moved away from a "command economy" to a version of "market socialism," major enterprises, even if state-owned and assisted, increasingly operated in a market environment. The large state-owned factories were granted more autonomy to manage themselves in an effort to increase their efficiency. Steps were taken to raise the prices of industrial inputs, such as energy and steel, to more realistic levels and to free the prices that industrial enterprises and retailers could charge their customers.

By the time of Deng's death in February 1997, China's economy had been growing by more than 9 percent a year for nearly twenty years. This was the fastest and longest period of growth of any country in the world in the last decades of the twentieth century. China's GNP was projected to be the world's second largest by early in the next century,[13] though shortly after that projection, China's economic growth began to slow, in part because of increasing bankruptcy of state industries. The majority of the population enjoyed an increase in their standard of living; a quarter of the population achieved middle-class living standards, especially in the densely populated coastal region. Yet China remained on average a poor country by per capita measures. Forty-two million citizens lived below subsistence level. As increases in farm income leveled off in the late 1980s, income gaps were also growing. The increasing disparities were not only between the coastal and inner provinces and between urban and rural areas, but also in the countryside, between those who worked in the fields and those who worked in small-scale enterprises and in the cities, between workers in state industries and those in non-state enterprises.

The Deng regime reversed Mao's repression of intellectuals, who were once again at least symbolically accorded their traditional high status. Scientists, engineers, and economists in particular were regarded as the key players in China's modernization. Virtually all the victims of Mao's campaigns were rehabilitated. Although intellectuals enjoyed greater individual, intellectual, and cultural freedom and access to the outside world, political dissidents continued to be persecuted either by imprisonment, labor reform, exile abroad, or enforced silence, though the number of those persecuted was in the hundreds or thousands rather than in the millions as in the Mao era. Those who attempted to set up alternative political parties or groups were severely punished with long prison terms.

Nevertheless, though political campaigns continued, they were allowed to fizzle out because neither party secretaries nor unit members were willing to disrupt normal routines for values in which they no longer believed. Nor were colleagues and family members willing to participate in such campaigns as they had done in the Mao era. The regime revitalized higher education, relaxed party control over intellectual life, sent students abroad to study, recruited technical experts into the government bureaucracy, tolerated cultural pluralism, and even encouraged an apolitical culture as a distraction from political activities.

Deng tried to avoid becoming another Mao by restricting himself to relatively modest official posts, by promoting others to the top political positions, and by insisting on regularized political procedures. But he never managed to shake the essentially personal nature of power in the party's top leadership. Until weakened by his final illness in the last few years of his life, he remained the supreme leader whose assent was needed for virtually all crucial decisions. Although Shanghai party chief Jiang Zemin replaced Zhao Ziyang as party general secretary after June 4, 1989, when Zhao was held responsible for the spring 1989 Tiananmen Square demonstrations, Jiang did not truly assume real power until Deng's death in 1997.

While Deng had finally put China on the road to wealth and power, the issue facing Jiang and his fellow leaders was whether they could continue in that direction long enough to fulfill China's goal of becoming prosperous and powerful. Deng left some of the most difficult problems for his successors: how to establish the institutions of macroeconomic and fiscal control needed to keep the vast economy from spinning through destructive economic cycles and from breaking up into economic regions; how to privatize the majority of bankrupt state enterprises without provoking worker unrest and without creating a dangerous class of unemployed; how to replace the social welfare obligations once handled by state enterprises and the communes; how to reform further the agricultural sector, whose productivity began to decline by the late 1980s; and how to deal with the destructive environmental impact of rapid industrial growth. The economy at century's end had achieved elements of a "soft transition" from a command economy to a market economy, but remained an unstable amalgam of "socialist" and "market" elements with some of the dysfunctional features of both, such as loss-making state enterprises and rampant corruption. Moreover, the slowing growth of the late 1990s ignited destabilizing labor protests all over the country, spreading peasant tax revolts and widespread criticism of official corruption.

An equally difficult problem facing the Jiang leadership was how to re-form China's obsolete political structure so that it could deal with this unrest and the shift to a market economy. The post-Deng leadership recognized that China's slowly changing political structure was inappropriate for its economic and social realities. But as China marked a number of politically sensitive anniversaries in 1999, and as the number of bankrupt state indus-tries and of their workers being laid off increased, the Jiang leadership delayed major political reforms for fear of further intensifying the unrest among workers and peasants. While Chinese communism under Deng and Jiang could no longer be called totalitarian, neither was it democratic. A sin-gle political party and its handful of top leaders still monopolized power. Though weakened, the apparatus of the party-state was able to repress any challenge to its authority or that of its leaders. Nevertheless, even though Deng Xiaoping and his colleagues had launched the economic reforms to strengthen the legitimacy of the Leninist party-state, at the conclusion of the twentieth century, it appeared that its mandate in its present form was limited.

The Democratic Impulse

Possible scenarios for China's future are: the Communist regime will col-lapse, perhaps during a power struggle among leadership factions; it will sta-bilize itself under a collective leadership willing to carry out political reform; it will disintegrate from within, leading to a decline of central government and growth of regionalism; or it will enter a gradual transition toward de-mocracy as one faction calls for liberalizing reforms or national elections to strengthen its hand against another seeking to maintain the present system, reinforced by demands from below. Reforms in the Deng-Jiang era percolat-ing up from below and from the National People's Congress (NPC) give cre-dence to the last scenario.

Clearly, a very different political climate exists in China at the start of the twenty-first century than during the Mao era. When Mao sent millions of urban young people to live among the peasants during the Cultural Revolu-tion, they were shocked by the poverty of the countryside, seemingly un-changed since the revolution. This experience plus the brutality of the Cul-tural Revolution laid the ideological basis not only for disillusionment with Maoism and the introduction of Deng's reforms, but also for grassroots de-mands for political change. Dissent emerged in the late Mao years in the form of scattered underground study groups and wall posters protesting the persecutions and upheaval of the Cultural Revolution. It grew louder and more daring with the April 5, 1976, Beijing protest against Mao's dictatorial policies. In the Democracy Wall movement of 1978–79, ex–Red Guards and workers put up large-character posters along the walls in Beijing and other cities, printed pamphlets, formed their own groups, and called publicly for political rights and the reform of the party as well as of the economy.

Deng at first welcomed these actions in order to promote his own reforms and eliminate his Maoist opponents still in the party leadership. But he suppressed the Democracy Wall movement in late 1979 when he no longer needed its support and it demanded more far-reaching political reforms than he wanted. He ordered the arrest of scores of participants, including Wei Jingsheng, who had warned in an article in his journal *Exploration (Tanso)* that Deng would turn into a dictator if the prevailing political system were not reformed. Nevertheless, while demonstrations and unofficial efforts to achieve political reform were suppressed, in intellectual circles, in the media, and at official public meetings in the 1980s, interrupted briefly by political campaigns that petered out, the demands for more democratic procedures were fairly freely expressed.

Although the post-Mao leadership gave priority to economic reforms, political reform was not totally dismissed. Even for China's Communist leaders, democracy was not an alien concept. The Chinese had admired democracy for a century. Mao claimed that socialist China was "democratic," though his conception of democracy was that of a far-sighted leader ruling in the interests of the people. Mao himself decided what the people should want. Popular consent was assumed rather than solicited; anyone who withheld consent was viewed as an enemy of the people. Deng's idea of political reform was likewise elitist. He believed that China needed the Communist Party and its leadership to hold it together. Nevertheless, because of his own persecution and that of his party colleagues, Deng emphasized that the party should rule through laws and institutions rather than by the whim of individuals.

To ensure that the kinds of abuse and repression that occurred during the Cultural Revolution would not happen again, Deng and his purported successors Hu Yaobang and Zhao Ziyang in the 1980s, and his actual successor, Jiang Zemin, in the 1990s, introduced procedures to redress individual grievances, regularize policy making, increase the flow of information, and allow more freedom in people's private, economic, cultural, social, and intellectual activities. Although the regime continued political education through campaigns, study groups, criticism sessions, and the state-controlled propaganda media, it no longer classified various groups as class enemies or demanded a high level of participation in political life from ordinary people. It tolerated people's opting out of politics to pursue private interests and allowed intellectuals inside and outside the party to debate sensitive issues within broad if shifting limits among themselves, though not publicly.

In the 1980s some establishment intellectuals, as well as non-establishment dissidents, articulated liberal-democratic ideas. They held that China could democratize only by establishing human rights, the rule of law, competitive elections, multiple parties, freedom of the press, and the separation of powers. These views, however, did not reach far into a Chinese population more concerned with making money than with changing the political system. Even so, they received considerable support among participants in the pro-democracy demonstrations in Beijing's Tiananmen Square and in other cities in spring 1989. Besides opposing corruption and inflation, the demonstrators demanded freedom of speech, denounced untruthful propaganda in the government-controlled media, called for political reforms, and urged the government to engage in open dialogue with its citizens. When ordinary citizens and workers joined these demonstrations, the leadership, fearing a Polish Solidarity-like movement of workers and intellectuals joining together to overthrow the party, suppressed the demonstrators with a violent military crackdown on June 4, 1989.

Despite the crackdown and arrest of the demonstration's leaders and dissident intellectuals and workers, several of the political reforms, started in the 1980s, continued and accelerated in the 1990s. Most notable were the village elections, begun in 1987, in which villagers were allowed to choose village committee members and village heads in multicandidate elections. With the dismantling of the communes, the decline of party authority, and the increasing chaos in the countryside, Deng and some of his Long March colleagues advocated competitive elections in the villages in an effort to reestablish authority. Even though the party leader in the village still had supreme authority and election fraud was widespread, as this practice spread to 60 percent of China's villages and to virtually every province by the late 1990s, China's peasants gained experience in democratic practices and in holding their leaders accountable.

At the central government level, the NPC, a rubber-stamp legislature during the Mao period, became more assertive and independent. Although its delegates were still appointed by the party leadership rather than elected, 30 to 40 percent of the delegates in the 1990s rejected or abstained on important party-initiated legislation.[14] The regime introduced thousands of new laws, a system of courts, and professional lawyers, though it still controlled the courts and implementation of the laws. Benchmark laws included the 1989 Administrative Litigation Law, which permits ordinary citizens to sue state officials who violate certain rights; the 1994 Prison Law, which, among other things, mandates at least on paper an end to torture in prisons; and the 1996 revision of the Criminal Procedure Law, which to some extent provides procedural safeguards for criminal defendants. These developments moved the country toward the rule of law on paper, though less markedly in practice.

Deng and later Jiang insisted, however, that these reforms were meant to save, not weaken, the authority of the Chinese Communist Party. Since the judiciary remained subservient to the party, and laws were vague enough and procedures flexible enough, the regime had a free hand in suppressing those it viewed as opponents. The army continued to be under the direct control of the party leader, as it had been under Mao, reporting directly to Deng and later to Jiang as chairman of the Military Affairs Commission. The military proved its loyalty to Deng when it moved as ordered against the peaceful demonstrators on June 4, 1989. In exchange, the military retained a strong voice in foreign and security policy and in succession politics, though the Standing Committee of the Politburo appointed at the Fifteenth Party Congress in October 1998 no longer contained military representatives.

At century's end, therefore, China was changing not only economically but also socially, culturally, and politically. The Deng-Jiang regimes' nearly twenty years of reform had brought about substantial economic development. With about 50 percent of China's GDP accounted for by industry, China is more industrialized than other poor and lower-middle-income countries. It is also more urbanized, with almost half the population living in high-density urban and suburban areas either as residents or as temporary workers. Owing to the initiation of an educational infrastructure during the Mao era, basic-level education is widespread and illiteracy is relatively low, especially among younger age cohorts, though there was a decline in female literacy in the last two decades of the twentieth century. Despite the growing polarization of wealth precipitated by the economic reforms, China still had a relatively equitable distribution.

In addition, the end of the cold war presented China with a completely altered international context and new external challenges. Soviet-American military bipolarity gave way to American dominance. Though more militarily secure than in the past, China remains a relatively vulnerable power. It has acquired some state-of-the-art weaponry from the former Soviet Union and may have stolen and/or developed advanced nuclear warheads. For the most part, however, the People's Liberation Army continues to be equipped with old-fashioned Chinese-made Soviet-style tanks and planes. The navy and air force lack blue-water ships, midair refueling capability, and aircraft carriers that can project power beyond China's coastal waters. The separate services lack the organizational and communications capabilities to enable them to coordinate in combat. Nevertheless, China's size, its large population, and its efforts to update its military weaponry have caused its neighbors to perceive a potential "China threat." This is especially true for the people on Taiwan, who see China's military modernization not as defensive but as offensive in nature.

In post–cold war international politics, cultural and ideological values have emerged as a major tool of influence. In human rights diplomacy and educational and cultural exchanges, China plays with a weak hand. Even though it promotes the idea of "Asian values," under its current system it is more of a receiver than a giver of ideas. It has not only endorsed the UN Declaration on Human Rights but also signed on to the Covenant on Social, Economic, and Cultural Rights and the Covenant on Political and Civil Rights in 1997–98. These covenants allow for independent labor unions and freedom of expression, association, and assembly, rights that, in fact, the regime continues to stifle. Although these covenants still have to be endorsed by the NPC in order to become operable, the fact that China has recognized them provides the international community as well as its own population—with norms that they can hold China to without being accused of interference in China's internal affairs.

Therefore, as the twenty-first century begins, China is more open to the outside world than ever before. With some limitations on sensitive political issues and on the position of Tibet and Taiwan, worldwide information and popular culture are spreading through mobile telephones, fax machines, computers, the Internet, E-mail, radio, television, and movies not just to China's large cities but to virtually every Chinese village. The spread of worldwide popular culture indirectly subverts the party-state because it fosters values alien to the emphasis on conformity of Marxism-Leninism and in the mainstream traditional Chinese culture.

A middle class is growing fast with rising incomes and educational levels. Although China's middle class is still not large enough to be independent of official patronage, it is becoming more educated and wealthy with the potential to exert political influence in its own interests. In a 1993 national survey, over 60 percent of the population reported themselves as interested in national affairs, and a similar percentage was able to identify top national officials, demonstrating a high level of political involvement and information.[15]

Nevertheless, despite these preconditions for the evolution to a democratic polity, it is not clear that China will move in that direction. The party-state is still strong enough to suppress any political challenge or opposition political party. Yet it is also weak in that it has not developed political institutions to deal with the forces of social change. This weakness could lead China in the direction of the former Soviet Union, where government, no matter how democratic it might be, is too feeble to implement laws. Or China could go the way of its East Asian neighbors, whose growing economic, social, and cultural pluralism led to political pluralism and in time to democratic political systems. The post-Confucian societies of East Asia have found that democratic reforms have effectively dealt with the social problems unleashed by economic reforms and made possible relative stability, even in times of economic downturns and social unrest, as evidenced during the Asian economic crisis of the late 1990s.

Yet China is qualitatively different from its neighbors. Its huge population was nearing 1.3 billion at the end of the century. The overwhelming majority of its technocratic bureaucracy is still trained in the former Soviet Union rather than in the West, and though the younger generation is being educated in the West, the majority have not returned to China. Moreover, there are still sectors of Chinese society and the bureaucracy which view themselves as losers in the decision to reform and open China to the West. Their influence over policy is receding, but their voices can still be heard. The further the benefits of international integration spread, however, the less realistic is the option of a return to autarky and the more probable is China's acceptance of the norms of the international community. Nevertheless, while China might not take the Russian route, it is still not clear that it will take the democratic path of its East Asian neighbors, either. While China has found the road to "wealth and power," it is not inevitable that this road will necessarily lead China in a democratic direction.

Selected Readings

Chan, Anita. *Children of Mao: Personality Development and Political Activism in the Red Guard Generation.* Seattle: University of Washington Press, 1985.

Chan, Anita, Richard Madsen, and Jonathan Unger. *Chen Village: The Recent History of a Peasant Community in Mao's China.* Berkeley: University of California Press, 1984.

Chang, Jung. *Wild Swans: Three Daughters of China.* New York: Anchor Books, 1992.

Economy, Elizabeth, and Michel Oksenberg, eds. *China Joins the World: Progress and Prospects.* New York: Council on Foreign Relations Press, 1999.

Goldman, Merle. *Sowing the Seeds of Democracy in China.* Cambridge, Mass.: Harvard University Press, 1994.

Goldman, Merle, and Roderick MacFarquhar, eds. *The Paradox of China's Post-Mao Reforms.* Cambridge, Mass.: Harvard University Press, 1999.

Harding, Harry. *China's Second Revolution: Reform after Mao.* Washington, D.C.: Brookings Institution, 1987.

Kim, Samuel S., ed. *China and the World: Chinese Foreign Policy Faces the New Millennium.* 4th ed. Boulder, Colo.: Westview Press, 1998.

Lardy, Nicholas. *China's Unfinished Economic Revolution.* Washington, D.C.: Brookings Institution, 1998.

Lieberthal, Kenneth. *Governing China: From Revolution through Reform.* New York: W. W. Norton, 1995.

MacFarquhar, Roderick. *The Origins of the Cultural Revolution.* Vols. 1, 2, and 3. New York: Oxford University Press and Columbia University Press, 1974, 1983, 1997.

Meisner, Maurice. *Mao's China and After: A History of the People's Republic.* New York: Free Press, 1986.

Nathan, Andrew J. *Chinese Democracy.* Berkeley: University of California Press, 1986.

Naughton, Barry. *Growing Out of the Plan: Chinese Economic Reform, 1978–1993.* New York: Cambridge University Press, 1995.

Oi, Jean. *Rural China Takes Off: Institutional Foundations of Economic Reform.* Berkeley: University of California Press, 1999.

——— *State and Peasant in Contemporary China: The Political Economy of Village Government.* Berkeley: University of California Press, 1989.

Riskin, Carl. *China's Political Economy: The Quest for Development since 1949.* New York: Oxford University Press, 1987.

Steinfeld, Edward. *Forging Reform in China: The Fate of State-Industry.* New York: Cambridge University Press, 1998.

Walder, Andrew G. *Communist Neo-Traditionalism: Work and Authority in Chinese Industry.* Berkeley: University of California Press, 1986.

CHRONOLOGIES

NOTES

CONTRIBUTORS

INDEX

Chronology of Modern Chinese History

1796–1804	White Lotus Rebellion in the northwest
1839–1841	Opium War (First Anglo-Chinese War)
1831–1844	Treaty of Nanjing and others (first treaty settlement)
1850–1864	Taiping Rebellion (Taipings capture Nanjing 1853)
1853–1868	Nian Rebellion
1856–1860	Second Anglo-Chinese War and treaty settlement
1862–1874	Tongzhi Restoration
1860s–1895	"Self-strengthening" movement
1894–95	Sino-Japanese War
1896–1898	Resurgence of imperialism
1898	Hundred Days of Reform of Kang Yuwei
1900	Boxer Uprising in North China
1900–1911	Late Qing reforms (examination system abolished 1905)
1905	Tongmenghui (Revolutionary Alliance) of Sun Yat-sen founded in Japan
1911	Republican revolution
1912–1916	Yuan Shikai president of the Republic
1916–1921	Warlord period
1916–1927	New Culture and May Fourth Movement
1921	Chinese Communist Party (CCP) founded
1923–1927	Guomindang (GMD)–CCP alliance
1926–1928	Northern expedition (Nationalist revolution)
1927–1937	Nanjing decade
1931	Japanese take over Manchuria
1934–35	Chinese Communists' Long March to Yan'an
1937–1945	Sino-Japanese War
1945–1949	Civil war
1949	People's Republic of China established
1956–57	Hundred Flowers period

1957–1959	Anti-rightist campaign
1958–1960	Great Leap Forward
1960	Sino-Soviet split
1966–1976	Great Proletarian Cultural Revolution
1972	U.S.-China rapprochement
1976	Death of Mao Zedong and Zhou Enlai
1972–1979	U.S.-China normalization of relations
1978	Deng Xiaoping comes to power
1978–79	Democracy movement
1979–84	Agricultural reforms
1983	"Spiritual pollution" campaign
1984	Urban reforms
1986	Debate over political reform
1987	Bourgeois liberalization campaign
1988	Price reform
1989	Tiananmen demonstrations and crackdown
1992	Revival of economic reforms
1997	Deng Xiaoping dies

Chronology of Modern Japanese History

1830s	Tempo era reforms of Tokugawa and domain policies
1853	U.S. Commodore Matthew Perry arrives in Japan
1858	U.S., then other nations, sign commercial treaties
1860–1868	Turbulent politics of rebellion and overthrow of Tokugawa
1868	Meiji Restoration; new government issues Charter Oath
1871	Iwakura mission leaves to study Western nations
1871–1876	Era of reforms: domains abolished, draft and compulsory education established, samurai class privileges eliminated
1877	Saigo Takamori leads the failed Satsuma Rebellion
1881	Emperor promises a constitution against backdrop of rising tide of Movement for Freedom and People's Rights
1884	People's rights movement declines; Liberal Party dissolves; major rebellion in Chichibu
1886–87	Peak of popular agitation for treaty revision
1889	Government promulgates Meiji Constitution
1890	Government issues Imperial Rescript on Education; first Diet elections
1894–95	Sino-Japanese War; Britain agrees to treaty revision
1902	Anglo-Japanese alliance initiated
early 1900s	First generation of socialists begins publishing and organizing
1904–5	Russo-Japanese War
1908	Gentlemen's Agreement virtually halts emigration to U.S.
1910	Japan formally annexes Korea as a colony
1911	Government executes socialists and anarchists for alleged plot against emperor
1912	Meiji Emperor dies; start of Taishō era
1913	Taishō political crisis brings down cabinet
1915	Twenty-one Demands addressed to China
1918	Nationwide protests over rice prices end in riots; Hara Takashi becomes first party prime minister

1923	Great Kantō earthquake and massive fires devastate Tokyo; thousands of Koreans murdered by vigilantes
1925	Government enacts universal suffrage for men, Peace Preservation Law
1930	London Naval Treaty continues naval restrictions first agreed to in 1922 with U.S. and Britain; Prime Minister Hamaguchi fatally shot
1931–32	Japanese military takes over Manchuria, establishes puppet state of Manchukuo
1932	Young military officers assassinate Prime Minister Inukai; end to party cabinets until after World War II.
1936	Young officers launch abortive coup, assassinate several state ministers
1937	Japan launches full-scale war in China
1941	Attacks on Pearl Harbor and Singapore open second front in Asian war
1945	U.S. drops atomic bombs on Hiroshima and Nagasaki; Japan surrenders
1945–1952	Allied occupation of Japan; major democratizing reforms imposed; occupation ends in shadow of cold war and Korean War with U.S.-Japan Security Treaty
1955	Liberal Democratic Party forms
1955–1973	Era of high-speed economic growth, over 10 percent annually
1959–60	Peak of domestic political upheaval over U.S.-Japan Security Treaty, student movement, and labor unrest
1961	Prime Minister Ikeda announces income-doubling goal by 1970
1964	Olympics held in Tokyo; bullet train begins operations
1968–1970	Second wave of major student protest; citizen movements over environmental damage surge
1971–72	"Nixon shocks" of devalued dollar and U.S. opening of relations with China
1972	U.S. returns control of Okinawa to Japan (excluding bases)
1973–74	First oil crisis jolts Japan; high growth era ends; high inflation
1978–79	Second oil crisis
1982	Nakasone Yasuhiro becomes prime minister, calls for administrative reform and more assertive international role; controversy over history textbooks
1985–1990	Economy surges, ends in "bubble" of speculative investment and loans
1989	Emperor Hirohito dies; his son Akihito takes throne, start of Heisei era
1993	Liberal Democrats lose power for the first time since 1950s; socialist prime minister heads coalition cabinet for the first time since 1947
1995	Earthquake devastates Kobe; adherents of Aum Shinrikyō religion launch deadly gas attack on Tokyo subways
1997–98	Banking crisis reaches nadir

Chronology of Modern Korean History

1392–1910	Chosŏn dynasty
1864–1873	Regency of the Taewongun, father of King Kojong
1864–1907	Reign of King Kojong (designated emperor 1897)
1876	Kanghwa Treaty
1881	Kojong sets up new office to push "enlightenment" reforms
1882	Korea and U.S. establish formal diplomatic relations
1884	Kapsin coup led by Kim Okkyun
1894	Tonghak uprising
1894–1896	Kabo reforms
1894–95	First Sino-Japanese War
1896–97	Kojong in residence at the Russian legation
1896–1898	Independence Club
1897	Kojong proclaims the Great Han empire (Taehan Cheguk)
1904–5	Russo-Japanese War
1905	U.S. recognizes Japan's authority in Korea in secret Taft-Katsura Agreement
1905	Japan establishes a formal protectorate over Korea
1907	Japan forces abdication of Kojong in favor of son Sunjong
1910	Japanese annexation of Korea
1910–1918	Japanese colonial government's cadastral survey
1919	March First Movement
1920–1931	Colonial reforms under new "enlightened" rule
1925	Communist Party of Korea founded
1931–1937	Japanese invasion of Manchuria and onset of colonial militarization
1937–1945	Wartime rapid assimilation and mobilization
1932–1941	Kim Il Sung active in anti-Japanese guerrilla warfare in Manchuria
1945	Liberation from Japanese colonial rule; American and Soviet partition of Korea along thirty-eighth parallel
1945–1948	Soviet and American occupations of north and south Korea

1948	Founding of Republic of Korea (ROK) in south, Democratic People's Republic of Korea (DPRK) under Kim Il Sung in north
1948–1960	First Republic under Syngman Rhee
1950–1953	Korean War
1960	April Nineteenth student revolution
1960–61	Second Republic (ROK)
1961	May Sixteenth army coup d'état led by General Park Chung Hee (ROK)
1965	ROK normalization of diplomatic relations with Japan
1961–1979	ROK rapid economic development and authoritarian rule under Park
1972–1979	Yusin political system (ROK)
1972	First joint statement on peaceful reunification; start of North-South dialogue
1979	Assassination of Park Chung Hee
1980	Kwangju massacre
1981–1988	Fifth Republic (ROK) headed by former general Chun Doo Hwan
1987	June Twenty-ninth democratic reforms (ROK)
1988–1993	Sixth Republic (ROK) headed by former general Roh Tae Woo
1988	Seoul Summer Olympics
1993–1998	Former political dissident Kim Young Sam elected ROK president
1994	Death of Kim Il Sung and succession of son Kim Jong Il (DPRK)
1994	DPRK nuclear crisis and "Agreed Framework" resolution
1996	Trials of former ROK presidents Chun and Roh
1997	Election to ROK presidency of another former dissident, Kim Dae Jung
1997–	ROK economic crisis and recovery

Notes

1. The Foreign Impact on East Asia

1. Richard W. Leopold, *Growth of American Foreign Policy* (New York: Alfred A. Knopf, 1962), p. 212.
2. For a fuller discussion of the Boxers, see Mary Backus Rankin's essay in chapter 2.
3. R. Bin Wong, *China Transformed: Historical Change and the Limits of European Experience* (Ithaca, N.Y.: Cornell University Press, 1997), p. 156.
4. Roosevelt to Spring Rice, March 19, 1904, in *Letters of Theodore Roosevelt*, ed. Elting Morison et. al., in 8 vols. (Cambridge, Mass.: Harvard University Press, 1951–1954), 4:760.
5. William Kirby, *Germany and Republican China* (Princeton: Princeton University Press, 1984), is the standard work on Chinese-German relations in this period. See also F. F. Liu, *A Military History of Modern China, 1924–1949* (Princeton: Princeton University Press, 1956), pp. 90–102.
6. On this point, see Waldo Heinrichs, *Threshhold of War: Franklin D. Roosevelt and American Entry into World War II* (New York: Oxford University Press, 1988), pp. 178–179.
7. Akira Iriye, *Power and Culture: The Japanese-American War, 1941–1945* (Cambridge, Mass.: Harvard University Press, 1981), p. 263.
8. For Korea, see Bruce Cumings, *The Origins of the Korean War*, vol. 1, *Liberation and the Emergence of Separate Regimes, 1945–1947* (Princeton: Princeton University Press, 1981). For China, see Odd Arne Westad, *Cold War and Revolution: Soviet-American Rivalry and the Origins of the Chinese Civil War* (New York: Columbia University Press, 1993).
9. For superb historiographic discussions of the occupation, its changing emphasis, and its conclusion, see Carol Gluck, "Entangling Illusions: Japanese and American Views of the Occupation," in *New Frontiers in American-East Asian Relations*, ed. Warren I. Cohen (New York: Columbia University Press, 1983), pp. 169–236; and Marc Gallicchio, "Recovery through Dependency: American-Japanese Relations, 1945–1970," in *Pacific Passage: The Study of American–East Asian Relations on*

the Eve of the Twenty-first Century, ed. Warren I. Cohen (New York: Columbia University Press, 1996), pp. 247–275.

10. John W. Garver, *Chinese-Soviet Relations, 1937–1945: The Diplomacy of Chinese Nationalism* (New York: Oxford University Press, 1988), pp. 238–239.

11. Hu Xigui, "Shiju bianhua ho wode fangzhen" (The changing political situation and our policy), mimeographed transcript of lecture to cadres, August 30, 1945. Archives of the Bureau of Investigation, Republic of China.

12. NSC 4/1, January 11, 1949, in U.S. Department of State, *Foreign Relations of the United States, 1949, The Far East: China,* 9 (1975), pp. 474–475.

13. See Warren I. Cohen, "Acheson, His Advisers, and China, 1949–1950," in *Uncertain Years: Chinese-American Relations, 1947–1950,* ed. Dorothy Borg and Waldo Heinrichs (New York: Columbia University Press, 1980), pp. 13–52; and Nancy Bernkopf Tucker, *Patterns in the Dust: Chinese-American Relations and the Recognition Controversy, 1949–1950* (New York: Columbia University Press, 1983).

14. This story is told best by John W. Lewis and Xue Litai in *China Builds the Bomb* (Stanford: Stanford University Press, 1988).

15. In October 1971 I reviewed the files of the Bureau of East Asian Affairs at the U.S. Department of State in an effort to understand why American actions had been kept secret from the Japanese. Every memorandum I saw argued for keeping the Japanese informed. When I asked Secretary of State William Rogers, he spoke of the need to preserve secrecy and of a Japanese government notorious for its leaks. Interviews with specialists in the department and with members of the National Security Council staff all pointed to Nixon's determination to embarrass Sato for his failure to deliver on textiles.

16. See, for example, Chalmers Johnson, *Japan: Who Governs? The Rise of the Developmental State* (New York: W. W. Norton, 1995).

17. Walter LaFeber, *The Clash: A History of U.S.-Japan Relations* (New York: W. W. Norton, 1997).

2. Social and Political Change in Nineteenth-Century China

1. See John K. Fairbank, Edwin O. Reischauer, and Albert M. Craig, *East Asia: The Modern Transformation* (Boston: Houghton Mifflin, 1965), pp. 404–406. Frederic Wakeman, Jr., uses the "High Qing" as an organizing concept in "High Ch'ing: 1683–1839," in *Modern East Asia: Essays in Interpretation,* ed. James B. Crowley (New York: Harcourt, Brace and World, 1970), pp. 1–61.

2. For a fuller discussion of the imperial Chinese state in comparison to Europe, see R. Bin Wong, *China Transformed: Historical Change and the Limits of European Experience* (Ithaca, N.Y.: Cornell University Press, 1997), chaps. 4–6.

3. Paul A. Cohen, *Discovering History in China: American Historical Writing on the Recent Chinese Past* (New York: Columbia University Press, 1984), chaps. 2 and 4.

4. Wong, *China Transformed,* pp. 38–52.

5. Ping-ti Ho, *The Ladder of Success in Imperial China: Aspects of Social Mobility, 1368–1911* (New York: Columbia University Press, 1962), p. 49.

6. On women in the seventeenth century, see Dorothy Ko, *Teachers of the Inner Chambers: Women and Culture in Seventeenth-Century China* (Stanford: Stanford University Press, 1994). On the eighteenth, see Susan Mann, *Precious Records: Women in China's Long Eighteenth Century* (Stanford: Stanford University Press, 1997).

7. Jerry Dennerline, *Qian Mu and the World of Seven Mansions* (New Haven: Yale University Press, 1988), pp. 112–113.

8. On Qing civil law, see Philip C. C. Huang, *Civil Justice in China: Representation and Practice in the Qing* (Stanford: Stanford University Press, 1996). On litigation, see Melissa A. Macauley, *Social Power and Legal Culture: Litigation Masters in Late Imperial China* (Stanford: Stanford University Press, 1998).

9. Relevant studies include Susan Mann, *Local Merchants and the Chinese Bureaucracy, 1750–1950* (Stanford: Stanford University Press, 1987); and Prasenjit Duara, "State Involution: A Study of Local Finances in North China, 1911–1935," *Comparative Studies in Society and History* 21 (January 1987): 132–161. For reevaluation of the sub-bureaucracy, see Bradly W. Reed, "Money and Justice: Clerks, Runners, and the Magistrate's Court in Late Imperial Sichuan," *Modern China* 21, no. 3 (July 1995): 345–382.

10. Yeh-chien Wang, "Secular Trends of Rice Prices in the Yangzi Delta, 1638–1935," in *Chinese History in Economic Perspective*, ed. Thomas G. Rawski and Lillian M. Li (Berkeley: University of California Press, 1992), p. 58.

11. John K. Fairbank, *Trade and Diplomacy on the China Coast: The Opening of the Treaty Ports, 1842–1854* (Cambridge, Mass.: Harvard University Press, 1953), chap. 2.

12. Pamela Kyle Crossley, "The Rulerships of China," *American Historical Review* 97 (1992): 1482–83; James L. Hevia, *Cherishing Men from Afar: Qing Guest Ritual and the Macartney Embassy of 1793* (Durham, N.C.: Duke University Press, 1995), pp. 37–52.

13. Hevia, *Cherishing*, p. 25.

14. Millenarian beliefs had already inspired the White Lotus uprising in western China (1796–1804) and the Eight Triagrams uprising in Beijing (1813).

15. The controversial argument that the Taipings were revolutionaries is made in Jen Yu-wen, *The Taiping Revolutionary Movement* (New Haven: Yale University Press, 1973).

16. Elizabeth J. Perry, *Rebels and Revolutionaries in North China, 1845–1945* (Stanford: Stanford University Press, 1980), chap. 4.

17. Kathryn Bernhardt, *Rents, Taxes, and Peasant Resistance: The Lower Yangzi Region, 1840–1950* (Stanford: Stanford University Press, 1992), chap. 4.

18. The phrase "ordering the world" comes from Robert P. Hymes and Conrad Schirokauer, eds., *Ordering the World: Approaches to State and Society in Sung Dynasty China* (Berkeley: University of California Press, 1993). For statecraft in the eighteenth century, see William T. Rowe, *Saving the World: Chen Hongmou and Elite Consciousness in Eighteenth-Century China* (Stanford: Stanford University Press, forthcoming), chap. 4.

19. James M. Polachek, *The Inner Opium War* (Cambridge, Mass.: Council on East Asian Studies, Harvard University, 1992), chaps. 1–2.

20. Ibid., chap. 4, deals particularly with bureaucratic politics and their intersections with Guangdong society. Frederic Wakeman, Jr., *Strangers at the Gate: Social Disorder in South China, 1839–1861* (Berkeley: University of California Press, 1966), focuses on Guangdong.

21. Hsiao Liang-lin, *China's Foreign Trade Statistics, 1864–1949* (Cambridge, Mass.: East Asian Research Center, Harvard University 1974), pp. 22–23.

22. Cohen, *Discovering History*, chap. 3.

23. On Fujian tea, see Robert Gardella, *Harvesting Mountains: Fujian and the China Tea Trade, 1757–1937* (Berkeley: University of California Press, 1994).

24. On restoration, see Mary Clabaugh Wright, *The Last Stand of Chinese Conservatism: The T'ung-chih Restoration, 1862–1874* (Stanford: Stanford University Press, 1957).

25. Charles Tilly, "Introduction," in *The Formation of National States in Western Europe*, ed. Charles Tilly (Princeton: Princeton University Press, 1975), pp. 6, 51–80.

26. Luke S. K. Kwong, *A Mosaic of the Hundred Days: Personalities, Politics, and Ideas of 1898* (Cambridge, Mass.: Council on East Asian Studies, Harvard University, 1984), pp. 38–40, 232–233.

27. Pamela Kyle Crossley, *Orphan Warriors: Three Manchu Generations and the End of the Qing World* (Princeton: Princeton University Press, 1990), pp. 170–171.

28. Bryna Goodman, *Native Place, City, and Nation: Regional Networks and Identities in Shanghai, 1853–1937* (Berkeley: University of California Press, 1995), p. 129.

29. Information in this discussion is drawn from Mary Backus Rankin, *Elite Activism and Political Transformation in China: Zhejiang Province, 1865–1911* (Stanford: Stanford University Press, 1986), chaps. 3–4. See also Goodman, *Native Place*, chap. 4.

30. Rankin, *Elite Activism*, pp. 129–133, 146, 164; Paul A. Cohen, *Between Tradition and Modernity: Wang T'ao and Reform in Late Ch'ing China* (Cambridge, Mass.: Harvard University Press, 1974), pp. 215–216.

31. This generalized characterization is not based on any one source. For an admirably nuanced discussion, see Benjamin Schwartz, *In Search of Wealth and Power: Yen Fu and the West* (Cambridge, Mass.: Belknap Press, 1964).

32. References to part of the large literature on nationalism appear in Prasenjit Duara, *Rescuing History from the Nation: Questioning Narratives of Modern China* (Chicago: University of Chicago Press, 1995), chaps. 1–2. Goodman, *Native Place*, pp. 46, 312–313, and Duara (pp. 51–56, 65–69) argue in different ways that nationalism combines with other identities and is a constructed, fluid, and in Duara's view reversible sentiment rather than a decisive modernizing break with tradition. The concept of "imagined communities" is from Benedict Anderson, *Imagined Communities: Reflections on Origin and Spread of Nationalism* (London: Verso, 1991), p. 37.

33. For this aspect of moral censure critiques and politics in the 1880s and 1890s, see Mary Backus Rankin, "Public Opinion and Political Power: Qingyi in Late Nineteenth-Century China," *Journal of Asian Studies* 41, no. 3 (May 1982): 453–484; John E. Schrecker, "The Reform Movement of 1898 and the *Ch'ing-i*: Reform as Opposition," in *Reform in Nineteenth-Century China*, ed. Paul A. Cohen and John E. Schrecker (Cambridge, Mass.: East Asian Research Center, Harvard

University, 1976), pp. 289–305. Both authors are indebted to the Korean-language scholarship of Min Tu-ki.

34. Joseph W. Esherick, *The Origins of the Boxer Uprising* (Berkeley: University of California Press, 1987), pp. 17–28, 63–67, 264–274.

3. Visions of the Future in Meiji Japan

1. On nativism, see H. D. Harootunian, *Toward Restoration: The Growth of Political Consciousness in Tokugawa Japan* (Berkeley: University of California Press, 1970), and *Things Seen and Unseen: Discourse and Ideology in Tokugawa Nativism* (Chicago: University of Chicago Press, 1987).

2. Miyachi Masato, "Fūsetsudome kara mita bakumatsu shakai no tokushitsu: 'Kōron' sekai no tanshoteki seiritsu" (The character of late Tokugawa society as seen in rumor notebooks: the first step toward the establishment of a realm of "public discourse"), *Shisō* (Thought) 831 (September 1993): 4–26.

3. Saitama-ken Iruma-gun Moroyama-machi Bunkazai Hogo Shingi Iinkai, ed., *Sōmō no shishi: Gonda Naosuke* (Grassroots Loyalist: Gonda Naosuke) (Saitama-ken Iruma-gun Moroyama-machi Kyōiku Iinkai, 1994).

4. Anne Walthall, "Off with Their Heads! The Hirata Disciples and the Ashikaga Shoguns," *Monumenta Nipponica* 50, no. 2 (Summer 1995): 137–170.

5. Edward S. Morse, *Japan Day by Day*, 2 vols. (Tokyo: Kobunsha, 1936), 2:36, describing his visit to Japan in 1877–78.

6. Quoted in Ivan Parker Hall, *Mori Arinori* (Cambridge, Mass.: Harvard University Press, 1973), p. 189; see also William R. Braisted, trans., *Meiroku Zasshi: Journal of the Japanese Enlightenment* (Tokyo: University of Tokyo Press, 1976).

7. Charles L. Yates, *Saigō Takamori: The Man behind the Myth* (London: Kegan Paul International, 1995).

8. Stephen Vlastos, "Opposition Movements in Early Meiji, 1868–1885," in *The Nineteenth Century*, vol. 5 of *The Cambridge History of Japan*, ed. Marius B. Jansen (New York: Cambridge University Press, 1989), pp. 386–387.

9. Ibid., pp. 414–419.

10. Irokawa Daikichi, *The Culture of the Meiji Period*, trans. and ed. Marius B. Jansen (Princeton: Princeton University Press, 1985).

11. Hasegawa Noboru, *Bakuto to jiyū minken: Nagoya jiken shimatsuki* (Gamblers and freedom and popular rights: the story of the Nagoya Incident) (Tokyo: Chūō Kōronsha, 1977), pp. 122–140.

12. On the Chichibu Rebellion, see Vlastos, "Opposition Movements in Early Meiji"; Roger W. Bowen, *Rebellion and Democracy in Meiji Japan: A Study of Commoners in the Popular Rights Movement* (Berkeley: University of California Press, 1980); and Irwin Scheiner, "The Mindful Peasant: Sketches for a Study of Rebellion," *Journal of Asian Studies* 32 (1973): 579–591.

13. Shinya Sugiyama, *Japan's Industrialization in the World Economy, 1859–1900: Export Trade and Overseas Competition* (London: Athlone Press, 1988), pp. 11 (silk exports), 46–47 (trade balances).

14. Coarse silk prices rose from 4.80 yen per roll in 1878 to a peak of 8.50 yen in 1882, then dropped steadily thereafter, to 6.00 yen in 1883, 4.50 in 1884, and 4.00 in 1885. Bowen, *Rebellion and Democracy in Meiji Japan*, p. 105.

15. Takeshi Fujitani, *Splendid Monarchy: Power and Pageantry in Modern Japan* (Berkeley: University of California Press, 1996).

16. E. Sydney Crawcour, "Economic Change in the Nineteenth Century," in Jansen, *The Nineteenth Century*, p. 615.

17. Imanishi Hajime, *Kindai Nihon no sabetsu to sei bunka* (Discrimination and the culture of gender in modern Japan) (Tokyo: Yūzankaku, 1998), pp. 66–69.

18. Quoted in Crawcour, "Economic Change in the Nineteenth Century," p. 614.

19. See Stewart Lone, *Japan's First Modern War: Army and Society in the Conflict with China, 1894–95* (New York: St. Martin's Press, 1994).

20. Quoted in John D. Pierson, *Tokutomi Sohō, 1863–1957: A Journalist for Modern Japan* (Princeton: Princeton University Press, 1980), p. 237.

21. Ibid., pp. 238, 239.

4. Korea's Transition to Modernity: A Will to Greatness

1. William James, *The Principles of Psychology* (Cambridge, Mass.: Harvard University Press, 1983), pp. 1098–1193, esp. 1167, 1180–81.

2. See, for example, John K. Fairbank, ed., *The Chinese World Order* (Cambridge, Mass.: Harvard University Press, 1968).

3. Quoted in Chai-Sik Chung, *A Korean Confucian Encounter with the Modern World: Yi Hang-no and the West* (Berkeley: Institute of East Asian Studies, University of California, 1995), p. 135.

4. Ibid., p. 8.

5. Ibid., p. 134.

6. Ibid., p. 206.

7. I acknowledge my debt here to Kyung Moon Hwang, whose doctoral dissertation deals with this subject. See Kyung Moon Hwang, "Bureaucracy in the Transition to Korean Modernity: Secondary Status Groups and the Transformation of Government and Society, 1880–1930" (Ph.D. diss., Harvard University, 1997).

8. Yu Kilchun, *Sŏyu kyŏnmun* (Observations of the West), vol. 1 of *Yu Kilchun chŏnsŏ* (The collected works of Yu Kilchun) (Seoul: Ilchogak, 1971), pp. 379–380.

9. Yun Ch'iho, *Yun Ch'iho ilgi* (The diary of Yun Ch'iho), 11 vols. (Seoul: Kuksa P'yŏnch'an Wiwŏnhoe, 1974), 359–60.

10. Yu Kilchun, *Sŏyu kyŏnmun*, pp. 310, 384; emphasis added.

11. Park Chung Hee, *Our Nation's Path* (Seoul: Hollym Corporation, 1970), p. 88; Pak Chŏnghŭi, *Uri minjok ŭi nagal kil* (Our nation's path) (Seoul: Tonga Ch'ulp'ansa, 1962), p. 96.

12. Yi Kwangsu, "Minjok kaejoron," in *Minjok kaejoron: Ch'uwŏn ŭi myŏngjak nonmunjip* (National reconstruction: a collection of the master essays of Ch'uwŏn) (Seoul: Usinsa, 1981), pp. 146–147.

13. Ibid., pp. 113, 117–127. See also Yi Kwangsu, *Na ŭi kobaek* (My confession), in *Yi*

Kwangsu chŏnjip (Seoul: Samjungdang, 1964), p. 197. *Sangnom* is a traditional pejorative term for Koreans (men) of the lower class, the opposite of *yangban.* The tendency to conceptualize Korea's place in the world as "master/slave," or *yangban/sangnom,* suggests that the Korean elite's traditional preoccupation with social status within their own society, so profound and so deeply rooted historically that one is hard-pressed not to see it as a kind of cultural fixation, may well have carried over into and informed their modern preoccupation with national greatness.

14. This topic deserves more detailed investigation. Hyung Gu Lynn's doctoral research at Harvard University on colonial policy making may shed some light on this subject.
15. Yi Hŭisŭng, *Kugŏ taesajŏn* (Unabridged dictionary of Korean) (Seoul: Minjungsŏgwan, 1975), p. 2641.
16. Don Oberdorfer, *The Two Koreas: A Contemporary History* (Reading, Mass.: Addison-Wesley, 1997), p. 233.
17. From a Pyongyang radio broadcast, October 15, 1996. Excerpted by *Naewoe Press* (November 1966).
18. *Analects* 9.5, quoted in Peter Bol, *"This Culture of Ours": Intellectual Transitions in T'ang and Sung China* (Stanford: Stanford University Press, 1992), p. 1.
19. See, for example, Carter J. Eckert et al., *Korea Old and New: A History* (Cambridge, Mass.: Korea Institute, Harvard University, 1990), chap. 20.
20. James, *Principles of Psychology,* p. 1099.
21. See, for example, Pak Chŏnghŭi, *Uri minjok ŭi nagal kil,* p. 128.
22. Bruce Cumings has made this same point with respect to North Korea. See his "Corporatism in North Korea," *Journal of Korean Studies* 4 (1982–83): 269–294.
23. Oberdorfer, *The Two Koreas,* p. 179.
24. I am grateful here for the many insights I received as a participant in a conference on the colonial period held at UCLA in the spring of 1996. The conference, "Beyond the Nationalist Narrative: Hegemony and Colonial Modernity in Korea, 1910–1945," was organized jointly by Gi-Wook Shin and Michael Robinson, and was funded by the National Endowment for the Humanities, the Social Science Research Council, and Yonsei University. The conference volume, *Colonial Modernity,* was published in December 1999 in the Harvard-Hallym Series on Korea from the Harvard University Asia Center Publications Program.
25. See Albert O. Hirschman, *Exit, Voice, and Loyalty: Responses to Decline in Firms, Organizations, and States* (Cambridge, Mass.: Harvard University Press, 1970).

5. State and Society in Interwar Japan

1. Ōkochi Kazuo, *Kurai tanima no rōdō undō* (The labor movement in the dark valley) (Tokyo: Iwanami shoten, 1970).
2. Quoted in Sheldon Garon, *The State and Labor in Modern Japan* (Berkeley: University of California Press, 1987), p. 42.
3. Tabuchi Toyokichi, House of Representatives, July 19, 1920, quoted in Sheldon

Garon, *Molding Japanese Minds: The State in Everyday Life* (Princeton: Princeton University Press, 1997), p. 124.

4. Carol Gluck, *Japan's Modern Myths: Ideology in the Late Meiji Period* (Princeton: Princeton University Press, 1985), p. 12.

5. Kano Masanao, *Taishō demokurashii no teiryū* (Undercurrents in Taishō democracy) (Tokyo: Nihon hōsō shuppan kyōkai, 1973), pp. 26–28.

6. Quoted in Garon, *State and Labor*, p. 49.

7. Tago Ichimin, quoted in Garon, *Molding Japanese Minds*, pp. 137–138.

8. Ida Iwakusa, quoted ibid., p. 140.

9. Yōsuke Matsuoka, "Dissolve the Political Parties," *Contemporary Japan* 2 (March 1934): 662.

10. Miriam Silverberg, *Changing Song: The Marxist Manifestos of Nakano Shigeharu* (Princeton: Princeton University Press, 1990), 164–167.

11. Robert J. Smith and Ella Lury Wiswell, *The Women of Suye Mura* (Chicago: University of Chicago Press, 1982), pp. 13, 15; Thomas R. H. Havens, *Valley of Darkness: The Japanese People and World War Two* (New York: Norton, 1978), pp. 24, 67.

12. Masao Maruyama, *Thought and Behavior in Modern Japanese Politics*, ed. Ivan Morris (London: Oxford University Press, 1963), pp. 73–74, 78–80.

13. Mitani Taichirō, *Taishō demokurashii ron* (A study of Taishō democracy) (Tokyo: Chūō kōronsha, 1974), p. 291.

14. Cited in Garon, *Molding Japanese Minds*, p. 142.

6. China in the Early Twentieth Century: Tasks for a New World

1. Liang's words are as translated in Xiaobing Tang, *Global Space and the Nationalist Discourse of Modernity: The Historical Thinking of Liang Qichao* (Stanford: Stanford University Press, 1996), p. 42.

2. John Fitzgerald, *Awakening China: Politics, Culture, and Class in the Nationalist Revolution* (Stanford: Stanford University Press, 1996), p. 117.

3. For a stress on the importance of the discourse of the modern nation-state system, interacting with historical narratives of community in the shaping of national identity, see Presenjit Duara, *Rescuing History from the Nation: Questioning Narratives of Modern China* (Chicago: University of Chicago Press, 1995). On the influence on Liang Qichao's thinking of new conceptions of space as China was placed in a larger world, see Tang, *Global Space*.

4. The translation is taken from Douglas R. Reynolds, *China, 1898–1912: The Xinzheng Revolution and Japan* (Cambridge, Mass.: Council on East Asian Studies, Harvard University, 1993), p. 203. Parenthetical references to the Chinese and Japanese forms of certain terms are omitted here.

5. Paul J. Bailey, *Reform the People: Changing Attitudes towards Popular Education in Early Twentieth-Century China* (Vancouver: University of British Columbia Press, 1990), describes both the progressive dilution of the classical curriculum in the new schools and the stress on forms of popular education beyond the regular

schools. On popular protest against the reforms, see Joseph W. Esherick, *Reform and Revolution in China: The 1911 Revolution in Hunan and Hubei* (Berkeley: University of California Press, 1976), pp. 117–142; and Roxann Prazniak, *Of Camel Kings and Other Things: Rural Rebels against Modernity in Late Imperial China* (Lanham, Md.: Rowman and Littlefield, 1999).

6. Reynolds, *China,* p. 48. For an account of the early years, see Paula Harrell, *Sowing the Seeds of Change: Chinese Students, Japanese Teachers, 1895–1905* (Stanford: Stanford University Press, 1992).

7. Min Tu-ki, *National Polity and Local Power: The Transformation of Late Imperial China* (Cambridge, Mass.: Council on East Asian Studies, Harvard University, 1989), pp. 89–136; John E. Schrecker, *The Chinese Revolution in Historical Perspective* (New York: Praeger, 1991).

8. For an insightful portrayal of one important group of constitutionalists, see Joan Judge, *Print and Politics: "Shibao" and the Culture of Reform in Late Qing China* (Stanford: Stanford University Press, 1996).

9. P'eng-yüan Chang, "The Constitutionalists," in *China in Revolution: The First Phase, 1900–1913,* ed. Mary Clabaugh Wright (New Haven: Yale University Press, 1968), p. 150; John H. Fincher, *Chinese Democracy: The Self-Government Movement in Local, Provincial, and National Politics, 1905–1914* (Canberra: Australian National University Press, 1981), pp. 100–102.

10. Roger R. Thompson, *China's Local Councils in the Age of Constitutional Reform, 1898–1911* (Cambridge, Mass.: Council on East Asian Studies, Harvard University, 1995), pp. 122, 133, 139–140.

11. Min, *National Polity,* pp. 182–216.

12. For a discussion of Liang Qichao's hostility toward the court (which refused to lift its ban on Liang) in 1911, see Ernest P. Young, "The Reformer as a Conspirator: Liang Ch'i-ch'ao and the 1911 Revolution," in *Approaches to Modern Chinese History,* ed. Albert Feuerwerker et al. (Berkeley: University of California Press, 1967), pp. 239–267.

13. Mary Backus Rankin, *Elite Activism and Political Transformation in China: Zhejiang Province, 1865–1911* (Stanford: Stanford University Press, 1986).

14. Esherick, *Reform and Revolution in China,* a compelling study of the 1911 revolution, emphasizes its local origins.

15. Harold Z. Schiffrin, "The Enigma of Sun Yat-sen," in Wright, *China in Revolution,* pp. 454–455.

16. For a discussion of the difference between older Chinese versions of racial distinction and the new sort espoused by Sun Yat-sen and Zhang Binglin (another revolutionary leader known for his emphasis on race), see Fitzgerald, *Awakening China,* pp. 120–122.

17. Scholarship stressing the importance of race in the 1911 revolution includes Pamela Kyle Crossley, *Orphan Warriors: Three Manchu Generations and the End of the Qing World* (Princeton: Princeton University Press, 1990), pp. 226–227; Frank Dikötter, *The Discourse of Race in Modern China* (Stanford: Stanford University Press, 1992), pp. 96–125; and Duara, *Rescuing History,* pp. 74–79, 115–146.

18. Crossley, *Orphan Warriors*, p. 197, cites the killing of Manchus also in Wuhan (eight hundred), Yichang (seventeen), and Hangzhou (a dozen).

19. For some, the anti-Manchuism went deep and lived on into the 1920s. Sun Yatsen did not reconcile himself to the early republican flag, with its five bars symbolizing an ethnically pluralist China, with the Manchus as one of the five constituent races. Fitzgerald, *Awakening China*, pp. 180–185.

20. Michael Gasster, *Chinese Intellectuals and the Revolution of 1911: The Birth of Modern Chinese Radicalism* (Seattle: University of Washington Press, 1969), pp. 76–84. See Duara, *Rescuing History*, pp. 115–146, for a different approach to the function of anti-Manchuism for the republican revolutionaries.

21. A famous revolutionary tract, while reifying the difference between Manchu and Han, claimed the Japanese as a branch of the Han race. Tsou Jung (Zou Rong), *The Revolutionary Army: A Chinese Nationalist Tract of 1903*, trans. John Lust (The Hague: Mouton, 1968), pp. 106–107.

22. For reference to Chen Tianhua as part of an argument about the central importance of racism to the republican revolutionaries, see Dikötter, *Discourse of Race*, p. 117; Duara, *Rescuing History*, pp. 75, 131–132.

23. Translated by Ernest P. Young, "Problems of a Late Ch'ing Revolutionary: Ch'en T'ien-hua," in *Revolutionary Leaders of Modern China*, ed. Chün-tu Hsüeh (New York: Oxford University Press, 1971), p. 222.

24. Ibid., pp. 240–241.

25. The case of Hunan is recounted in Esherick, *Reform and Revolution in China*, pp. 202–210.

26. On these and other aspects of Yuan's rule, see Ernest P. Young, *The Presidency of Yuan Shih-k'ai: Liberalism and Dictatorship in Early Republican China* (Ann Arbor: University of Michigan Press, 1977).

27. Liang Qichao, *Yinbingshi wenji* (Collected essays from the Ice Drinker's Studio) (Taibei: Taiwan Zhongguo shuju, 1960), 12.34:4–19.

28. See the argument of Edward A. McCord, *The Power of the Gun: The Emergence of Modern Chinese Warlordism* (Berkeley: University of California Press, 1993), pp. 1–15.

29. Cited in Ernest P. Young, "Politics in the Aftermath of Revolution: The Era of Yuan Shih-k'ai, 1912–1916," in *The Cambridge History of China*, vol. 12, ed. John K. Fairbank (Cambridge: Cambridge University Press, 1983), p. 250.

30. For accounts of reform coexisting with warlordism, see Winston Hsieh, "The Ideas and Ideals of a Warlord: Ch'en Chiung-ming (1878–1933)," *Papers on China* (Cambridge, Mass.: Harvard University, East Asia Research Center), 16 (1962): 198–252; Donald G. Gillin, *Warlord: Yen Hsi-shan in Shansi Province, 1911–1949* (Princeton: Princeton University Press, 1967); Diana Lary, *Region and Nation: The Kwangsi Clique in Chinese Politics, 1925–1937* (Cambridge: Cambridge University Press, 1974); Leslie H. Chen, "Chen Jiongming (1878–1933) and the Chinese Federalist Movement," *Republican China*, 17, no. 1 (November 1991): 21–37; Eugene William Levich, *The Kwangsi Way in Kuomintang China, 1931–1939* (Armonk, N.Y.: M. E. Sharpe, 1993).

31. *Mao's Road to Power: Revolutionary Writings, 1912–1949*, vol. 1, *The Pre-Marxist Period, 1912–1920*, ed. Stuart R. Schram (Armonk, N.Y.: M. E. Sharpe, 1992), p. 545. Various of Mao's writings on this theme appear ibid., pp. 543–612. For a close study of activity on behalf of provincial autonomy and federalist structures in another province, see R. Keith Schoppa, "Province and Nation: The Chekiang Provincial Autonomy Movement, 1917–1927," *Journal of Asian Studies* 36, no. 4 (August 1977): 661–674. On Hunan, as well as the exemplary Guangdong case, including the conflict between Sun Yat-sen and Chen Jiongming, see Duara, *Rescuing History*, pp. 177–204.

32. Chen Duxiu, "Call to Youth," translated in Ssu-yü Teng and John K. Fairbank, *China's Response to the West: A Documentary Survey, 1839–1923* (Cambridge, Mass.: Harvard University Press, 1954), pp. 240–245.

33. For discussions of the continuing influence or understanding of the May Fourth Movement, see Vera Schwarcz, *The Chinese Enlightenment: Intellectuals and the Legacy of the May Fourth Movement of 1919* (Berkeley: University of California Press, 1986); and Jeffrey N. Wasserstrom, *Student Protests in Twentieth-Century China: The View from Shanghai* (Stanford: Stanford University Press, 1991).

34. Fitzgerald, *Awakening China*, pp. 118–119.

35. Hao Chang, *Liang Ch'i-ch'ao and Intellectual Transition in China, 1890–1907* (Cambridge, Mass.: Harvard University Press, 1971), pp. 192, 242–253.

36. Andrew Nathan, *Chinese Democracy* (Berkeley: University of California Press, 1986), pursues this theme from Liang Qichao to Deng Xiaoping.

37. Schwarcz, *Chinese Enlightenment*, pp. 118–121.

38. For Lu Xun's interest in the writings of the American missionary Arthur Smith, see Lydia H. Liu, *Translingual Practice: Literature, National Culture, and Translated Modernity: China, 1900–1937* (Stanford: Stanford University Press, 1995), pp. 45–76.

39. Arif Dirlik, *The Origins of Chinese Communism* (New York: Oxford University Press, 1989), pp. 74–94.

40. Maurice Meisner, *Li Ta-chao and the Origins of Chinese Marxism* (Cambridge, Mass.: Harvard University Press, 1967), pp. 80–89.

41. Mao Zedong, "The Great Union of the Popular Masses," in *Mao's Road to Power*, 1: 378–389.

7. The Nationalist Regime and the Chinese Party-State, 1928–1958

1. Kuo Heng-yü, *Die Komintern und die chinesische Revolution* (The Comintern and the Chinese revolution) (Paderborn: Schöningh, 1979), p. 284.

2. Arif Dirlik, *The Origins of Chinese Communism* (New York: Oxford University Press, 1989), p. 153. The opening and now partial publication of the Comintern archives in Moscow has demonstrated anew the massive influence of the Soviet Union on China's domestic political landscape in the 1920s. See *Die Komintern und die national-revolutionäre Bewegung in China* (The Comintern and the na-

tional-revolutionary movement in China), *Dokumente* (Documents), vol. 1, *1920–1925* (Paderborn: Schöningh, 1996); vol. 2, *1926–27*, pts. 1 and 2 (1997).

3. Hans J. van de Ven, *From Friend to Comrade: The Founding of the Chinese Communist Party, 1920–1927* (Berkeley: University of California Press, 1991), p. 56.

4. On party-government structures, see Hung-mao Tien, *Government and Politics in Kuomintang China, 1927–1937* (Stanford: Stanford University Press, 1972), p. 18. Indeed, the party's role was to "construct" the state *(yi dang jian guo)*: see John Fitzgerald's illuminating account in his *Awakening China: Politics, Culture, and Class in the Nationalist Revolution* (Stanford: Stanford University Press, 1996), pp. 185 and 180–213 passim.

5. Su Shaozhi, paper presented to the conference "Construction of the Party-State and State Socialism in China," Colorado College, 1993.

6. Broadly, see Ch'ien Tuan-sheng, *The Government and Politics of China, 1912–1949* (1950; Stanford: Stanford University Press, 1970).

7. See Wen-Hsin Yeh, *The Alienated Academy: Culture and Politics in Republican China, 1919–1937* (Cambridge, Mass.: Council on East Asian Studies, Harvard University, 1990), p. 174.

8. C. Martin Wilbur, *Sun Yat-sen, Frustrated Patriot* (New York: Columbia University Press, 1976), p. 278.

9. Sun Yat-sen, *The International Development of China* (New York: Putnam, 1922), p. 191.

10. Thomas G. Rawski, *Economic Growth in Prewar China* (Berkeley: University of California Press, 1989), p. 116.

11. Sun Yat-sen, *International Development*, p. 192.

12. Generally, see Michael R. Godley, "Socialism with Chinese Characteristics: Sun Yatsen and the International Development of China," *Australian Journal of Chinese Affairs*, no. 18 (July 1987): 109–125.

13. Richard Louis Edmonds, "The Legacy of Sun Yat-sen's Railway Plans," *China Quarterly* 111 (September 1987): 442.

14. Sun Yat-sen, *International Development*, pp. 66–67.

15. The term "developmental state" is appropriated from Chalmers Johnson's study of Japanese industrial policy of the same and later periods, *MITI and the Japanese Miracle: The Growth of Industrial Policy, 1925–1975* (Stanford: Stanford University Press, 1982), pp. 17–25. On the aspirations of modern states to "the administrative ordering of nature and society" in the era of "high modernism," see James C. Scott, *Seeing Like a State: How Certain Schemes to Improve the Human Condition Have Failed* (New Haven: Yale University Press, 1998), pp. 88 and 87–102 passim.

16. *Shoudu jihua* (Plan for the capital) (Office of Technical Experts for Planning the National Capital) (Nanjing: Guodu sheji jishu zhuanyuan banshichu, 1929).

17. Ibid., passim. The quotations are from Min-Ch'ien T. Z. Tyau, ed., *Two Years of Nationalist China* (Shanghai: Kelly and Walsh, 1930), pp. 389–394. The restoration of the Ming city wall—without a highway atop it—would not begin until 1995. New China News Agency, May 16, 1995.

18. Barry Till, *In Search of Old Nanking* (Hong Kong: Joint Publishing Co., 1982), p. 203.

19. This took place at a party congress in 1920. See Alec Nove, *An Economic History of the USSR* (New York: Penguin, 1969), p. 71.

20. Generally, see Zhang Li, "Yijiusanling niandai Zhongguo yu Guolian de jishu hezuo" (China's technical cooperation with the League of Nations during the 1930s), *Zhongyang yanjiuyuan jindaishi yanjiusuo jikan* (Quarterly of the Institute of Modern History of the Academia Sinica), no. 15 (December 1986): 281–314; Norbert Meienberger, *Entwicklungshilfe unter dem Völkerbund: Ein Beitrag zur Geschichte der internationalen Zusammenarbeit in der Zwischenkriegszeit unter besonderer Berücksichtigung der technischen Hilfe an China* (Wintherthur, 1965); and Jürgen Osterhammel, "'Technical Co-operation' between the League of Nations and China," *Modern Asian Studies* 13, no. 4 (1979): 661–680.

21. Terry M. Weidner, "Local Political Work under the Nationalists: The 1930s Silk Reform Campaign," *Illinois Papers in Asian Studies*, no. 2 (1983): 67, 70, 79. See also Lillian Li, *China's Silk Trade: Traditional Industry in the Modern World, 1842–1937* (Cambridge, Mass.: Council on East Asian Studies, Harvard University, 1981), p. 200.

22. See League of Nations Archives, Geneva, General 50/R5669–71, Reports of the Engineering Mission of the League of Nations in China, 1932–1935; J. L. Buck, *The 1931 Floods in China* (Nanking: Department of Agricultural Economics of the University of Nanking, 1932). On the Huai River projects, see David Pietz, "Engineering China's Rivers: The Huai River Valley in Republican China" (Ph.D. diss., Washington University, St. Louis, 1998).

23. Sun Yat-sen, *International Development*, p. 192.

24. Noel Miner, "Chekiang: The Nationalists' Effort in Agrarian Reform and Construction" (Ph.D. diss., Stanford University, 1973), p. 237.

25. See William Kirby, "Engineering China: Birth of the Developmental State, 1928–37," in *Becoming Chinese: Passages to Modernity and Beyond, 1900–1950*, ed. Wen-hsin Yeh (Berkeley: University of California Press, 2000).

26. Wang Shijie, "Education," in *The Chinese Yearbook, 1937* (Shanghai: The Commercial Press, 1937), p. 1032.

27. Zhang Ruide (Chang Jui-te), *Zhongguo jindai tielu shiye guanli de yanjiu* (Research on modern Chinese railway management) (Taipei: Zhongyang yanjiuyuan jindaishi suo, 1991); Julia Strauss, *Strong Institutions in Weak Polities: State Building in Republican China, 1927–1940* (Oxford: Oxford University Press, 1998).

28. See Strauss, *Strong Institutions*.

29. Douglas S. Paauw, "The KMT and Economic Stagnation, 1928–1937," *Journal of Asian Studies* 16, no. 2 (1957): 214.

30. Lloyd E. Eastman, *The Abortive Revolution: China under Nationalist Rule, 1927–1937* (Cambridge, Mass.: Harvard University Press, 1974), p. 171.

31. Quoted ibid., p. 170.

32. See Frederic Wakeman, Jr., *Policing Shanghai, 1927–1937* (Berkeley: University of California Press, 1995).

33. Ch'ao-ting Chi, *Wartime Economic Development of China* (New York: Institute of Pacific Relations, 1940), p. 8.
34. See Lloyd E. Eastman, *Seeds of Destruction: Nationalist China in War and Revolution, 1937–1949* (Stanford: Stanford University Press, 1984), pp. 112, 119.
35. Ch'ien Tuan-sheng, *Government,* p. 186.
36. Ibid., p. 140.
37. See William Kirby, "The Chinese War Economy," in *China's Bitter Victory: The War with Japan, 1937–1945,* ed. James C. Hsiung and Steven I. Levine (New York: M. E. Sharpe, 1992), pp. 185–212.
38. Mao Tse-tung (Mao Zedong), "On Coalition Government," in *Selected Works* (Peking: Foreign Languages Press, 1961–1964), 3: 282–285, quoted in Suzanne Pepper, *Civil War in China: The Political Struggle, 1945–1949* (Berkeley: University of California Press, 1978), p. 220.
39. See Arlen Meliksetov, "'New Democracy' and China's Search for Socio-Economic Development Routes (1949–1953)," *Far Eastern Affairs,* no. 1 (1996): 75–92, esp. 82–83; Bo Yibo, *Ruogan zhongde juece yu shijian de huigu* (A review of some important policies and events), vol. 1, *1949–1956* (Beijing: Zhonggong zhongyang dangxiao chubanshe, 1991), pp. 234–242.
40. On the plight of smaller opposition parties, see Roger Jeans, ed., *Roads Not Taken* (Boulder, Colo.: Westview, 1992).
41. For a stimulating comparison between the party-states that argues for a "single-state, two regime" model, see Robert E. Bedeski, *State-Building in Modern China: The Kuomintang in the Prewar Period* (Berkeley: Center for Chinese Studies, University of California, 1981). For the textbook description, see Kenneth Lieberthal, *Governing China: From Revolution through Reform* (New York: W. W. Norton, 1995), p. 77.
42. Bedeski, *State-Building,* p. 20.
43. See the paper by Konstantin Schevelyoff on Chinese policy making in the 1950s, presented to the conference "Construction of the Party-State and State Socialism in China," Colorado College, 1993.
44. Chiang quoted in Hsiao-shih Cheng, *Party-Military Relations in the PRC and Taiwan: Paradoxes of Control* (Boulder, Colo.: Westview, 1990), p. 136, cited in Steve Tsang, ed., *In the Shadow of China: Political Developments in Taiwan since 1949* (London: Hurst & Co., 1993), p. 65.
45. Chen Yi to Chen Lifu, May 10, 1944, in *Minguo dang'an* (Republican archives), no. 3 (1989): 20–21.
46. On degrees of Leninism in the post-1950 GMD, see Steve Tsang, "Chiang Kaishek and the Kuomintang's Policy to Reconquer the Chinese Mainland, 1949–1958," in Tsang, *In the Shadow of China,* p. 67.
47. Quoted in Pepper, *Civil War in China,* p. 227.
48. See William Kirby, "Continuity and Change in Modern China: Economic Planning on the Mainland and on Taiwan, 1943–1958," *Australian Journal of Chinese Affairs* 24 (July 1990): 121–141.
49. Simon Kuznets, "Growth and Structural Shifts," in *Economic Growth and Struc-*

tural Change in Taiwan: The Postwar Experience of the Republic of China ed. Walter Galenson (Ithaca, N.Y.: Cornell University Press, 1979), pp. 15–131.

50. See Thomas B. Gold, *State and Society in the Taiwan Miracle* (Armonk, N.Y.: M. E. Sharpe, 1986), pp. 76–77.

51. See John Wilson Lewis and Xue Litai, *China Builds the Bomb* (Stanford: Stanford University Press, 1988).

52. See the compelling argument of David Shambaugh, "Building the Party-State in China, 1949–1965: Bringing the Soldier Back In," in *New Perspectives on State Socialism in China*, ed. Timothy Cheek and Tony Saich (Armonk, N.Y.: M. E. Sharpe, 1997), pp. 125–150.

53. Lieberthal, *Governing China*, p. 204.

8. The Search for Social Cohesion in China, 1921–1958

1. I would argue that the Cultural Revolution was markedly different in goal from the efforts to find social cohesion in the period up to the Great Leap Forward. The central dynamics of the Cultural Revolution were the settling of political scores, the purposeful introduction of chaos and destruction, and the purge of the party. However the Great Leap Forward turned out, and whatever its effects, its intended goal was the construction of a large, socially cohesive unit that was envisioned as the basis for the Maoist version of a communist utopia.

2. Core zones refer to those areas that were most urbanized, populated, and economically developed. In *Chinese Elites and Political Change* (Cambridge, Mass.: Harvard University Press, 1982), I set forth a paradigm of four zones from highest to lowest degree of development, inner and outer core, and inner and outer periphery. In the revolutionary activities of the 1920s, the inner periphery generally included most of the hinterland areas to which party organizers traveled. The outer periphery was still at this stage of the revolution generally too remote for involvement.

3. C. Martin Wilbur, "The Nationalist Revolution: From Canton to Nanking, 1923–28," in *The Cambridge History of China*, vol. 12, *Republican China, 1912–1949*, pt. 1, ed. John K. Fairbank (Cambridge: Cambridge University Press, 1983), p. 564.

4. R. Keith Schoppa, *Blood Road: The Mystery of Shen Dingyi in Revolutionary China* (Berkeley: University of California Press, 1995), p. 103.

5. Christina Kelley Gilmartin, *Engendering the Chinese Revolution* (Berkeley: University of California Press, 1995), pp. 153 and 157.

6. Statistics on union and association members come from Wilbur, "Nationalist Revolution," pp. 590–592.

7. Simon Leys, "The Art of Interpreting Nonexistent Inscriptions Written in Invisible Ink on a Blank Page," *New York Review of Books*, October 11, 1990, p. 12.

8. Christian Henriot, *Shanghai, 1927–1937*, trans. Noel Castelino (Berkeley: University of California Press, 1993), p. 239.

9. See, for example, Bryna Goodman, *Native Place, City, and Nation: Regional Networks and Identities in Shanghai, 1853–1937* (Berkeley: University of California

Press, 1995); R. Keith Schoppa, "Province and Nation: The Chekiang Provincial Autonomy Movement, 1917–1927," *Journal of Asian Studies* 36, no. 4 (August 1977): 661–674; and Prasenjit Duara, *Rescuing History from the Nation: Questioning Narratives of Modern China* (Chicago: University of Chicago Press, 1995), pp. 177–204.

10. Schoppa, *Blood Road*, p. 218.

11. R. H. Tawney, *Land and Labor in China* (Boston: Beacon Press, 1966), pp. 92–96.

12. See, for example, Gregor Benton, *Mountain Fires: The Red Army's Three-Year War in South China, 1934–1938* (Berkeley: University of California Press, 1992); and Odoric Y. K. Wou, *Mobilizing the Masses: Building Revolution in Henan* (Stanford: Stanford University Press, 1994).

13. Lyman Van Slyke, "The Chinese Communist Movement during the Sino-Japanese War, 1937–1945," in *The Cambridge History of China*, vol. 13, *Republican China, 1912–1949*, pt. 2, ed. John K. Fairbank and Albert Feuerwerker (Cambridge: Cambridge University Press, 1986), p. 631.

14. Tony Saich, ed., *The Rise to Power of the Chinese Communist Party: Documents and Analysis* (Armonk, N.Y.: M. E. Sharpe, 1996), p.370.

15. Ibid., p. 604.

16. Jerome Ch'en, "The Communist Movement, 1927–1937," in Fairbank and Feuerwerker, *Cambridge History of China*, vol. 13, pt. 2, p. 195.

17. Jonathan Spence, *The Search for Modern China* (New York: Norton, 1990), p. 376.

18. Saich, *Rise to Power*, p. 372.

19. This information on the Three-Year War comes from Gregor Benton, "Under Arms and Umbrellas: Perspectives on Chinese Communism in Defeat," in *New Perspectives on the Chinese Communist Revolution*, ed. Tony Saich and Hans van de Ven (Armonk, N.Y.: M. E. Sharpe, 1995), pp. 124–126. See also his *Mountain Fires*.

20. Benton, "Under Arms and Umbrellas," p. 126.

21. See the compelling analysis by Pauline Keating, "The Yan'an Way of Co-operativization," *China Quarterly* (December 1994): 1025–51.

22. John Wilson Lewis, *Leadership in Communist China* (Ithaca, N.Y.: Cornell University Press, 1963), p. 110, cited in Van Slyke, "Chinese Communist Movement," p. 620.

23. Saich, *Rise to Power*, p. 1007.

24. Mark Selden, *The Yenan Way in Revolutionary China* (Cambridge, Mass.: Harvard University Press, 1971), p. 215.

25. For Yancheng, see the magisterial study of Ch'en Yung-fa, *Making Revolution* (Berkeley: University of California Press, 1986), p. 127; for Nanniwan, see Saich, *Rise to Power*, p. 977. Reportedly by 1943, it was producing up to 80 percent of those needs.

26. Saich, *Rise to Power*, p. 1123.

27. Wang Shiwei, "Wild Lilies," pt. 2, quoted in Dai Qing, *Wang Shiwei and "Wild Lilies"* (Armonk, N.Y.: M. E. Sharpe, 1994), p. 19.

28. The phrase is Chen Yung-fa's, *Making Revolution*, p. 220.

29. The examples from Henan are in Odoric Wou's magisterial study *Mobilizing the Masses*.

30. Ch'en Yung-fa, *Making Revolution*, p. 221.

31. Keating, "The Yan'an Way of Co-operativization," p. 1032.

32. Quoted in Edwin E. Moise, *Land Reform in China and North Vietnam* (Chapel Hill: University of North Carolina Press, 1983), p. 106.

33. Keating, "The Yan'an Way of Co-operativization," pp. 1029–31.

34. Issue of February 4, 1948, quoted in Moise, *Land Reform*, p. 59.

35. Steven I. Levine, "Mobilizing for War: Rural Revolution in Manchuria as an Instrument for War," in *Single Sparks: China's Rural Revolutions*, ed. Kathleen Hartford and Steven M. Goldstein (Armonk, N.Y.: M. E. Sharpe, 1989), p. 175.

36. Saich, *Rise to Power*, pp. 1300 and 1305.

37. Merle Goldman, *Literary Dissent in Communist China* (Cambridge, Mass.: Harvard University Press, 1967), pp. 70–86.

38. Saich, *Rise to Power*, p. 1311.

39. Suzanne Pepper, "The KMT-CCP Conflict, 1945–1949," in Fairbank and Feuerwerker, *Cambridge History of China*, vol. 13, pt. 2, p. 781.

40. R. Keith Schoppa, *Xiang Lake: Nine Centuries of Chinese Life* (New Haven: Yale University Press, 1989), p. 225.

41. Moise, *Land Reform*, p. 144.

42. The phrase is from Frederick C. Teiwes, "Establishment and Consolidation of the New Regime," in *The Cambridge History of China*, vol. 14, *The People's Republic*, pt. 1, *The Emergence of Revolutionary China, 1949–1965*, ed. Roderick MacFarquhar and John K. Fairbank (Cambridge: Cambridge University Press, 1987), p. 87.

43. Kenneth Lieberthal, *Governing China* (New York: W. W. Norton, 1995), p. 120.

44. Quoted in Teiwes, "Establishment and Consolidation of the New Regime," p. 94.

45. John Wong, *Land Reform in the People's Republic of China* (New York: Praeger, 1973), p. 204.

46. This information on the revolution in Guangdong localities is from Helen F. Siu, *Agents and Victims in South China* (New Haven: Yale University Press, 1989), pp. 160–161 and 168–169.

47. Quoted in Allen S. Whiting, "The Sino-Soviet Split," in MacFarquhar and Fairbank, *Cambridge History of China*, vol. 14, pt. 2, p. 500.

48. Issue of October 25, 1958, cited in Roderick MacFarquhar, *The Origins of the Cultural Revolution*, vol. 2, *The Great Leap Forward, 1958–1960* (New York: Columbia University Press, 1983), p. 103.

49. See the discussions in Christina K. Gilmartin et al., eds., *Engendering China* (Cambridge, Mass.: Harvard University Press, 1994). Especially helpful are Gao Xiaoxian, "China's Modernization and Changes in the Social Status of Rural Women," and Lisa Rofel, "Liberation Nostalgia and a Yearning for Modernity." The term "national woman" is Tani Barlow's.

50. Siu, *Agents and Victims*, p. 176.

51. Quoted in MacFarquhar, *Origins of the Cultural Revolution,* pp. 101–102.

52. Benton, *Mountain Fires,* p. 5.

53. Saich, *Rise to Power,* p. 201.

9. Society and Politics from Transwar through Postwar Japan

1. Robert J. Smith, *Kurusu: The Price of Progress in a Japanese Village, 1951–1975* (Stanford: Stanford University Press, 1978), pp. 6–7, 79–83; Ronald P. Dore, *Shinohata: Portrait of a Japanese Village* (New York: Pantheon, 1978).

2. See entry on "nuclear family" *(kaku kazoku)* in Sasaki Takeshi et al., eds., *Sengo shi daijiten* (Encyclopedia of postwar Japan, 1945–1990) (Tokyo: Sanseidō, 1991), p. 114.

3. Kawasaki City, ed., *Kawasaki rōdō shi* (History of labor in Kawasaki) (Kawasaki, 1987), p. 200, cites one such survey showing that women averaged 139 minutes a day for sewing and 179 minutes for cooking, but just 58 minutes for shopping and 57 minutes "spent with children."

4. Irokawa Daikichi, *Shōwa shi: sesō hen* (A social history of the Shōwa era) (Tokyo: Shogakkan, 1990), pp. 25–32, on births, weddings, deaths, funerals, and other rituals.

5. The text of the constitution can be found in John Maki, *Government and Politics in Japan* (New York: Praeger, 1962), and in many other sources.

6. Haruko Taya Cook and Theodore F. Cook, *Japan at War: An Oral History* (New York: New Press, 1992), p. 428.

7. John W. Dower, "Peace and Democracy in Two Systems," in *Postwar Japan as History,* ed. Andrew Gordon (Berkeley: University of California Press, 1993), pp. 3–33.

8. John D. Dower, *Empire and Aftermath: Yoshida Shigeru and the Japanese Experience, 1874–1954* (Cambridge, Mass.: Council on East Asian Studies, Harvard University, 1979), esp. chaps. 8–12.

9. Chalmers Johnson, *MITI and the Japanese Miracle: The Growth of Industrial Policy, 1925–1975* (Stanford: Stanford University Press, 1982).

10. Ken Ruoff, *The Symbolic Monarchy in Japan's Postwar Democracy* (Cambridge, Mass.: Harvard Asia Center Monographs, forthcoming).

11. Known as "three *chan*." *Chan* is a diminutive suffix attached to the words "grandma," "grandpa," and "baby."

12. Thomas P. Rohlen, "Is Japanese Education Becoming Less Egalitarian? Notes on High School Stratification and Reform," *Journal of Japanese Studies* 3, no. 1 (Winter 1977): 41.

13. Ezra Vogel, *Japan's New Middle Class: The Salary Man and His Family in a Tokyo Suburb* (Berkeley: University of California Press, 1963).

14. Classic and recent studies of urban Japan include Ronald Dore, *City Life in Japan: A Study of a Tokyo Ward* (Berkeley: University of California Press, 1958); Theo-

dore C. Bestor, *Neighborhood Tokyo* (Stanford: Stanford University Press, 1989); and Jennifer Robertson, *Native and Newcomer* (Berkeley: University of California Press, 1991).

15. Vogel, *Japan's New Middle Class,* pp. 175–178.

16. Irokawa, *Shōwa shi: sesō hen,* pp. 25–32.

17. Walter Edwards, *Modern Japan through Its Weddings: Gender, Person, and Society in Ritual Portrayal* (Stanford: Stanford University Press, 1989).

18. For the text of this plan, see David Lu, *Sources of Japanese History* (New York: McGraw-Hill, 1974), pp. 250–252.

19. For analysis of the various events surrounding Hirohito's death, see especially Takeshi Fujitani, "Electronic Pageantry and Japan's 'Symbolic Emperor,'" *Journal of Asian Studies* 51, no. 4 (November 1994): 838–848.

10. Searching for the Appropriate Model for the People's Republic of China

1. This section draws on Andrew J. Nathan and Robert S. Ross, *The Great Wall and the Empty Fortress: China's Search for Security* (New York: W. W. Norton, 1997).

2. Nicholas R. Lardy, "Economic Recovery and the 1st Five-Year Plan," in *Cambridge History of China,* vol. 14, ed. Roderick MacFarquhar and John K. Fairbank (Cambridge: Cambridge University Press, 1987), p. 179.

3. This section draws on Andrew J. Nathan, "Totalitarianism, Authoritarianism, Democracy: The Case of China," in *Asia: Case Studies in the Social Sciences: A Guide for Teaching,* ed. Myron L. Cohen (Armonk, N.Y.: M. E. Sharpe, 1992), pp. 235–256.

4. Li Zhisui with Anne F. Thurston, *The Private Life of Chairman Mao* (New York: Random House, 1994).

5. Gordon H. Chang, *Friends and Enemies: The United States, China, and the Soviet Union, 1948–1972* (Stanford: Stanford University Press, 1990).

6. See Merle Goldman, *China's Intellectuals: Advise and Dissent* (Cambridge, Mass.: Harvard University Press, 1981).

7. Xiong Xianghui, "Dakai ZhongMei guanxi de qianzou," *Zhonggong dangshi ziliao,* no. 42 (Beijing: Zhonggong dangshi chubanshe, 1992), pp. 56–96.

8. Lu Feng, "The Origins and Formation of the Unit *(Danwei)* System," issue of *Chinese Sociology and Anthropology* 25, no. 3 (Spring 1993).

9. Liu Binyan, *A Higher Kind of Loyalty: A Memoir by China's Foremost Journalist* (New York: Pantheon, 1990), p. 89.

10. Economist Intelligence Unit, *Country Report: China, Mongolia* (First Quarter 1998): 28.

11. Ibid., p. 33.

12. See Dorothy Solinger, *Contesting Citizenship in Urban China: Peasant Migrants, the State, and the Logic of the Market* (Berkeley: University of California Press, 1999).

13. World Bank, *China 2020: Development Challenges in the New Century* (Washington, D.C.: The World Bank, 1997), pp. 6–8.

14. See Murray Scot Tanner, *The Politics of Lawmaking in Post-Mao China* (Oxford: Clarendon Press, 1999).

15. Codebook of the "Comparative Research Project on Political Culture and Political Participation," Columbia University, Duke University, People's University, May 1995. The survey was done in 1993 for a project of which Andrew J. Nathan was one of the investigators.

Contributors

Warren I. Cohen is Distinguished University Professor of History at the University of Maryland, Baltimore County, and Senior Scholar at the Woodrow Wilson International Center for Scholars. His best-known book is *America's Response to China*.

Carter J. Eckert is Professor of Korean History and Director of the Korea Institute at Harvard University. He is the author of *Offspring of Empire: The Kochang Kims and the Colonial Origins of Korean Capitalism* and co-author of *Korea Old and New: A History*.

Sheldon Garon is Professor of History and East Asian Studies at Princeton University. He is the author of *State and Labor in Modern Japan* and more recently *Molding Japanese Minds: The State in Everyday Life*.

Merle Goldman is Professor of Chinese History at Boston University and Associate of the Fairbank Center at Harvard. Her most recent books are *Sowing the Seeds of Democracy in China* and, with John K. Fairbank, the enlarged edition of *China: A New History*.

Andrew Gordon is Professor of History and Director of the Edwin O. Reischauer Institute of Japanese Studies at Harvard University. He has recently published *Wages of Affluence: Labor and Management in Postwar Japan*.

David L. Howell is Associate Professor of East Asian Studies and History at Princeton University. He is the author of *Capitalism from Within: Economy, Society, and the State in a Japanese Fishery*.

William C. Kirby is Geisinger Professor of History and Director of the Asia Center at Harvard University. His works include *Germany and Republican China* and *State and Economy in Republican China* (co-edited), as well as numerous articles on China's economic and political development in an international context.

Andrew J. Nathan is Professor of Political Science at Columbia University. He is the author or co-author of a number of works on contemporary China, including *Chinese Democracy, Human Rights in Contemporary China, China's Crisis, The Great Wall and the Empty Fortress: China's Search for Security,* and *China's Transition*.

349

Mary Backus Rankin is an independent historian of late imperial and early republican China. Her publications include *Early Chinese Revolutionaries: Radical Intellectuals in Chekiang and Shanghai, 1902–1911* and *Elite Activism and Political Transformation in China: Zhejiang Province, 1865–1911.*

R. Keith Schoppa occupies the Edward and Catherine Doehler Chair in Asian History at Loyola College in Maryland. He is author of *Chinese Elites and Political Change, Xiang Lake: Nine Centuries of Chinese Life,* and *Blood Road: The Mystery of Shen Dingyi in Revolutionary China.*

Ernest P. Young is Professor of History at the University of Michigan. He is the author of *The Presidency of Yuan Shih-k'ai: Liberalism and Dictatorship in Early Republican China* and has published articles on late Qing intellectual and political history.

Index

DATE DUE

NOV 2 1 2002		
JUN 3 0 2001		
APR 0 8 2004		
OCT 1 2 2006		